Jonathan Blundell

Cambridge IGCSE® Sociology Coursebook

CAMBRIDGE UNIVERSITY PRESS

CAMBRIDGE
UNIVERSITY PRESS

University Printing House, Cambridge CB2 8BS, United Kingdom

Cambridge University Press is part of the University of Cambridge.

It furthers the University's mission by disseminating knowledge in the pursuit of education, learning and research at the highest international levels of excellence.

Information on this title: education.cambridge.org

First published 2014
5th printing 2016

Printed in the United Kingdom by Latimer Trend

A catalogue record for this publication is available from the British Library

ISBN 978-1-107-64513-4 Paperback

Contents

Introduction

This book has been specifically written for the new Cambridge International Examinations IGCSE® Sociology syllabus which will first be examined in 2015. Its global and international scope also makes it ideal for introducing Sociology to young people studying similar courses.

The book is written in language carefully designed to be clear and accessible to 14 to 16 year olds. Sociology involves the use of many specialist terms and these are explained where they occur first in the book.

The Cambridge International Examinations IGCSE syllabus is examined by two examination papers. The first three chapters of the book, on Theory and Methods, Culture, Identity and Socialisation and Social Inequality are fundamental to the study of sociology. All students should study these three chapters, which are examined by the first paper. Together, these three chapters provide students with the basic sociological skills and knowledge needed for studying topic areas. The four topic areas on the syllabus are covered in the next four chapters of the book and are examined by the second paper. In the examination, students are only required to answer questions on two of these.

The final chapter focuses on the skills needed to prepare for and to sit the examinations.

The book shares with the syllabus the aim of making this exciting subject accessible to young people around the world. It brings together the knowledge gained from classic studies in the development of the subject and more recent research findings. It uses examples and case studies from around the world. It reflects contemporary developments such as globalisation and the growth of new media. Students are encouraged to reflect on their learning and to apply their sociological understanding to their own nation and social situation.

To help students through the book, we have used a number of features:

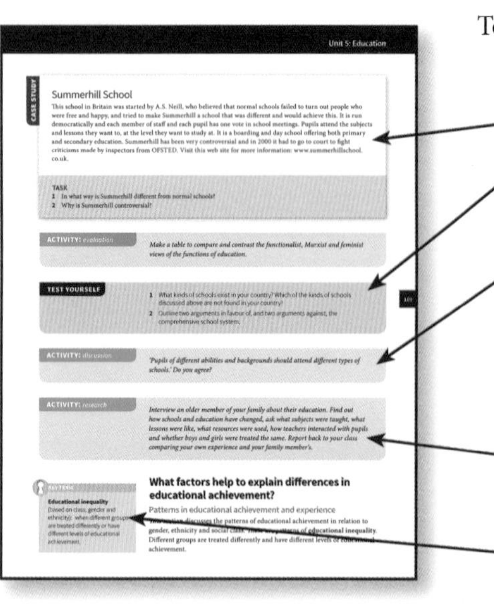
Unit 5: Education

CASE STUDY

Summerhill School

This school in Britain was started by A.S. Neill, who believed that normal schools failed to turn out people who were free and happy, and tried to make Summerhill a school that was different and would achieve this. It is run democratically and each member of staff and each pupil has one vote in school meetings. Pupils attend the subjects and lessons they want to, at the level they want to study at. It is a boarding and day school offering both primary and secondary education. Summerhill has been very controversial and in 2000 it had to go to court to fight criticisms made by inspectors from OFSTED. Visit this web site for more information: www.summerhillschool.co.uk.

TASK
1 In what way is Summerhill different from normal schools?
2 Why is Summerhill controversial?

ACTIVITY: evaluation

Make a table to compare and contrast the functionalist, Marxist and feminist views of the functions of education.

TEST YOURSELF

1 What kinds of schools exist in your country? Which of the kinds of schools discussed above are not found in your country?
2 Outline two arguments in favour of, and two arguments against, the comprehensive school system.

ACTIVITY: discussion

'Pupils of different abilities and backgrounds should attend different types of schools.' Do you agree?

ACTIVITY: research

Interview an older member of your family about their education. Find out how schools and education have changed, ask what subjects were taught, what lessons were like, what resources were used, how teachers interacted with pupils and whether boys and girls were treated the same. Report back to your class comparing your own experience and your family member's.

KEY TERM

Educational inequality (based on class, gender and ethnicity): when different groups are treated differently or have different levels of educational achievement.

What factors help to explain differences in educational achievement?

Patterns in educational achievement and experience

[illegible] the patterns of educational achievement in relation to gender, ethnicity and social [illegible] **educational inequality**. Different groups are treated differently and have different levels of [illegible] achievement.

- Case studies with questions.
- Other questions to check knowledge and develop understanding at the end of each section within each chapter.
- Suggestions for discussion and debate, to help students develop confidence verbally in using sociological language, apply ideas to issues relevant to them and appreciate the opinion and arguments of others.
- Suggestions for research, allowing students to develop their understanding through carrying out their own research.
- Key terms help students identify and understand important concepts. These terms are those listed in the syllabus and each is explained in a separate box when it is first used in the book.

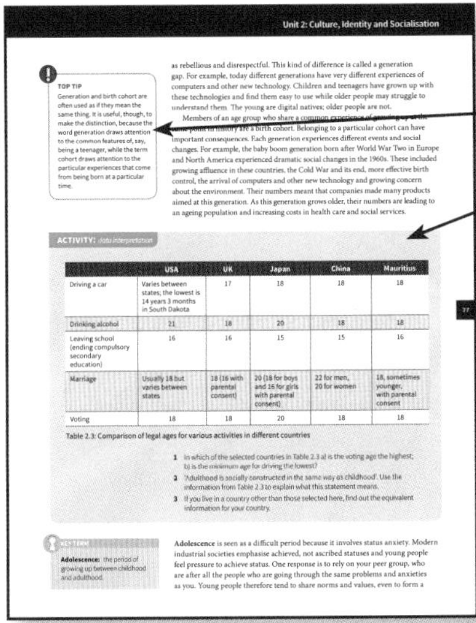

- Hints and tips.
- Practice in interpreting data in a variety of formats, such as tables, charts and graphs; this is an essential skill in sociology.

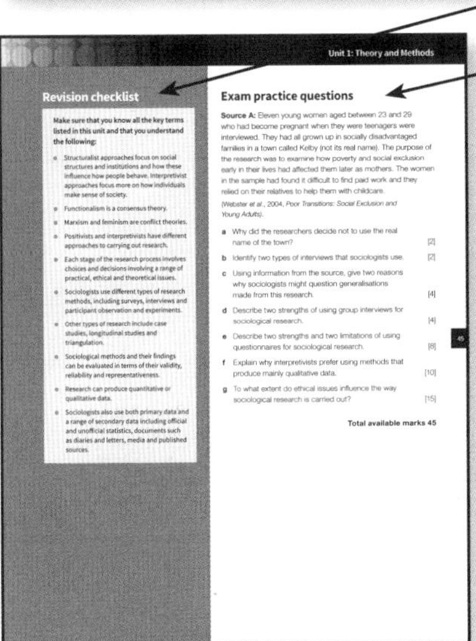

- Checklist of key points at the end of each chapter.
- Examination style questions at the end of each chapter.

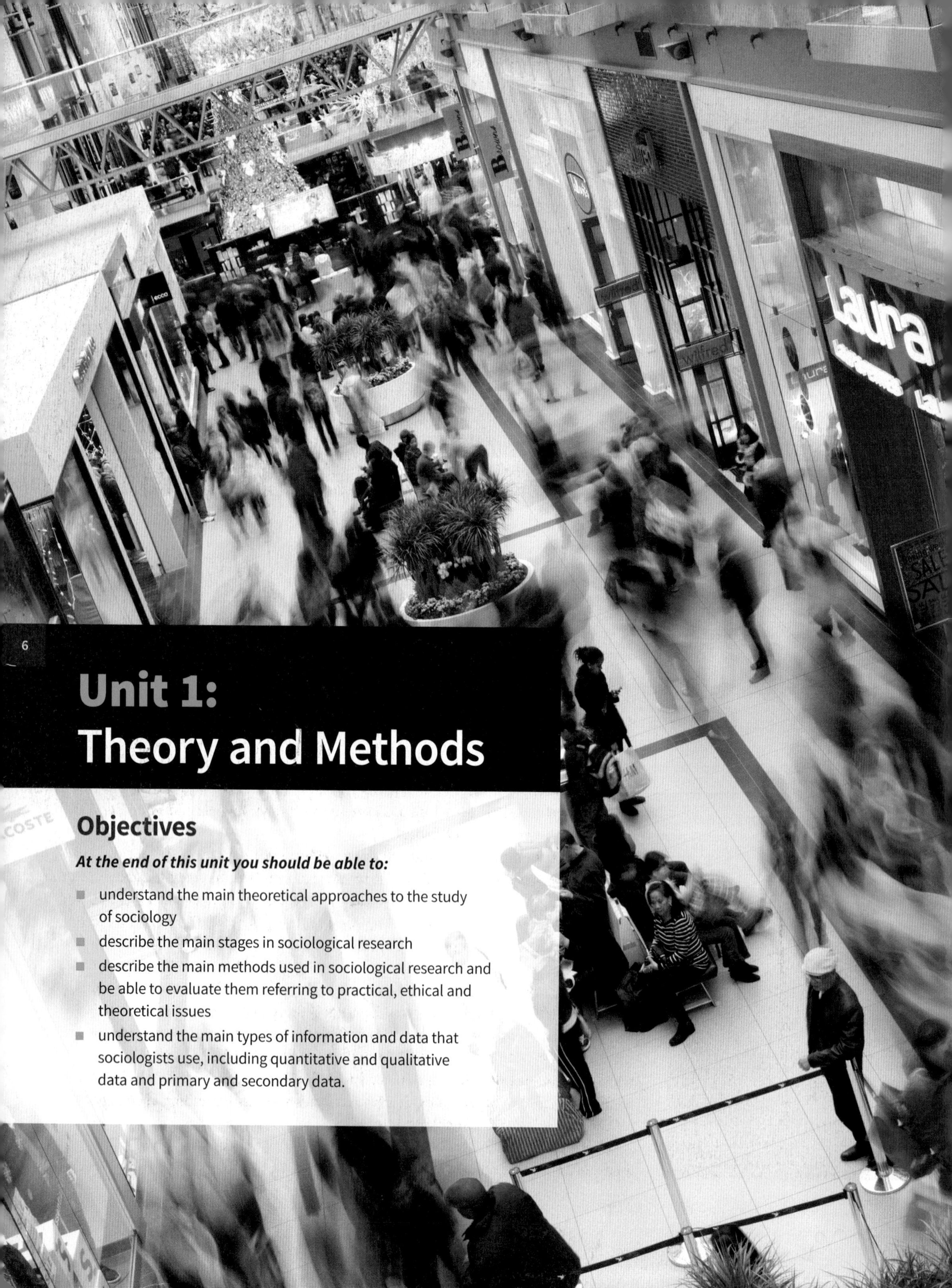

Unit 1: Theory and Methods

Objectives

At the end of this unit you should be able to:

- understand the main theoretical approaches to the study of sociology
- describe the main stages in sociological research
- describe the main methods used in sociological research and be able to evaluate them referring to practical, ethical and theoretical issues
- understand the main types of information and data that sociologists use, including quantitative and qualitative data and primary and secondary data.

Introduction

Sociology tries to understand and explain the relationship between people and the societies they live in. A society is the group to which you belong; it can be a small unit like the family or a large one like your country, and anything in between. People can be grouped by the things they have in common: for instance, their level of education or their religious attitudes, whether they are recent migrants to a country or whether they are male or female. The subject matter of sociology consists of the actions and beliefs of people in social groups, the relationships between social groups and the ways in which people's actions can change society, as well as the ways that social change in the whole society affects different social groups.

To study the complex behaviour of people in social groups sociologists use different kinds of tools. The main tools are of two types: theories about society and methods used to explore those theories. This unit looks at the main theories and methods used. Notice that the theories are based on very different ideas about what the relationship between people and the societies they live in could be and the methods they use are also very different from each other. To study sociology you need to have a good understanding of these differences as well as understanding the content of each main theory discussed here. This book will try to help by pointing out the important features of each.

KEY TERMS

Structuralism: an approach focusing on the large-scale social structures in which people play defined roles.

Macro/micro approaches: macro approaches focus on the large scale of whole societies, micro approaches on small-scale social interaction.

Emile Durkheim

How do different sociologists interpret society?

Structuralist and interpretivist approaches: the individual, identity and society

Structuralism

There are two main approaches to sociology: **structuralist** and interpretivist. Structuralist approaches focus on large-scale (**macro**) social structures and institutions rather than individuals. Structuralists see societies as a set of structures in which individuals play definite roles. In this approach it is the social roles and the actions that people carry out in fulfilling these roles that are important, not the individuals themselves. Sociologists use these theories to discover social structures that may be hidden from individuals.

A well-known example of a structuralist approach is the work of Emile Durkheim on suicide published over 100 years ago. He chose to study suicide because we usually think of it as an individual act motivated by private troubles but he wanted to show it is linked to the way societies are organised. Durkheim noticed that suicide rates – the proportion of the population who committed suicide each year – in a country did not change much. However, there were significant differences in suicide rates between countries. Durkheim tried to show that social forces (or the social causes of actions) lay behind individual actions like suicide. These social forces led to the different suicide rates. A social force, for example, is the connection between individuals and support networks such as families and religious organisations. Strong connections lead to lower suicide rates and weak connections lead to higher rates. Suicide rates thus show us something about the nature of a society, not about individuals.

Durkheim was working within the framework of the positivist method that is used in natural science. Like other structuralists, he looked for

KEY TERMS

Correlation: when two variables are related to each other but causation cannot be proved; for example, ill-health is related to poverty. This is not a causal relationship because some sick people are not poor and some poor people are not sick.

Causation: where a strict link can be proved between variables in a time sequence; such as, heating water to 100°C causes it to boil. Causation is hard to find in sociology.

Interpretivism: approaches that start at the level of the individual, focusing on small-scale phenomena and usually favouring qualitative methods.

Identity: how a person sees themselves, and how others see them, for example as a girl and a student.

correlations and **causation** between variables. According to the structuralist approach, individuals have little freedom of thought or action (though they may think that they do). Society controls our lives. Individuals are puppets, and hidden social forces are pulling the strings that make individuals behave as they do.

Interpretivism

In contrast, interpretivists start with the individual rather than society and focus on the **micro** rather than the macro scale. **Interpretivists** believe individuals are in control, pulling the strings of society. People make the societies they live in and change them through their actions. We are born into particular societies and learn the norms and values of the society we grow up in but we do not have to accept them, and the values themselves also change continuously over time as people's ideas change. Interpretivists are interested in how individuals make sense of society and of social actions – the things that they do.

Interpretivists start their study of society from the level of the individual, unlike structuralists. They are interested in how people see themselves and what makes up their **identity** (who we think we are). In all societies we are given labels, and these can be part of our identities. We choose among the identities that are socially available to us and reject others, and these labels carry different meanings for us. For instance, someone may see themselves primarily through their religious identity or their age identity. Similarly, we may see other people in terms of labels that they might accept or reject. Socially available labels include:

- sex and gender identities
- ethnic identity – membership of an ethnic group
- age
- social class
- nationality
- occupation
- roles within a family, such as parent
- membership of a religious or political organisation.

We have some choice about aspects of our identities and may also decide for ourselves how important different aspects of our identities are to us. In the case of national identity, some people may be very patriotic but others may not see their nationality as important, or may identify more strongly with a religious or ethnic identity. So interpretivists believe our identities are not imposed by society, as structuralists would argue, but come from the interaction between our own thoughts and actions and those of others. Our identities bind us to certain social groups and to certain ways of behaving.

Interpretivists use research methods that try to discover what meanings people give to their actions and how they interpret the world around them. Interpretivist researchers try to understand how people see the world. For example, in researching crime an interpretivist would want to know what the people involved had to say about what they did, not just what happened.

TEST YOURSELF

1 Summarise the main differences between structuralism and interpretivism.
2 The picture on page 9 shows puppets and strings. Think of another way of showing the different approaches in a visual way, using as few words as possible.

Approaches to studying society and individuals

How different theories on conflict and consensus create alternative sociological perspectives

Sociologists have different views on the nature of society and social life. These are referred to as **perspectives**. In this section we discuss the different underlying ideas about conflict and consensus in functionalist, Marxist and feminist perspectives.

> **KEY TERMS**
>
> **Perspectives:** ways of viewing social life from different points of view.
>
> **Consensus:** basic agreement on a set of shared values.
>
> **Conflict:** disagreement between groups with different interests.

Consensus and conflict

One major difference between perspectives in sociology is the extent to which they emphasise either social **consensus** or social **conflict**.

There is social consensus when people generally share values and there are no major disagreements between the main groups. This is possible only if either all the groups in a society have similar levels of wealth, status and power or if it is widely accepted that it is right for each group to have the level of wealth, status and power that it does. A society built on consensus will be stable and harmonious. The values that are shared may be based on a religion or a belief system, or perhaps on political ideas, and there are likely to be shared practices and rituals that bring everyone together and make them feel a sense of belonging so they identify strongly with their society and its values.

Social conflict occurs when major disagreements arise about important issues such as wealth, status and power. In a society based on conflict there will be significant and important differences between groups, which may become open conflicts, and there will be no overall set of shared values held by all groups. A society based on conflict will be unstable, though there may be long periods where one group in power is able to suppress others that challenge it.

Because interpretivist approaches are more interested in individuals and small-scale (micro) social interaction than in the overall nature of a society, the debate about conflict and consensus does not apply to them. However, this means that they are sometimes criticised for not taking into account the wider issues such as power, which may influence the situations they study.

Functionalism

The main sociological perspective based on a consensus view of society is functionalism. Functionalists emphasise social functions and ask, 'What function does this aspect of society carry out that keeps this society stable and allows it to continue?' They might say, for example:

- The function of schools is to give young people the skills they need for work, which helps the economy of a society.
- The function of families is to socialise children into the norms and values of the society so that the next generation will have these values.
- The function of prisons is to remove temporarily from society people who do not keep the laws and who therefore upset the smooth running of society.

Functionalists perceive human society as being like the human body. This is called the organic or biological analogy because it compares society to a living organism. The different parts of the human body – the brain, heart, liver, skin and so on – all have jobs to do to keep you healthy. In the same way, each part of society is seen as having functions that all help the society as a whole to be healthy and survive. If something goes wrong in one part of your body it may affect other parts and it may be a warning sign that you need to do something. So, in a human society, an increase in crime might become a problem that needs to be tackled, perhaps by getting schools to be better at teaching people to obey the law.

Functionalism was the most important perspective in sociology for many years, especially in the early and mid-20th century. It was the way that most sociologists thought societies worked. It is often referred to as structural functionalism. The main sociologist associated with it is the American Talcott Parsons (1902–1979).

Marxism

Marxism is a perspective that argues that modern industrial societies are based on a fundamental conflict between different social classes. Marxists argue that there is a permanent and continuous conflict of interest between social classes that takes the form of strikes and other protests by the working class, and can lead to revolution. Marxists refer to the two main classes as the bourgeoisie (the owners of wealth and property) and the proletariat (the working class). The bourgeoisie has power and wealth and exploits and oppresses the proletariat, who are 'wage slaves'. This means that the proletariat have no choice but to work if they are to survive but that they are never paid the full value of their work – this is taken by the ruling class as profits.

Where functionalists look at parts of society and see how they keep society stable and harmonious, Marxists look at the same phenomena and see how they allow the bourgeoisie to keep their wealth and power. Marxists might say, for example:

- Schools ensure that some people fail and that they think this is their own fault so that they then accept a low position in society.
- The mass media distract people's attention from what is really going on and make people interested only in celebrities, sport and trivial issues.

Karl Marx

So Marxists agree with functionalists that parts of society have functions although they disagree completely about their interpretation.

Marxism is much more than a sociological perspective; it is also important in politics, history and economics. Marxism inspired the political movements of socialism and communism, which involve attempts to create new societies based on equality rather than class divisions. Marxists are in favour of radical social changes that will end exploitation and make everyone equal. Critics of Marxism argue that this is probably impossible and that the attempts to create equal societies have led to even greater oppression.

Marxism is named after Karl Marx (1818–1883). Marxist ideas have developed considerably since his time, as later Marxists have tried to adapt his ideas to explain what has happened since, particularly why the revolutions in modern industrial societies that Marx expected did not happen. Modern Marxist writers are often called neo-Marxists.

Feminism

A second sociological perspective that emphasises conflict is feminism. Like Marxists, feminists see a fundamental division between two groups in society, but for feminists this division is between the two sexes rather than two classes. Feminists argue that it is men who control society and who have wealth and power in all aspects of society – in relationships, families, the world of work, education, and so on. The control of society by men is called patriarchy. Feminist sociologists research on gender differences; for example, they are interested in why, although girls tend to do better in school than boys, it is still boys who, when they are men, will be in higher paid jobs.

Like Marxism, feminism is much more than a sociological perspective; it is important in other subjects and it is a broad social and political movement with a long history. Feminists have campaigned for equality between men and women for many years. They have achieved advances in many societies but argue that there is not yet full equality. Feminism has sometimes been seen as being anti-men but many feminists argue that equality will bring benefits for men as well.

TOP TIP

Throughout this book you will study the ways that these different approaches have been applied to different topics in sociology (families, education, crime and so on). For questions on theory and methods, you can bring in relevant examples from any of the topic areas.

Feminism covers such a very wide range of ideas that there are several strands within feminism. They include:

- liberal feminists, who believe that major advances have been made and that equality can be reached through further changes such as new laws; their view does not emphasise conflict
- radical feminists, who believe that despite these advances, societies remain fundamentally patriarchal and men still have power; though this may now be less obvious, radical changes are still needed

- Marxist (or socialist) feminists, who bring together the insights of both Marxism and feminism, focusing on how class and gender work together to produce fundamental divisions in society.

TEST YOURSELF

1 Marxism and feminism are both broad political movements as well as sociological perspectives. Why might those who adopt these perspectives want to change society as well as study it?

2 How might Marxists and functionalists interpret differently the functions of (a) the government and (b) the police force?

ACTIVITY: *discussion*

Which of the consensus and conflict approaches discussed here do you think is the most relevant today? Be prepared to justify your choice.

How do sociologists study society?

The distinction between positivist and interpretivist approaches to research methods

In all subjects the methods used to carry out research are important. Sociologists use a range of different methods. They choose methods that are appropriate for what is being studied and for what they want to find out. If the methods are appropriate and have been implemented well other people are more likely to accept that the research findings add to our knowledge. If the method has not been chosen and carried out well, the research will be criticised by others and the findings may be rejected.

Positivism

Positivism is an approach that concentrates on producing **quantitative data**, usually in the form of statistics. It is based on the belief that, as far as possible, sociology should use the same research methods as the natural sciences such as physics, chemistry and biology.

This approach in sociology goes back to 19th and early 20th century sociologists such as Auguste Comte and Emile Durkheim. They witnessed the growing ability of the natural sciences to understand and predict the workings of the natural world. They believed that there were laws of social behaviour that could be discovered by using similar methods and so they advocated the use of scientific methods in sociology.

Scientists try to be objective. They try to be neutral and to discover the truth rather than being guided by their values and by what they would like to be true. If a researcher can be objective the results will be **unbiased** and should be an accurate account of what really happened. Critics have pointed out that this is probably impossible; for example, scientists' research is influenced by their values from the very beginning, when they choose to research something they think is important. Positivists reply that even scientists cannot attain **objectivity** yet sociologists should always aim to be objective.

Positivists favour experiments, as these are typical methods used in the natural sciences. However, it is often difficult to carry out experiments in sociology. Positivists tend to use instead social surveys and questionnaires, which also produce quantitative data.

KEY TERMS

Positivism: an approach to sociology based on studying society in a scientific manner.

Quantitative data: information and facts that take a numerical form.

Bias: prejudice that distorts the truth when research is influenced by the values of the researcher or by decisions taken about the research, such as the sampling method used.

Objectivity: absence of bias; the researchers do not allow their values or feelings to influence the research.

Surveys using questionnaires

Interpretivism

Interpretivists take a different view from positivists. They argue that there is a difference between the subject matter of sociology and natural science. Humans are active, conscious beings; they make choices. What makes a social event social is that those involved in it give it broadly the same meaning.

It follows that if we want to understand people's actions we have first to understand these actions in the way that the participants do. Social reality does not exist separately from human actions. It is embedded in social actions. Sociologists need to understand how people make sense of the social reality around them before they can understand their actions. Interpretivists say that if the subject of sociology is so different from that of the natural sciences, sociologists need to use different methods. Positivist methods are not appropriate. Positivists may be able to describe the social world, but interpretivists think it is more important to understand why people behave as they do.

Where positivists prefer experiments and surveys, interpretivists prefer to use unstructured interviews and participant observation, which are more helpful in uncovering why people behave as they do. For example, a positivist may be able to say how many people commit what types of crime, while an interpretivist will want to find out why they commit crimes.

An interview

TEST YOURSELF

1 What do you think positivists mean by the 'laws of social behaviour'?
2 Why do interpretivists prefer different research methods to those preferred by positivists?

The main steps in devising and implementing a research strategy

In this section we discuss research aims and selection of topic; hypothesis setting and revision; pilot studies; and sampling.

TOP TIP

Sociologists study sociological problems. These are not the same as social problems, which are the difficult issues that a society faces, such as how to tackle crime or poverty. Sociologists may study these but the main aim is to understand them, not to provide answers about what to do about them.

Research aims and selection of topic

Sociological research starts with the identification of a problem. The best research often involves problems that are also puzzles: not just a lack of information, but a lack of understanding. A research problem could be, for example, why girls do better than boys at school. Research projects do not stand alone; they are always related to or even arise directly from earlier research.

In deciding what to research, sociologists may be influenced by factors such as:

- their personal interests, experiences and observations
- what is already known about the topic and what is not yet known about it
- social changes and developments – there may be something new that we know little about
- whether funding is available, which may depend on how important funders think the topic is
- how practical it will be to do the research; for example, will it possible to identify and contact respondents?
- what ethical issues are raised by this topic.

Doing research can be costly, so obtaining funding for the research is important. The costs include not only travel and materials such as paper but the time spent on the research. Most research is carried out by sociologists employed by universities and other educational or research bodies, though the money may come from government, businesses and companies or from charitable organisations. To be able to start the research the sociologist may have to convince the funding bodies that it is a worthwhile project by writing them a proposal, including estimates of what the study will cost.

KEY TERM

Hypothesis: a theory or explanation at the start of research that the research is designed to test.

Hypothesis setting and revision

Having identified the problem or puzzle, the next stage is to review the available evidence. This involves finding out what is already known. Who else has identified the same problem and how have they gone about investigating it? The evidence will be in books and academic journals. This stage is often called the literature review. Drawing on the ideas of others helps the sociologist clarify the issues and make decisions about how to proceed.

The next stage is to turn the ideas into a clear **hypothesis** that can be investigated. A hypothesis is a statement that the research will attempt to find evidence to support or disprove; it is a sort of educated guess, often about how two or more variables are connected. The hypothesis might suggest a cause and effect relationship but sometimes research is only able to establish a correlation. While a research investigation using a positivist approach will probably have a hypothesis, a more interpretivist approach may have a looser and broader aim, such as to find out what a group of people thinks about something.

Now the sociologist has to decide the research method and plan its implementation. A range of different methods is available and the sociologist has to choose among them, influenced by practical, ethical and theoretical issues. The method chosen must be able to produce material that will provide evidence supporting or disproving the hypothesis or achieving the aim.

Pilot studies

Whatever method is chosen, it is important whenever possible to test it with a small number of respondents or in a limited way to see if there are any problems in the design or if the research plan can be improved. This is a **pilot study**. For example, a pilot questionnaire might be given to a small number of people to see if they can understand all the questions, and whether the answers available cover the responses they want to give. Putting problems right at an early stage saves money, time and effort later.

KEY TERMS

Pilot study: a small-scale test of a piece of a research project before the main research.

Survey population: all those to whom the findings of the study will apply and from which a sample is chosen.

Sampling frame: a list of members of the population from which the sample is chosen.

Sampling

The researcher has to choose an appropriate sample for the research by selecting some of all possible respondents. It is usually expensive and impractical to include all of them in the research so a number of them are chosen. Samples make research more manageable by making it possible to do research with smaller numbers of participants.

The people that the research is about are called the **survey population**. A list of everyone in the population is called a **sampling frame**. Commonly used sampling frames include the following.

- The electoral roll (also called the electoral register): this is the list of everyone registered to vote in elections, with their address. It therefore includes most adults, though it will not include anyone who is not registered or not allowed to vote.
- Telephone directories: these are easily available in countries where many people have land-line telephones and they give addresses as well as telephone numbers. However, they usually list only one person in each household. They do not tell you how many people live at an address and they do not include people who do not have telephones or who have chosen not to be in the directory.
- School registers: for research in a school there will be lists of children, with other information such as their gender, but these lists will be available only to genuine researchers and permission from those in authority, such as the head teacher, is needed.

All these sampling frames have problems. Getting a good, useful sampling frame can be difficult. But sometimes samples are not necessary. If you are in a small or medium-sized school you might find it possible to ask questions of everyone in your year group. Many countries have a census, which is a social survey carried out by the government to get information about every single person in the country. Censuses collect information from the whole population, not a sample.

Samples are usually chosen so that they are representative, that is, so that the researcher can claim that the results apply to the whole population, not just the sample. To be representative, the sample has to be a cross-section of the population. For example, if there are equal numbers of males and females in the

KEY TERMS

Generalisability: when the findings about a sample can be said to apply to a larger group of people sharing their characteristics.

Random sampling: when each person has an equal chance of being selected.

population, there should be equal numbers of males and females in the sample. The sample then has **generalisability**.

Types of sample

Samples can be chosen in several different ways. Some of the most common are:

1 **Random samples**. This is when everyone in the sampling frame has an equal chance of being chosen. This can be done by drawing names from a hat. It is the method used in making draws for sports competitions and for lotteries (you would be annoyed if you chose a number and found later that it was less likely to be chosen than others). Random samples are not always representative; for example, by chance, a sampling frame containing equal numbers of boys and girls might produce a sample dominated by one sex.

Random samples

KEY TERM

Stratified sample: when the sampling frame is divided, for example, by gender or age.

2 **Stratified samples**. To overcome the problem that random samples are not always representative, the sampling frame can be divided (for example, into boys and girls) and a random sample is then taken from each division of the sampling frame. Stratifying samples can be done by sex, age, ethnic group or any other characteristic. In draws for sports competitions, seeding is a way of stratifying the sampling frame and keeping the top players or clubs apart in the early stages of the competition. If the sampling frame is first stratified, then a random sample taken, this is a stratified random sample.
3 Systematic samples. This is when there is a regular pattern to the choice – for example, every tenth name in the sampling frame is chosen. It is not random because other names in the frame have no chance of being chosen.
4 Cluster samples. These are used when the population is spread out over a large area, such as a whole country. Certain areas are chosen for the sampling frame (for example, a city area and a rural area) and random samples taken in those areas to avoid the expense and time involved in travelling around the whole country.
5 Opportunity samples. These are simply the people who are available at the time to take part in the research. They are used, for example, when researchers stop people on the street and ask them questions. This is not random, because people who are not there at the time have no chance of being chosen, and because the researcher

will make decisions about who to ask (for example, by not asking people who look too busy or as if they would not want to take part). Opportunity samples are very often used by students who do not have the time to get a random sample.

6 **Quota samples**. This is when a researcher is sent out with instructions to find people with certain characteristics, for example, 10 teenagers taking IGCSE Sociology. This is often used in market research. If you are stopped in the street by someone asking questions they may well be finding out whether you are a suitable person for their survey.

7 **Snowball samples**. This has become a well-known way of contacting people when normal sampling will not work. It involves finding one respondent and getting them to put you in touch with one or more others. It has been used, for example, in interviewing gangsters – for whom there is no sampling frame.

KEY TERMS

Quota sampling: deciding in advance how many people with what characteristics to involve in the research and then identifying them.

Snowball sampling: when one respondent puts the researcher in contact with others.

Sampling methods: the different ways in which samples can be created.

Notice that the last three **sampling methods** described above do not involve a sampling frame.

After a pilot study and the choice of a sample, the research is carried out. The data are collected and the information recorded. Having collected the data, the sociologist has to analyse them and work out what they mean for the research problem. This is often far from straightforward; most research raises further questions because it is not clear what the findings mean, and they can be interpreted in different ways.

The research findings then have to be reported so that they can be read and used by others researching the same or related areas. Findings are usually published in academic journals or in books. This is the end of the individual research, but all research continues in the sense that it is part of the continuing process taking place within the worldwide sociological community.

TOP TIP

The Cambridge syllabus only refers to four sampling methods: random, snowballing, quota and stratified. Three other methods are explained here to give you an idea of the range of sampling methods sociologists use.

TEST YOURSELF

1 Why is it important for sociologists to choose their sampling method and sample carefully?

2 Why are pilot studies important?

Difficulties in implementing a research strategy

The stages involved in planning and preparing for research have been outlined above. Each stage involves problems. Some of these are listed in Table 1.1.

Research stage	Potential problem
Identifying a topic for research	There may be practical problems that can be foreseen, such as finding respondents. It may be difficult to get funding.
Reviewing existing evidence	It may be difficult to find existing evidence; the researcher may have to check many possible sources.
Developing a hypothesis or aim	At this stage difficult choices must be made about the overall approach; for example, what kinds of data are required.
Choosing a method	The method chosen may not produce data that can confirm or disprove the hypothesis or does not fulfil the aim of the project.
Implementing the research method	The problems with each method are explained in the sections on individual methods. The problems can be classified as practical, ethical or theoretical.

Table 1.1: Problems encountered in planning a piece of research

KEY TERM

Ethical issues: issues that have a moral dimension, such as when harm or distress may be caused to the participants.

The British Sociological Association

Ethical issues affecting the choice and implementation of a research strategy

Sociological research involves people, and so it raises issues about the welfare of both the researchers and respondents involved. Sometimes some research or some activities that might be part of the research should be avoided. **Ethical issues** involve decisions about what is right and wrong, and therefore involve values. Because it is possible to make wrong decisions and to carry out research that might harm people or damage the reputation of the university or organisation they work for, or of sociology as a discipline, the main professional associations in sociology have codes of conduct that guide researchers through these difficult areas.

ACTIVITY: *research*

The professional association for sociology in the UK is the British Sociological Association (BSA). You can find their code of conduct online at http://www.britsoc.co.uk/media/27107/StatementofEthicalPractice.pdf.

You will notice that these are guidelines rather than rules. This is partly because there are disagreements over what is and is not ethically acceptable, but also because there are some situations where breaking the guidelines might be justified. The guidelines exist to help researchers make the right decisions, not to tell them what to do in a particular situation.

Some of the main ethical guidelines that almost all researchers keep to are:

1 The participants must not be harmed.
2 The participants' informed consent should be obtained.
3 The researcher should not invade the participants' privacy.
4 Participants should not be deceived.

The researcher must also ensure that as far as possible and whenever appropriate the research is:

- anonymous – the participant's name (or anything else which might identify an individual) does not appear on the survey form; this is not always done if it might be necessary to contact someone again for further information
- confidential – it is not possible to trace an individual's answers from the published findings.

These main guidelines are considered one by one.

1 Harm. It is wrong to harm participants in a study but it is not easy to decide what harm means or to know in advance that harm will be caused. Harm does not have to be physical. It might include making participants feel angry or upset. This could happen if they are asked about something that disturbs them. Participants can be protected by confidentiality.
2 Informed consent. The respondent must agree to take part, having fully understood what is involved. Informed consent includes explaining the purpose of the research, when and where the findings will be available and what they might be used for. People have the right to refuse to take part in research or to refuse to answer particular questions, and the researcher should not try to persuade them if they do not want to. It is sometimes not necessary or possible

to get informed consent from everyone involved in research; for example, in observing a large number of people. Some kinds of research bring the researcher into contact with all sorts of people. However, the rule of obtaining informed consent rules out covert observation (see next section). There is also a problem about how much information has to be given to the participant in order for the consent to be informed. Explaining everything is time-consuming and probably not necessary. In fact, researchers probably break this guideline in minor ways quite frequently. For example, researchers may well underestimate how long an interview is likely to take when telling a participant. There also is sometimes a question of whose consent is needed. For a study of children of school age, should respondents get informed consent from the children, their parents (and which parent) or both?

3 Invasion of privacy. After they have obtained participants' informed consent the researcher still needs to respect their privacy. If a participant has agreed to be interviewed, they can still refuse to answer particular questions, and this may be because the questions seem to invade their privacy, for example by asking them about their earnings, their religious beliefs or their sexual activity.

4 Deception. A researcher may present their research as something different from what it is. This can involve lying about what the research is about, but it can also mean not giving full information in order to try to get the participant to respond more naturally. For example, a researcher observing a classroom may tell the pupils that they are helping the teacher rather than that they are researching the children's behaviour. This is deception.

TOP TIP

Students often think anonymity and confidentiality are the same, but they are different. When someone completes a census form, for example, they are asked to give their name so their information is not anonymous, but it is confidential, as the findings of the census are published as statistics from which it is impossible to find out what answers any individual has given.

TEST YOURSELF

1 Write an introduction to a questionnaire in which you ask the respondents for their informed consent. Start by asking them to complete the questionnaire but tell them that they do not have to do so, and go on to explain about other aspects of informed consent and about anonymity and confidentiality.

2 You decide to observe a class in a primary school to see whether the teacher treats boys and girls differently. What ethical issues would you have to consider, and how would you ensure you keep to the ethical guidelines?

The main methods used in sociological investigation; their strengths and limitations

The main methods used in sociological investigation are:

- **questionnaires/social surveys**
- interviews
- experiments
- case studies
- longitudinal studies
- participant observation
- non-participant observation
- content analysis
- triangulation.

KEY TERMS

Questionnaires: a standardised list of questions used in social surveys.

Social surveys: the systematic collection of information from a sample, usually involving a questionnaire or structured interviews.

In this section we look at the strengths and limitations of each method and assess their usefulness in sociological research and examine the types of evidence each produces.

Questionnaires and social surveys

Types of questions in questionnaires and surveys

Most surveys use different types of question. It is important to choose the right type of question for the information you want to collect and to make it easier to analyse your data. The main types of question are:

- **Closed or pre-coded questions**. The researcher provides a set of answers from which the **respondent** can choose one (or sometimes more), so the researcher limits the responses that can be given. Each answer is coded by being given a number or value that is then used for analysing the responses. The advantage of this is that it makes it easy to analyse the results and produce statistical tables. The disadvantage is that some respondents may want to give answers that are not available in the options provided. This disadvantage can be reduced by introducing an 'other (please specify)' option among the answers.
- Scaled questions (a particular form of closed-ended question). A common set of possible responses is: agree strongly/agree/neither agree nor disagree/disagree/strongly disagree. There is a debate about whether it is better to have an odd or even number of possible responses. If you have an odd number of responses – if there are, say, five options – most respondents will probably choose the middle one (in the example above, this would be 'neither agree nor disagree') because this avoids making a decision. If there are even numbers – if you eliminate the middle option – you push your respondents into making a decision. This helps to produce data that seem to prove something, but runs the risk of making people agree (or disagree) when they really do not have a preference.
- **Open questions**. The aim of a survey is always to produce mainly quantitative data. However, in order to probe more deeply into why people believe or do particular things it is possible to use open-ended questions where the respondents can write their own response. This produces some limited **qualitative data** but it does make it more difficult to analyse the data. It is normal in a questionnaire to code answers to open-ended questions so they can be analysed.

KEY TERMS

Open, closed and pre-coded questions: closed or pre-coded questions are those where the researcher has set out which responses can be recorded. In open questions the respondent can reply freely in their own words to give their responses.

Respondent: someone who provides information to researchers, usually used for surveys and interviews rather than other methods.

Qualitative data: information and facts (like attitudes or kinds of actions) that are not able to be presented in numerical form.

Self-completion questionnaires: questionnaires that are completed by the respondent on their own, with the researcher not present.

Postal questionnaires: self-completion questionnaires that are sent out and returned by post.

Response rate: the proportion of responses obtained out of a sample.

Ways of administering surveys

1 **Self-completion questionnaire**, also known as a self-administered questionnaire. Respondents answer the questions without any additional guidance from the researcher, who is not present. The most common type of self-completion questionnaire is by post, but in a school, for example, you might distribute questionnaires by asking teachers to give them to their classes. **Postal questionnaires** can reach large numbers of people so you can have a large sample, depending on your sampling method, which should make your results more representative and allow you to generalise. However, the **response rate** for postal questionnaires is often very low and this calls into question the representativeness of the findings. It might be the case that those who return the questionnaire are in some way different from those who do not; for example, they may have a particular interest in what the questionnaire is about. Because the researcher is not present, sometimes questionnaires are returned on which some questions have not been answered or the respondent has given inappropriate answers or clearly did not understand the question.

Ways of improving the response rate:

- sending a letter explaining the research in some detail, which not only gets informed consent but makes it more likely that the participant will answer
- sending a stamped, addressed envelope
- following up those who do not respond with a further letter reminding them about the questionnaire
- making the questionnaire as short and easy to complete as possible, so it is more likely to get a response
- giving clear instructions and questions that are likely to be relevant to or of interest to participants
- using people's names in a letter (rather than 'dear sir or madam') to make the participants feel more personally involved; the researcher could also individually sign each letter
- offering the participant an incentive of money or the chance of being entered in a prize draw if the questionnaire is returned.

2 **Structured interviews** (also called standardised interviews). It may at first seem strange to include interviews here, but this kind of interview is really just an alternative way of administering a questionnaire. In a structured interview the researcher reads out the questions, including the answers allowed in closed questions, and records the respondents' answers for them. This can be done as a **telephone questionnaire** or face-to-face. If the interviews are face-to-face, the location where they are held (administered) is very important. Ideally, the time and place for the interview should have been agreed in advance and the interviewee should be made to feel at ease. For a structured interview the questions need to be standardised (that is, the same questions are asked in the same order). Structured interviews normally have a higher response rate than postal questionnaires because the researcher can explain the purpose of the research and reassure the participants about any issues they may have. The researcher may also be able to give the interviewer prompts. However, structured interviews take up much more of the researcher's time than postal questionnaires do and are therefore more expensive. The researcher may employ assistants to carry out the interviews, in which case clear and detailed instructions need to be given to them.

KEY TERMS

Structured interview: an interview in which the questions are standardised (the same questions asked in the same order) and the replies codified to produce quantitative data.

Telephone questionnaires: when the researcher reads the questions to a respondent over the telephone and records their answers.

TOP TIP

The best way to learn about research methods is to try them out. The sections here on guidelines for good questionnaires and interviews and on the types of question to ask should be helpful if you try out these methods yourself.

Some guidelines for good questionnaire design

- A questionnaire should be as short as possible, with a clear layout that is easy to follow.
- Instructions for completing it should be easily understood and it should be easy to follow and complete.
- There should only be as many questions as necessary to obtain all the information required.
- You should start with short questions that need simple answers and that are likely to interest participants.
- There should be just enough alternative answers to allow participants to express their views and to provide the information required.
- Questions should not be leading questions that suggest to the participant that a particular answer is expected or is right.
- Questions should avoid words that might not be understood by everyone, including sociological terms.
- Questions should only be asked about things that participants are likely to know about and be able to give meaningful answers to.

- It is best to leave personal information (such as asking for the participants' name and age) to the end.

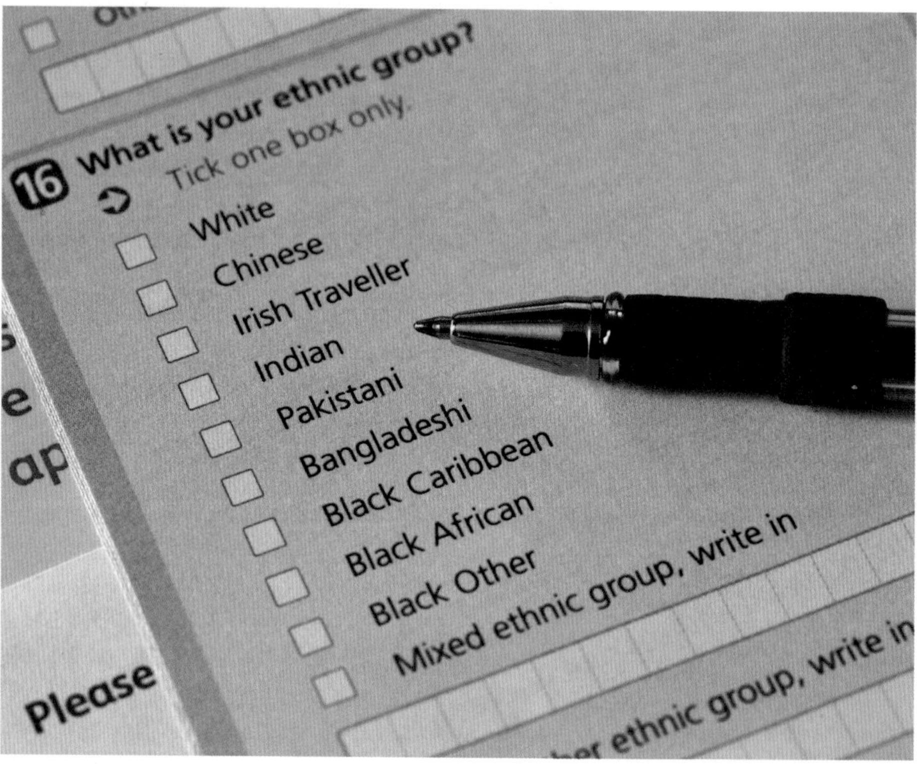

A question from the UK census

Strengths and limitations of self-completion questionnaires

Strengths:

- They are cheaper than structured interviews because they can be distributed by post.
- Large numbers of questionnaires can be posted to participants who may be geographically distant.
- The researcher is not present so cannot influence the answers given.
- They are convenient for participants who can complete the questionnaire when they choose.

Limitations:

- The response rate is low compared to structured interviews.
- Questions may be misunderstood and if a participant does not understand a question there is no one present to explain it.
- The researcher cannot be sure who answered the questions.
- Participants often leave some questions unanswered.

Strengths and limitations of structured interviews

Strengths:

- If the participant does not understand a question the interviewer can explain it.
- The interviewer can ask additional questions, probing deeper, or avoid questions that are not relevant to the participant.

- There is a higher response rate to structured interviews than to self-completion questionnaires.
- The interviewer may be able to set up a good relationship with the participants, winning their trust and getting valid answers.

Limitations:

- The interviewers may themselves influence the answers given either through their own social characteristics (such as their age, sex, ethnic group and so on) or through interaction with the participant.
- They take more time and are therefore more expensive than self-completion questionnaires.
- Participants may give socially desirable answers; that is, the answers that they think are the right ones, which give the interviewer the impression of them that they want.
- If several interviewers are used they may approach their work in different ways.

KEY TERMS

Reliability: when the research can be repeated and similar responses will be obtained.

Validity: when the findings accurately reflect the reality that it is intended to capture.

Social surveys are usually high in **reliability**; that is, they can be repeated and similar responses will be obtained. However, they are not always valid – the findings are not necessarily true. This was shown by research in the 1980s to find out how many unsuitable films children had watched. These films were horror films known as 'video nasties' and at the time there was concern in the media that young children who saw these films were being influenced by them. Surveys found that many children did say they had seen some of these films but to check the **validity** of the research a number of films that did not exist had been included in the survey. Children claimed to have seen these and so their answers must have been invalid. The children were claiming to have seen these films as a way of showing off to their peers, trying to seem more experienced and grown up than they really were.

CASE STUDY

A survey: the UK census

Like many countries, the UK holds a census to gather statistical information about everyone living there. The UK census is carried out every 10 years, most recently in 2011. Every household has to answer many pages of questions on a range of subjects, from the number and ages of people living there and their ethnic group and religion to how people travel to work. See online at http://www.ons.gov.uk/census/index.html.

You can find the actual questions asked in 2011 by clicking on Downloads then 2011 Census questionnaire online at http://www.ons.gov.uk/ons/guide-method/census/2011/the-2011-census/2011-census-questionnaire-content/index.html.

TASK

1. Using the website, put together a page of information about the census that answers these questions (and any information that you think is important): what is the census? How many households took part? When was the first census? What sorts of the questions does the census ask? Who has to fill in the census? What is the information from the census used for? How is the information kept confidential?
2. What strengths and limitations of the survey method does the census show?

KEY TERMS

Unstructured interview: an interview without set questions that usually involves probing into emotions and attitudes, leading to qualitative data.

Semi-structured interview: an interview with some standardised questions but allowing the researcher some flexibility on what is asked in what order.

Focus group: a group brought together to be interviewed on a particular topic (the focus); a special type of group interview.

Group interview: any interview involving a group interviewed together.

Interviews

The main types of interviews for qualitative research are **unstructured interviews**, **semi-structured interviews**, **focus groups** and **group interviews**. They are different from the structured interviews discussed above in several ways:

- Interviewers do not have to keep to a schedule of questions.
- The interviews are much more flexible and more like a conversation.
- The interviewer can follow up things that the interviewee says by asking new questions. In fact, if the interviewee goes off the point this may be seen as a good thing, because it reveals what the interviewee, rather than the interviewer, sees as important.

A typical unstructured interview

In *unstructured interviews* the interviewer has only a brief set of prompts. The aim is to get the interviewee to talk freely and the interviewer will try not to say very much except for encouraging the interviewee or probing a bit deeper at times.

In *semi-structured interviews* the interviewer has an interview guide, that is, a list of questions or fairly specific topics to be covered. The order of questions may vary and questions not in the guide may be asked, but all the questions in the guide will be used with a fairly similar wording.

While it is useful to identify different types of interview, in reality many interviews contain both types of approach.

Unstructured and semi-structured interviews are extreme types of interview research but most interviews are close to one type or another. Both types are flexible and clearly different from structured interviews, where there is no flexibility.

Some guidelines for good interviews

Interviewing is a skill. Good interviewers have to be flexible and good listeners, knowing when to intervene and when not to. They may be able to strike up a rapport with the interviewee, which will lead to rich, detailed and valid responses. They are likely to try to do the following things.

- Make the interviewee feel comfortable with the research situation, reassuring them about the purpose of the interview and that their anonymity and confidentiality will be preserved.
- Create a certain amount of order, so the questions flow reasonably well (but the order can be altered in the interview).
- Make sure the language used is understandable and relevant.
- Avoid leading questions or questions that make assumptions.
- Keep a fact sheet record, including the interviewee's name, age and gender to contextualise people's answers.
- Make sure the interview takes place in a quiet and private setting so that the interviewee feels at ease and able to talk freely and so that what they say can be heard (including on a recording).
- Use a good quality recording machine and microphone. It is always good to record and transcribe interviews whenever possible (remembering respondents have the right to refuse to speak into the microphone) because it helps correct the natural limitations of the interviewer's memory and it allows them to examine thoroughly what people say. The data can then be looked at again and used by others. However, recording and transcribing is time consuming – the usual estimate is that transcribing takes about five or six times as long as the interview itself.

Some types of questions used in interviews

- Introductory questions such as, 'Can you tell me about . . .? Have you ever . . .?'
- Follow-up questions to get the interviewee to elaborate, such as, 'What do you mean by . . . ? You mentioned . . . ?'
- Probing questions, such as, 'Could you say a bit more about . . . ?'
- Specifying questions asking for detail or elaboration, such as, 'What did you do then?'
- Indirect questions. For example, 'Why do many people feel that . . . ?' is probably a roundabout way of asking 'Do you feel that . . . ?'
- Silence, so that interviewees can reflect on and amplify an answer.
- Interpreting questions such as, 'Do you mean that . . . ?'

Focus group interviews

Focus group interviews are a particular kind of group interview. While some group interviews simply consist of a number of respondents who are interviewed together to save time and money, focus group interviews are about one particular topic. They were first used in market research but are now being used more often in sociology. The researcher will have an interview guide with different types of questions. Focus groups enable researchers to find out not just what individuals say but what they say as members of a group and how they respond to the views of others. This is closer to real social life than individual interviews, because we form our opinions through being aware of the views of others and through discussion with others, rather than on our own.

A focus group in action

Focus groups bring out a wide variety of views. Group members bring out the issues they think are important and their views may well be challenged by others in the group. The researchers need to decide how much they will be involved. Allowing a group to discuss freely is good because they can decide what is important but this runs the risk of much irrelevant discussion, so the researcher may intervene to keep discussions on track. The researcher may need to decide how to deal with silences and with reluctant speakers as well as with those who speak too much. Recording and transcribing focus group interviews are even more difficult than with individual interviews. It can be difficult to decide who said what and people often talk over each other.

Strengths and limitations of qualitative interviews

Strengths:

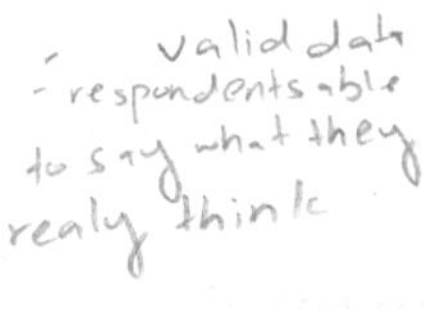

- Interviews, conducted well, provide detailed and valid data on the point of view of respondents, who are able to say what they really think.
- The flexibility of the interview allows the interviewer to probe more deeply or to follow new directions.
- Interviewers can often assess the honesty and validity of the answers as they are given.
- They can bring out information for further investigation.

Limitations:

- Interviews are time consuming, both to carry out and then to transcribe and analyse.
- It can be difficult to make generalisations when standardised questions are not used.
- They are less reliable than structured interviews because they are difficult to replicate.

KEY TERM

Interviewer bias: intentional or unintentional effect of the way that the interviewer asks questions or interprets answers.

- The interviewers need to be highly skilled.
- The responses may be a affected by **interviewer bias**; that is, by the intentional or unintentional effects of the way that the interviewer asks questions or interprets answers.
- The responses may also be affected by **interviewer effect**; that is, the answers are affected by, for example, the interviewer's sex, age or ethnicity.

CASE STUDY

Interviews: *Hard Labour* (2004) by Caroline Gatrell

This research, published as *Hard Labour* in 2004, studied how women in top professional jobs in the UK combined work with being a mother. Gatrell carried out 20 in-depth unstructured interviews with women and 18 with their male partners. The women all had at least one baby or preschool child. Gatrell asked questions about becoming a parent, housework and the problems the women faced at work because they were mothers and whether they felt there were conflicts between motherhood and work. She found that the women faced far more problems than men in combining being a parent with paid work and that laws on equality were not very effective and did not prevent discrimination (for example, a hospital consultant was demoted because she wanted to work part time) and that the women had to find complex ways of balancing work and motherhood. The women were willing to talk openly because Gatrell won their trust: this increased the validity of the findings. This was particularly important when asking about sensitive topics such as whether the women thought they were good parents. The sample was small and the couples were not representative of the whole population because of their high status and earnings.

TASK

1. Why is this type of interview good for researching sensitive topics?
2. Gatrell used individual interviews, partly because the women lived all over the UK. If focus group interviews had been held with groups of the same women, consider how the research and findings might have been different.

Experiments

Experiments are in many ways a neglected method in sociology but they are a valid way of studying social behaviour. They are the closest we can get in sociology to the methods of the natural sciences. They are usually a positivist method, producing quantitative data, and are often used to find cause and effect relationships or correlations.

Natural sciences such as physics and chemistry are traditionally associated with experimentation. Scientists, usually working in a laboratory, control the variables they are interested in, quantify the data and test their hypotheses, thus isolating causal links and minimising **subjectivity**. The experiments involve manipulating one independent variable and creating change in a dependent variable. Provided that all other factors can be held constant (controlled), changes in the dependent variable can then be said to be caused by the change to the independent variable. The aim of the experimenter is to test a hypothesis. The results of the experiment determine whether the hypothesis is accepted or rejected. Scientists claim that experiments have a high degree of reliability and experiments are always reported in a way that makes it possible for other scientists to replicate the research and check the findings. Scientists also claim experiments have a high degree of validity – they tell us something true about what is being studied.

There are very few **laboratory experiments** in sociology. Laboratory experiments are deeply flawed from a sociologist's point of view. People live

KEY TERMS

Interviewer effect: ways in which an interviewer may influence participants' responses, by their characteristics or appearance or by verbal cues such as facial expressions and tone of voice.

Subjectivity: lack of objectivity; the researcher's view influences the approach taken.

Laboratory experiments: experiments taking place in a laboratory, that is, an artificial setting created for the research where external variables are excluded as far as possible.

KEY TERMS

Hawthorne or Observer Effect: the unintended effects of the researcher's presence on the behaviour or responses of participants.

Field experiments: experiments that take place in the natural setting of the real world rather than in a laboratory.

in societies, not in laboratories, so studying how they behave in laboratories when they know they are being observed is not very helpful (people's behaviour changes when they know they are being observed – this is known as the **Hawthorne or Observer Effect**).

Because of this, sociologists use **field experiments** ('the field' being naturally occurring settings) more often than laboratory experiments. These experiments are often used by non-positivists and the results can be qualitative.

Field experiments

- These can present ethical problems: is it right to deceive people about the existence of the experiment or to manipulate their behaviour?
- They can involve risk: people may become angry about strange and new situations.
- The researcher can lose a large degree of control over what happens once the experiment is under way.
- They are a very effective way of getting inside group behaviour.

CASE STUDY

Laboratory experiment: Bandura and the Bobo dolls

A number of studies claim to have proved a link between watching violent acts and imitating them. Many of these were experiments conducted in laboratory conditions so that an imitative effect can be established. In the early 1960s Bandura and his colleagues carried out the best known of these experiments. They set up an experiment with four groups of preschool children, as follows:

- Group 1 saw real-life adult men and women attacking a self-righting inflatable doll with mallets.
- Group 2 saw a film of adult men and women attacking a self-righting inflatable doll with mallets.
- Group 3 saw a TV film of cartoon characters attacking a self-righting inflatable doll with mallets.
- Group 4 was the control group. The children saw no violent activity.

Following this experience, each child was deliberately mildly frustrated by being put in a room with lots of exciting toys but was told, on beginning to play with them, that they were reserved for other children. The child was then put in a room with only a doll that was like those seen by groups 1, 2 and 3. Each child spent 20 minutes in this room and was observed by judges seated behind a one-way mirror. The researchers found that the first three groups were all equally aggressive towards the dolls, and all were more aggressive than the control group. In other words, most of the children used the mallet to hit the doll, which was taken to prove that the children who had seen aggressive behaviour were more likely to be aggressive towards the Bobo dolls (the control group was less aggressive).

Here are some of the problems with this research:

- What is meant by violence or aggression here? Is it violence if no one is hurt? The children hit the dolls but this does not mean they would hit a real person.
- Children do not normally watch television in a laboratory with researchers watching – they watch at home with their parents, who can explain what is happening.
- If the media do affect people, it is likely that this is a long-term process – the 'slow drip effect' rather than being something that can be detected in their behaviour immediately afterwards.

TASK

1. Add to the list of problems given above. Think particularly of ethical problems.
2. Why would it not be possible to carry out an experiment to see if the children were violent towards real people?

CASE STUDY

Field experiment: *Pygmalion in the Classroom* (1968) by R. Rosenthal and L. Jacobson

In this experiment the researchers went to a primary school in San Francisco. They claimed to have a new intelligence (IQ) test that could predict which children would become 'high attainers' in the near future. The teachers were told that about 20 per cent of the age group would fall into this category of 'very able children' and were invited to administer the test. The researchers then told the teacher which pupils had been identified by the test as likely to become high attainers. In fact, the names had been chosen at random.

Over the next 18 months, the researchers went to the school regularly. At the end of the time the named children had made significant progress compared to others in the class, more than could be explained by chance. The researchers claimed that the dramatic improvement in performance was due to increased teacher expectations of the children in question. So teacher expectation was shown to be an important variable in shaping the child's self-image.

TASK

1. What was the main purpose of the experiment?
2. What was the main finding of the experiment?
3. What ethical problems arose from this experiment?
4. Why do you think this research has never been repeated?

KEY TERM

Case study: a detailed in-depth study of one group or event.

Case studies

Case studies involve detailed research on one or more examples of people or things. Case studies can involve any method or combination of methods, quantitative or qualitative. Many research projects involve a case study.

It is usually not possible to generalise from case studies or to use them to prove or disprove a hypothesis. There are some exceptions, however, where these are possible. One very famous case study in sociology was the affluent worker study in 1968 by John Goldthorpe and David Lockwood. They investigated whether car factory workers in the UK, because they were paid well compared to other factory workers, were starting to behave more like middle-class people than working-class people. Although only one factory (the 'case' in this case study) was researched, it was the where workers were paid most. Therefore, if embourgeoisement was not happening there the researchers could be sure it was not happening at other factories. This is an example of an extreme case being used to draw wider conclusions.

Strengths:

- Case studies allow different aspects of the case being studied to be explored using appropriate methods.
- Case studies can provide a deep and detailed account of the case.
- If the case is carefully chosen it may be possible to draw wider conclusions.
- Case studies can produce findings that can be tested by other research elsewhere.

Limitations:

- The findings may only apply to the case so generalisations cannot be made.
- The findings cannot be replicated.
- The deep involvement of the researchers may lead to them being influenced by their own feelings.

KEY TERM

Longitudinal survey: a survey taking place at intervals over a long period.

Longitudinal studies

Longitudinal studies are carried out periodically over a period of time, rather than as a one-off piece of research. Longitudinal research is often used by government-funded research organisations to ask basic questions about changing lifestyle, health, illnesses, education and employment. Most longitudinal research employs surveys. Examples of these in the UK include the:

- British Social Attitudes survey
- British Crime Survey
- British Household Panel Study (BHPS).

Panel studies

In some longitudinal research the same sample is used each time. The group of people or households being studied is called the panel or the panel sample. Panel members are interviewed on a regular basis with a period of months or years between each interview. The key requirement of panel studies is that as far as possible the respondents are the same people throughout the study.

CASE STUDY

Longitudinal panel research: the National Child Development Study (NCDS)

This follows the lives of 17 000 children in the UK all born in one week in March 1958. There have been eight follow-up surveys (or 'sweeps') when the respondents were 7, 11, 16, 23, 33, 42, 46 and 50 years of age. The data collected have been used to understand the importance of class and education, among other factors, in a person's life. Using NCDS data we know that the sons of professional fathers are more likely to get professional jobs than sons of working-class parents. We also know that working-class children who achieve A-level qualifications are far more likely to move up the social scale than working-class children who leave school with few GCSEs. Other topics that have since been studied include medical care, health, home environment, family relationships, economic activity, income, training and housing and even sleep patterns.

TASK

1. In what ways are the data gathered in longitudinal research more useful than that gathered in a one-off survey?
2. How might being involved in the NCDS affect members of the sample?

Strengths and limitations of longitudinal research

Strengths:

- One of the standard criticisms of survey research is that it only gives us a snapshot view of society. A survey based on questionnaires or interviews may tell us how a certain number of people think or behave in specific respects. But longitudinal research is like a film. It can show us how people's lives change over time. This is a great advantage of this type of research.
- It becomes possible to see what factors may have brought about changes in people's lives over time.
- Because the respondents have to be committed to the research there is a good chance that they will provide valid data.

Limitations:

- This kind of research requires a considerable commitment of time and research over a long period.
- There is an inevitable drop out from the research (also known as sample attrition), as individuals die or move away or decide they do not want to take part any more. The BHPS deals with this by following individuals wherever they go and also by including new household members to top up the original sample (for example, when a child becomes adult and marries, their partner will be invited to join the survey). This keeps the total numbers roughly the same but there is some movement of individuals in and out of the study at each wave. To motivate participants the BHPS keeps in touch with them by newsletter and written reports. Some panel surveys even send their members birthday and greetings cards.
- Being part of research like this may also change the participants. Sociologists call this the Hawthorne Effect described above. Someone taking part in this kind of research may well start to think more about aspects of their lives they are questioned about and may act differently as a result.

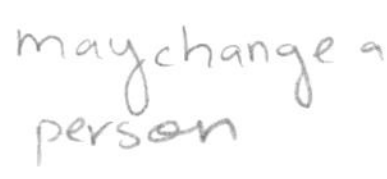

CASE STUDY

7 Up

Although it is not, strictly speaking, a piece of sociological research, the British television series *7 Up* is a good example of a panel survey. It began as a one-off documentary made in 1964, in which 20 7 year olds from very different backgrounds are shown talking to each other, going to the zoo and playing in a park. Every 7 years the same group is visited and interviewed about the progress of their lives. *7 Up* has given us some dramatic life histories and given us an insight into career and family choices and ageing in modern Britain. This type of programme has since been made in other countries and with new groups of children born later.

TASK

1. How does this case study illustrate the strengths of panel studies?
2. How might a) the Hawthorne Effect and b) sample attrition affect *7 Up*?

ACTIVITY: *research*

The Centre for Longitudinal Studies in London also runs the 1970 British Cohort Study *and the* Millennium Cohort Study. *Find out more about all three projects by visiting the website at* http://www.cls.ioe.ac.uk.

ACTIVITY: *research*

Find out if an equivalent of 7 Up *has been shown on television in your country. If you can, watch it and think about how much useful information it provides for sociologists about how people live.*

Participant and non-participant observation

Participant observation

Participant observation is used to develop an understanding of the world from the point of view of the subjects of the research. In this case researchers put themselves in the same position as those they are studying. The idea is to get inside people's heads to see the world as they do and how they make sense of it. It involves joining a group of people and living as they do. The stages of participant observation can be summed up in terms of getting in, staying in and getting out of the group concerned.

KEY TERMS

Overt participant observation: when the group being studied is aware that research is taking place and of who the researcher is.

Covert participant observation: covert means 'hidden'; in such research the group being studied is unaware of the research and is deceived into thinking the researcher is a real member of the group.

1 Getting in. Joining a group raises many questions about the researcher's role. Researchers adopt an **overt** role where they declare their true identity to the group and tell them that they are being studied. Alternatively, the researcher may adopt a **covert** role (by concealing their identity) or produce a cover story (partially declaring their role as a researcher, but concealing elements of it). To participate successfully, particularly if adopting a covert role, the researcher needs to share some of the personal characteristics of the group, such as their age, gender or ethnicity. After deciding what role to play, the next problem is getting access to the group. The presence of a stranger needs explanation. This may involve gaining friendships with key individuals, known as gatekeepers.
2 Staying in. The observer has to develop a role that will gain the trust and cooperation of those observed, so that they can continue to participate in and observe the group. At first this will involve learning, listening and getting a sense of what is going on. Problems encountered in staying in include the need to take notes, which may disrupt the natural behaviour of the group, and also deciding how far to be involved without either losing the trust of the group or the objectivity of a researcher. To maintain the group's trust, researchers may be expected to participate in acts that they do not agree with.
3 Getting out. Getting out of the group involves issues such as leaving it after the research observation without damaging relationships, becoming detached enough to write an impartial and accurate account and making sure members of the group cannot be identified.

Covert and overt participant observation

In covert participant observation the group being observed does not know that research is taking place. They assume that the participant observer is a new member of their group. This involves deceiving the group by concealing the truth about what the researcher is doing. The members of the group do not give their informed consent although the published research is likely to protect their anonymity. There are advantages to adopting a covert role in participant observation. It is most likely to be used where criminal or deviant activities are involved. It avoids the risk of changing the behaviour of the group under study because they do not know they are being studied. However, if the covert role is used and maintained, the researcher has little choice but to become a full participant in the group, because the research may be ruined if the researcher's real identity and purpose are discovered. This may involve participating in illegal or unpleasant activities. It is also difficult to ask questions and take notes without arousing suspicion, and there are moral and ethical concerns about observing and reporting on people's activities in secret without obtaining their consent first. The covert participant observer is likely to have to work hard at passing as a member of the group and making sure that the groups cannot discover that research is taking place.

Adopting an overt role means that the group is aware that research is taking place. The participant observer may well introduce themselves, explain the purpose of the research and obtain the group's informed consent. The advantage is that the researcher may be able to ask questions or interview people, and avoid participating in illegal or immoral behaviour. It is ethically and morally right for people to be aware they are being studied. However, adopting an overt role does have problems. For example, there is always the possibility that the group being studied may behave differently from normal, perhaps trying to make a particular impression on the participant observer. This raises questions over the validity of the research. The behaviour being observed and recorded is not how the group would behave if the participant observer was not there.

Strengths and limitations of participant observation

Strengths:

- They are usually high in validity, because the normal behaviour of the group is observed in its natural setting over a period.
- A deep understanding can be obtained, seeing things from the point of view of those involved.

Limitations:

- The presence of the participant observer may affect the behaviour of the group, but the researcher will not know in what ways it is doing so.
- Reliability is low because the research is very difficult to repeat or check.
- It is unlikely that generalisations can be made about other groups.
- There are problems throughout the research in gaining access to the group, winning acceptance, recording information, leaving the group and analysing the data.
- The researcher needs to have the social characteristics (such as age, gender, ethnicity) that will allow them to join the group and be accepted.
- Covert research involves the researcher devoting a lot of their time and energy to maintaining their cover, rather than gaining information.
- Researchers may lose their objectivity if they come to identify strongly with the group and see things from its point of view.

CASE STUDY

Participant observation: *Gang Leader for a Day* by Sudhir Venkatesh

As a young sociology student in Chicago, USA, Venkatesh decided to research the lives of people living in a poor area in the city. The area had many social problems including a high rate of crime and drug use and poor quality high-rise housing. The people in the neighbourhood there were African–Americans living in poverty. People at his university thought that Venkatesh was brave or foolish even to visit the area, which they considered dangerous. Almost by chance, Venkatesh was able to win the support of J.T., the leader of the Black Kings gang, who acted as the gatekeeper, taking Venkatesh around with him and in effect showing him how the gang and social life in the area worked – which was very different from what might have been expected from media and other accounts by outsiders. Venkatesh found that the gang played an important part in the life of the area, providing support to some of the most needy people and also punishing people whose actions harmed others in the community. For several years he spent most of his time in the neighbourhood.

TASK

1. In what ways does this research show some of the problems and advantages of participant observation?
2. This research was largely overt. People knew Venkatesh did not belong in the area, though they did not all know he was doing research. What issues could the covert researcher encounter in an area like this?

KEY TERM

Non-participant observation: when the researcher observes a group but does not participate in what it is doing.

Non-participant observation

Some sociological research is carried out by observation alone (without the researcher participating), which is known as **non-participant observation**. The main reason for this is to reduce or eliminate the risk that people will be affected by the presence of a researcher or a new member of their social group. It may also be used when groups might be unwilling to cooperate in the research, though this raises ethical issues. It is often used to produce quantitative data, with the observer, for example, counting the number of times something happens.

Non-participant observation also allows sociologists to observe people in their normal social situations and avoid the Hawthorne Effect. This can be achieved fully only when the observation is carried out without the knowledge of the observed, for example from a distance, by blending into the background, through one-way glass or using video cameras. If the observer is visibly present, even though they are not participating, there is still the possibility that their presence will influence what is happening.

A problem with this method is that it does not allow the researcher to investigate the meanings people attach to the behaviour that is being observed. The data produced may well simply reflect the assumptions and interpretations of the researcher, raising issues over the reliability and validity of the data.

KEY TERM

Content analysis: a method of studying communication and the media, which involves classifying the content and counting frequencies.

Content analysis

Content analysis is a research method used specifically to study the content of documents and the mass media, such as books, newspapers and magazines, television and films and websites. A researcher using content analysis defines a set of categories and then classifies the material being studied by how frequently it appears in the different categories. This can involve counting the number of times particular words are used or the amount of space or time given to a particular item or type of story.

For example, the Glasgow Media Group uses content analysis findings as evidence to support its claims about bias in the media, showing that striking trade unionists were given less time to explain their case than management representatives. Content analysis has also been used to show that disabled people are underrepresented in almost every genre of television programmes.

Strengths and limitations of content analysis

Strengths:

- It provides information about content of the media in statistical form and this can be used both to test sociological theories and to change the content of the mass media. For example, television stations might decide to improve provision for people with a disability as a result of content analysis findings.
- It is reliable.
- It does not involve people as respondents, so avoiding ethical issues.

Limitations:

- It produces quantitative data, that is, statistics. These can be interesting but will not tell us why a media text is the way it is or whether or how this affects audiences.
- It can be difficult to decide what categories to use.
- It can be difficult to allocate material to different categories.

CASE STUDY

Content analysis: *Viewing the World* (2000)

The UK government's Department for International Development commissioned research into the way that developing countries were reported on British television. The researcher recorded all the main news programmes on the five main terrestrial television channels for three months and then analysed them, counting the number and length of news stories that mentioned developing countries and also the tone of the story – what impression it gave of the country being reported on. They also analysed the content of some non-news programmes that had some coverage or mention of the developing world. It was found that the developing world was underreported (that is, there were few stories on these countries) and that the coverage was overwhelmingly negative, focusing on wars, disasters and deaths. Visits to these countries by famous Americans or Europeans and stories about wildlife were also reported. Nearly half of all the 137 developing countries were never mentioned at all in this period. There were also differences in coverage between the channels. Channel 4 had more news about countries in the developing world and was more likely to go beyond the normal negative coverage.

TASK

1. What decisions would these researchers have had to make when recording their data?
2. How do you think they measured the tone of the news stories?
3. What other content in the mass media could be analysed in this way?

KEY TERM

Triangulation: use of two or more methods in the same research project.

Triangulation

Triangulation is when a researcher decides to use a variety of research methods. For example a study may be conducted based on both observation and structured interviews, or on both closed questionnaires and diaries.

Strengths and limitations of triangulation

Strengths:

- Triangulation can allow the researcher to support quantitative data with qualitative examples, thereby providing a study with reliability and validity.
- It can be used to check the validity of the research.
- It can be used to check the reliability of the research using different sources.
- It can be used for cross-referencing the researcher's interpretations to other data collected to check for accuracy.
- It can provide balance between methods, where one may be weaker than another in that particular area of research.

Limitations:

- Using several methods is time consuming and expensive.
- The researcher needs to be skilled in several research methods.
- Positivist and interpretivist approaches are based on very different ideas, so it may be difficult to combine them in one piece of research.

TEST YOURSELF

1 In what ways are structured interviews more like questionnaires than unstructured interviews?
2 What are the advantages of longitudinal research over research carried out at one time?
3 Compare the differences between participant and non-participant observation in relation to practical, ethical and theoretical issues.
4 Draw a diagram showing the main research methods. Arrange them so that each method is placed closest to the other methods that it is in some ways similar to, and further away from those from which it is most different. You can use arrows and up to six words for each method.

The importance of analysing and evaluating research

This section examines issues of validity, reliability, **representativeness** and research bias in sociological research.

When you evaluate a research method you must consider three types of issues: practical, ethical and theoretical. Practical issues involve, for example, the resources, time and money the project needs, the response rates you have and the difficulties of transcribing long interviews. Ethical issues involve anonymity, confidentiality, informed consent, potential risks and harm. Theoretical issues include the overall positivist or interpretivist approach that is taken, but also validity, reliability, representativeness and bias. Usually researchers want their research to be both valid and reliable but it is difficult to achieve this because as you increase one you tend to lose the other.

KEY TERM

Representativeness: the degree to which research findings about one group can be applied to a larger group or similar groups.

Validity

Validity refers to the extent to which the research findings accurately reflect reality. The findings of participant observation and unstructured interviews are usually said to be valid because these methods allow the researcher to develop a detailed, in-depth understanding of the respondents and the research topic. In these situations it is unlikely that the respondents could mislead the researcher or provide false information. However, while these methods produce valid findings, their reliability is not as strong. These methods are favoured by interpretivists, who see validity as being more important than reliability.

TOP TIP

Many students think that reliability and validity, because they are both important, are similar or even the same. They are very different and it is essential to understand the differences.

Reliability

Reliability refers to the extent to which the findings of the research can be confirmed by repeating the study. Some research can be replicated. For example, science experiments can be carried out again in exactly the same way and in the same conditions, and if the experiment is reliable the same results should be obtained. This is hard to achieve with sociological research, but research repeated with a similarly representative sample should, with some allowance for individual differences within a sample, produce broadly similar results. Surveys are more reliable than participant observation and unstructured interviews but they tend to be less valid. This is because respondents do not always give truthful information.

Representativeness

Most research involving samples will use a representative sample. This means that the sample must be in effect a smaller version of the population being studied, with the same proportions of people of different gender, age and so on, according to what is relevant to the research. The researcher can then claim that the findings of the research apply not only to the actual sample but to the whole population being studied. This is generalisation. However, samples cannot be the same as the whole population, so there will always be a difference between the results for a sample and the results for the whole population. This is called sampling error. Sampling error can be reduced by having a large random or stratified random sample.

Research bias

Bias may come from the researcher's values, such as their political views. Positivists argue that researchers should be neutral and objective so that the findings would be the same regardless of who carries out the research and analyses the findings. However, interpretivists argue that because sociology is about people it is not possible to be completely unbiased. Even deciding what to research is likely to be influenced by the researcher's values. So researchers should be completely open about their bias to their readers and let them make their own decisions about the validity and reliability of the findings. This approach has been adopted by many feminist researchers.

The ways in which researchers can influence the findings is called the imposition problem; that is, the problem of the researcher imposing themselves or their values on the research. This can happen through the social characteristics of the researcher (gender, age and so on) influencing the answers given or the behaviour observed, or through the ways in which researchers word questions or analyse data. The findings of sociological research do not speak for themselves; they have to be interpreted. To assess the research we need to be aware of any possible bias in the interpretation.

TEST YOURSELF

1 Choose any of the case studies of research methods in this unit and assess how valid, reliable and representative the findings are likely to have been.
2 In which research methods does it make most difference who the researcher is (in terms of their gender, age and so on)? Are there any methods where this is not important?

ACTIVITY: *evaluation*

Evaluate the relative importance of the different factors sociologists consider when choosing a research method.

ACTIVITY: *discussion*

Is it possible for any research in sociology to be completely free of bias? Consider the case studies in this unit and any other sociological research you know.

What types of data and information do sociologists use?

The difference between primary and secondary data

Primary and secondary data have different uses and their strengths and limitations also differ.

KEY TERMS

Primary data: information collected by the sociologist at first hand.

Secondary data: information collected earlier by others and used later on by a sociologist.

Primary data and secondary data

Primary data are collected by the researcher. **Secondary data** are data that already exist, having previously been gathered by an earlier researcher (at which time they were primary data). In most research projects, the researcher first studies all the published research on the topic under investigation. By doing this they start by using secondary data. They then carry out research that produces new primary data, adding to knowledge on the topic and supporting or questioning the secondary data.

Sociologists use four main types of secondary data:

- official statistics produced by government or official organisations
- other research by other sociologists, by journalists and by the government
- the media (television, radio, internet, newspapers and magazines)
- other sources, mainly of qualitative data, such as diaries, letters and photographs.

Qualitative and quantitative data

This section discusses the strengths and limitations of different kinds of data. Qualitative data include historical and personal documents, diaries and media content. Qualitative data include numerical data such as official statistics and data in tabular and graphic form, including diagrams, charts and graphs.

Both primary and secondary data can be either quantitative or qualitative. Quantitative data are produced as numbers that can be used for statistics; qualitative data are usually in the form of words describing phenomena. Positivists tend to prefer quantitative data while interpretivists prefer qualitative data.

KEY TERM

Official and non-official statistics: official statistics are produced by government and official agencies, non-official statistics are produced by other organisations, such as charities and think tanks.

Quantitative secondary data: official statistics

Official statistics are the main source of secondary quantitative data for sociologists and are widely used. They consist of numerical data produced by national and local governments and by official bodies. It is useful to make a distinction between hard and soft statistics. Hard statistics are those that, apart from any errors or incompleteness in compiling, should be completely accurate. For example, records are kept in most countries of all births, marriages and deaths. The number of people found guilty of a particular crime is also a hard statistic, as all that is involved is counting all the cases found guilty in all the courts.

Soft statistics, on the other hand, depend on people making decisions about what to record and how, so that these decisions may lead to different statistics. These include crime and unemployment statistics because decisions are made about what to include and how to compile the statistics.

Strengths and limitations of official statistics

Strengths:

- They are readily available, often free of charge and on the internet, and therefore cheap and easy to use. Governments have spent more time and resources collecting these statistics than a sociologist would be able to.
- They are usually produced by research that is well planned and organised, using large samples. They are likely to be valid, reliable and representative.
- They are often part of longitudinal research so they show changes over time, for example, in crime, unemployment and divorce rates. This makes it possible to identify **trends**; that is, the general direction in which something develops or changes over time.
- They allow comparisons to be made, such as between men and women or between different areas of a country.

KEY TERM

Trend: A change over time in a particular direction.

- They are widely used to help governments and other organisations plan ahead. They provide information that is useful to policymakers as well as sociologists.

Limitations:

- Interpretivists argue that statistics are socially constructed, rather than being objective facts, and that therefore we should be very cautious about using them, especially about taking them at face value. For example, statistics showing an increase in motoring offences such as speeding may not really mean there has been an increase in the offence. They may mean that the police have been cracking down on motorists and so more offences are being recorded.
- Statistics are often not as complete or accurate as they may appear to be or may claim to be. For example, it is thought that the 2011 UK census, conducted with a huge budget and when it was an offence not to complete a census form, missed out about a million people.
- Official statistics have been produced by others and are unlikely to contain exactly what a sociologist would like to know. For example, sociologists might want to know how many marriages break down but official statistics will only count divorces and not separations.
- Official statistics are funded by a government, which means that politics can affect the statistics. Statistics may be biased in favour of the government, massaged (or altered, subtly or not) to show things in the best light. When statistics would be embarrassing for the government, they may not be published or they may never be collected in the first place.
- Comparisons over time can be made only if the same phenomenon has been measured in the same way at every stage. For example, a rising crime rate could be explained by a government passing new laws making more activities illegal. Official statistics are therefore very useful for **comparative studies**, which involve comparing different areas, groups or periods of time, looking for similarities and differences.
- Marxists argue that statistics reflect the interests of the ruling class; they help to maintain and justify the way things are. For example, the way laws are made and the statistics put together has the effect of drawing attention away from crime committed by the ruling class.

KEY TERM

Comparative study: in research, looking at two or more different groups or events in terms of their similarities and differences.

Non-official statistics

As well as official statistics, other widely available statistics are of use to sociologists. These include research commissioned by organisations such as religious groups and charities and the work of organisations such as policy institutes (often called 'think tanks' in the media) that carry out research. In the UK, for example, the Sutton Trust and the Joseph Rowntree Foundation carry out research on social issues.

ACTIVITY: *research*

Visit the website of the Joseph Rowntree Foundation. Make a list of the kinds of research project the foundation carries out. Choose one project to investigate in detail and make a summary of the methods and findings.

Diagrams, charts, graphs and tables

Statistics and quantitative data can be presented in a number of formats. Researchers have to decide the most appropriate format for presenting data and for making their findings accessible to their readers. Sociological researchers use various types of diagrams, charts, graphs and tables. Students of sociology need to be able to interpret these tables accurately and extract information, and if you carry out your own research you may also need to be able to construct diagrams, charts, graphs and tables. The activity on the following page gives examples of some of the most common ways of presenting statistical data. Answer the questions to see if you can interpret the data.

ACTIVITY: *data interpretation*

Graphs

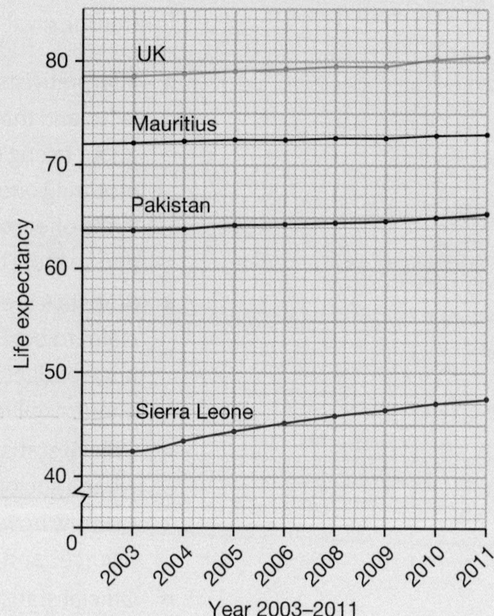

Life expectancy at birth, total (years) from 2003 to 2011 for four selected countries

1 Which country has the highest life expectancy throughout the period?
2 In which country did life expectancy increase most over the period 2003 to 2010?

Tables

Country	Literacy rate	
	2000/2001	2010
Mauritius	84	89
Sri Lanka	91	91
Bangladesh	47	57
Singapore	93	96
Italy	98	99
The Gambia	37	50
China	91	94
Saudi Arabia	79	87

World Bank literacy rate; adult total (% of people ages 15 and above), 2000/2001 and 2010

Note: Adult (15+) literacy rate (%). The total is the percentage of the population age 15 and above who can, with understanding, read and write a short, simple statement. Generally, 'literacy' also encompasses 'numeracy', the ability to make simple arithmetic calculation.

1 Which countries in the table had the highest and lowest literacy rates in each year?
2 Which country made the greatest improvement between 2000/1 and 2010?

Bar charts

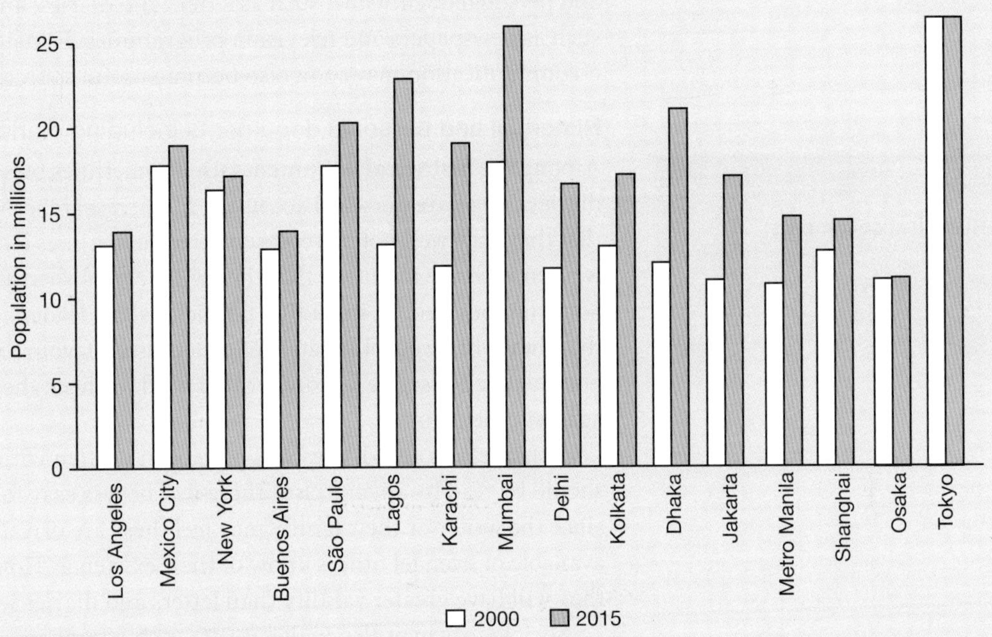

Growth of megacities

1 What was the largest city in 2000?
2 Which other city will also have a population of over 25 million by 2015?
3 Identify the four cities that will have grown the least between 2000 and 2015.

Pie charts

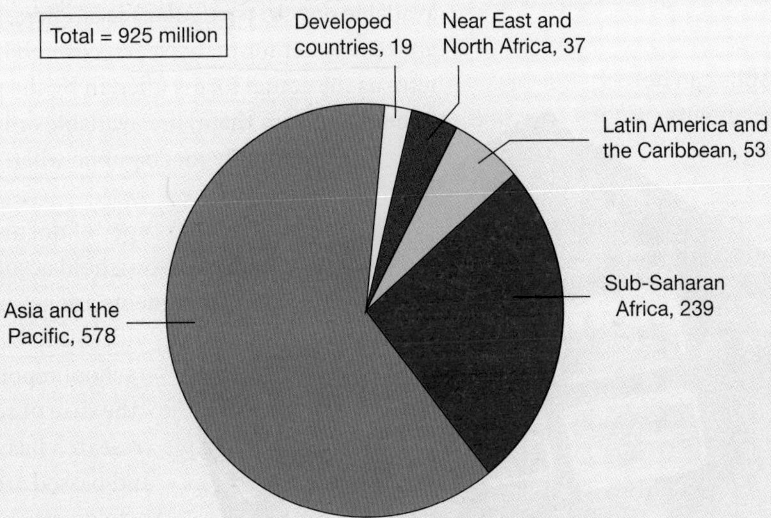

Undernourished people in the world by region, 2010

1 Which regions of the world have (a) the highest number of undernourished people and (b) the lowest number?
2 What would you need to know to calculate which regions of the world had the highest rates of undernourishment (that is, per number of people in the population)?

Types of qualitative data and their strengths and limitations Qualitative secondary data include a wide variety of sources. The main ones are historical and personal documents, such as letters and diaries, and media sources such as newspapers and television programmes. E-mails, tweets and other e-communication may soon also become useful sources as more people use them.

Historical and personal documents including diaries

KEY TERM

Historical documents: a wide range of documents from the past used as sources of information by sociologists.

Among the **historical documents** used sometimes by sociologists are letters and diaries. These are personal accounts, so the researcher will need to bear in mind that they may well not be representative. Sometimes letters and diaries have been written with the intention that they will be published at some time in the future. Some famous people, including politicians and leaders, have done this. It is likely that they will give, deliberately or otherwise, a favourable view of themselves and their actions. The researcher will need to check the validity of their accounts against other sources.

Other letters and diaries will have been written with no intention that they should be read by anyone else. These will be less easy for the researcher to obtain, since the writer or their family may feel these are private and may not make them available or even let others know of their existence. However, if they can be used they will have greater validity than letters and diaries written for publication.

Sociologists may also make use of autobiographies, people's published accounts of their lives. As with diaries and letters intended for publication, these need to be treated with caution as the writer may have been more concerned with giving their own version of events and presenting themselves in a favourable light than with writing an accurate account. Autobiographies are also likely to be written many years after the events they describe, so they may be affected by a faulty memory. The validity of autobiographies is therefore questionable.

Governments and other official organisations produce documents of many types. Some of these are available immediately to the public but others are made available only to particular researchers, not the general public and still others are kept secret for many years, covered by official secrecy laws. In the UK census returns the actual forms filled in by the public (not the statistical summaries compiled from them) are available only after a hundred years. Most documents are eventually made public when they are no longer seen as confidential or sensitive.

Other types of documents can be useful in sociological research, such as household accounts, wills and even shopping lists. Documents are not necessarily written: photographs and home videos can be useful sources. Some documents such as school reports may also contain quantitative data (in the case of school reports, exam or test grades). Some research has even used notes written by pupils in class and passed around when the teacher was not looking. Sociologists are always curious about social life and will use whatever sources of information are available.

Sometimes researchers ask people to keep diaries, which can then be used alongside data from interviews or questionnaires. One of the best known examples of this was the Mass Observation research in the UK in the 1930s in which large numbers of people were asked to keep diaries, providing a rich source of

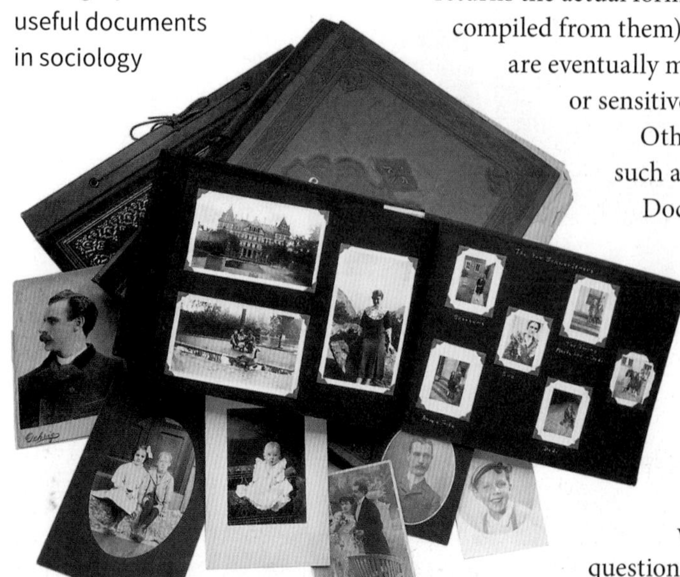

Photographs can be useful documents in sociology

information about life at the time. In the Mass Observation these were primary data, but they became secondary data when used by later researchers.

Strengths and limitations of qualitative secondary data such as letters and diaries

Strengths:

- They may be high in validity.
- They offer first-hand accounts by people involved.
- They provide descriptive detail and insight missing in statistical sources.

Limitations:

- They may be unrepresentative.
- They need to be checked against other sources.
- They may be biased, intentionally or otherwise and may reflect the emotional state of the writer at the time.

Media content

The media (such as newspapers, magazines, television, film, recorded music and the internet) provide a vast amount of material of interest to sociologists. The media can be a source of information on a topic being researched. The sociologist may use a relevant documentary television programme, for example, as part of their literature review at the start of a research project together with printed material, to find out what is already known about a topic. The researcher needs to be aware of possible bias and selectivity in the content of the programme.

The media can be a source of information

Media such as novels and films explore themes of interest to sociologists. Sometimes these are intended to be accurate descriptions of what life was like in a particular time and place and they can bring that experience to life in a way factual writing cannot. It can, however, be difficult for the sociologist to separate what is based on reality and on detailed research from work that comes from a writer's imagination.

Interpreting and evaluating evidence from qualitative sources

A sociologist using qualitative secondary sources needs to be able to interpret and evaluate the sources. These are some of the questions that sociologists may ask to help them do this:

- Who produced the source? For historical sources we need to evaluate whose point of view is promoted, and take into account groups whose points of view are not available. Many sources will be written by people coming from the middle and upper classes, and the point of view of those lower down the social scale and who are more likely to be unable to write may be missing.
- Why was the source produced; for example, was it intended to be read by others or not?
- Was the author in a position to know about what they are writing about (for example, is it a first-hand account of an event?)
- Does the source seem to be biased?
- Does it seem to be typical of this kind of social actor and how can this be decided?
- Are there other sources that corroborate or conflict with the source?
- Is it clear how the author meant the document to be interpreted?

ACTIVITY: *evaluation*

Evaluate the usefulness of different types of secondary data in sociological research.

TEST YOURSELF

1. Explain the difference between primary and secondary data.
2. List all the types of a) hard statistics and b) soft statistics you can think of. Use a newspaper or news website to find some statistics and work out whether they are hard or soft. Even football league tables are statistics.
3. How can qualitative secondary sources be evaluated for validity, reliability and representativeness?

Revision checklist

Make sure that you know all the key terms listed in this unit and that you understand the following:

- Structuralist approaches focus on social structures and institutions and how these influence how people behave. Interpretivist approaches focus more on how individuals make sense of society.
- Functionalism is a consensus theory.
- Marxism and feminism are conflict theories.
- Positivists and interpretivists have different approaches to carrying out research.
- Each stage of the research process involves choices and decisions involving a range of practical, ethical and theoretical issues.
- Sociologists use different types of research methods, including surveys, interviews and participant observation and experiments.
- Other types of research include case studies, longitudinal studies and triangulation.
- Sociological methods and their findings can be evaluated in terms of their validity, reliability and representativeness.
- Research can produce quantitative or qualitative data.
- Sociologists also use both primary data and a range of secondary data including official and unofficial statistics, documents such as diaries and letters, media and published sources.

Exam practice questions

Source A: Eleven young women aged between 23 and 29 who had become pregnant when they were teenagers were interviewed. They had all grown up in socially disadvantaged families in a town called Kelby (not its real name). The purpose of the research was to examine how poverty and social exclusion early in their lives had affected them later as mothers. The women in the sample had found it difficult to find paid work and they relied on their relatives to help them with childcare.

(Webster *et al.*, 2004, *Poor Transitions: Social Exclusion and Young Adults*).

a Why did the researchers decide not to use the real name of the town? [2]

b Identify two types of interviews that sociologists use. [2]

c Using information from the source, give two reasons why sociologists might question generalisations made from this research. [4]

d Describe two strengths of using group interviews for sociological research. [4]

e Describe two strengths and two limitations of using questionnaires for sociological research. [8]

f Explain why interpretivists prefer using methods that produce mainly qualitative data. [10]

g To what extent do ethical issues influence the way sociological research is carried out? [15]

Total available marks 45

Unit 2: Culture, Identity and Socialisation

Objectives

At the end of this unit you should be able to:

- understand the key terms culture, norms, values, roles, beliefs and identity, appreciate that these are social constructions and understand how they influence human behaviour
- understand the terms conformity and non-conformity and how agencies of social control work
- know examples of rewards and sanctions applied in different societies and organisations
- explain the nature of sub-cultures and how these impact on consensus and conflict
- describe and account for diversity and variations in human behaviour and culture, including issues related to cultural relativism and multiculturalism
- assess the view that globalisation is creating a global culture
- explain the ways in which childhood is socially constructed
- describe the processes of learning and socialisation, both primary and secondary
- explain the different agencies of socialisation and their impact on individuals, including the consequences of inadequate socialisation
- assess the different views in the nature/nurture debate
- assess role, age, gender, ethnic group and class as influences on social identity.

Introduction

What is it about human beings that makes us what we are? We all belong to a single species, *Homo sapiens*, the only survivor of a number of species of ape that we call human. We have a lot in common with other species of animals yet we feel we are different. We have grown in numbers and become the dominant species on the planet, expanding into areas very different from the original habitat of our distant ancestors on the plains and in the forests of Africa. We live in complex societies that are increasingly interconnected. Increasingly, we control (or fail to control) our own destiny as a species and the destiny of our planet and all its life forms.

For sociologists, what makes us distinctively human is our relationships with other people, how we live in groups and societies and how we reflect and act upon our lives. This unit explores the relationships between individuals and societies, and how much we are shaped by the social influences around us. It looks at how our sense of our own identity is shaped by those around us, and at how, in learning to live with others, we are learning to be human. In doing so this unit will sometimes look at other possible alternative influences, looking beyond sociology and putting sociological ideas in a wider context.

What is the relationship between the individual and society?

Culture, norms, values, roles and beliefs

KEY TERMS

Culture: the way of life of a society.

Beliefs: statements that people hold to be true.

This section examines the social constructions of **culture**, norms, values, roles and **beliefs** and how these influence human behaviour.

There is no agreed definition of the term culture but it is used in two main ways. In everyday speech it usually refers to things like art, music and literature. Sometimes it also refers to things such as the media, fashion and advertising – which are sometimes called popular culture. In this unit we are using the term in a broader way to mean the whole way of life of a society. In this sense every aspect of human life is influenced by culture because we constantly refer, consciously or unconsciously, to our society or social group for guidelines about how to think and behave. Culture includes:

- what you eat and drink, with whom and when
- how you dress and the care you take over your appearance
- the language, spoken and unspoken, that you use to communicate with others
- the way you spend your leisure time
- the kind of home and family you live in
- religious and spiritual beliefs and practices
- festivals and celebrations.

All societies have ideas about the right and wrong ways of doing these things.

Elements of culture: norms, values, roles and beliefs

Each human culture can be thought of as having these five elements:

1 Symbols. These are anything that carries particular meaning recognised by people who share the same culture. For example, a cross worn on a chain is a symbol of Christian religious beliefs and a shirt with a particular colour and crest may show that the person wearing it supports a particular football team. Some countries have national symbols.

KEY TERMS

Values: standards shared by members of a culture and used to judge whether behaviour is right or wrong.

Norms: the behaviour that societies expect of their members in particular situations.

Social interaction: any situation in which two or more people have social contact with each other.

Customs: norms in a particular society that are widely accepted and carry on over time.

Laws: rules that are given force by being formalised by governments.

Status: a position that someone has in a society; status can be ascribed (fixed by others) or achieved.

2 Language. A system of symbols with sounds and words carrying meanings that allows people to communicate with one another.
3 **Values**. These are standards of what is considered good and right that act as guides for what people should think and believe and how they should act. Many people claim to have their own values but these will be shared with others.
4 Beliefs. These are statements that people hold to be true. They are more specific than values.
5 **Norms**. These are the kinds of behaviour that a society expects of its members in particular situations. Sometimes norms are divided into two types, mores and folkways. Mores are norms that are widely observed and carry more of a sense of what is right or wrong. Folkways are norms for routine, casual **social interaction**. Norms that are widely accepted and continue over time are sometimes called **customs**. In addition, some norms are given extra weight by being used as the basis for rules, regulations and **laws**. Norms are usually enforced by informal means, laws by formal means.

Values, beliefs and norms (including mores and folkways) are not always easy to separate in reality. They all provide guidelines for how people should behave but they differ in how specific or general they are. Values include things like personal space and privacy. In some modern industrial societies these are highly valued. From these values derive beliefs, such as that it is wrong to move into someone's personal space. Knowing what the values are makes it possible to work out what the norms will be, even in a new situation. Norms derived from these values include how far away you stand when talking to someone and where you sit, for example, on a bus or in a train. Norms can usually be traced back to an underlying belief or value.

Values and norms vary between societies so they are social constructions. For example, in some societies people stand closer to each other when talking than is normal in modern industrial societies. There are also societies where it is normal and right to sit next to a stranger on a bus, even if there are empty seats somewhere else. The norms here are based on values about personal space.

One distinctive value in modern industrial societies is the desirability of being wealthy and owning material goods. North American Indians also placed a high value on possessions but this is not for personal enjoyment. At festivals known as potlatch celebrations, wealthy Indians gave away lavish gifts to their guests. In return, the gift giver received the approval of the recipients and was looked up to and highly respected. Possessions were considered to have little value other than to be given away, by which the owner could acquire **status** and respect. An individual in a modern industrial society who gave away most of their possessions in this way would be considered eccentric or even insane.

Norms and values also change over time in a society. Norbert Elias described in his book *The Civilising Process* how in the Middle Ages there were fewer constraints on individual behaviour than there are today. The state was weak and unable to control individual behaviour to any great extent and those with power could use violence and force to get their own way. But as the state grew in power a 'civilising process' started. It had been common for strangers to share a bed in an inn, for people to eat with their fingers from common bowls and for people to go to the toilet in public. By the late medieval period books on etiquette were advising the nobility that burping, breaking wind, spitting and picking one's nose in public were uncouth and bad manners. By the 19th century such behaviour was unacceptable in all but the lowest classes. We still distinguish classes by their refinement in manners and personal behaviour.

TOP TIP

Values and norms are the most commonly used of these terms. Think of values, beliefs and norms as lying along a continuum with no clear distinction between them.

In modern society there are more norms that cover more areas of life. Elias also suggests that it became the norm to control emotion. People still have violent and intense emotions but are now shocked by emotional display when they would not have been centuries ago. Because norms and values are different in different societies around the world and differ in different periods of history we can say that they are socially constructed. They are made by societies not by individuals and they are not natural in the way that scratching an itch is natural (dogs and cats scratch as well).

Because people in a society share values and norms, most of the time social life is orderly and predictable. Not everyone shares all the values or conforms to all the norms but societies have ways of expressing disapproval of those who break the norms and of encouraging or forcing people to conform.

Elements of culture: status, role and identity

Most norms are associated with status, which is the position someone has in a society. You have the status of a sociology student. Your teacher's status is that of a teacher. But you both have other statuses too. For example in your family your status is son or daughter, brother or sister. In traditional societies, most statuses were ascribed; that is, they were decided at birth, with individuals unable to choose or decide their status for themselves. In modern industrial societies some statuses are now achieved. Individuals make decisions or follow courses of action that lead to particular statuses. With each status goes a set of norms called a **role**. The role of a student includes norms such as attending classes, asking questions and learning. Students are expected to sit at a desk and listen to what the teacher says. A role is like a script to follow in a play but it is one that gives you some choice over how you act it out (you may be a good student or a lazy one, for example).

> **KEY TERMS**
>
> **Role:** the patterns of behaviour expected of someone because of their status in society.
>
> **Social institutions:** parts of society that have their own sets of norms and values, such as the family and the school system.
>
> **Social identity:** individuals' perception of themselves, based partly on ideas about how others see them.
>
> **Gender:** the roles and expectations associated with being male or female.

At this stage it is helpful to think more about what is meant by society and culture. They are very closely related and sometimes interchangeable terms, but they are different. Cultures and societies cannot exist without each other. Society is made up of **institutions**, both formal ones such as the legal and educational systems and informal ones such as families. Culture is about how these institutions work, setting norms and expectations about the roles people should play. At the macro level we talk about culture and society; at the micro level about individuals and identities. Identities refers to our sense of who we are, how we see ourselves and the ways in which we think we are similar to and different from other people. An inescapable part of this is about how other people see us and judge us. In other words, our sense of ourselves comes to a large extent from others. Other people may give us feedback about ourselves and our behaviour but even without feedback we can put ourselves in the position of others and imagine how they would see us. The norms and values of our culture are part of our identity, because if we conform we will be seen as good and will see ourselves as good.

Our **social identity** or image of ourselves is therefore formed through interaction with others – 'no man is an island' (sociologists would add 'or woman'). Identifying ourselves as male or female is our **gender** identity. We also develop identities in groups and situations such as the family, at work, at school. We see ourselves as having certain characteristics such as being a good friend or being a tough boss. Identities connect individuals to the macro level in the sense that through our identity we can see ourselves in the context of our culture, linking our inner selves (who we think we really are) with the roles we occupy in society.

We can choose how to respond to the identities we see ourselves as having. For example, a person with a disability may see their disability as an important aspect of their identity because such people are often treated differently from others.

Stuart Hall (see page 50)

They can choose how to deal with this, for example, by passively accepting inferior treatment or by rejecting the label and fighting back to emphasise their abilities. Stuart Hall has argued that in the 21st century people are often more uncertain about their identities than they were before. For example, ethnic identities are no longer as clear as they once were and more people have mixed backgrounds and are familiar with different cultures. We also have more roles and sometimes there is more uncertainty about what these roles involve. This can be experienced as disorientating or as liberating, in that it breaks down old **stereotypes**.

KEY TERM

Stereotype: the attributes that people think (often wrongly) characterise a group.

ACTIVITY: *research*

Interview several older people and ask them how your society's culture has changed over their lifetimes. What changes in values and norms do they think there have been?

TEST YOURSELF

1 What is the difference between a society and a culture?
2 How are our identities connected to the culture that we live in?
3 In what ways is social life like performing in a play?

KEY TERMS

Social control: ways in which members of society are made to conform to norms and values.

Rewards: a positive sanction so that someone is praised or is better off.

Sanctions: ways of rewarding or punishing acceptable or unacceptable behaviour, usually used in the sense of punishment (negative sanctions).

Sub-culture: a group within a larger culture that has its own distinctive norms and values.

Youth sub-culture: a sub-culture of adolescents or young adults that is usually distinguishable by their style, dress and musical preference.

Value consensus: general agreement across a society on a set of values.

Social conformity: acting in accordance with norms and social expectations.

Informal social control: ways of controlling behaviour imposed by people without a formal role to do so (such as peers).

Conformity and nonconformity

This section examines the agencies and processes of **social control** and gives examples of the **rewards** and **sanctions** applied in different societies and organisations (such as schools and the workplace). It looks at the existence of **sub-cultures** (like **youth sub-cultures** and religious sub-cultures) in society and how these impact on social consensus and conflict.

Conformity and non-conformity: the agencies and processes of social control

Nearly all people conform to most norms most of the time. People conform because through socialisation they have internalised the norms and values of their culture. There is a **value consensus**; nearly all people in a society agree on shared values, and also on the norms derived from them. Even criminals will often disapprove of the actions of other criminals, which suggests that they share part of the overall value system. However, societies need to have ways of ensuring **social conformity**. All societies have ways of making their members conform to norms. This is achieved by systems of sanctions. Positive sanctions are often referred to as rewards and so sanctions usually mean negative sanctions (punishments).

Informal social control is exercised by individuals and groups who do not have any official power to do so. It includes, for example, any way in which you might express disapproval of something your friends have done that you do not like. You might make a negative comment about them or refuse to speak to them until they apologise. Informal social control can seem minor but is often very effective. It can be exercised through glares and comments like 'that was rude' or expressions of anger or disgust. One common form of informal social control in **peer groups** of young people is **ostracism** or social rejection; that is, an individual is excluded from the group and made aware that they are not welcome.

Some types of informal social control are:

- shame
- ridicule
- sarcasm
- criticism.

When informal social control does not work, then **formal social control** may be used. This needs to be done by someone who has authority in that situation, such as a teacher, employer or police officer. Agencies of formal social control include the police and the criminal justice system. They can impose a wide range of formal sanctions, such as fines and imprisonment.

Agencies of social control are also **agencies of socialisation**. They pass on norms and values but they are also able to make people conform. The main agencies of social control are as follows.

- Families. It is through **primary socialisation** in the family that children absorb norms and values. The strong bonds between parents and children and the impressionability of young children make this the most important period of socialisation. Children learn to regulate their own behaviour so as not to offend others. They internalise values so that they feel guilt and remorse if they break norms that are based on them.
- Schools. In the school system children are controlled in many ways. They are told what to do and when, most of the time. Unit 5 explores the idea of the **hidden curriculum**, which suggests that at school learning to obey the rules and conform to education is as significant for children as learning knowledge and skills.
- Religion. For those with religious beliefs, religions offer guidelines and laws for how to behave and offer both rewards and punishments for behaviour. The values of a society are often based on the main religion.
- The media. The media offer role models as well as constant messages about how to behave and reminders about rewards and punishments through offering examples of good and bad behaviour, both in factual news reporting and in fiction.
- Workplaces. There are rules and regulations at places of work and other norms that people may need to learn as they settle into a new job.
- Peer groups. These are powerful agencies of social control because people feel the need to belong to groups. The threat of being rejected is often a powerful one. When we feel we have been pushed into behaving in ways that our peers will approve of, this is called **peer pressure**.

If these agencies fail to control behaviour then societies have more powerful sanctions. The police and the criminal justice system can be used to enforce laws. Police forces are set up with the explicit purpose of social control. They are able to use **coercion** (force) when they decide it is necessary. By arresting and charging people the police bring people into the criminal justice system where judges and juries, acting on behalf of society, have the power to impose sanctions. The range of sanctions available is discussed in Unit 6 on crime and deviance. In some countries if it seems that the police are unable to control behaviour the armed forces may be used to do so.

KEY TERMS

Peer group: people of the same status (for example, they are the same age).

Ostracism: excluding someone from the community or group.

Formal social control: social control imposed by a person or organisation (such as a teacher or a police officer) who has the authority to implement rules or laws.

Agencies of socialisation: institutions in which people are socialised.

Primary socialisation: the first and most important period of socialisation in which the individual learns the basic norms of behaviour.

Hidden curriculum: what pupils learn in schools apart from the content of lessons, such as the importance of following rules and the consequences of not doing so.

Peer pressure: the influence that a peer group has to force or persuade its members to conform.

Coercion: the use or threat of force or violence.

TOP TIP

Some agencies of social control can use both formal and informal methods to control deviance. For example, schools have formal punishments such as detentions, but also control behaviour in more informal ways, for example, a disapproving look or warning by a teacher.

Functionalist and Marxist views of social control

One way of viewing social control is to say that it is most effective when it involves persuading people to conform by convincing them that this is the right thing to do. People internalise the norms and values of their society, thinking of them as their own. If this persuasion does not work there is the threat of sanctions. Functionalists believe this process is positive and is essential to the continued stability of the society, whereas Marxist see it as negative in that it allows the ruling class to continue in power, keeping the working class controlled.

For functionalists like Emile Durkheim societies need a set of shared values to hold them together as functioning societies and in order to prevent anomie. Anomie happens when individuals lack the guidance of norms and values and are unable to regulate their behaviour so that the bond between the individual and society breaks down. Durkheim argued that societies need a collective conscience, shared by all or nearly all. In the traditional societies in Australia studied by Durkheim, the clan or tribe joined together in worshipping a totem and this gave them a sense of shared identity. The clan's values were their own. In modern societies, and especially during periods of rapid social change, there is a risk that the bonds that hold society together will break down.

The Marxist Louis Althusser referred to schools, the media and religion as the ideological state apparatus, that is, institutions that make people believe that it is right to conform. However, the norms and values they conform to are those that suit the ruling class and help to keep the ruling class in power. For example, working-class people might accept the belief that people who are born into a high status deserve their status and should be respected and obeyed. This is in effect a form of brainwashing and the working class concerned is in a condition of false consciousness, by accepting beliefs that are against its own interests. The state keeps in reserve the use of the repressive state apparatus of the police, the criminal justice system and the armed forces when the ideological state apparatus does not work.

Examples of rewards and sanctions in different societies and organisations

Here are just some of the rewards and sanctions that can apply in different societies and organisations. As well as the positive sanctions that apply to individuals, organisations often offer incentives that apply to all their members and are designed to increase motivation. In a school, for example, a pleasant working environment and an ethos of caring for all pupils may help reduce the need for sanctions. In a workplace the company may offer health care, paid holidays, pensions and other benefits. These are offered to make the workers feel loyal to a company that treats them well and to encourage them to work hard because they want to, rather than because of threats of sanctions.

Rewards and sanctions in schools

Most schools display their rules on notice-boards and elsewhere, and will have a policy on rewards and sanctions. Increasingly, in modern industrial societies rewards are emphasised more than sanctions. Schools find they get a better response by reinforcing positive behaviour than by punishing negative behaviour. The rewards include verbal praise, positive comments on written work, positive letters to parents, merit badges or stickers, positive points, certificates of achievement and success in exams.

Sanctions include looks of disapproval by teachers, verbal comments by teachers, negative comments on written work, making students sit or work alone, sending them out of the classroom, keeping them in at break, lunchtime or after school (detention), making them write lines, contacting their parents to report their misbehaviour or concerns, confiscating their property such as cigarettes. In the past, and still today in some countries, students are given corporal punishment (beating).

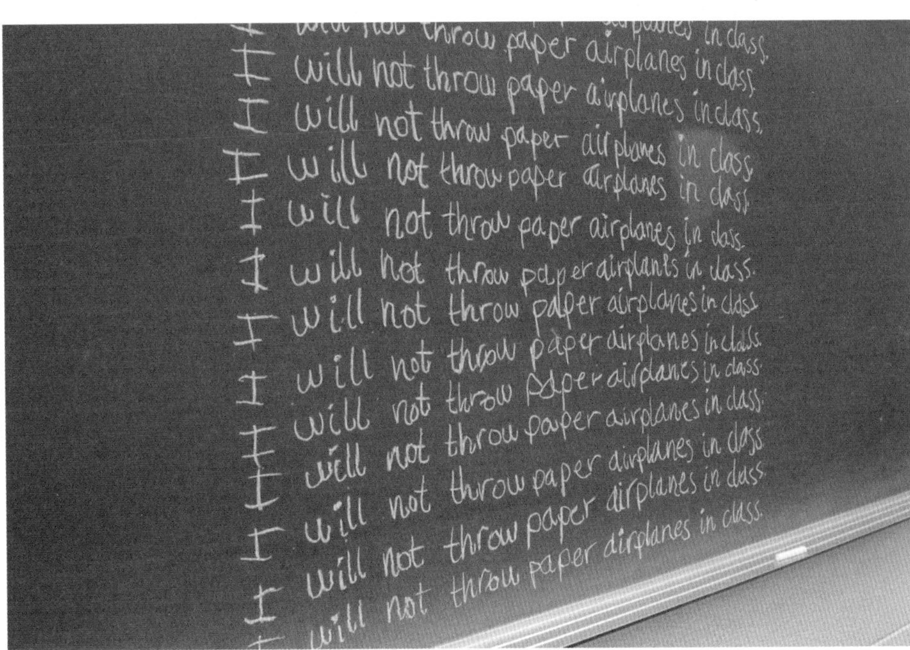

School punishments

Rewards and sanctions in the workplace

Like schools, all workplaces have rules, for example about starting and finishing times and about what to wear. The ultimate sanction is being fired. There are laws to prevent workers being fired unfairly so if being dismissed is threatened there may well be a disciplinary hearing first at which the workers can put their case. If the worker belongs to a trade union, the union can offer support in this process.

Rewards in the workplace include promotion to a better post, a pay increase, performance-related pay, bonus payments, commissions or being given shares in the company.

Sanctions include the loss of pay, having to face a disciplinary hearing, being closely monitored at work, being demoted to a lower post, being given less pleasant work and being fired.

Rewards and sanctions in traditional societies

In traditional societies social control is mostly informal in character. Sanctions for breaking rules can be extreme, for example by putting the offender to death. There is usually no equivalent of prison as this would require people to run the prison and would take time and resources. Punishments are therefore often physical punishments that are over fairly quickly. In medieval Europe offenders could be put in the stocks where they were unable to move while the community showed its disapproval by throwing dirt or rotten fruit at them. Once the punishment was over the offenders would be free to resume their role in the community. Traditional societies usually have common laws that are not written down and are part of the cultural tradition of the group. Public sanctions against offenders remind the community of these laws. Sanctions are more about enabling the community to regain the stability that has been upset by the offence than to punish wrongdoing at the individual level.

Collective sanctions or rewards are also common in traditional societies. This means that sanctions are applied not to an individual offender but to other members of their group, such as their family. This meant that wrongdoing had serious consequences for other people close to the offender and they were likely to try to regulate the offender's behaviour for their own benefit. Collective punishments have also been used in the army (punishments for a whole army unit for the wrongdoing of one soldier) and in schools (keeping a whole class in detention when one or a few pupils have misbehaved).

Rewards include being given a position of responsibility in the community, respect, status and gifts to show appreciation.

Sanctions include being shunned by the community, being expelled from the community (sent away), having your possessions taken away, being punished physically, including beatings, having your head shaved, being mutilated or killed or having to pay blood money (the murderer is made to pay the family of the victim).

Rewards and sanctions in modern industrial societies

> **KEY TERM**
>
> **Social order:** the ways in which societies and their institutions remain stable over time.

Social order in modern industrial societies depends on a complicated system of formal sanctions. This is because these societies are diverse and complex so informal sanctions cannot be relied upon. Unlike in traditional societies, sanctions often take the form of imprisonment. For this a police force or equivalent, courts and prisons are needed. In the UK today there are four main types of sanction:

- Discharge. This is when individuals are found guilty but are not punished. If the discharge is conditional they may be punished later for this offence if they commit further offences.
- Fine. This is the most common sanction and is used for many minor offences. The offender is punished financially according to the severity of the offence and their ability to pay. Fines are often imposed for offences such as driving and traffic offences and criminal damage.
- Community service. This covers a wide range of sanctions where offenders do not go to prison but are required to do certain things or their actions are restricted in some way. They may have to do unpaid work or get training or treatment, live in a particular place, be put under a curfew and be made to avoid activities like attending football matches. They may have to report to a police station or see a probation officer regularly. The purpose of these sanctions is to try to prevent reoffending and to punish the offender.
- Prison sentence. This is reserved for the most serious offences. Prison sentences can be for any length of time or for life.

The UK has used many other sanctions in the past that are not considered suitable today. These include:

- Execution. The death penalty has been abolished. The last execution by hanging was in 1964. Some modern industrial societies, notably the USA and Japan, still have the death penalty.

- Transportation. Offenders in the 19th century could be transported to a colony (in the UK this was usually Australia) as punishment. This is a form of exile. It was considered a humane alternative to execution.
- The pillory and the stocks, described on page 53.

The formation and existence of sub-cultures

So far we have discussed cultures, their norms and values, informal and formal social control and the sanctions and rewards they impose. As well as cultures there are sub-cultures. Sub-cultures are groups of people in a culture whose norms and values are different in some ways from the overall culture. This may show in their different value systems, different behaviour and different style of dress and appearance. The members of a sub-culture are influenced by the culture of the society and their own position in it but they reject or rebel against aspects of it in some way. In the eyes of the wider society the members of the sub-culture may appear not to be conforming but they do conform to the norms and values of the sub-culture. Sub-cultures may even use informal social control to regulate the behaviour of members, for example refusing to accept them as members.

Youth sub-cultures

The term youth sub-culture is mainly associated with groups of young people who adopt a style and culture that is partly at odds with the main culture. Some sub-cultures identified in the UK since the 1950s are:

- beatniks
- mods and rockers
- skinheads
- hippies
- punks
- Goths
- emo.

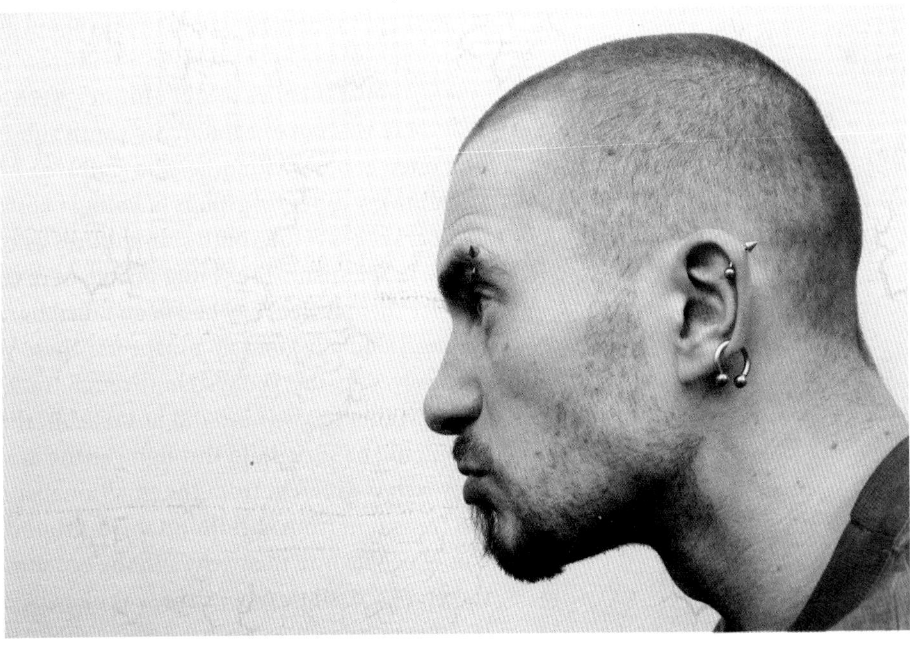

Skinheads – a youth sub-culture

Clothing, music, appearance and speech can act as symbols of these sub-cultures. All these groups attracted considerable media attention and were widely considered to be deviant. These youth sub-cultures were often identified as threats by the main culture because their values and behaviour were seen as deviant. They were therefore subject to sanctions. For example, a student might be excluded from classes for dressing in the style of the sub-culture. In addition to this the police might deal more severely with deviance by youth sub-culture members than with others who did not fit police stereotypes.

The existence of sub-cultures suggests that not everyone in a society holds the same values and norms. However, there will be dominant norms and values to which the sub-cultures are a reaction. From a functionalist point of view, sub-cultures offer a kind of safety valve. Growing up is a difficult period for many and a youth sub-culture may help adolescents to manage this period. Young people need to develop a sense of autonomy and independence from their parents and so they turn to the support of their own age group. Within the strong peer groups of young people the norms and values may be different to some extent from those of the rest of society. This period, during which individuals are less dependent on their parents than in childhood, is functional both for the individual and society.

Some functionalists also use the idea of sub-culture to explain the higher rates of crime among working-class boys. Joining a sub-culture is functional for some individuals whose route to success seems to be blocked, for example because they have not done well at school or cannot find a job. The sub-culture gives them a group in which they can win status and respect. It gives such people an alternative opportunity structure. The members of the sub-culture may start by having the same values as everyone else but it is because they cannot achieve their goals by socially acceptable means that they form sub-cultures. Most people belong to sub-cultures for a limited period only. Employment, marriage and adult responsibilities make people leave the sub-culture and adopt mainstream norms and values. While too much crime and deviance is dysfunctional and can destabilise a society, sub-cultures can therefore carry out valuable functions.

While functionalists tend to talk about a youth culture, Marxists and interactionists refer to youth sub-cultures. This is because the Marxist and interactionist theories of sub-cultures were formed in the 1960s when it was clear that there was not one but many youth sub-cultures, all with very different styles and often at odds with other sub-cultures. Marxist approaches therefore tried to explain why different groups of young people adopted different sub-cultures.

Marxists saw the youth sub-cultures as rebellions by working-class youth against capitalism. The young people were reacting against a system that seemed to offer them little. They had been failed by the education system and had no jobs (or dead-end jobs) and no prospects. These young people could not try to defend themselves against the system through trade unionism as their parents might have done. Middle-class youth did not rebel in the same way because they could see that they could be successful through getting academic qualifications and a career. This approach is different from the functionalist one because it is not concerned with the transition from **childhood** to **adulthood** generally, but with the place in which young people find themselves in the economic system and class structure. Marxists therefore see youth sub-cultures as one way in which deep conflicts within society become visible.

KEY TERMS

Childhood: the period before adulthood, in which individuals are not granted full adult rights.

Adulthood: when an individual is accepted by their culture as a full member.

CASE STUDY

Phil Cohen: *Sub-cultural Conflict and Working-Class Community* (1972)

Phil Cohen studied working-class communities in the east end of London in the early 1970s. These communities were changing rapidly. People were being rehoused and moved away from the area where they lived; older industries and small businesses were closing so there were few jobs and new immigrants were arriving into the area. The old way of life was disappearing. Teenage boys could no longer assume they would have jobs for life in a stable community. They were angry and confused about their situation and they reacted by forming sub-cultures. One of these was the skinhead sub-culture, which was based on being aggressive, defending the community against all outsiders and showing fierce loyalty to the group. Cohen argued that the appearance of skinheads was an exaggerated version of how men in those areas had always appeared – with hair cut very short and wearing heavy boots and baggy trousers with braces. The heavy boots had been needed for work on the docks or on building sites but now the skinheads wore them as a symbol of aggressive **masculinity**. The skinheads defended their area against ethnic minorities and outsiders and Cohen saw this also as a version of older working-class values.

TASK

1 Why would middle-class boys be less likely to form a sub-culture?
2 Why did the skinhead sub-culture adopt the signs and symbols (appearance, dress and so on) that it did?

KEY TERM

Masculinity: the expected behaviour associated with being male.

Although youth sub-cultures attracted a lot of media and sociological attention it should be remembered that most young people never belonged to any of these sub-cultures. Most young people conform most of the time to norms and values of the main culture. In addition, some of those who seem to be members of a sub-culture move between the sub-culture and the main culture so that they may dress and behave as a sub-culture member at the weekend but at work they look like everyone else and their work colleagues may not even know they are different outside work. Some writers have suggested that the sub-cultures quickly became little more than fashion, created by the mass media and marketing so that in any case the sub-culture's values have little depth; they are more style than substance. They may have begun as real rebellions, as suggested by the Marxists, but they soon became incorporated into the system. For example, early punks rejected fashion by making their own clothing from ripped old clothes, safety pins and even bin liners but before long mass-manufactured punk clothing could be bought in fashion shops.

Sociologists have also tried to explain why girls do not seem to form sub-cultures in the way boys do. All the youth sub-cultures seem to have been very male-dominated, with fewer committed girl members or girls who were only there because their boyfriends were. However, this may be because girls' behaviour was seen as less deviant or threatening and so got less media attention or because the male sociologists studying these sub-cultures did not see the girls' sub-cultures as relevant or interesting. Parents and others also tend to keep greater control over girls than boys. Angela McRobbie suggested that there were female sub-cultures but that girls got together in their homes, not on the streets as boys tended to. She called this a bedroom sub-culture. Teenage girls met to listen to music and experiment with make-up. The girls created a sub-cultural space away from adults but also from boys. McRobbie saw this as rebelling against sexual subordination. Girls were more in evidence in some of the later sub-cultures, such as Goths. This can be explained by the changing gender roles in society.

ACTIVITY: *research*

The internet and new media provide ways for young people to interact online with others who share their interests. Investigate the idea that new youth sub-cultures are being created in this way.

Other sub-cultures

As well as youth sub-cultures, there are other types of sub-cultures within societies. For a sub-culture to be said to exist, it has to break away from the dominant norms and values so that from the point of view of the main culture the sub-culture is deviant or eccentric. Some types of sub-cultures are:

- Religious. Many religious beliefs and practices fit into the main culture. Some, however, such as sects that place strong demands on members, can be seen as sub-cultures.
- **Ethnic minority** groups. The cultures of immigrant or indigenous groups that are markedly different from the main culture can be seen as a sub-culture.
- Class sub-cultures. Some sociologists have argued that the working class has a set of values and norms that are sufficiently different from the main, middle-class culture for it to be considered a sub-culture.
- Sub-cultures based on interests. These have to be strong enough to take up a considerable part of members' time and become an important aspect of their identities. An example would be bodybuilding. The interests can be social or political.

The internet and the new media have allowed sub-cultures based on interests to grow stronger as it has become much easier for geographically distant people to share their enthusiasms via online communities, forums and chat rooms. These sub-cultures can now be global.

KEY TERMS

Ethnic minority: an ethnic group that is relatively small in number compared with the majority in a society and is seen as different.

Globalisation: the complex process by which different cultures around the world are increasingly aware of, interact with and influence each other.

Global culture: the idea that as a result of globalisation there is or will be a single culture shared by people all around the world.

ACTIVITY: *discussion*

What different sub-cultures are there in your society today? How similar or different are they to those discussed in this unit?

TEST YOURSELF

1. In what ways does social control tend to differ between modern industrial and traditional societies?
2. Why are female youth sub-cultures different from male ones?

ACTIVITY: *evaluation*

In what ways are functionalist and Marxist accounts of youth sub-cultures different from each other and why?

Diversity and cultural variation in human behaviour

This section deals with diversity and cultural variation and the issues related to cultural relativism or multiculturalism. The debate about whether **globalisation** is creating a **global culture** is discussed.

CASE STUDY

The Amish

The Amish are groups of traditional Christians, who live mainly in the USA and Canada, with a distinctive way of life based on their religious beliefs and practices. They reject many aspects of modern life, including most modern technology, and largely keep themselves apart from mainstream society. They dress very plainly and the men wear wide-brimmed hats. The Amish place a high value on humility, calmness, rural living, simplicity and hard manual labour. The use of electricity, telephones and cars (they prefer horse-drawn carriages) is frowned upon by this community and they refuse to perform military service. They have religious objections to commercial insurance and to social security, although they pay sales and property taxes. Social control over their members includes shunning (social rejection aimed at getting the offender to want to be readmitted into the community) and excommunication. In some Amish communities teenagers are allowed a period called *rumspringa* (running around) when they can behave in ways that would, for an adult, result in shunning.

Amish family

TASK

1 In what ways is the Amish way of life different from that of most Americans today?

2 How might *rumspringa* be functional for the Amish way of life?

KEY TERM

Diversity: where there are many differences; cultural diversity refers to the wide differences between human cultures.

Diversity and cultural variation in human behaviour

Different societies around the world have developed different cultures, some in close contact with each other and trading and marrying people of other societies, while others developed in relative isolation for many thousands of years, such as the Australian Aborigines. Cultures are rooted in communities and in the past people learnt their culture in informal, everyday situations in their home and community. Most cultures were always in contact with others but cultural interactions have increased over the last 200 years. The increased contacts between peoples means that people around the world now have more knowledge of other cultures.

Human cultures are very diverse. What is considered normal in one culture may be considered strange, deviant or offensive in another. Areas of cultural variation include:

- language
- norms of dress and appearance
- food and drink
- traditions such as rituals and festivals
- ideas about morality.

Here are some cultural variations in food:

- Cultures have different ideas about what people should and should not eat, such as insects, and animals such as dogs and monkeys. Horse meat is eaten in many countries in Europe but not usually in the UK.
- All the main world religions have some followers who keep to dietary rules. For example, Muslims do not eat pork or drink alcohol. Jains follow beliefs about the sanctity of all life and so do not eat meat, poultry, fish or eggs and even avoid eating root vegetables, as the whole plant is killed when the root is dug up.
- Meat and fish are usually cooked before eating, but there are exceptions such as raw fish eaten in Japan and Rastafarians only eat lightly cooked food.
- There are cultural variations in meal times and in who should eat with whom; for example, men and women may eat separately.
- Western cultures tend to avoid eating with their hands and use cutlery such as knives, forks and spoons. East Asian cultures use chopsticks and in Africa and South Asia eating with the hands is common.

Knowledge about other cultures has spread rapidly, both through travel and migration and through electronic mass communication. We are now more aware that we live in a diverse multicultural world and many people are able to access and appreciate aspects of other cultures, such as their food, music and clothing. This has been called the global village, as we have all become closer. For example, people from all around the world are aware of and able to watch mega-events such as the 2012 Olympic Games in London. There are now very few groups of people living traditional **lifestyles** that are relatively isolated from other cultures.

KEY TERM

Lifestyle: the typical way of life of an individual, group or culture.

The main flow of cultures is from the West and especially the USA to the rest of the world. Elements of Western or American culture and influence can be seen in all cultures. There are fears that this may lead to cultural uniformity, which is the opposite of cultural diversity. Globalisation is said to be reducing cultural diversity and may be leading to the development of a single human culture based on Western values. This view is considered in the section on globalisation on page 62.

KEY TERM

Cultural relativism: considering all cultures on their own terms rather than from a Western point of view.

Cultural relativism and multiculturalism

Cultural relativism

Sociologists often study and write about cultures other than their own. When they do this, it is important not to be ethnocentric; that is, the sociologists should not judge other cultures by comparing them with their own. The sociologists should try to see how the other culture, which may seem strange and different, will have some of the same features as their own society; for example, there will be families and sanctions against those who break norms and rules. The differences need to be understood in the context of the other culture's own situation. Cultural relativism involves not judging the other culture as an outsider but on its own merits.

Multiculturalism and other responses to diversity

The movement of groups of people between regions and countries means that in many nations today there are different cultures. For example, in the UK there are at least four cultures based on national identities (English, Scottish, Welsh and Irish) and also cultures of immigrant groups, such as African-Caribbean and Asian. In some countries this has happened to a much lesser extent; for example, Japan has relatively few immigrants.

People and societies can adapt to cultures existing alongside each other in different ways. Assimilation and integration take place when immigrant cultures or others over time gradually lose their separate identity and become part of the dominant culture. This has happened with some groups that immigrated to the USA. The USA in the 18th and 19th centuries was described as a 'melting pot'. This means that immigrants from all over Europe and from elsewhere gradually became more American than German or Russian or whatever their national origin. They were assimilated into being American, which involved conforming to American norms and values. Some aspects of their culture blended with American culture, so that American culture changed by absorbing these new influences.

KEY TERM

Multicultural society: a society in which many different cultures or sub-cultures exist alongside each other.

Many people felt that the assimilation of cultures in a melting pot meant that important aspects of culture were lost. From this came the idea of a **multicultural society** made up of many different cultures existing alongside each other without losing their distinctive features. Each group would keep its own language and cultural practices and would not have to abandon its heritage in order to be accepted. In the USA some immigrant groups have held onto the culture of their country of origin and may even, because they feel it is under threat, assert it more strongly than in their country of origin.

Two multicultural countries are India and Mauritius. In India an astonishing variety of different cultures and sub-cultures exist alongside each other but also overlap. Some aspects of this diversity are:

- their religions; while most Indian people are Hindus there are followers of many other faiths, including Islam, Christianity, Buddhism, Sikhism and Jainism
- their regions; because of India's great size there are big differences in culture between different states and regions within India
- their languages; Hindi is the official language and English a subsidiary official language but more than 30 native languages are spoken by more than a million Indians and there are hundreds of other languages too (several different writing systems based on different languages are used).

There have been many conflicts resulting from this diversity. However, India is unlikely to split into different countries based on different cultures and there is no sign that a single dominant Indian culture will wipe out all the others.

Mauritius has a very ethnically diverse population. Most Mauritians are of Indian, African, Chinese or European descent. Mauritian Creole is the most widely used language but many people are multilingual, speaking French, English or Asian languages as well.

In some modern industrial societies there has been a movement away from multiculturalism in recent years. This is connected to concerns about immigration. Some politicians and others have argued that it is not desirable to have distinct ethnic cultures in a nation-state. Criticisms that have been made of multiculturalism include:

- It gives too many rights to minority communities; for example, if they have the right for their children to be educated in their home language this would be expensive to provide.
- Minority communities may stay too separate from the host community, so there is insufficient integration.
- It is too idealistic. It is unlikely that very different cultures can exist alongside each other in peace, harmony and equality.
- The host culture becomes just one of many cultures, when it should provide the value system that holds the society together.
- It may lead to conflict between groups.

In the UK multiculturalism became linked to immigration and became less popular in the worsening economic situation after 2008 and as a result of media reporting of these issues. On 7 July 2005 bomb attacks in London carried out by British-born Muslims killed 52 civilians. It was argued that if assimilation rather than multiculturalism had been followed, radical Islam could not have become so strong in the UK.

Other ways in which some countries have moved towards assimilation rather than multiculturalism include the following:

- Citizenship tests, which were introduced in the UK for people wishing to live in the UK or become naturalised British citizens. These tests are intended to ensure that people know about British history and culture and can use the English language.
- Community cohesion. This refers to attempts to integrate minority groups by involving them in community programmes.
- Acting against the expression of some aspects of minority cultures. For example, in 2010 France banned the wearing in public of anything that covered the face. The effect of this was to prevent the wearing of the *niqab*. An aspect of Muslim culture (though not necessarily of Muslim religion) was banned.
- Increasing nationalism. In some countries nationalism has been based on asserting a single culture. This happens when a region wants to break away from a country and the people are ethnically, linguistically or religiously distinct from the national culture. Examples include the province of Quebec in Canada (where French rather than English is spoken) and Catalonia in Spain (where Catalan rather than Castilian Spanish is spoken). It can also take the form of opposing immigration and wanting to expel minorities. This can result in ethnic cleansing, which means the expulsion of an ethnic group and its culture (for example, by destroying its buildings) so as to create an ethnically pure state. Ethnic cleansing often involves persecution and violence and in its extreme forms involves genocide (the extermination of an ethnic group).

Muslim woman wearing a niqab

Globalisation and global culture

Globalisation is a concept used by sociologists to describe the process in which geography ceases to be a limitation on human behaviour and people become increasingly aware of this. It involves the feeling that the world seems to be getting smaller, because people and cultures around the world have more contact with each other and are more aware of each other. Globalisation is often described as involving changes in politics, economics and culture. In practice it is very difficult to separate these because the globalisation of culture is made possible by economic and political changes. Examples of cultural globalisation include:

- world information systems such as satellite communications, the internet, telecommunications and e-mail
- global mass media such as news, films, television programmes and recorded music being available around the world
- global patterns of consumption and consumerism, where people have cosmopolitan life styles and feel at home in different cultures
- global sport, such as the Olympic Games and the football World Cup
- world tourism, where people now travel long distances for tourism
- clothing and appearance; for example, people all around the world wear T-shirts, jeans and baseball caps
- food; the types of food and styles of cooking from different places are available everywhere
- some brand names associated with cultural goods are global like McDonalds, Coca Cola and Walt Disney.

It can be said that many people now see the world as one place; a perception encouraged by the media (for example, now we can see news from around the world as it is happening) and by people's personal experiences. Even poor people in developing countries are likely to have friends and relatives living in other countries and even on other continents, so more people feel that we live on one small planet that we all share. This change in thinking can be seen even in popular media, such as in science fiction films, where all humans are united in facing an enemy, such as alien invaders or an asteroid heading for the planet.

How far has cultural globalisation gone? Many people are still excluded from all or some aspects of cultural globalisation. Much of the writing about globalisation is by people in the developed world, where, for example, a much greater range of food is available, and fruit and vegetables that are out of season are flown around the world to meet demand. However, the experience of globalisation in developing countries is more economic than cultural – working hard for little reward to supply the rich world. For example, global tourism brings relatively ordinary people with very different socioeconomic backgrounds and expectations into contact with one another. This can lead to frustration and a sense of injustice.

Does globalisation mean Westernisation? One view of cultural globalisation is that it means the spread of Western, or specifically American, culture so that the flow of culture is all one way. This can either be seen as good, because it spreads values about human rights, freedom and gender equality; or as bad, because it brings exploitation and the end of local cultures which cannot survive against Western culture. When it is seen as a bad thing it is often referred to as cultural imperialism. This implies that, rather than ruling the rest of the world directly as they did in the age

This photograph, taken by an astronaut in a spacecraft orbiting the moon, has been said to have changed the way we see ourselves – we all inhabit one small planet and all the differences between us are insignificant in this context

of colonialism, the rich countries now dominate the world through their cultural influence. Table 2.1 lists points that support and oppose the view that globalisation means Westernisation.

New media or technology may not be interpreted or used in the same way. Each culture makes a different use of what is available. For example, mobile phones are used in different ways in parts of Africa and in Europe. In Africa, phones are often shared and are used, for example, by farmers to find out prices at markets and to spread news about when weddings and other festivities will take place.

Those who oppose Westernisation argue that the values it brings are destructive. Through Westernisation people are encouraged to want a consumer-driven lifestyle and aspire to possess goods they do not need. People who have always drunk water may absorb a message from films that water is not as good as fizzy drinks, which are associated with the desired Western lifestyle. This may have long-term health consequences and may in any case be something they cannot afford. The globalisation of American culture can seem like a vigorous attempt by powerful transnational corporations to persuade the rest of the world that it needs and wants to adopt American consumerism and materialism. The spread of the American lifestyle is also bad for the environment as it depends on the heavy use of energy that depletes natural resources and contributes to climate change.

Evidence for globalisation as Westernisation	Evidence against
Hollywood films are seen all over the world and they tend to glorify an American way of life and American values. They are also accompanied by merchandising such as toys, which may particularly influence children.	Other countries have film industries, for example India has Bollywood. Bollywood films are watched globally but mainly by audiences of Indian origin.
Most of the world's most successful music performers are Western or European.	Bob Marley, from Jamaica, was the first superstar from a developing country. In early 2012 Korean star Psy found a global audience, and world (non-Western) music has a following in the rich world.
A western style of dress, with T-shirts, jeans and trainers has become almost a young people's uniform around the world.	Many people still value traditional styles of dress, such as the sari, *salwar kameez* and *dhoti* in India, and kimonos in Japan. Ethnic designs and jewellery are popular in the West.
English has become a global language. Most web pages are in English.	Although some languages are dying, there are still thousands of languages. Chinese is close behind English in numbers of internet users.
Some Western foods have become popular globally, led by brands such as McDonalds and Kentucky Fried Chicken.	Foods from other parts of the world have become popular in the West, with many restaurants that offer Chinese, Indian, Thai, Japanese and other food, and the ingredients of different cultures are on sale in shops.
Football originated in Europe and has become the world's most popular team sport, and European teams often win the World Cup.	Brazil has won the football World Cup most times. American sports such as basketball and baseball have not become globally popular.
World news is supplied mainly by a small number of American companies and press agencies and tends to reflect American interests.	News organisations from non-Western countries, such as al Jazeera, based in Qatar, are increasingly important.
Most global tourism is by Western tourists to destinations designed to cater for them.	Pilgrimages such as the *haj* to Mecca in Saudi Arabia and to the *kumbh mela* in India involve millions of people.

Table 2.1: Evidence for and against the view that globalisation means Westernisation

Some countries and peoples have reacted by vigorously to reject Western ideas. Here are some examples:

- The small Himalayan kingdom of Bhutan has tried to minimise some modern influences; for example it did not allow televisions until 1999.
- Muslim fundamentalists and jihadists such as the Taliban in Afghanistan and *boko haram* (which means 'Western education is sinful') in Nigeria violently reject Western culture.
- Some countries try to block access to the internet and censor Western media, such as magazines, to prevent their people being 'corrupted'.
- France limits the amount of English language television that can be broadcast and English language music that can be played on the radio (to protect the French language).
- Some countries, such as the People's Republic of China, use a variety of methods to restrict their citizens' access to internet sites that they do not approve of.

KEY TERMS

Ethnicity/race: ethnicity refers to cultural differences such as language and religion as well as place of origin; race refers to supposed biological differences between different groups of people.

Social construction: the idea that social situations and events are constructed – made – by societies: they do not exist in nature as independent things.

Globalisation seems to sometimes weaken local cultures by bringing in Western influences. On the other hand, the flow of culture is not always one way. Europe and North America are influenced by cultures from outside, in music, food, fashion and much more. Philosophical and religious traditions and practices from Asia, such as meditation and yoga, have become popular. Some sociologists describe what is happening as the creation of hybrid cultures; that is, when two cultures meet, a new culture emerges that has features of both. This is seen as positive, even exciting. We cannot expect traditional cultures to remain the same (it is unlikely that they ever have) but elements of them will survive and enrich new emerging cultures. For example, aspects of traditional cultures acquire a new value when tourists want to see them. An African dance that may have celebrated a harvest or coming of age ceremony may not be used for those purposes any more, but may be performed for tourists, creating an income for the dancers.

ACTIVITY: *evaluation*

Consider the impacts of globalisation on your society's culture. In what ways and for whom have these been positive or negative?

TEST YOURSELF

1 Suggest two reasons why European countries such as the UK are now less likely to see multiculturalism as a good thing.
2 Give two examples of ways in which cultures may resist Americanisation.

KEY TERMS

Age groups: ways in which people of the same or similar age share a status and associated roles.

Elderly: belonging to the age group of those advanced in years.

Age group as an example of social construction

Social construction

Age, like gender, **race** and **ethnicity**, is **socially constructed**. Different societies divide their members into **age groups** in different ways and the roles assigned to them vary and are not always directly linked to biological abilities. In modern Western societies children spend a long period relative to most other societies undergoing socialisation into adult roles before they enter the adult world. **Elderly** people enter a phase of retirement at a legally specified age. In some other societies, children start working alongside adults at much earlier ages and there is no formal retirement age: people work as long as they are physically able.

Social construction of childhood

Children are physically immature people; this is biological. But the ways in which children are thought of, the way they are treated and the ways they are expected to behave vary between cultures and in different time periods, so childhood is socially constructed. The way in which childhood is socially constructed has, according to historical research, changed completely in the last 500 years. The French historian Philippe Ariès went so far as to argue that childhood in the modern sense did not exist in the medieval period in Europe. Children were not seen as different from adults. They wore the same clothes, worked alongside adults and shared the same recreations. Children learnt news as adults did, from travellers or from those with access to information such as priests. Children were not protected from the adult world. They were aware early on of violence, death and sex. There was no period of formal education for most of them and no set age at which they became adults.

This changed around 500 years ago. The invention of the printing press and the growth of formal education created a new, separate world of childhood. In this new period children were thought to be different from adults and needed to be trained and taught to control their nature so as to behave in a civilised way. They were protected from many aspects of the adult world. Many British children worked long hours in harsh conditions during the Industrial Revolution but gradually new laws stopped this. More children went to school and stayed there longer. Today, whole professions (including educational psychologists, paediatricians, teachers and child psychiatrists) are based on the assumption that children are not yet fully developed people and that they are vulnerable and need protection and guidance. Modern industrial societies have become **child-centred**, and children are considered to be at least as important as adults and to deserve special attention and protection. Ariès says that this idea of childhood is a modern invention.

Neil Postman has developed Ariès's ideas and argues that childhood has been changed again by the growth of television, computers and new technology. These mean that children are exposed to the adult world at an early age (as they were in the past). They cannot be kept isolated and innocent any more. Postman cites increases in crime by children and the tendency for children to dress and behave sexually more like adults and at a younger age as evidence that childhood is changing as society changes.

KEY TERM

Child-centred: a society in which children are highly valued and a lot of time and effort are devoted to their well-being.

TEST YOURSELF

1 What does it mean to say that childhood is socially constructed?

2 Make a list of features of childhood in the medieval period in Europe, according to Ariès and then compare them to the situation today. What similarities and differences are there?

How do we learn to be human?

Primary and secondary socialisation

Socialisation happens throughout life. However, the most important period is that of primary socialisation, which takes place mainly within the family and from birth to infancy. This is when children learn the basics of interacting with other

KEY TERM

Secondary socialisation: later socialisation, usually involving learning more specific norms for particular statuses and roles.

people. For example, they learn how to smile and how other people will react to this. Human beings are born helpless and have to become aware of themselves and learn to live in the culture they have been born into. This makes it possible for societies to survive over time. In early childhood we learn the main norms and values of the culture we live in; for example, how to eat and how to relieve ourselves in approved ways.

The main agencies of **secondary socialisation** are also the agencies of social control discussed above. They are schools, religion, workplaces, the media and peer groups. Each time a person faces a new situation, such as starting school, starting a new job or getting married there are new roles and accompanying norms to be learnt, and these are learnt through secondary socialisation. Some situations may require people to change their behaviour a lot: in these situations re-socialisation takes place. Examples of re-socialisation are joining the armed forces or being imprisoned.

Socialisation is not a simple process of absorbing ideas and messages. Rather, whether as children or adults, we are actively involved in our own socialisation, thinking about how the messages apply to us and about how we can or should amend our behaviour and about how others see us. Even young children are not blank slates on whom messages can be written. We can reject some of the messages; indeed, we almost have to, since in modern industrial societies the messages from different agencies of socialisation may be different.

Processes through which children learn social expectations

Children learn social expectations through processes like manipulation and exposure to the hidden curriculum.

KEY TERMS

Imitation: young children learning by copying the behaviour of others.

Role modelling: acting as an example so that this behaviour is copied by others.

Sex: being male or female (based on biological indicators such as XX and XY chromosomes).

Manipulation: how parents and others encourage some behaviour and discourage other behaviour.

Canalisation: channelling children towards activities that are considered appropriate for them (for example, because of their gender).

From a very early age children try to conform to social expectations. They learn from parents and others. One of the main ways this happens is through **imitation**. Young children see someone doing something and copy it. Behaviour is more likely to be imitated if the child sees the behaviour is positively sanctioned; that is, the other person is rewarded in some way. In this way the child learns what behaviour is approved of. When parents or others apply sanctions to behaviour, this is called reinforcement. When children see older children and adults behaving in ways that they then try to copy themselves, these others act as **role models**. For example, a child may see their mother being polite or kind and try to emulate this because they have learnt that this is good behaviour. Role models can also be people that the child sees or learns about through the media, such as sports players and celebrities. In school your teachers should be role models in the sense that they are not expected to set a bad example, for example, by being late often.

The feminist sociologist Ann Oakley argued that children learn the social expectations that go with their **sex** roles (that is, the behaviour expected of their sex) in four main ways:

- By **manipulation**. Parents encourage and praise some activities and discourage others. For example, a boy may be praised for taking part in a hazardous physical activity while a girl might be discouraged from even trying.
- By **canalisation**. Parents channel their children towards activities they consider appropriate. Boys may be encouraged to play football, girls to take up ballet dancing. Girls may be encouraged to take greater care over their appearance than boys.

- By verbal appellations. These are the ways in which parents address their children. For example, the word naughty may be used more often with boys than with girls; pretty may be used for a girl and handsome for a boy.
- Through different activities. These are the different activities that boys and girls take part in; for example, girls helping their mother with cooking while boys help their fathers with do-it-yourself tasks around the home.

Oakley developed these ideas specifically to explain how we are socialised into sex roles but the ideas can be applied more widely. Regardless of gender, children learn from their parents what are considered appropriate activities, games and behaviour.

Since Oakley developed these ideas in the 1970s there have been significant changes in the way children are brought up. In the late 20th century, influenced by feminist thinking, many parents tried to ensure that their children were not brought up in gender stereotypical ways. This tended to apply more to girls than to boys; that is, girls were encouraged to behave in ways that until then had been more associated with boys rather than boys being encouraged to take up girls' activities. For example, many parents deliberately chose clothes for young children that were not gendered in design or colour (pink or purple for a girl, blue for a boy) and encouraged children to read stories where a girl lead character was resourceful and adventurous. Parents found this was harder to achieve than expected. Possible reasons for this are that:

- gendered behaviour is not only about how children are socialised; it may also be in the nature of boys and girls to want to follow what is considered to be gendered behaviour
- the family, even during primary socialisation, is not the only agency and children may learn conflicting expectations from other agencies, such as their peer group
- the marketing of goods and messages from the media tends to be strongly gendered and this counters parents' efforts to be gender neutral; for example, it may be difficult to buy non-gendered clothing for children.

The American Barrie Thorne is a feminist sociologist who tried, with her husband, to bring up her two children (a boy and a girl) in a gender-neutral way but found it much harder than she expected. She researched children's behaviour in classrooms and playgrounds, where boys and girls tend to play and interact separately in single sex groups. She argued that schools tend to encourage this behaviour in the different ways they treat boys and girls. This could be something as simple as a boys versus girls quiz or game. Children learn that gender is important and then work out in groups for themselves what this means for how they should behave.

These messages about gender that children receive in school are part of the hidden curriculum. This refers to how some of the most important things children learn in school are not part of the formal curriculum of lessons, but come from the way that the school, classrooms, lessons and playgrounds are organised and the expectations adults have of children. For example, children learn that it is important to be on time and to speak politely to adults. The ideas above about how children are socialised into sex roles can also be applied to socialisation into other roles. For example, there are class roles and race or ethnic roles.

ACTIVITY: *data interpretation*

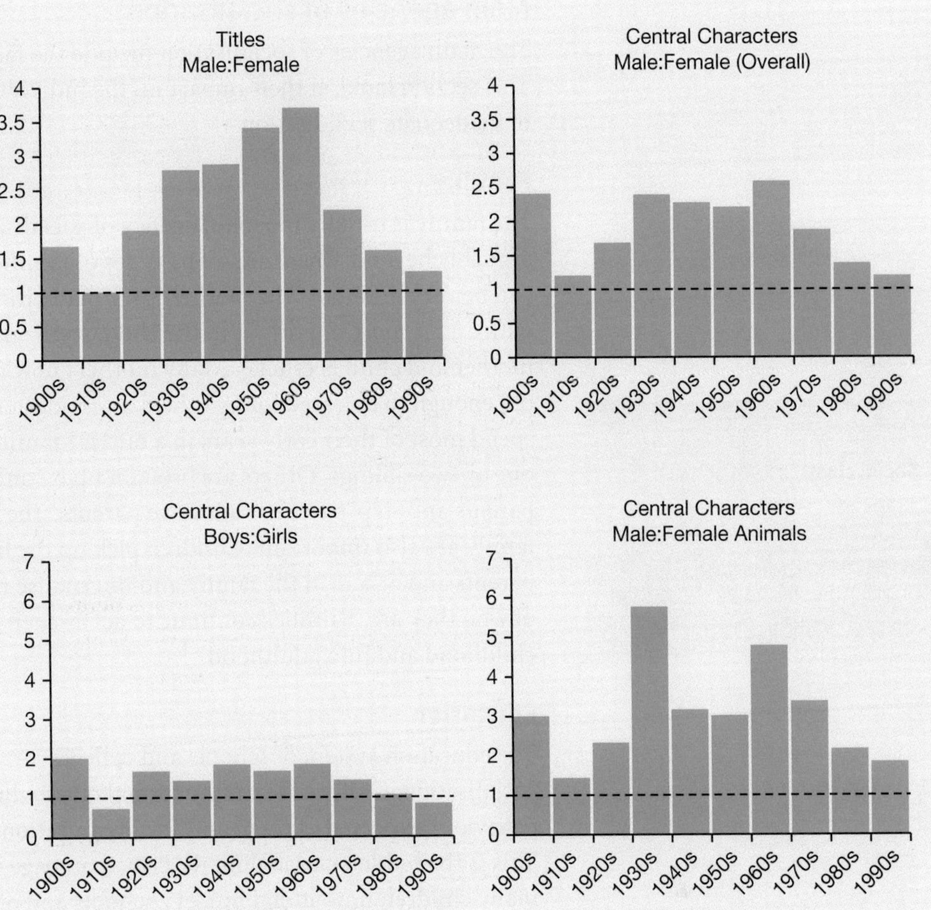

Ratios of males to females in titles, overall central characters, child central characters, and animal central characters

The researchers analysed more than 5,000 children's books in the USA from the 20th century, looking at the sexes of the characters named in the title, of all central characters, of child (boy and girl) central characters and of animal central characters. The ratio of 1, indicated by a dotted line on these graphs, indicates that the ratio of males to females is 1. Above the dotted line there are more male than female characters.

1 Describe how the ratio changed for titles and central characters from the 1950s to the 1990s.

2 In which two decades were there more girls than boys as central child characters?

3 'Representation of the sexes is becoming more equal in children's books.' To what extent do the data here support this claim?

TEST YOURSELF

1 According to Ann Oakley, what are the four ways in which young children learn about sex roles?

2 Give examples of how the hidden curriculum works in your school.

Main agencies of socialisation

The main agencies of socialisation include the family, education and the media. This section looks at their impact on the individual and some of the consequences of inadequate socialisation.

Families

The family is usually the main agency of socialisation throughout childhood and arguably beyond. There are many types of families so the experience of children can be very different. The mother is normally the person who has most contact with and is most important to the child, so the nature of the relationship between mother and child is crucial. Many mothers now return to work when their child is old enough to be cared for by others. In modern industrial societies, many children spend most of their early years in a nuclear family of mother, father and perhaps one or two siblings. Others are brought up by only one parent or by both biological parents and step-parent or adoptive parents. The **social class** and ethnicity of the family are also important. Children pick up the language and behaviour of their parents and others in the family and internalise them so that they become part of who they are. Families continue to act as agencies of socialisation throughout childhood and into adulthood.

KEY TERM

Social class: a form of social stratification in which people are grouped at different levels in the social hierarchy, the most common of which are the upper, middle and working classes.

Education

The education system of schools and colleges is another important agency of socialisation. Children learn the formal curriculum but they also learn the behaviour expected of them and the organisation of the classroom and the school. This is the hidden curriculum described on page 68. In modern industrial societies many children now attend nursery schools and other preschool institutions where they begin to learn these things. In traditional societies education is more informal and is carried out by adult members of the family and community.

Peer relationships

Peer groups are made up of people of the same age and status. In traditional societies there are often age groups based on rites of passage and ceremonies, for example before they become accepted as adults. Experiencing these ceremonies together binds the age group into a peer group that can strongly influence the group members' behaviour.

In modern industrial societies children are brought together in classes in schools based on their age. Children in the same class at school often spend a lot of time together and form strong friendship bonds that may even last throughout their lives. These bonds may now form earlier than in the past as more children attend nursery schools or day-care centres, playing and learning together.

Peer groups continue to be important in adult life, whether as continuations of earlier friendships or in new peer groups based on work colleagues or people met through other interests.

The media

The media are now an important part of socialisation throughout life. In traditional societies the equivalent of the media is the oral storytelling tradition, in which many stories have messages from which children learn. Today, the media are increasingly important in childhood as more children interact with the media for longer periods. There are more films and television programmes aimed at children, for example.

For a long time sociologists have wondered whether the socialisation of children by the media might be faulty or have negative effects. For example, children might watch violence on television programmes and copy it, thinking it was acceptable behaviour or they might copy bad language. In fact, research suggests that children can be thoughtful and discriminating viewers. They do not passively accept media messages; they work at making sense of them, often with help from their family and peers. The importance of the media continues throughout life. For example, the news coverage of crimes and court cases reminds people of the limits of acceptable behaviour and the consequences of breaking the law.

Religion

Religious organisations are often important agencies of socialisation. Many children learn moral values from attending mosques, churches and other places of worship, or from hearing and reading holy books and teachings.

Workplaces

When starting a new job, people have to learn not only what the employer wants and expects them to do, but also how to get on with their fellow workers. This can involve in effect being socialised into new norms and values.

Inadequate socialisation: feral and isolated children

One of the ways we can be certain that primary socialisation is extremely important is that in cases where it does not happen the consequences are severe. Children who have been **inadequately socialised** are unable to fit into society. Wild or **feral children** have not been socialised. There are many legends and stories around the world about feral children, such as the story of Mowgli, the boy brought up by wolves in Rudyard Kipling's *Jungle Book*.

About one child a year has been discovered who has been deprived of human contact for an extended period. Some cases are better documented than others and there are differences between each. For example, some children have had different amounts of human contact before living alone for a long period. Some seem to have been cared for by animals and some have even adopted some animal behaviour. Some are cases of extreme neglect, where a child has been confined and deprived of human contact but given food. Where children have had some human contact, for example, kept in a house but fed and hearing some language, they are referred to as isolated children. Some cases are eventually found to have been frauds. In some sociology textbooks there was a report of two girls in India, Amala and Kamala, who were supposed to have been brought up by wolves in the 1920s and who were known as the wolf children. This was later proved to have been a deception with the aim of raising money for the orphanage where the girls (who had mental problems and were orphans but not feral children) lived.

Despite the differences between the individual cases, most feral and isolated children:

- find it difficult to speak a language; this has led to the belief that there is a crucial period in the development of children when they need to hear and start to speak a language and that if this does not happen they will never learn to speak
- find it hard to adapt to normal food; for example, they may prefer uncooked meat
- do not like wearing conventional clothing

KEY TERMS

Inadequate socialisation: when socialisation is incomplete or ineffective.

Feral children: 'wild' children who have not been socialised.

- may not walk upright, preferring to walk on all fours
- may seem uninterested in other people and unable to understand how others might see them and react to them
- may not learn to use a toilet, instead relieving themselves at will.

The study of feral and isolated children shows that humans are naturally social. We need other people around us. The way we communicate and interact with other people varies between cultures but it is still a fundamental human need. Children who live isolated from other people (whether or not they are with animals) cannot interact, speak a language or learn to love. They cannot develop normally and are damaged by the experience. They have difficulty adjusting to life in a human culture. In some cases the damage may be so great that they never learn to do the things most humans do, especially to communicate. In a sense, these children are not completely human. They are biologically human but they are unable to be part of the essential human experience.

The case of a Cambodian woman, Rochom P'ngieng, suggests that secondary socialisation is also very important. She disappeared from home when she was aged 8 and had therefore completed primary socialisation. She was thought to have been killed by wild animals but reappeared nearly 20 years later. However, having been deprived of human contact she had lost her ability to speak. She preferred to crawl than to walk and could not readjust to human society. This is only one case and there have been doubts as to whether the woman is the same girl who disappeared, but this case does suggest that we need human contact not only in the crucial period of primary socialisation but throughout our lives.

CASE STUDY

Genie

Genie (not her real name) suffered extreme abuse and neglect and did not go through many of the important parts of primary socialisation. She was discovered in California in 1970 when she was 13. Her father believed she was mentally retarded and kept her in a bedroom, tied up most of the time. No one in the neighbourhood knew of her existence. Her mother (who became blind) and older brother were also terrorised by her father and forbidden to speak to her. Throughout her childhood Genie had very little sensory stimulation. When she was discovered (after she and her mother escaped) she was studied by many researchers and her abilities and progress documented. At this time she was described as walking like a rabbit (with hands held up in front of her). She could not stand upright, focus on anything not close to her or chew food. While being cared for in hospital and then in foster homes she made good progress and learnt to speak in simple sentences. Genie did not make enough progress to live in normal life and continues to live in institutions. However, it is difficult to be sure if her problems arise only from inadequate socialisation or from mental problems from birth or are the result of abuse and neglect.

TASK

1. How does Genie's story show the importance of primary socialisation?
2. What skills had Genie not learnt?
3. Compare Genie's experience to Rochom P'ngieng's. Can people forget their primary socialisation?

A feral child?: American girl Dani was neglected by her parents and kept in a closet until she was seven years old

Studies of feral and isolated children leave some unanswered questions because of the variety of cases and doubts about the validity of some reports. Media reports tend to emphasise how different feral children are from socialised children; for example, commenting on their wild appearance. But children living wild could hardly be expected to cut their hair or trim their nails. The study of feral and isolated children raises important questions, including the following:

- How much behaviour is natural rather than learnt in a specific culture?
- How do children who have never learnt a language learn to communicate?
- Can feral children think logically?
- Can feral children see how others might see them?
- What differences are there between a feral child and an animal such as a wolf or monkey? (Is it interaction with other humans that makes us more than animals?)

TEST YOURSELF

1. Are the problems feral children have in adapting to society the result of missing out on primary and secondary socialisation? How do we know this?
2. Why do you think feral or isolated children struggle to adapt in society?
3. Which agencies of socialisation are the most important in modern industrial societies? How is this different from traditional societies?

ACTIVITY: *research*

Use the internet or other resources to find out about another feral or isolated child. You could research:

- *Oxana Malaya, the Ukrainian 'dog girl'*
- *John, the Ugandan 'monkey boy'*
- *Suchet, the 'bird boy' of Fiji*
- *Dani, the American girl*

These children are the subjects of programmes in the television series Raised Wild.

KEY TERMS

Nature: the influence of biological factors on human behaviour in the nature/nurture debate.

Nurture: the influence of society and culture on human behaviour in the nature/nurture debate.

The nature/nurture debate

The **nature/nurture** debate focuses on the extent to which our personality, attitudes and behaviour are decided by what we have inherited in our genes (our nature) or by our social environment (nurture). This is a long-running debate with arguments on either side. Although there can probably be no clear conclusion, recent research on genes suggests that there is a complex relationship between nature and nurture – in other words, that both sides are partly right. We live in societies and so our genes are expressed only in social situations, so it is difficult, and perhaps a mistake, to separate the two. Sociologists concentrate on nurture but that is because it is part of the subject matter of sociology, so perhaps the sociological preference for nurture as the main explanation of behaviour is just the outcome of the nature of the discipline.

The two extreme positions in this debate are called determinism. Those who argue that nature is all important are biological determinists; those who argue that nature is all important are social determinists.

On the nature side of the debate, sociobiologists argue that all social behaviour is directed by natural instincts or biological drives. We have known for many years that aspects of our appearance, such as eye colour and hair colour, are determined by the genes encoded in our cells and are therefore inherited. The nature theory takes this a step further and argues that more abstract traits such as intelligence, personality, aggressiveness and sexual orientation may also be inherited. Some of the traits that sociobiologists have said may be biologically determined are:

- Criminal behaviour. There may be a genetic predisposition to violent, aggressive or rule-breaking behaviour.
- Intelligence. There may be a genetic component to intelligence.
- Sexual orientation. Whether people are heterosexual, bisexual or homosexual may be determined by their genes.

Sociobiologists argue that humans, like all living things, have evolved through the process of natural selection, in which traits that help survival are more likely to be passed on to the next generation.

On the nurture side, sociologists argue that while we do inherit tendencies, these do not determine how we behave. It is possible for people who are genetically very similar to become, through socialisation, very different people. As thinking, reflexive people we are able to make decisions about how we behave, even about the sort of person we are. It is therefore possible that someone will inherit a trait that means they may be more likely than another person to respond aggressively in a difficult situation. However, this does not mean they cannot control this behaviour. Equally, the aggression may be the result of being socialised into a culture in which aggression is the expected response.

Sociobiology, or biological determinism, is rejected by most sociologists. For example, we can all accept that adults have sex drives. But the existence of a biological drive cannot explain the diversity of human responses to it, such as monogamy, polygyny, polyandry and celibacy. The fact that some people (such as Christian monks and nuns) practise celibacy shows that we can suppress our biological drives because of the patterns of behaviour established by our culture. Moreover, people do not have instincts in the usual sense of complex patterns of behaviour that are genetically determined. There is, for example, no human equivalent of the ability of weaver birds to build complex nests that are identical to the nests of other weaver birds, even when they have been raised away from weaver birds. Humans need to learn from other humans. Human babies are able to do very little by themselves. We do have biological needs but how we satisfy them, if at all, depends on our culture. Inherited genetic factors (our nature) and our social environment (nurture) interact and depend on each other. Thinking of them as opposites or alternatives is not helpful.

Discussions of sex and gender differences often involve the nature/nurture debate. The anthropologist G.P. Murdock looked at 224 societies ranging from hunter gatherers to modern nation-states. He argued that men and women had different social roles because of their biological differences, such as women's childbearing and men's greater physical strength. He found that men tended to do work such as hunting, land-clearing and quarrying, which require physical strength, and to range further afield than women, who did lighter work nearer home.

The feminist Ann Oakley uses Murdock's own findings to argue against him that there is no such universal division of labour. There are societies in which, for example, land-clearing is done by women and cooking by both sexes. The Mbuti pygmies have no rules dividing labour. Men and women hunt together and responsibility for caring for children is shared. Oakley concludes that there are no exclusively female roles and that biological characteristics do not bar women from any roles.

Biology is also the starting point of the functionalist Talcott Parsons's analysis of gender roles. He argues that because mothers bear and nurse children they have a closer and stronger relationship with them. In modern industrial society the absence of the father who goes to work reinforces this. Parsons calls the woman's role expressive, which means she provides emotional warmth and security. These expressive qualities are also shown in her relationship with her husband – the second function of the wife and mother is to provide love and understanding to the weary breadwinner whose role at work is instrumental. Ann Oakley uses the example of the people of the island of Alor in Indonesia to show that women are not tied to their offspring and that the separation has no harmful effects. She accuses Parsons of basing his analysis on the beliefs and values of his own culture, particularly the myths of male superiority and of the sanctity of marriage and the family. The expressive role is not necessary for the functioning of the family; it exists for the convenience of men.

Sociobiologists have argued that men and women have different reproductive strategies. They argue that it is in the biological interest of men to produce as many offspring as possible to carry their genes. Men compete with other men to win mates, just as male animals do. Women have to invest time and energy in their offspring so they need to choose a partner carefully. Thus, argue sociobiologists, men are more likely than women to be promiscuous and aggressive. Women can be sure their offspring are theirs so they are willing to spend time and devote attention to childcare. In modern times this means to be a housewife. Men cannot be sure of this and so are less tolerant of infidelity. War and territoriality, say sociobiologists, have their roots in the aggressive attempts of men to win women against competition from other men.

Sociobiology has been criticised on several counts. Firstly, it has been pointed out that instinct is relatively unimportant in humans and that much more human behaviour is learnt than is the case with animals. War and hunting are probably only 500,000 years old. For most of history humans survived by gathering vegetables. It has been said that sociobiology is ethnocentric and that it assumes that all human behaviour corresponds to the modern capitalist world. In fact there is plenty of evidence that men are not always aggressive and women are not always docile. The examples from the animal world are selective. Sociobiologists ignore anything that does not fit their case. Many feminists dismiss sociobiology as a sophisticated attempt to justify male power.

TOP TIP

The term sociobiology is now used less often than evolutionary psychology, which studies whether human behaviour can be traced back to evolutionary adaptations, that is, whether we behave as we do because our ancestors who behaved in those ways survived as a result.

TEST YOURSELF

1. How would (a) biological determinists and (b) social determinists explain why boys and girls play with different kinds of toys?
2. The nature/nurture debate has sometimes been described as a false debate. What does this mean?

Role, age, gender, ethnic group and class as influences on social identity

Role

Identities are how we perceive ourselves and how we are perceived by others. Everyone has a number of statuses and roles and most people have multiple roles. Roles are based on our relationships with others. For example, I am a husband, father, teacher and author; for my bank I am a customer and for my doctor a patient. Each of these

KEY TERM

Role conflict: when someone finds that the demands of two or more of their roles clash with each other.

TOP TIP

People's lives are constantly changing and roles and identities are not fixed for life. Your roles will change as you become an adult, enter work or continue as a student

roles is part of my identity, though some are more important than others, and there are occasions and situations where the relative importance or unimportance of that aspect of my identity changes. In modern industrial societies people experience **role conflicts** where the norms attached to roles seem to pull them in different directions. For example, a woman may experience conflict between her work role (the need to be at the office, working hard) and her role as a mother (the need to nurture her children).

Sociologists are particularly interested in those aspects of identity that we all have: ethnic and gender identities, our age and our age group. We also all belong to a social class, though this is sometimes less clear. The rest of this section considers the relationships between identities and age, gender, ethnic group and class. Sociologists are also interested in other aspects of identity such as sexual orientation, adherence to religious groups and ability and disability. These features are not discussed in this course.

Age and identity

In traditional societies many people had little idea how old they were. More important was the age set they belong to: the group of people with whom they went through important stages in life, especially initiation into adulthood. In some traditional African societies there were three main stages in men's lives – as children, warriors and elders. Boys of roughly the same age were initiated into adulthood and became adults at the same time. The initiation may have involved instruction in traditions and lore and adult responsibilities and an ordeal or test of strength. There were equivalent ceremonies for girls. African elders were seen as sources of knowledge and experience and were valued members of the community and integrated into extended families.

Industrial societies also place a great emphasis on age in terms of years, but the age often has very different implications for people's sense of identity. Children become adults at a set age, usually 18, rather than according to their maturity as in traditional societies. At other ages, different rights and responsibilities are acquired. In the UK ages at which rights are acquired are shown in Table 2.2.

Age	Right or responsibility
10 (12 in Scotland)	Age of criminal responsibility (can stand trial and be convicted of a criminal offence)
13	Can work for limited hours that do not interfere with education
16	Age of consent for sex
17	Can drive a car
18	Can vote in elections
21	Can drive a bus, lorry or train

Table 2.2: Stages of rights in the UK

Members of the same age group are a generation. The difference between generations is usually thought of as about 25 years. In modern industrial societies there is often a significant difference in experiences and attitudes between generations and this can lead to conflict. For example, teenagers may think that older people are out of touch and 'past it' and older people may see teenagers

TOP TIP

Generation and birth cohort are often used as if they mean the same thing. It is useful, though, to make the distinction, because the word generation draws attention to the common features of, say, being a teenager, while the term cohort draws attention to the particular experiences that come from being born at a particular time.

as rebellious and disrespectful. This kind of difference is called a generation gap. For example, today different generations have very different experiences of computers and other new technology. Children and teenagers have grown up with these technologies and find them easy to use while older people may struggle to understand them. The young are digital natives; older people are not.

Members of an age group who share a common experience of growing up at the same point in history are a birth cohort. Belonging to a particular cohort can have important consequences. Each generation experiences different events and social changes. For example, the baby boom generation born after World War Two in Europe and North America experienced dramatic social changes in the 1960s. These included growing affluence in these countries, the Cold War and its end, more effective birth control, the arrival of computers and other new technology and growing concern about the environment. Their numbers meant that companies made many products aimed at this generation. As this generation grows older, their numbers are leading to an ageing population and increasing costs in health care and social services.

ACTIVITY: *data interpretation*

	USA	UK	Japan	China	Mauritius
Driving a car	Varies between states; the lowest is 14 years 3 months in South Dakota	17	18	18	18
Drinking alcohol	21	18	20	18	18
Leaving school (ending compulsory secondary education)	16	16	15	15	16
Marriage	Usually 18 but varies between states	18 (16 with parental consent)	20 (18 for boys and 16 for girls with parental consent)	22 for men, 20 for women	18, sometimes younger, with parental consent
Voting	18	18	20	18	18

Table 2.3: Comparison of legal ages for various activities in different countries

1. In which of the selected countries in Table 2.3 a) is the voting age the highest; b) is the minimum age for driving the lowest?
2. 'Adulthood is socially constructed in the same way as childhood'. Use the information from Table 2.3 to explain this statement.
3. If you live in a country other than those selected here, find out the equivalent information for your country.

KEY TERM

Adolescence: the period of growing up between childhood and adulthood.

Adolescence is seen as a difficult period because it involves status anxiety. Modern industrial societies emphasise achieved, not ascribed statuses and young people feel pressure to achieve status. One response is to rely on your peer group, who are after all the people who are going through the same problems and anxieties as you. Young people therefore tend to share norms and values, even to form a youth culture, but this is functional since it helps people through the transition to adult life. This functionalist view of adolescence and youth came into question with the development from the 1950s onwards of youth sub-cultures that were seen as rejecting or rebelling against the dominant culture's values. Neo-Marxists developed the idea that working-class youth sub-cultures were a form of resistance to capitalism at a time in life when the grip of hegemony is the weakest. One example of this kind of work is Phil Cohen's account of youth sub-cultures discussed in a case study on page 57.

Gender and identity

In traditional societies gender roles are usually fixed and there is little scope for individuals to negotiate them. However, the anthropologist Margaret Mead found surprising variations in gender roles in traditional societies in New Guinea:

- Among the Arapesh people both men and women were peaceful in temperament and neither men nor women made war.
- Among the Mundugamor people both men and women were warlike; the opposite of the Arapesh.
- Among the Tchambuli people the women left the villages to work while the men stayed at home and spent time on their appearance.

To these we could add Western society at the time of Mead's research, which seemed the opposite of the Tchambuli pattern, with men working and women being more concerned with appearance. Mead's findings have been taken as proof of the importance of nurture rather than nature. It seems that men and women can have different temperaments and different roles depending on the culture in which they are brought up. However, Mead's research has been questioned, with the suggestion that she may have wanted these patterns to exist and thought she saw them when they were not really so clear.

In modern industrial societies gender is an essential aspect of identity. It is helpful to distinguish sex from gender, although they are closely interconnected. Sex relates to the body and biological characteristics; in particular, male and female humans have different chromosomes. Gender is about how these biological differences affect our social lives. Until recently, gender roles and identities were quite strict. Men took what functionalists call the instrumental role, looking after the practical and economic needs of the family, such as food, shelter and money. Women took the expressive, domestic role, looking after the home and the emotional needs of the family.

KEY TERM

Femininity: the expected behaviour associated with being female.

Men who conform to the expected gender role of their society are masculine, while women who conform to the expected gender role are feminine. In modern industrial societies, masculinity and **femininity** have often been thought of as opposites (as in 'the opposite sex'). This can be seen in some of the words commonly used to describe the two sexes:

> Masculinity: strong, competitive, aggressive, unemotional, active, confident, hard
> Femininity: weak, emotional, passive, quiet, dependent, soft

These are stereotypical ideas though at times in the past people would have wanted to live up to the stereotypes. Today they seem unrealistic. Not many men or women fit these stereotypes. There have been huge changes in gender in the last 50 years or so, so that sociologists now talk about masculinities and femininities to show that there are different ways of being masculine or feminine, rather than simply conforming to a stereotype.

In business, politics and culture more women have reached senior positions and are important decision-makers. Young women increasingly expect to work and have financial independence, and they do not see their futures only in terms of becoming a wife and mother. But the situation is still far from equal and many feminists are sceptical of these changes. Patriarchal culture is deeply embedded. Both men and women see culture through the male gaze, and sometimes accept that women will be represented as sexual objects and that it is natural for them to be enjoyed by men in this way. Women who work in previously male-dominated areas may still be thought of as unfeminine. In some modern industrial societies young women are also acting in ways that are similar to those of some young men, such as drinking alcohol to excess and being involved in delinquency.

For men in modern industrial societies the traditional and expected role was to be strong physically and emotionally, to support the family. This has been referred to as hegemonic masculinity – an idea about what a 'real man' should be like. The word hegemonic means that it was widely accepted and very difficult to escape from. For example, boys were expected to be able to fight, to be interested in competitive sports like football and to think of themselves as better than females. Males who could not live up to this could be seen as failing to achieve masculinity, not being a real man.

This has changed and it has become much more acceptable for males to behave in ways that might once have been seen as feminine, such as:

- showing emotion publicly, such as crying
- taking care over their appearance, following fashions and using cosmetics
- talking about their relationships and emotions
- for fathers, having a close emotional bond with their babies or infants.

More men are stay at home dads, and those who work full time are spending more time with their children and helping more with housework. These changes are seen as a good thing in many ways, freeing men from a restrictive role and allowing individuals to negotiate the form of masculinity that is right for them. They may also lead to a fall in domestic violence by men against women and children and to greater willingness to talk and negotiate rather than fight. It may also lead to less harmful attitudes towards the environment. There has, however, been a negative side with new pressures on men, especially with regard to appearance. The old hegemonic male took little care over his appearance, but today value is placed on looking good. The cosmetics industry for men has grown and advertising pushes males into caring more about their appearance. This can lead to feelings of inadequacy shown, for example, in a rise in eating disorders among boys. There may also be greater role conflict as men try to combine success at work with being a good husband and father.

These changes have happened at the same time as it has become harder to carry out some of the requirements of hegemonic masculinity. As traditional working-class industries such as coal mining and steel works closed down or moved to other countries, in Britain many men lost their jobs in the late 20th century. More men were unemployed. It became harder to be a breadwinner supporting a family, partly because more women were bringing up children alone. Feminism was influential and made it seem that men were not needed any more. It seemed that the things for which men had been valued in the past were not in demand or valued as much. This led to a crisis of masculinity. This may make it harder for young men to find a role and may contribute to anti-social behaviour and delinquency.

Ethnic group and identity

Throughout history when different groups of people have encountered each other they have responded by making a distinction between themselves and the other group. The Romans saw everyone who lived outside the Empire as barbarian, in contrast to civilised Roman citizens. Those in the Islamic world saw all outsiders as infidels and the Chinese saw all Europeans as barbarian. One detailed study of this is Edward Said's *Orientalism,* which describes how a concept of the Orient (the East) as 'other' was developed by Europeans, who saw it as mysterious, exotic, cruel, unpredictable and lacking in sexual restraint – all in contrast with how the Europeans liked to think of themselves.

In the past (during the period of slavery and afterwards) racism was based on alleged physical differences. More recently, cultural differences have become a greater source of tension. In the UK this takes the form of expressing support for a mythical traditional British way of life based on freedom of speech, tolerance and fair play combined with the idea that ethnic minorities threaten this by trying to preserve aspects of their own culture (such as their religion) and failing to integrate. People who hold this view claim it is not racist, just common sense. By blaming minorities such people see them as the enemy within and misunderstand and stereotype them.

Ethnicity is a social construct. Ethnic groups exist only because people identify themselves and others as members of groups and reinforce boundaries between groups. In most modern industrial societies today there is much greater ethnic diversity than in the past because of migration. For example, the UK has significant African-Caribbean and Asian ethnic minorities. Within each of these there are several groups and using terms like Asian to describe too many big groups is not useful. Asians in Britain are not one group or even three (Indian, Pakistani and Bangladeshi). There are many possible distinctions between people based on their language, religion, social class and national origin. New hybrid cultures are being created as cultures meet. For example, there are now British Bangladeshis who are both British by citizenship and Bangladeshi by part of their culture. There are also now growing numbers of people from mixed backgrounds (for example, with one British Asian and one White British parent) who live in both cultures and who have some choice in creating new identities for themselves.

Closely related to ethnic identity is national identity. It might be expected that globalisation would lead to the end of the nation-state and to national identities. In fact, nationality has become a more central part of many people's identities in recent years and nationalism has been a factor in both world wars, in anti-colonial struggles, in the fall of eastern European communism and in debates over the future of Europe.

> **TOP TIP**
> Everyone has an ethnicity. Those who belong to a majority ethnic group have an ethnic identity just as much as those who belong to a minority.

Nationalism developed in modern times as a way of uniting the diverse peoples of nation-states. For example, the UK needed to unite the people of England, Scotland, Wales and Ireland, who had different religions, languages and cultures. Benedict Anderson argues that nations and nationalism are socially constructed and calls them 'imagined communities'. In real communities people know each other or interact regularly but nations are too big for this to happen. Creating a sense of national identity is particularly important where:

- there are several sub-cultures or ethnic groups within the nation as the sense of national identity needs to be stronger than loyalty to the sub-culture; some civil wars start when a group tries to break away because they reject the national identity

- the national boundaries are artificial, that is, they do not correspond to natural dividing features such as rivers and mountains or to where people actually live; in Africa the borders drawn up in the colonial period by European states have led to problems because the boundaries drawn on maps divided people from the same group from each other.

States persuade people to accept a national identity using means such as:

- national symbols such as flags, emblems, money and postage stamps
- a head of state such as a king who acts as the national figurehead
- national anthems
- national rituals such as parades, festivals and holidays, either regularly or for special occasions
- national sports teams; for example, although they involve individuals and teams competing against each other in the Olympic Games, the nationality of the competitors is always emphasised
- broadcasting and mass media; these often involve a national broadcaster, such as the British Broadcasting Corporation.

In the UK it is not easy for members of ethnic minorities to assert a British national identity. Racist media portray being non-White and being British as mutually exclusive. Even people born in Britain or with a British passport and nationality may find that they are seen as 'a threat to our way of life'. Welsh and Scottish people often find that they tend to be forgotten. For many non-British people, British means English (English people sometimes make this mistake too).

Social class and identity

Social class can be less immediately obvious from an individual's appearance than their age, group, ethnic group and gender. Sociologists have different ways of deciding which social class people belong to and neither they nor the people concerned always agree with each other where the distinction should be made. This is partly because there are no clear boundaries between classes. However, our social class decides many of our life chances and this is widely recognised, though it may be expressed simply as rich and poor.

We usually refer to three classes: upper, middle and working class. Members of the upper class are likely to think of themselves as belonging to a sort of exclusive club, based on the ability to spend considerable amounts of money. Spending conspicuously can be a way of signalling their wealth to everyone else; for example, by owning luxurious houses, expensive cars and jewellery.

The middle class has grown enormously in the last hundred years or so. Rising living standards have allowed this expanded class to demonstrate its status in many ways. Members of the middle classes often try to show their class status through conspicuous consumption in the same way as the upper class. For example, their class may be shown through their house, car, the type of holiday they take and where they shop. Those recently upwardly mobile from the working class may be most keen to prove their new status.

Being working class was a powerful source of identity for many in the 20th century. In the UK there were strong working-class communities based on industries such as coal, steel, car-making and ship-building, where boys would often follow their fathers to work in the local industry and marriages often were made within the community. Membership of trade unions and shared working and living conditions created a strong sense of collective identity that was stronger than in other classes. The working class were aware of their lower living standards but, by asserting their values, were able to place a strong positive value on their way of life. These collective identities have been weakened by the loss of jobs in these industries and the fragmentation of the communities based on them. Media reporting of the working class has become very negative, representing them stereotypically as lazy and scrounging off welfare. The term 'chav' came into use, as Owen Jones put it in the title of his book, to demonise the working class. It has become harder to claim being working class as a positive identity.

ACTIVITY: *discussion*

What do you think are the main influences on an individual's identity in your culture today – age, gender, ethnic group or class?

Coal mining areas in the recent past had strong working class communities

Linguists found that David and Victoria Beckham have changed the way they speak so that they no longer sound working class

TEST YOURSELF

1 Suggest ways in which a sense of national identity can be created.
2 Examine some of the ways that gender identities have changed in the last 50 years or so.

Revision checklist

Make sure that you know all the key terms listed in this unit and that you understand the following:

- All societies have cultures but these vary over time and place.
- Norms, values, roles and beliefs are all social constructions, are parts of all cultures and influence behaviour.
- Agencies and processes of social control try to enforce conformity through the rewards and sanctions applied in different societies and organisations, such as schools and workplaces.
- Some individuals and groups resist social control and do not conform.
- Within many societies there are sub-cultures with distinct norms and values.
- There is considerable diversity in multicultural societies in cultures and behaviour.
- There is debate about the extent to which globalisation may be leading to a single global culture based on Western values.
- Childhood and old age are socially constructed.
- People learn to be human through primary and secondary socialisation.
- Socialisation is carried out by a range of agencies.
- Socialisation can be inadequate; feral children, for example, may be unable to learn to be fully human.
- There is debate about the extent to which human behaviour is shaped by nature or by nurture (socialisation into a culture).
- People's identities are shaped by role, age, gender, ethnic group and social class.

Exam practice questions

Each society socialises its children into its norms, values and roles. Boys and girls are often treated differently, and are socialised into their expected gender roles. The agencies of socialisation can also be agencies of social control, applying rewards and sanctions to encourage children to behave in the expected ways. In spite of this, some individuals and groups do not conform.

a What is meant by the term 'norms'? [2]

b Describe two agencies of social control. [4]

c Explain how one agency of social control can use rewards and sanctions. [6]

d Explain why some individuals and groups do not conform to the culture of their society. [8]

e To what extent are gender roles shaped by nature rather than by nurture? [15]

Total marks available 35

Unit 3: Social Inequality

Objectives

At the end of this unit you should be able to:

- describe social stratification and the different forms that stratification can take in modern industrial society: class, age, ethnicity and gender
- explain the difference between achieved and ascribed status
- describe life chances and account for differences in life chances among and within stratified groups
- explain the main features of inequality and how it is created
- assess evidence of and reasons for the distribution of wealth and income in different societies
- assess the impact of the welfare state and other government measures, including equal opportunities legislation, to reduce inequality
- explain the problems involved in defining wealth and poverty
- explain the causes of poverty and the consequences of being rich or poor in a global context
- discuss examples of racial prejudice and discrimination in education, employment and housing
- discuss scapegoating and the consequences of racism for ethnic groups
- discuss the effects of gender on the life chances of males and females and the changing role of women in modern industrial societies, including gender discrimination in employment
- assess explanations of gender discrimination
- assess different ways of defining and measuring class
- discuss the changing nature and role of different classes and class cultures
- discuss the nature, extent and significance of social mobility.

Introduction

Living together as members of a society brings many benefits to us as individuals. We can achieve more together than we can alone. Our media and culture tend to present great achievements to us as the work of individuals – scientists, inventors, discoverers, writers, artists and composers – but all their accomplishments have been made possible by their social background and by building on the earlier work of others. However, not everyone has an equal chance to achieve. Most societies are organised so that they are unequal. Individuals and groups are ranked or graded in a hierarchy that gives some an advantage over others. This is called social stratification. The ways in which societies are organised are not neutral. Some individuals and groups benefit more than others. This unit explores the nature of social stratification and inequality, focusing mainly on inequalities between men and women, between social classes and between ethnic groups.

What is social stratification?

Forms of social stratification

In this section we explain the ways in which **social stratification** occurs through **social class**, **age**, ethnicity and gender.

Human beings living in groups have always divided functions and labour to achieve greater efficiency. In hunter-gatherer groups long before recorded history, individuals performed the different tasks needed by the whole group, such as gathering food, preparing food, constructing shelters and watching out for danger. In all societies past and present it is women who bear the children but beyond this, **statuses** and roles are socially constructed and groups and societies make their own decisions about who should do what. This is called social differentiation. Societies become more differentiated as they develop because there are more tasks that need to be done and therefore more statuses and roles.

Social differentiation refers only to differences in roles and statuses. It does not mean that one individual is considered to be superior to another. People with different statuses and roles are different but they are not necessarily higher or lower in rank than others. Social differentiation does, however, lay the foundations for ranking people in groups so that there is a hierarchy in which some are seen to be superior or they have greater **power** or possessions than others. At this point differentiation becomes stratification. The word stratification is borrowed from geology, where the strata are the different layers of rocks, deposited one on top of the other. Sociologists use the word to sum up how social groups are like layers in society and some are higher than others.

Social stratification is found in all societies, based on rules, norms and values that can be enforced by sanctions. In modern **industrial societies** stratification is dynamic rather than static. That is, there are constant changes as groups try to improve their status and power relative to others. The main forms of stratification are class, age, ethnicity and gender. These are in practice difficult to separate. **Minority groups**, which can be based on ethnicity, age, disability or other factors, often have less power than other groups and are in a lower position in society.

Social class is important in modern industrial societies but social stratification has taken other forms in the past, such as **slavery**, estates and caste.

- Slavery. Many early societies were stratified into citizens and slaves, where citizens had rights that slaves did not (including the right to own slaves). Slaves were treated as property, forced to work and had no freedom.

KEY TERMS

Social stratification: a hierarchy in which groups have different statuses and different levels of privilege.

Social class: a group of people having the same social and economic status.

Age: age is a form of stratification.

Status: a position that someone has in society.

Power: the ability to influence people's behaviour.

KEY TERMS

Industrial societies: societies that use technology for mass production, in contrast to traditional societies.

Minority group: a category of people lacking power; can be based on factors such as religion, disability and age.

Slavery: a stratification system in which one group is treated as the legal property of another group.

Slavery in the past

KEY TERM

Caste: a closed stratification system traditionally found in India.

- **Caste**. This was the stratification system in India and in some other places, similar to the estate system, explained below, in that people inherited their status at birth and could not change it. They also had to marry within their caste. There were thousands of castes, mostly based on a particular occupation. Members of lower castes were considered inferior by the higher castes and there were strict rules about ritual, purity and contact between different castes, because having contact with someone from a lower caste was thought to pollute a higher caste member.

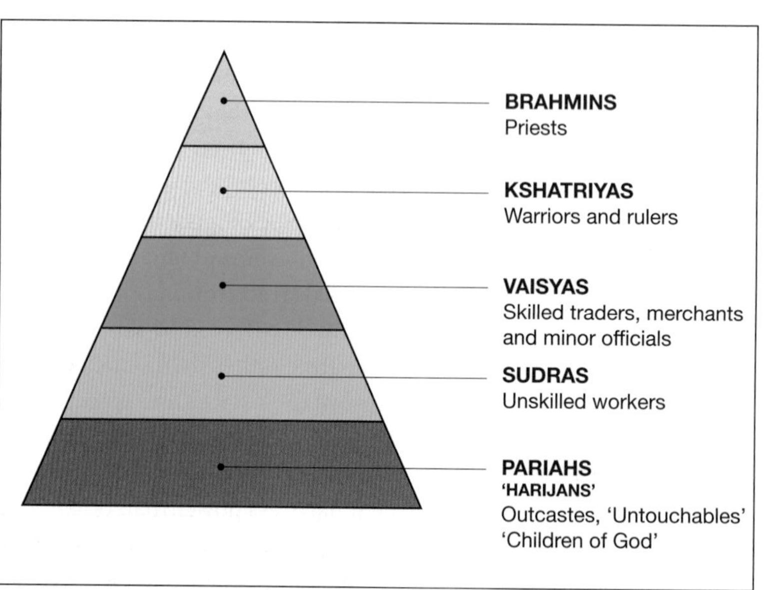

The Indian Caste System

- Estates. This was a later form of stratification in feudal societies in Europe in the medieval period. Individuals were born into a social layer called an estate, from which they could not move. The three estates were the clergy (priests), the nobility or aristocracy and the commoners. There was some intermarriage and mobility, so this system was slightly more open than the caste system.

These three systems were to a large extent **closed** systems, which means that people had great difficulty in changing their status. Social class, which has replaced these systems in modern industrial societies, is more open, because it allows some mobility between classes. No systems are completely open or closed. In most modern industrial societies competition for statuses is limited to some degree by gender, ethnicity and social class. This is considered later in this unit. Although there is some movement of individuals and sometimes groups in open systems, the system itself remains stratified. Social stratification continues over time.

In all societies gender adds another dimension to social stratification. In all societies there are inequalities between men and women. In many societies today there are also ethnic and racial divisions. Stratification, gender and ethnicity work together to produce different patterns of inequality.

KEY TERMS

Closed society: a society in which mobility between different levels of stratification is not possible.

Ascribed status: a status that is given to individuals by their society or group, over which they have little or no control.

Traditional societies: societies that are still predominantly agricultural and have not yet become industrial.

Discrimination: when an individual or group suffers a disadvantage because of their characteristics, for example being refused a job.

Ageism: prejudice or discrimination against someone based on their age.

Achieved status: a status that individuals acquire through their own effort.

Ascribed and achieved status

Ascribed statuses are given to people by their group or society and people usually have little control over them. Age, sex, ethnic group, religion and social class are ascribed to people at birth but they may later be able to change some of these. Ascribed statuses are common in **traditional societies**, where people's life chances can be largely determined at birth. Age differs from other statuses in that it changes over time. Adults have a higher status than children and in many societies there are rites of passage to mark the transition to adulthood. Age often brings greater status in societies where the younger members of the group look after the elders, value their experience and treat them with great respect. In modern industrial societies, however, old age often brings a loss of status because statuses that are attached to work are lost when someone retires. When there is **discrimination** against older people this is called **ageism**.

Achieved statuses are those that people acquire through choice and competition. These include changing some of the statuses that may have been ascribed at birth, such as by being upwardly mobile in social class or converting to a different religion. Other achieved statuses are more specific than ascribed status. Examples of this are an occupational status such as a teacher or an engineer.

A master status is the most important status in a person's interactions and relationships with others. Sex and age (especially for children) are often master statuses.

TOP TIP

The term traditional societies is misleading because it implies that they do not change. All societies, including traditional ones, constantly change, so that what appears to be a tradition may in fact be of fairly recent origin.

TOP TIP

Ageism can also refer to discrimination against children and young people, for example, when they are unfairly denied some of the rights that adults have or when their views are not listened to by adults.

TEST YOURSELF

1 Using examples, explain the difference between achieved and ascribed status.
2 What are the similarities and differences between slavery, caste and the estates system as systems of stratification?

KEY TERM

Life chances: the opportunities that people have to improve their lives.

Life chances

This section explains what **life chances** are and discusses how and why these differ between and within stratified groups.

Life chances are the opportunities that people have to improve their lives. Life chances depend upon aspects of stratification such as social class, gender and ethnicity. People who share these aspects are likely to also have similar life chances.

Life chances include opportunities for:

- employment
- education
- good health and well-being
- housing
- social mobility
- life expectancy.

Taken together these indicate an individual's quality of life.

KEY TERMS

Human rights: a wider category than civil rights, including political rights.

Civil rights: rights that protect the freedom of individuals.

Working class: manual or blue-collar workers.

Fatalism: individuals' belief that they cannot control what happens to them.

Life chances are affected by the nature of stratification in a particular society and by norms, values and laws. Laws may limit the **human** and **civil rights** of groups, preventing them from improving their life chances. In South Africa in the apartheid period (1948–1994), the life chances of Black South Africans were limited by segregation laws. In the USA in the 1960s the African-American civil rights movement campaigned against segregation and against violence such as lynching and for the right to vote in the southern states. The denial of these civil and human rights had severely restricted the life chances of African-Americans until then.

One factor in life chances is the individuals' perception of their life chances. Some social groups, such as the **working class**, may have a pessimistic attitude towards life, feeling that they have little control over what happens to them. This attitude is called **fatalism**. Marxists argue that working-class fatalism comes from false consciousness, where the workers have been socialised into accepting that the capitalist society is fair, that their own lowly position is their own fault and that those who have power and wealth deserve their position. A fatalistic outlook is likely to become a self-fulfilling prophecy; that is, if people do not believe that they can improve their life then it is unlikely that they will do so.

KEY TERMS

Deferred gratification: being able to set long-term goals, planning for the future.

Immediate gratification: choosing instant satisfaction rather than waiting for a greater reward in the future.

Another feature of the outlook of some stratified groups relates to gratification. Those who are able to plan for the long term, for example by saving money, practise **deferred** (also known as delayed) **gratification**. For example, students at university usually have a lower income than they would have got had they gone to work instead of continuing to study after leaving school. However, in years to come they are likely to have a higher standard of living because their degree-level qualifications allow them to hope for high-paid occupations.

On the other hand, some groups practise **immediate gratification**. If there is a sudden change for the better in their fortunes, like inheriting money or winning a lottery, the new wealth will be spent straightaway rather than being invested to ensure longer term affluence. It has been suggested that working-class people are more likely to practise immediate gratification. This may be because their standard of living is lower so an immediate improvement is highly desirable.

An example of life chances: life expectancy

Life expectancy is the average number of years a person can expect to live. Historically, and in some parts of the world today, life expectancy was low because many infants and children died, for example of infectious diseases. This brought down the average life expectancy but it did not mean that people were likely to die at that age, because those who survived childhood would be likely to live for several decades.

Life expectancy measures illustrate how life chances vary between societies and stratified groups. Life expectancy varies by gender, by social class and by ethnic group.

- Gender. Women tend to live longer on average than men. In many modern industrial countries women live about 5 years longer on average. Possible reasons for this are as follows:
  - Men are more likely to be in high-risk situations so have a higher risk of accidental death, including in car accidents.
  - Men in many societies consume more alcohol, tobacco and other drugs than women, making them more likely to suffer from serious disease.
  - Men's work exposes them to risks, such as risks of accidents in mining and factory work.
  - There are biological reasons for differences between the life expectancy of men and women.
- Social class. Working-class people have lower life expectancy than **middle-class** people in the same society. For example, in the UK life expectancy at birth for those whose parents were in routine occupations such as cleaners and labourers was 74.6 years in 2008 to 2010, whereas for those whose parents were higher managers and **professionals** it was 80.4. Possible reasons for this are as follows:
  - Working-class occupations are more dangerous so there is a work-related risk.
  - Working-class people may live in unhealthy environments, such as near sources of pollution or in damp, cold houses.
  - Working-class people may be unable to afford good health care.
- Ethnicity. **Minority ethnic groups** tend to be low down the socioeconomic scale and so are affected by the same factors as those that influence social class and life chances. There can also be specific ethnic factors, such as the prevalence of particular health conditions. For example, Britain's African-Caribbean population has much higher rates of sickle cell anaemia than the average for the population. Racial discrimination in access to services may also be a factor.

KEY TERMS

Middle class: professional and other non-manual workers, below the upper class and above the working class.

Professional worker: someone who works as a professional, such as a lawyer and architect.

Minority ethnic group: a minority group with a distinct national or cultural tradition.

ACTIVITY: *discussion*

What do you think are the main factors affecting life chances in your society today?

TEST YOURSELF

1. Explain the difference between immediate and deferred gratification.
2. What are some reasons why working-class people tend to die younger than middle-class people on average?

What are the main features of social inequality and how are these created?

Wealth and income

This section discusses the evidence and reasons for the distribution of wealth and income in different societies and the impact of welfare states and other government measures to reduce **inequality**. The problems of defining wealth and poverty are described together with the causes of poverty and the consequences of being rich or poor in a global context.

Wealth

KEY TERMS

Social inequality: the inequality between groups in a stratification system, for example in income or wealth.

Wealth: money, savings and property that can be bought and sold to generate income.

Wealth refers to the ownership of financial savings and of things that can be bought and sold to generate income. There are many different forms of wealth other than money. Some of the most important of these are ownership of:

- stocks and shares in companies
- land
- houses and other buildings
- works of art, jewellery and other valuable items.

Having these forms of wealth is an important indicator of social class position. Some of these forms of wealth create more wealth. For example, shares produce dividends and works of art often grow in value. The very wealthy do not need to work because their wealth creates more wealth. Wealth is often inherited; that is, the wealthy have not acquired their wealth themselves but it has been passed down to them by their parents or other relatives.

In the UK wealth is distributed very unequally. The wealthiest 10 per cent of adults own about 40 per cent of the wealth while the least wealthy 10 per cent own about 1 per cent of the wealth and the lowest 40 per cent own less than 10 per cent. These figures have not changed much in recent years (see http://www.hmrc.gov.uk/statistics/wealth/personal-wealth.pdf).

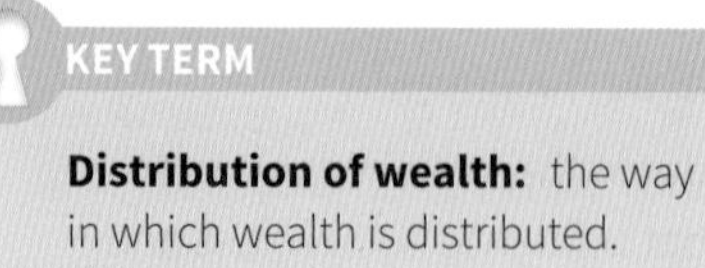

KEY TERM

Distribution of wealth: the way in which wealth is distributed.

These figures probably underestimate the wealth owned by the wealthiest. This is because wealthy people tend to be secretive about the extent of their wealth and may employ tax advisers to help them appear less affluent than they are so that they pay less tax.

Despite this strikingly unequal **distribution of wealth**, large numbers of people in many modern industrial societies do have some wealth. Many people have bank or building society savings accounts; smaller numbers have other personal investments. Most households also own consumer durables such as televisions, computers and cars that are a form of wealth. Other common forms of wealth are:

- Housing. Many people own their own houses and for many this is their main form of wealth. However, it is difficult to turn this into money that can be used if it is your only house and you need to live there.
- Pensions. Many people now have pensions so that when they retire they will have a reasonable income. The money saved is a form of wealth but it is kept in pension funds and cannot be used before retirement.
- Shares. More people own shares in businesses than in the past but the largest numbers of shares are usually held by a small number of very wealthy investors.

For many families, the main form of wealth they own is their home

Income

KEY TERM

Income: the sum of earnings from work and other sources.

For many people their main **income** is pay from their employment but other types of income include:

- social security and other state benefits
- pensions
- interest on building society and bank accounts
- dividends on shares.

People do not receive all their income. This is because tax has to be paid on most income and other deductions may be made such as national insurance and pension contributions. The income that remains after these deductions is called disposable income. It is the amount of money that people get directly and can spend or save.

Income is important because it has huge consequences for people's life chances. For example, those with high incomes are able to live in a larger house and pay for private health care and education.

In the UK the people in the top 10 per cent get 31 per cent of all income in the UK while the bottom 10 per cent get just 1 per cent. The UK has become more unequal over the last 20 years at both ends of the income scale. The poorest have fallen further behind on average while the richest have pulled further ahead. The distribution of income is therefore very unequal, though not as unequal as the distribution of wealth. The falling behind of the poorest has led to an increase in poverty, which is considered later.

Inequalities in different countries

KEY TERM

Welfare state: the way in which governments try to provide for the less well off and reduce social inequality.

Different countries have different levels of inequality. In many modern industrial societies, including the UK, there was a trend during the 20th century towards a reduction in inequality; that is, the distribution of income and wealth became more equal. This was helped by the expansion of the **welfare state** and by governments in power that were committed to making the society more equal. This trend was reversed towards the end of the century and inequality widened in most countries. Those at the lower end of society continued to be better off because of economic growth but those at the top pulled further ahead.

Among the more equal modern industrial societies are Japan, Norway, Sweden and Finland. In these countries the richest 20 per cent of the population are about four times richer than the poorest 20 per cent. In Singapore they are about 10 times richer and in the USA more than eight times richer.

The effects of inequality on societies have been studied by Wilkinson and Pickett in *The Spirit Level* (2010). They argue that many aspects of society are decided not by how wealthy a country is, but by how equal or unequal it is. Societies in which there is a considerable gap between rich and poor people are societies that score poorly on a range of measures, such as:

- physical and mental health and obesity
- educational performance
- levels of violence and other crime, and the number of people imprisoned
- lack of opportunities for social mobility.

These negative consequences also apply to those at the higher end, so it seems that greater equality benefits everyone in a society.

Welfare states and other government measures to reduce inequality

Governments do not see inequality in itself as a problem. In modern industrial societies, which see themselves as **meritocracies**, it is widely accepted that people should be rewarded according to their talent and effort. However, it is also widely accepted that these inequalities should not be extreme and that governments have a duty to ensure that the living standards of the poorest are not too low.

> **KEY TERM**
>
> **Meritocracy:** a society in which individuals achieve the level that their talents and abilities deserve.

Modern industrial states are all welfare states to some extent. This means that they take some responsibility for the security and well-being of all citizens. Through taxation, those who are well off contribute some of what they have to provide for those in need. While most welfare is provided by the government, voluntary organisations and charities, religious organisations and informal social groups often provide a large amount of welfare.

The reasons why welfare states were introduced and continue today are:

- Moral. It is seen as wrong to let others live in poor conditions and on low incomes while others prosper. This is supported by world religions, which see charity as a virtue.
- Political. Welfare has been seen as necessary to prevent the working class uniting in anger against an unjust system that creates such inequalities and injustices. Governments and political parties can also win support and votes by giving benefits to particular groups. Functionalists see welfare as necessary for maintaining a society's value system and preventing it from becoming dysfunctional.

The strongest welfare states are probably those of the Scandinavian countries – Sweden, Norway, Denmark, Iceland and Finland. There are differences between these countries but they all have highly developed welfare states that give people generous benefits. This is paid for by taxing the wealthy and high-income earners more than in other countries, and as a result Scandinavian countries have relatively low levels of inequality. In these countries and elsewhere in Europe, welfare states have often been expanded by social democratic parties who see welfare as a way of reducing class struggle and achieving a **redistribution of wealth** and power. In contrast, the USA's approach, based on its value system of individualism, is to encourage people to look after themselves with the support of their family and religion. It provides a safety net for the most needy rather than, as European countries have done, trying to reduce inequalities.

> **KEY TERMS**
>
> **Redistribution of wealth:** advocated by Marxists and others to achieve greater equality by giving some of the wealth of the better off to those who are less wealthy.
>
> **Dependency culture:** a set of values leading people to lose the ability to look after themselves so they become dependent, for example, on welfare benefits.

The welfare state in the UK started just before World War One with the introduction of old age pensions and national insurance. Workers, employers and governments paid into a fund that could support the sick and unemployed. The welfare state was then greatly extended by the Labour government after World War Two with the introduction of free universal secondary education, a free National Health Service, extended benefits and pensions and better and affordable housing that was provided by the government. While some benefits were means tested (that is, given only to those who met certain criteria), many were universal.

The high levels of welfare established in the UK in the mid-20th century were hard to maintain as costs went up and the economic situation declined. Right-wing politicians and writers argued that the welfare state was too expensive and encouraged a **culture of dependency**. The coalition government elected in 2010 argued that austerity was needed and cut many benefits, restricting them to those who can meet strict criteria, and encouraged the privatisation of the welfare services. This can be seen as moving the UK closer to the type of welfare state in the USA rather than those in Scandinavia. More benefits are means tested. For example, there are controversial new tests for people with disabilities to determine whether they should work to support themselves or receive support.

Welfare states have been strongly criticised by conservative and right-wing politicians and writers. They argue that:

- welfare encourages a something for nothing dependency culture in which people feel they do not need to look after themselves
- welfare payments have become too generous, for example, discouraging unemployed people from looking for jobs
- the welfare system has become expensive because it now provides more for more people when it should support only those who are most in need
- there is a risk of producing an **underclass** whose values are based on reliance on welfare
- the system is open to abuse, with some people fraudulently claiming benefits that they are not entitled to; this is really an argument for reform and clamping down on fraud rather than not having welfare at all
- when the state becomes involved in providing for high proportions of its citizens it becomes a nanny state; it interferes too much and does more than states should do.

KEY TERMS

Underclass: a group below the working class that is effectively cut off from the rest of society.

Marxism: a theoretical perspective that sees conflict between classes as the most important feature of society.

In addition, there are **Marxist** and left-wing criticisms. Welfare softens the harshest effects of the capitalist economic system and so reduces demands for radical change. It gives the impression that the system is less unjust than it really is. Welfare can be seen as a form of bribery, making revolution less likely. From this point of view it would be better if there were no welfare, as this would make the unjust nature of the system clear to everyone and lead to demands for changes.

Governments also try to reduce inequality by:

- Progressive taxation. People who are wealthy or have a high income pay a greater proportion of their income or wealth in taxation than those who are not.
- Subsidising or providing free of charge goods or services for poorer members of society. For example, in the UK people who receive a state pension can travel free on buses during the day and get financial help towards fuel bills in winter so that they can keep warm.
- Providing state education. They attempt to help children from poorer backgrounds get training and skills so that they can work their way to a higher standard of living.
- Setting a minimum wage that prevents anyone from being paid too little.
- **Equal opportunities** legislation that tries to remove discrimination against minorities. In the UK the Equality Act 2010 brought together earlier laws aimed at preventing discrimination based on sex and gender, age, **disability**, religion and other protected characteristics.

KEY TERMS

Equal opportunities: when all people are given the same chances (for example, in applying for a job) regardless of differences such as age, gender and social class.

Disability: covers a wide range of types of impairment in how the body functions in carrying out activites.

As well as government attempts to reduce inequality, the actions of voluntary agencies, charities and religious organisations are also important. In some countries governments give strong support to these groups as they are seen as being more effective in tackling problems than governments can be. These agencies often begin with individuals or small groups taking action on issues they see as important, but many grow into well-funded national organisations with highly skilled professional staff. For example, Barnardo's is a British charity that spends around £200 million per year helping vulnerable children and young people.

ACTIVITY: *research*

Use the internet or other sources to find out the main forms of welfare provided by the government in your country. These may include education and health care. Which are universal and which are means tested?

The problems of defining wealth and poverty

Among the groups most likely to live in poverty in modern industrial countries are:

- lone parents and their children
- unemployed people, especially the long-term unemployed
- workers who are low paid or do not have skills and qualifications
- chronically ill or disabled people
- people who are dependent on welfare benefits
- refugees, asylum seekers and recently arrived immigrants.

In addition, women, children, older people and members of ethnic minority groups have a high risk of living in poverty.

KEY TERMS

Relative poverty: being poor in relation to others in the same society.

Absolute poverty: being without some or all of the basic necessities of life.

It is very difficult to define poverty. For example, living standards are higher in modern industrial countries than in developing countries, yet there are poor people in both types of society. One way of defining poverty is to talk about absolute and **relative poverty**. People living in **absolute poverty** do not have some of the basic necessities of life such as:

- food
- safe drinking water
- sanitation (toilets or latrines near the home)
- shelter (somewhere to live)
- health (access to treatment for serious illnesses and in pregnancy)
- education
- information (access to the media).

Absolute poverty is a standard that can be applied in all times and places. It is estimated that more than one billion of the world's seven billion people live in absolute poverty.

Relative poverty is a way of measuring poverty that takes into account its social context, that is, when people can be considered poor in comparison to others in the same society. This means that in a modern industrial society people can be considered poor if they do not have a standard of living considered desirable or essential in that society, even though in a different society they might be considered wealthy. Relative poverty is often used as a measure for researching poverty in modern industrial societies. It is not usually as extreme as absolute poverty. Those in relative poverty have the basic necessities of life such as food, shelter, water and sanitation but their standard of living is significantly lower than that of most people in their society.

There are different ways of calculating what the poverty level is in a society. A commonly used official measure is having an income less than 60 per cent of the median income. Measured in this way, poverty becomes closely connected to inequality, since an unequal society will have high levels of relative poverty. Poverty levels can also be calculated from the total costs of the necessities for life in that society. This method was used by Peter Townsend in his famous studies of poverty in the UK. Townsend found that what people considered as necessities changed over time. For example, in the late 20th century refrigerators and washing machines became thought of as essential rather than things that only the relatively well off could afford. Researchers using this kind of approach might today consider things like how many hot meals people have a week, whether older children have their own bedroom and whether families can afford a holiday away from home each year. The level below which people are considered poor in a particular society is called the **poverty line**. In the UK just under 20 per cent of people are in poverty, using the definition of having an income that is less than 60 per cent of median income. The proportion of the population in poverty roughly doubled during the 1980s but has since fallen a little due to measures such as the introduction of the minimum wage.

KEY TERM

Poverty line: the level of income below which people are judged to be in poverty.

CASE STUDY

Mack and Lansley

In their famous *Breadline Britain* study in 1985, these researchers asked a sample of the whole population about essentials for living. Their list of items included living conditions such as a damp-free home and activities such as outings for children and was called the deprivation index. People were considered to be in poverty if they lacked three or more of the items on the list (excluding ones they had chosen not to have). They found that 7.5 million people or over 10 per cent of the population were living in poverty in the UK.

TASK

1 Mack and Lansley found that a smaller percentage of the population were living in poverty than was found in Townsend's research a few years earlier. Suggest two reasons for this.

2 Make a list of items that you would include on a deprivation index for your society.

The causes of poverty

Poverty is a complex phenomenon that does not have a single cause. Some of the main reasons for people being in poverty are:

- not having paid work
- being in low-paid work
- receiving benefits that still leave people below the poverty line.

KEY TERM

Cycle of poverty: when poverty tends to be inherited, so the new generation cannot escape the poverty of their parents.

In addition, the chances of being in poverty as an adult are increased by having been born into poverty. The **cycle of poverty** refers to families that have been in poverty for at least three generations, because the factors causing their poverty do not change and instead perpetuate it. For example, a child born into poverty is not likely to do well at school and to get the skills and qualifications needed to move up the class ladder compared with children not born in poverty. Poor people often do not have the resources to get out of poverty and suffer disadvantages that tend to keep them in poverty. They tend to lack social and cultural capital as well as money. A similar phenomenon occurs at the other end of the scale, as the children of wealthy parents are likely to become wealthy adults.

People in poverty can become trapped and find it difficult or impossible to escape from the **poverty trap**. This is because it is expensive to be poor. People have to spend a lot just to keep their existing standard of living. Some of the ways this works are listed below:

KEY TERM

Poverty trap: when poor people are unable to escape from being poor.

- The poor cannot afford to travel to cheap supermarkets and so they have to use expensive local shops.
- They cannot afford to buy in bulk, which is cheap.
- They cannot afford to insulate their homes so they pay a lot for fuel.
- They buy old or secondhand goods that are likely to break down and need to be replaced.
- They cannot afford facilities that would enable them to take up opportunities; for example, to pay a childminder so they can work longer hours.
- They may be unable to borrow from a bank so to pay their bills they may have to borrow from someone who will charge high rates of interest.

One explanation of the cycle of poverty is that there is a **culture of poverty,** that is, that poor people have a set of values that tend to keep them in poverty. Characteristics that have been said to be part of the culture of poverty include:

KEY TERM

Culture of poverty: when poor people have a set of values that keep them in poverty.

- having low levels of literacy and education
- being unable to plan for the future
- desiring immediate gratification rather than deferring it
- fatalism (not believing they can change their lives for the better)
- feeling marginalised and dependent on others
- not using resources and facilities such as banks and hospitals.

The explanation above is controversial, because some research has shown that the poor have the same values as the rest of society, rather than a separate set of values. Some characteristics such as poor education are not the fault of the poor person, so the culture of poverty approach seems to be wrongly blaming the poor for their situation. The idea of a culture of poverty has sometimes been used by politicians as a reason for not attempting to tackle poverty, on the grounds that spending money on alleviating poverty will make no difference if the value system cannot be changed.

Social exclusion refers to the ways in which people are systematically excluded from rights, opportunities and resources that are available to others. Poverty refers to material disadvantage, although it is often linked to other disadvantages; social exclusion refers to a wider set of disadvantages, which together prevent people from fully engaging in the life of their society and often result in poverty. Those who are socially excluded may miss out on:

KEY TERM

Social exclusion: people who are unable to take part in the society in the same way as most people are excluded from social goods.

- housing
- employment (being employed not only brings in income but also a sense of identity and self-esteem; people who are socially excluded miss out on both)
- health care
- transport (lack of transport can prevent people from taking up employment opportunities and can even make it difficult to shop).

To tackle social exclusion governments need not only to provide financial help in the form of welfare benefits but also find ways in which people who are excluded can become more involved in society. For example, giving a young unemployed man a bicycle may mean that he can find work, visit friends and go to shops. Welfare benefits on their own may even make social exclusion worse. In some societies the economic problems of recent years have made the majority less sympathetic to the restrictions faced by welfare claimants. Claimants are increasingly stereotyped and marginalised and so their social exclusion increases as well.

Social exclusion can be part of the poverty trap because the social support that can help people move out of poverty is missing. When people fall into poverty it can become difficult to escape from it. For example, for those in work on low wages and receiving some benefits, a pay rise may mean that they receive fewer benefits and will be worse off. There is then an incentive for them to try to avoid moving to better paid work or getting promoted. Being on welfare benefits can prevent people from becoming self-sufficient.

ACTIVITY: *evaluation*

What are the strengths and limitations of each of these ways of defining and measuring poverty: absolute poverty, relative poverty, social exclusion?

Sociological theories and poverty

- Functionalists see inequality as a positive thing that is functional for the whole society. To make the best use of the different qualities and abilities that people naturally have, society has to reward some people more than others. The existence of poverty means that unpleasant or poorly paid jobs will be done, since the poor have no choice but to take them. Poverty reminds the rest of society of the importance of values such as hard work, honesty and a stable family life and warns them of the consequences of straying from these values. It also increases social solidarity among those who are not poor by showing that they are different from those who deserve charity or blame.
- Marxists see inequality and poverty as inevitable consequences of **capitalism**: 'the rich get richer and the poor get poorer'. Capitalists (the **bourgeoisie**) will always try to pay their workers as little as possible so as to increase their profits and will try to bring in automation and mechanisation to save themselves labour costs. So the working class find that their wages fall and some become unemployed. It also suits capitalists to have a **reserve army of labour** who may be needed again.
- Right-wing thinkers use the culture of poverty argument to blame the poor for being poor. They believe that poverty is caused by culture rather than by the structure of society, as Marxists do.
- Feminists draw attention to the higher proportions of women than men who live in poverty. This has been called the feminisation of poverty. This is partly caused by the poverty of lone mothers but is also because women tend to be paid less on average than men and because women have more limited employment opportunities.

KEY TERMS

Capitalism: the economic system of most countries today based on private ownership of the means of production.

Bourgeoisie: the ruling or upper class in Marxist class theory.

Reserve army of labour: people who are employed when an economy is booming or when they are needed, but then are out of work when they are not required.

The consequences of being rich or poor in a global context

The global measure of poverty (by which is meant absolute poverty) used by the World Bank is living on less than US$1.25 a day. This figure is adjusted slightly to take account of the different prices of essentials in different countries. In all, 1.2 billion people live below this line. This figure has fallen considerably since 1990.

Mukesh Ambani's house in Mumbai

Dharavi, a slum area of Mumbai

The world has achieved the Millennium Development Goal of halving the number of people in extreme poverty. The same number (1.2 billion) lives on between US$1.25 and US$2 a day.

In some developing countries there is a very wide gap between rich and poor and sometimes there are striking contrasts when rich and poor people live close to each other. For example, India's richest man, Mukesh Ambani, who is one of the wealthiest people in the world with a fortune of US$27 billion, owns a 27-storey house in the city of Mumbai, a city where millions of people live in slums.

Many of the world's poorest people live in India and China and in these countries economic growth is lifting many people out of poverty. However, in Africa economic growth is often slower and starts from a lower base, so many people there will continue to live in poverty. The world's poorest people face many risks. Some of these are listed below:

- Those living in slums in cities often have temporary homes with few services and facilities and no security. At any moment the city authorities may decide to bulldoze their home.
- Those living in rural areas often have limited access to health, education and other services.
- Political instability and civil wars often affect poorer people most. Wealthier people can afford to escape.
- The areas that poorer people live in are often at risk of flooding, landslips and pollution; this is because the people cannot afford to move away from these risks.
- Climate change is affecting the poor people first and worst (for example, rising sea levels may flood farmland and homes). Again this is because they face risks they cannot escape from.

By contrast, the world's wealthiest and most powerful people can move easily from one country or continent to another. Increasingly, they share cosmopolitan lifestyles based on the consumption of luxury goods and services. They use private transport, often live in gated communities and go to exclusive clubs, restaurants and resorts. The sociologist Leslie Sklair has suggested, based on interviews with some of these people, that there is a fairly new transnational capitalist class that consists of the following main groups:

- owners and controllers of transnational corporations
- politicians and bureaucrats, such as those working for the United Nations and other global organisations
- professionals
- consumerist elites (such as those in the media).

KEY TERMS

Lifestyle: the way of life of an individual, group or culture.

Privileged groups: groups enjoying higher status than others or material advantages.

This class is a sort of global bourgeoisie, in Marxist terms. More broadly, most inhabitants of the more developed countries have a significantly higher standard of living than the majority of the world's population. Their **lifestyle** is based on consumerism and they consume a high proportion of the world's energy and other resources. They are the one billion or so most **privileged** people in the world. We used to examine inequality and stratification within individual countries but because of globalisation it is now important to examine them on a global scale.

TEST YOURSELF

1 Why is it difficult for some people to break out of poverty?
2 What are some of the ways that governments can try to reduce inequality between classes?
3 What are some of the difficulties involved in researching the distribution of wealth?

TOP TIP

The term ethnicity is usually preferable to race because race means an ascribed status. Ethnicity recognises that there can be some degree of choice. For example, a White European converting from Christianity to Islam would adopt an Islamic ethnic identity.

Ethnicity

In sociology the term race is now rarely used and has largely been replaced by ethnicity. Race refers to the once common belief that humans could be divided into biologically distinct races. One common division was into Caucasoid (White), Negroid (Black African) and Mongoloid (Asian). These labels allegedly go together with physical characteristics and often mental and behavioural traits, decided by the unique biological make-up of the group. Although few people now believe that humans can be divided into races in this way, we still use the term race when people act as if race did exist, for example in the terms **racism** and racial discrimination.

KEY TERMS

Racism: prejudice or discrimination against an individual or group because of their ethnicity or perceived race.

Prejudice: an unexamined opinion that a group of people are inferior or different.

Institutional racism: when the way that an organisation works has racist results, even when individuals do not intend this.

Elite: a privileged group at the top of a stratification system.

Racial **prejudice** refers to beliefs that another racial group is inferior in some way. Racial or race discrimination is when someone suffers disadvantage because of their ethnic or perceived racial group. Someone who is prejudiced may be in a position to discriminate against people, for example by not giving them a job or a promotion. Racism is a more general term used interchangeably with racial discrimination. **Institutional racism** refers to racism that is built into the way that an organisation or system works so that discrimination is not the result of individual's prejudice or discriminatory actions.

During the colonial period when European states established empires, racial inequality was common and expected. The European rulers and administrators formed a privileged **elite** while the life chances of the indigenous people were limited. In some countries, when independence was achieved and colonialism ended the Europeans left or stayed on as a less privileged minority. In the lands of White settlement (such as the USA, Canada, Australia and New Zealand) the indigenous people often faced discrimination and second-class status. In South Africa this was formalised in the **apartheid** system of racial segregation. South Africa's inhabitants were classified into four racial groups (Native, White, Coloured and Asian). Laws kept the groups apart in terms of where they lived, their work and their access to health and education services. Services for the Black South African majority (who made up three-quarters of the population) were inferior and they had few political rights. There was a long struggle for freedom from apartheid and the system was eventually abolished. When Black South Africans were finally able to vote the White minority lost power. The apartheid period represents an extreme form of racial stratification.

KEY TERM

Apartheid: the stratification system in South Africa until 1994 based on keeping racial groups apart.

Signs of Apartheid in South Africa in 1989

Functionalism and ethnicity

Functionalists see societies in terms of stability and consensus based on shared values. Differences between racial or ethnic groups are dysfunctional since they upset the smooth running of society. Functionalists tend to see such problems as temporary, occurring during periods of immigration. Newly arrived immigrant groups who are ethnically distinct need to become assimilated; that is, over time they will gradually lose their distinct cultural identity as they adopt the norms and values of the host society. There are at least four aspects to assimilation:

- Socioeconomic status. Members of the immigrant group are at first likely to be in relatively low-paid and **unskilled work** but over time move into better paid, **skilled work**.
- Residential concentration. Newly arrived immigrant groups often live in distinct areas so that they are among people who share their culture and values. Over time, the members of the group spread out and live among the host population.
- Language attainment. Newly arrived immigrants are likely to be more proficient in their mother tongue than in the host country language. The next generation may be bilingual and the third may speak only the host community's language or may prefer to use it.

KEY TERMS

Unskilled worker: workers who need no or minimal training to perform their work.

Skilled worker: workers who need skills acquired through training to perform their work.

- Intermarriage. Marriages initially take place within the immigrant community but over time more members marry outside the community and it becomes harder to pass on their original culture to the next generation.

The ideas about assimilation were developed mainly in the USA, which received waves of immigrants. In the USA assimilation does not necessarily take place and some communities remain relatively distinct. In some cases, assimilation is blocked by the barriers placed in the way of the immigrant community. For example, discrimination may make it impossible for them to improve their socioeconomic status. In this case the community may react by asserting its own culture more strongly. A third possibility is that the disadvantages are so strong that the immigrant community's position actually worsens and as a group they may experience downward mobility.

There are also differences of opinion as to whether assimilation is a good thing. Functionalists see it as a way by which society returns to a stable consensus based on shared values but by assimilation a community may lose its distinctive culture.

Marxism and ethnicity

Marxists see racism as a result of the capitalist economic structure. The idea of race, they say, is part of capitalist ideology. It has been used to justify the bad treatment of particular groups of workers. The ruling class persuade the working class that some of the problems they face, such as unemployment, are the fault of immigrant or other ethnic groups, thus **scapegoating** these groups. If the working class believe this (as part of their false consciousness), then it becomes divided against itself. This strengthens the position of the ruling class and makes revolution less likely.

KEY TERM

Scapegoating: when individuals or groups are blamed and sometimes punished for something which is not their fault.

Racism is in the interests of the ruling class so it is not surprising that it continues to be perpetuated through, for example, negative images in the media. Marxists are less interested in the cultural characteristics of groups and more in their class position in capitalist societies. Minority ethnic groups can also form a reserve army of labour. They can be used as workers when the capitalist system needs them but can be discarded and remain unemployed if not. They suffer all the disadvantages associated with this identity and are vulnerable to exploitation. Ethnic minorities are usually part of the working class but they are more disadvantaged than the indigenous working class because of the ideology of racism.

The right-wing view: minority ethnic groups as an underclass

The underclass is an idea used by right-wing thinkers. The underclass is seen to be clearly separated from the working class by a structural break. The underclass is, for these writers, characterised by:

- multiple deprivation such as a low income, unemployment, poor housing, poor education and racial discrimination for minorities
- social marginality – they lack the normal means of voicing grievances or exercising power and are less likely to vote and less aware of their rights than the indigenous working class
- a culture of fatalism and despair – they feel alienated and are suspicious of the police and authority in general
- dependency on the welfare state.

Most writers see the underclass as made up of various groups, including lone parent families and old people who depend on state pensions to survive but some see the structural break as being between the White working class and ethnic minorities, so that the minorities appear to be an underclass.

Some right-wing thinkers see the underclass as mainly a Black phenomenon. In the USA Charles Murray has argued both that African–Americans are on average less intelligent than other Americans and that their culture leads to births outside marriage, single parenthood and the inadequate socialisation of boys. The African–American underclass is associated with high levels of criminality, violence and drug-taking. In the UK there is much media concern about immigration (although the concern has switched in recent years to focus mostly on White European immigrants). This is linked with nationalism, where an English or British national identity is linked to the dominant culture so that non-natives are seen as different and a threat. This supposed national culture is highly selective, owing more to imagination than to real history. For example, there has been considerable concern in the media about whether Muslim minorities in the UK threaten British culture. The whole approach is based on an oversimplified view of cultures, which are seen as fixed and separate.

Ethnicity and education, employment and housing

Education, employment and housing are three areas of social life in which minority ethnic groups may face discrimination. This is often because those who are in positions of power and authority hold prejudiced views. There will be laws against racial discrimination in all three areas but in practice it can be very hard to prove that what has happened is discrimination.

In education, teachers are likely to be from the majority group and may stereotype ethnic minority pupils as lazy or deviant. These pupils may internalise these views and are then likely not to succeed in education. The school may also have a curriculum that is based on the history and culture of the majority group.

In employment, applicants for jobs may face discrimination. They may not be selected for interview if their name suggests they are from a minority or they may not be offered the job after an interview even if they are the best candidate, perhaps being told that they would not fit in. If they are given employment they may find they are not given opportunities to take training courses and they do not get promotion.

In housing, where local government has a stock of housing available for rent, members of ethnic minorities may find that the rules about who has priority may mean they are rarely offered housing, In privately owned housing there can be informal segregation when members of minorities planning to move to a new area are made aware that they will not be welcome.

Gender

This section looks at the effect of gender on the life chances of males and females with particular reference to gender discrimination in employment. The changing role of women in modern industrial societies and explanations of gender discrimination are discussed.

Effects of gender on life chances

We are all born male or female. This is perhaps our most basic ascribed status. It has huge implications for the rest of our lives. All societies are to some extent patriarchal; that is, men have a higher status than women and some degree of power over women. These are some of the ways in which women's life chances differ from those of men around the world:

KEY TERM

Domestic labour: the work that has to be done within the home, such as housework; understanding how domestic labour is divided is important for understanding gender inequality in families.

- Women have a triple burden of work: they work for an income, do **domestic labour** and take on emotional work, including the care of children.
- In most countries women earn far less than men, even for the same work.
- Women's health differs. Pregnancy and childbirth can be serious risks to health where medical facilities are inadequate. The risks are increased when girls marry at a very young age.
- Women experience violence. As well as domestic violence, this includes practices such as female genital mutilation, sometimes euphemistically called circumcision.
- In some countries the preference for boy children has led to the abortion of female foetuses. Later this can lead to an imbalance in the population, so that there are more boys than girls.
- Girls are less likely to go to school than boys in many developing countries.
- Girls are more likely than boys to marry young. This often ends their education and may lead to health problems if there is an early pregnancy.
- Women are more likely to be in poverty than men.
- Women live longer; on average about 5 years longer than men in most societies.

Changing role of women in modern industrial societies

Women now play a greater part in the workforce and as a result their roles have changed. The traditional female gender role of housewife and mother has not disappeared but it is now more likely to be combined with paid work. Men have often taken on a greater share of housework and childcare to accommodate this. However, women still face discrimination in employment. Women are more likely than men to work part time. They also spend time away from work when children are born and while the children are young and this can affect their opportunities for promotion. Many women find they experience role conflict between the demands of their family and the demands of work.

Feminism and gender inequality

KEY TERM

Feminism: political movement and sociological perspective advocating equality of the sexes.

Feminism is not a single set of ideas. There are at least four broad tendencies in feminism. These can be dated back to the 1970s when the Women's Liberation movement achieved considerable success.

- Liberal feminists are most concerned with getting equal rights with men and the need to overcome prejudice and discrimination through legislation and changes in our lives.
- Radical feminists see a basic conflict between men and women and see all societies as patriarchal (male dominated). They believe that male power is deeply embedded in society and that radical changes are needed to change this. Some radical feminists advocate that women live separately from men.
- Marxist and socialist feminists combine Marxist and feminist views, seeing the exploitation of women as an aspect of the class structure of capitalism. Employers use women as a reserve army of labour, male workers try to exclude women from skilled work and husbands benefit from their wives' unpaid work. Radical feminists see **patriarchy** as the problem but for Marxist feminists it is both patriarchy and capitalism.

KEY TERM

Patriarchy: the dominance of men over women and children in society.

- Black feminism. Some African-American and African-Caribbean women have formed their own groups distinct from the main feminist movement in reaction to the assumption by some feminists that all women are essentially in the same exploited situation. They see racism and ethnicity as part of the explanation of the situation of ethnic minority women.

By the late 20th century men tended to assume that women had achieved equality and that it was therefore no longer necessary to take gender into consideration. Some felt that feminism had gone too far; others that the main goals had been achieved. Some feminists felt that feminism was becoming seen as too negative. While it was clear what feminism opposed, the solutions it sought were not. Many feminists had been strongly critical of nuclear families yet it was clear that many women valued them. At the same time there was a growing backlash in the media, with scare stories about how career women were sacrificing the joys of motherhood and marriage.

Gender discrimination in employment

In pre-industrial societies the family was the unit of production, and all members of the family were involved. For example, in making cloth the husband wove, the wife spun and dyed and the children did the housework. There was no housewife role. During the Industrial Revolution the factory replaced the family as the unit of production. At first men, women and children worked in factories. In the early 19th century laws were made to restrict children working. The care and supervision of children then became the responsibility of the mother, who was then sometimes unable to work herself. Later there were restrictions on female employment. For example, the Mines Act of 1842 stopped women working in coal mines. The dominant ideology of the Victorian period saw women's place as being in the home. Men in work began to see women as rivals and women were excluded from trade unions. The result of all this was that women were pushed into the mother-housewife role.

From World War One onwards women began to return to employment and there was a gradual extension of their legal and political rights (including the right to vote, acquired in 1928) but the mother-housewife role remained their primary role.

Oakley sums up the effects of industrialisation as follows:

- Men were separated from the daily domestic routine.
- Women and children became economically dependent on men.
- Housework and childcare became isolated from other work.

Towards the end of the 20th century the numbers of women working grew significantly in most modern industrial countries. Some of the reasons for this are listed below:

- Under the influence of feminist ideas, including dissatisfaction with the housewife role, women wanted to work.
- Women who had worked, for example during World War Two, valued the experience and wanted to work.
- There were changes in the socialisation of girls so that more girls saw their future in terms of work as well as or instead of being a housewife and mother.
- Changes occurred in national economies so that skills and jobs traditionally associated with women became more numerous and more valued.

- Laws, for example laws preventing sex discrimination, led to changes.
- There were changing attitudes in workplaces, as employers began to value their female staff more.
- There were more female role models in occupations for girls and young women to aspire to.

KEY TERMS

Vertical segregation: occupying different levels within a hierarchy.

Horizontal segregation: differences in the number of people from different groups (such as the sexes) in different occupations.

Gendered division of labour: the way that societies expect women to be responsible for some. tasks (such as cleaning and preparing food) and men for others.

There is still both **vertical** and **horizontal segregation** in workforces. Horizontal segregation means that women tend to have different occupations from men. For example, most of the secretarial, nursing and primary school teaching jobs are held by women. Women are more likely than men to work in the service sector. Vertical segregation means that even when they work in the same occupations or workplaces as men women tend to be concentrated in the lower levels of the hierarchy. For example, in schools in the UK, although many teachers are women, most head teachers and senior managers are men. Taken together, these mean that there is a **gendered division of labour**.

Women are more likely than men to work part time and more married than unmarried women work part time. Childless women are the most likely to work and women with children under the age of five are the least likely to do so. The proportion of women returning to work after having children has increased but the biggest change has been that time spent away from work has fallen sharply. Women are more likely to return to work between the birth of their children. More women see having paid work as a normal part of married life although many still see motherhood as their main responsibility.

In the UK two important new laws increased equality at work:

- The Equal Pay Act 1970 specified that women were entitled to the same pay as men if they were doing the same or broadly similar work or if a job evaluation scheme showed their work was of equal value. The Act was strengthened in 1984 after the European Court ruled that it did not conform to the law in the rest of Europe.
- The Sex Discrimination Act 1975 barred discrimination on the grounds of sex in employment, education and the provision of goods and services. Women were to be given equal access to jobs and equal chance of promotion but some types of jobs were excluded from the Act.

In addition, maternity leave and maternity pay reduced the loss of income women experienced when they had children and ensured that after having children women were able to return to work at the same level and the same pay as before.

KEY TERM

Glass ceiling: the unseen barrier that seems to prevent women from achieving the highest positions at work.

Despite these advances, in many areas of work women seem to be able to rise to a fairly high level but then they are unable to move up to the very highest level, regardless of their qualifications and achievements. This has been called the **glass ceiling**, because it is as if there is an invisible barrier preventing their advancement. Some aspects of the glass ceiling are:

- Women who apply for promotions are not seen as serious candidates.
- Women have not taken these positions before, so employers see appointing a woman as a risk.
- The appointments are made by men, who may have sexist attitudes.
- The small group of men at the top of a company or organisation may not want to work with someone who they see as different to them.
- A woman may be seen as a threat – she may do a better job than the men.

- Men may believe that because of family responsibilities a woman may not be able to give the time the job requires and also cannot work at certain times (such as the weekend).

Research by Ryan and Haslam into women who manage to break through the glass ceiling found that their experiences were different from those of men. Women were more likely than men to find themselves in jobs where there was a high risk that they would fail, either because they had been appointed to run companies or organisations that were already in difficulty or because they were not given the resources to do a good job. The researchers referred to this as the glass cliff, meaning that these women were at greater risk than men of failing and of losing their position.

Christine Lagarde

Women at the top: some examples

At the time of writing no woman has been president of the USA, Russia or China. There has been no female secretary-general of the United Nations. Some women who have reached very high positions include:

- Hillary Clinton, US Secretary of State 2009–2013
- Margaret Thatcher, British Prime Minister 1979–1990
- Christine Lagarde, Managing Director of the International Monetary Fund since 2011
- Dilma Rousseff, President of Brazil since 2011
- Margaret Chan, Director of the World Health Organization since 2007
- Angela Merkel, Chancellor of Germany since 2005.

Consequences of gender inequalities at work

- There are marked gender differences in earnings. The advantage men have is carried over into old age. Women are likely to have considerably lower occupational pensions.
- Women are more vulnerable to poverty. Many more women than men earn wages that are so low they are in or close to poverty. This is particularly true of women who are heads of households.
- From the 1990s there has been a widening of inequalities in each sex. While women working full time at both the top and the bottom of the scale have had some success in narrowing the gap with men, the gap between the winners and the losers among women has become wider than the equivalent gap for men.

Explanations of gender inequalities at work

Conventional sociological explanations see women's position as being due to their labour market position:

- They have discontinuous careers due to childbirth.
- They are usually the secondary breadwinner (it is assumed that women can be paid less than men because men are the main breadwinners for families).
- They are less geographically mobile than men. (Families will move house for the male to take up a promotion or new job but are less likely to move for the woman's work).
- The existing large reserve of employable women keeps wages down.
- Cultural factors may also contribute, for example the widespread ideas that men should not be subordinate to women (so a man should not have to work for a female boss) and that work groups should be based on one gender.

Functionalists tend to say that women's lack of commitment to paid employment is a cause of their disadvantages. Women are likely to interrupt or abandon their careers and they may not put themselves forward for training. They are less likely than men to be in continuous employment for many years. However, this approach cannot explain why even women who do work continuously and have qualifications still tend to end up in lower positions than men. So we need to look at the structure of the labour market.

The dual labour market theory moves the explanatory emphasis from family to work. Unlike legislation, which focuses on individual acts of discrimination, it stresses the limitations on women's opportunities generally and the continuation of a gendered division of labour.

Marxist and Marxist feminists use the ideas of deskilling and the reserve army of labour in their explanations of women's disadvantages. Jobs that have been deskilled are those that used to require skills and initiative but no longer do so. An example of deskilling in office work is that typing used to be considered a skill, and good typists were proud of the number of words per minute that they could type, but these days word processing and other computer tasks are now seen as tasks anyone can do. The reserve army of labour idea explains how women were able to enter the workforce during the two world wars to take up jobs previously held by men who were away in the armed forces. It cannot, however, explain horizontal segregation or the fact that many women remained in the workforce during the recent hard economic times. Some writers believe the male-run trade unions play a role in restricting women's opportunities.

Radical feminists see women's position at work as another example of the patriarchy. Society fails to offset women's disadvantages, for example by funding childcare facilities better. Like functionalists, some radical feminists see the disadvantages as originating in the home: marriage and motherhood reduce women's chances of success in paid work.

ACTIVITY: *discussion*

To what extent do women still face discrimination in some types of employment?

ACTIVITY: *research*

Interview an older female member of your family and ask how life chances, especially with regard to family and work, have changed for women in her lifetime.

Men

Most sociology in the past was about men, though this was rarely made clear. Sylvia Walby has argued that this tends to lead to women being seen as a deviant minority while men are gender neutral (so that, unless we specify that we are talking about a woman, it is automatically assumed that it is a man). Recently there has been more research into masculinity and male roles. Men's roles in society have changed at the same time as, and in ways related to, changes in women's roles.

Barbara Ehrenreich argued that in the USA some men began rejecting conventional masculine gender roles even before women began to reject feminine roles in the 1970s. Some men rejected the role of breadwinner, the rat race and the road to an early heart attack and looked for a more fulfilling life, often giving a higher priority to family life.

Traditional male roles have become even more difficult in recent years for the following reasons:

- Working-class masculinity had been threatened by the decline of the manufacturing industry. There are fewer jobs involving traditional working-class male work and more workplaces are mixed. Male unemployment has risen while female employment has risen.
- The violence and sexual abuse of women and children by men has become more visible and is widely condemned.
- The value of men's role within the family is increasingly being questioned. For example, many women bring up children successfully on their own.
- Feminism has brought masculinity into question, exposing men as self-interested abusers of power rather than heroic conquerors of nature.
- The dominance of heterosexual White men in modern industrial societies has been increasingly challenged not only by feminism but also by Black and gay radical politics.

There have been many reactions to the changing situation. Rutherford says two such reactions are:

- Retributive man. In this reaction the man reasserts traditional masculinity, trying to turn the clock back to a period that has passed.
- New man. This involves men today acknowledging their emotions, sharing domestic work with their wives or girlfriends and taking a greater role in fatherhood.

Different jobs and working environments

ACTIVITY: *discussion*

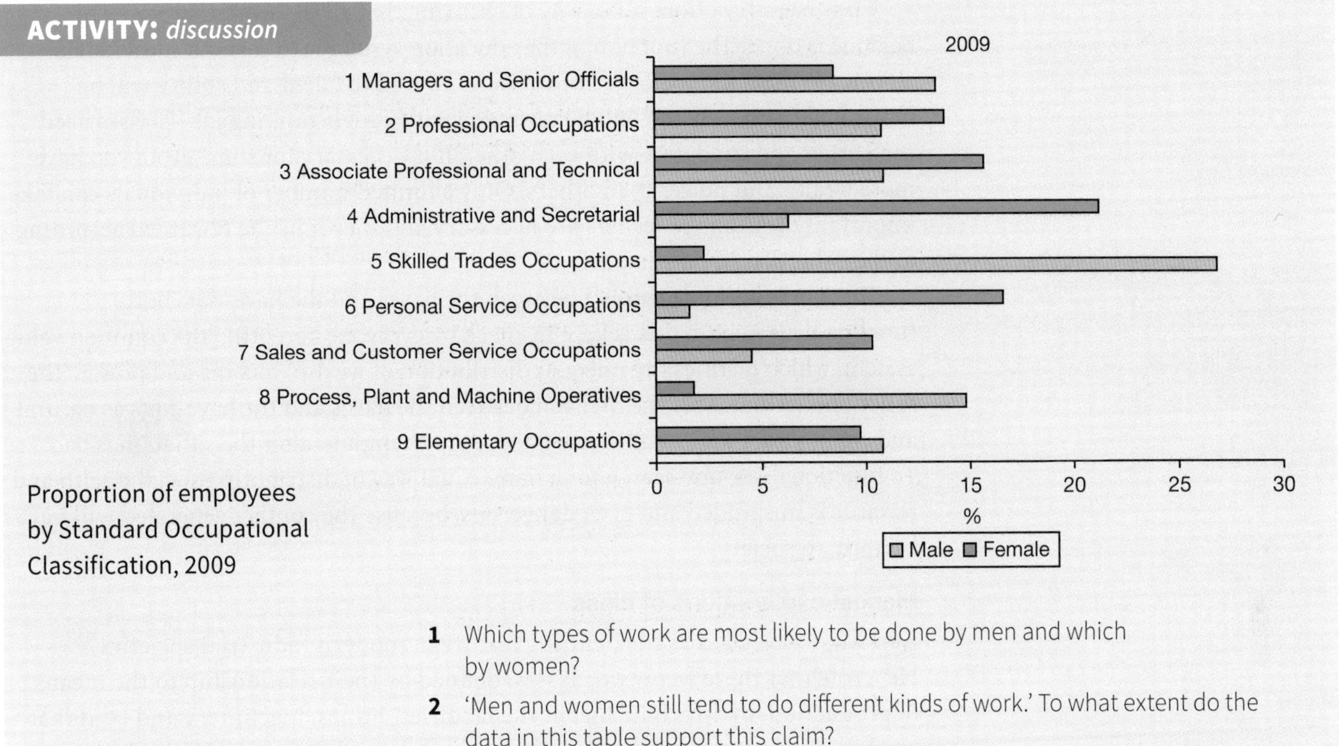

Proportion of employees by Standard Occupational Classification, 2009

1. Which types of work are most likely to be done by men and which by women?
2. 'Men and women still tend to do different kinds of work.' To what extent do the data in this table support this claim?

TEST YOURSELF

1. Suggest three ways in which members of minority ethnic groups may face discrimination at work.
2. What is the glass ceiling that faces women at work and why do women find it difficult to break through it?

Social class

In this section we describe ways of defining and measuring social class. We examine the changing nature of different classes and class cultures and discuss the nature, extent and significance of social mobility.

Ways of defining and measuring class

There is less agreement about the definition and measurement of social class than about other dimensions of stratification. It is possible for individuals to define themselves as being in one social class when a sociologist might decide they belong to another. People's own ideas about their social class position are their subjective class. Sociologists are more concerned with their objective class position. However, tracing people's objective class position depends on decisions about how to define and measure social class.

Functionalist explanations of class

The most famous functionalist work on class is by American sociologists Kingsley Davis and Wilbert E. Moore. They argue that social class is inevitable in any complex modern society. Because a society has a common value system, individuals can be ranked and so a stratification system emerges. For example, Western capitalist societies value individual achievement, efficiency and production so there are high rewards for successful business executives.

Class has a function. It is a way of ensuring that all the work that needs to be done is done. The function of the education system is to sort out individuals' abilities to meet the society's needs. Those who have talent and ability will be motivated to do well and will be rewarded with a high-ranking job. Classes need each other and cooperate with each other. It is necessary for some groups to have more wealth and power than others. Only a limited number of individuals can take important decisions so leaders are necessary and they must be rewarded according to the value placed on what they do.

There may be some conflict between the haves and the have-nots but functionalists believe this is kept in check by everyone accepting the common value system, which justifies the unequal distribution of wealth, income and power. The functionalist view sees the division between the haves and the have-nots as natural and right. Order and stability are good. Any attempt to alter the situation is bad. To functionalists, any search for a more equal way of distributing social wealth and rewards is misguided and even dangerous, because the conflict generated will be harmful to society.

Marxist explanations of class

Karl Marx saw class as the defining feature of modern industrial societies. He wrote that there were two classes, defined by their relationship to the means of production, by which he meant the factories, mines, machinery and land that can be used to create wealth. The bourgeoisie owned the means of production and the proletariat or working class owned nothing but their ability to work. The working class had to become wage slaves, working to live but never earning the true value of their work, which was taken as profits by the bourgeoisie. The state ruled on behalf of the bourgeoisie. The working class were not fully aware of their situation because they were taught that the system was fair and that they themselves were to blame for their lowly position. Marx thought that eventually the gulf between the two classes would become so clear that the working class would revolt and bring in a new and more equal system. Many governments feared that he was right and tried to reduce inequalities to prevent this from happening.

Marx recognised the existence of other classes as well as the bourgeoisie and proletariat. At the time when he was writing there was a large middle class, but Marx argued that this would disappear over time, as its members either moved up into the bourgeoisie or were pulled down into the working class. There was also a lumpenproletariat, by which he meant those at the lower end of society who did not work, such as criminals and beggars, and so were not working class.

Contemporary Marxist analyses of class have been faced with the problem of where to locate the many new and greatly expanded service sector occupations (a development in the class structure that Marx did not anticipate). This has led to the **proletarianisation** argument, which we will consider when we study the working class.

> **KEY TERM**
>
> **Proletarianisation:** the theory that the lower levels of the middle class are becoming working class.

One recent Marxist approach is that developed by the American Erik Olin Wright, who sees a basic division still exists between the capitalist class and the working class. Wright argues that there are three dimensions of control of economic resources – control of investment, control of the physical means of production and control of labour power. Wright says that the bourgeoisie control all these things and the working class control none, but in between there are many groups who may have access to one area of control but not others. He describes them as being in contradictory class locations. There are then many different groups and in his theory Wright has moved a long way from the basic Marxist dichotomy of the bourgeoisie and the proletariat and closer to the Weberian view.

Weberian explanations of class

Max Weber's approach to the study of class has two basic similarities to Marxism but also several differences. The similarities are that:

- class is situated in the economic structure of societies
- both are conflict approaches – they see conflict between groups is inevitable.

Weber, however, recognised the existence of more classes than Marx. Weber expected the number of people in middle-class occupations to grow whereas Marx thought the middle classes would gradually merge into the bourgeoisie or proletariat as society polarised the two main classes.

Weber believed that social class is based on the economic marketplace, in which positions vary according to your income, skills and qualifications. While it is possible to make out broad classes within which people share broadly similar life chances, there is also a finely graded ladder of classes based on occupations. He distinguished between **market situation** (income, degree of security and chances of advancement in a particular occupation) and the work situation (the extent and ways in which an occupation is controlled or authority is exercised). An individual's position on the ladder involves not only income but also their status. A priest, for example, often has a low income but considerable status as a well-known and trusted person in the community. Weber said that status groups competed against each other for status. Workers in a trade union demanding a pay rise are likely to compare their wage with that of another group of workers as they do not want to earn less than them – rather than, as Marxists would say, seeking an overall redistribution of wealth. So for Weber, class, status and power do not always go together, whereas for Marxists they do.

KEY TERM

Market situation: the economic position of a group of workers in relation to others.

Weber's ideas have proved very influential in sociology and he was right about the growth in middle-class occupations. Most sociologists today see social class in similar terms to Weber, as involving several different classes rather than just two.

Max Weber

Feminism and social class

Many class studies have been gender blind and assumed that class categorisation is based on the head of the household, meaning the male breadwinner. More recent research has used either individual (each individual classified separately) or joint classifications (looking at the situation of both partners together). Both have shortcomings but they produce different models of class from that of the traditional approaches.

Some sociologists have defended the traditional gender-blind approach to class on the grounds that the paid work of women is relatively insignificant compared to that of men and that gender is less important than class. Women were more likely to have part-time jobs and to be out of the workforce for long periods. They were more likely to be economically dependent on a man. Not surprisingly, this view has been strongly contested by feminist sociologists like Michelle Stanworth. They point out that in many societies there are many households in which the woman's income is essential to maintaining living standards. There are even families where the woman is the only breadwinner. There are dual-class families too, where the man and woman are, in theory, in different classes and families where the combined income of both partners means the family has a significantly higher standard of living than if only one of them worked.

A more radical view is that rather than devising ways of measuring class that take more account of women, we should change our ideas of class. Some radical feminists see all women, because of their exploitation and oppression by men, as forming a class in conflict with another class – men. Most would not go so far but would say that class analysis has not taken sufficient account of women. Sylvia Walby argues that married women are in a dual-class position – in one class at home, because husbands exploit the domestic work of their wives, and in another at work, where women have the same interests as men working at the same level.

ACTIVITY: *evaluation*

Compare and contrast the four theoretical approaches to social class above. Which has the strongest explanation of class today? Give reasons for your choice.

Measuring class

For Marxists there are only two main classes, the bourgeoisie and the proletariat. Most other sociologists find it difficult to operationalise the idea of social class by deciding where the boundaries lie between the classes and putting individuals into these classes. There is no agreement on the best way of measuring class. Factors that can be taken into account when deciding which class someone belongs to are:

- wealth
- income
- housing (number of houses, size and location)
- occupation
- level of education and qualifications
- status
- lifestyle – some research has even used the type of car people drive or their choice of shops to buy their goods.

KEY TERMS

Occupational structure: the hierarchy of occupations in a society.

Professions: occupations that require specialised higher level education.

White-collar worker: a non-manual worker, member of the middle class.

Blue-collar worker: a manual worker, member of the working class.

The most commonly used category of these is the person's occupation. This is because occupation is closely connected to income, status and living standards. Occupations can be ranked in a hierarchy, with the highest paid and most rewarding occupations at the top and others below. This is called the **occupational structure**. Occupations are either non-manual or manual. Non-manual jobs involve mental rather than physical work, such as the **professions** and office and sales work. These are **white-collar** occupations and are seen as middle class. Manual jobs are **blue-collar** jobs and involve some physical effort. They are seen as working class. These two broad groups can be further divided according to the level of skill involved and the qualifications or training required.

For a long time the most commonly used scale in the UK was the Registrar-General's Scale, which was based on status as much as on pay. An example of this scale is shown in Table 3.1.

This scale is now quite dated in some ways. The distinction between manual and non-manual work is not as important as in the past, and because there are fewer semi-skilled and unskilled manual jobs there are now many people in the middle of this table. The scale was based on the assumption that there would be a male householder. Now that more women work there are more couples whose work would put them in different classes.

Social class	Examples
I Professional and managerial	Accountant, doctor
II Intermediate	Teacher, farmer
III a Non-manual skilled	Police officer, sales representative
b Manual skilled	Electrician, bus driver
IV Semi-skilled	Farm worker, postal delivery worker
V Unskilled manual	Labourer, cleaner

Table 3.1: The Registrar-General's Scale of Social Class (1913)

In the UK nowadays the Standard Occupational Classification is widely used. This is similar to the Registrar-General's Scale but it is based on nine major types of occupations, from managers, directors and senior officials at the top to elementary occupations at the lower end. Many other countries use similar classifications adapted to the occupations in that country. There is also an international standard classification of occupation used by the United Nations' International Labour Office, which can be used to compare countries.

All occupational scales have some problems:

- They usually miss out important groups at both ends, such as those who are so wealthy they do not need to work and long-term unemployed and disabled people. Those who do not have jobs make up around half the population so it is important to include them in some way.
- They miss out other important aspects of inequality, such as how much wealth people have.
- Many people have other sources of income so their financial situation is different from others in the same occupation.
- They are based on the occupations of individuals but most people live in families, in which there may be more than one wage earner with occupations at different levels on the scale.
- Many women are in routine non-manual work (class IIIa on the Registrar-General's Scale). Should their classification be based on their own employment or that of their husband or partner? Whichever is chosen, the classification systems find it hard to account for the fact that they may share their income.

The upper class

KEY TERM

Upper class: the highest class in society that is wealthy enough not to need to work.

The **upper class** tends to be less visible than the other classes, although our common use of the term middle class implies there must be a higher group. The upper class does not appear in accounts of class based on occupation, such as the Registrar-General's Scale. Peter Saunders argues that it is too small to count as a class but most sociologists feel this small group deserves special attention because of its immense wealth and power.

Giddens suggests there are three groups in the upper class:

1 The landowning aristocracy. This consists of people with titles and inherited wealth including, at the summit, the royal family. Despite inheritance taxes and, in some cases, their need to open their stately homes to the public, they remain rich and powerful.

2 The jet set or pop aristocracy. This consists of people who have usually made their money in sport, the media and entertainment. Their income is unpredictable and often limited to a fairly brief period of their lives. The aristocracy – 'old money' – tend to look down on what they see as 'new money'.
3 The entrepreneurial rich. This consists of people involved in business as owners and directors in retail, publishing and communications, banking and finance, property development and manufacturing.

Giddens also suggests that the top 1 per cent of owners of wealth in the UK form the upper class. Their wealth gives them access to power and leading positions. The Marxist sociologists Westergaard and Resler, in their classic 1970s study of class in Britain, *Class in a Capitalist Society*, argued that the upper class was made up from between 5 and 10 per cent of the population. To reach this apparently high figure they included directors, top managers, senior civil servants and higher professionals on the grounds that these people are often large shareholders of companies and therefore own a share of the means of production, making them members of the bourgeoisie.

While many sociologists believe the ownership of wealth is the deciding factor in membership of the upper class, elites theorists argue that the top groups in society derive their power not from wealth but from their occupation of the top jobs. Those who occupy the top positions, as politicians, judges, civil servants, military officers, directors and so on, are drawn from a small minority who have very privileged backgrounds. In the UK this can be seen in the high numbers of top civil servants who went to top public schools and to Oxford or Cambridge universities. High-ranking politicians, especially in the Conservative Party, also tend to be from the same high class self-recruiting background. This is popularly referred to as the old boys' network. In Britain a small group of people owns a totally disproportionate amount of wealth today and this elite group of wealthy people overlaps considerably with the few thousand people who take all the important political, financial and administrative decisions.

The middle class

The phrase middle class covers people in a very wide range of occupations, from office clerks or secretaries to lawyers or architects. The middle class has expanded rapidly in all advanced capitalist countries in this century, as anticipated by Weber but not Marx. Sociologists often divide the middle class into three distinct parts:

1 The petty bourgeoisie or old middle class. They are small business owners, not just shops and workshops but also self-employed people, landlords and small farmers. Marx expected this group to disappear as large capitalist companies drove smaller ones out of business. Indeed, it has shrunk but it survives, partly due to government encouragement and incentives.
2 The upper middle class – the professionals and managers. Weber describes these people as the intelligentsia and specialists. Their high income is usually derived from the education and training they have received. This group grew in the 20th century, especially in the public sector, with professionals working in schools, hospitals, social services and national and local government.
3 The lower middle class working in a very wide range of jobs, including routine clerical and service sector jobs, foremen and nurses. They are sometimes referred to as white-collar workers. This group has undergone downward block mobility – a decline in status and pay relative to other groups – over the last century and has

become larger and feminised (that is, it contains a higher proportion of women). It has even been argued that there is little difference in practice between those in routine non-manual work and working-class occupations, which means that this group has been proletarianised. The term pink collar is sometimes used for lower middle-class work that has traditionally been done by women, such as secretarial and clerical work.

Giddens argues that there is only one middle class, clearly distinguishable from the upper class by the fact that it does not own the means of production and from the working class by its possession of educational or technical qualifications. Other sociologists emphasise the differences within the middle class and describe it as fragmented. Their differences include political ones. The petty bourgeoisie tends to be very conservative while public sector professionals are often left wing.

The proletarianisation debate

Proletarianisation is essentially a Marxist idea. Part of the group that used to be considered middle class is now, according to this argument, really part of the working class. The groups usually thought of as having been proletarianised are:

- clerical and administrative workers in offices, including specialised work such as receptionists
- shop and sales workers
- sometimes higher groups such as teachers.

A century ago these jobs carried more status than they now do. They involved indoor work and skills that were then less common than they are now and they were better paid than working-class jobs at the time. Since then the gap between working-class jobs and these lower middle-class jobs has narrowed so that writers such as Braverman claim that the latter have been proletarianised. If this theory is right, the working class is still the largest class, the real middle class is quite small, society is divided between the bourgeoisie and the proletariat and there is still the possibility of revolutionary change. The term **new working class** is used by sociologists who think that the old working class has now merged with the lower middle class to form a larger working class.

KEY TERM

New working class: the supposed new class formed by lower middle-class workers merging with the traditional working class.

Proletarianisation involves:

- formerly middle class jobs having lower status than they used to have
- middle class wages falling relative to working-class wages
- conditions of employment changing, like job security and benefits such as sick leave
- jobs having less autonomy; that is, managers exercise more control and there is less freedom over, for example, when to have a break or in which order to do tasks in these jobs
- work changing through mechanisation and automation, so that the work requires less skill – this may lead to fewer jobs; for example, banks need fewer workers as more customers use automated teller machines or internet banking
- workers in these jobs are starting to think of themselves as working class; for example, by joining a trade union.

The evidence for proletarianisation is mixed. On the one hand, clerical work has been deskilled. The skills required are often not much more than being able to read and write and follow instructions. Wages for such work have also fallen relative to other work. However, these types of jobs are still advertised as being skilled and with chances for promotion, unlike a lot of manual work. People in these jobs enjoy greater job security and a more pleasant working environment and are more likely to have pensions and other benefits than people in working-class jobs.

Men in these jobs may have a better chance of moving up the career ladder. Women are held back by domestic commitments, their inability to move geographically and a lack of post-entry qualifications (so they cannot go on management training courses at head office) and this creates more opportunities for men. It could be argued that, because of the temporary nature of their status, female clerks have been proletarianised even if male ones have not.

The working class

The working class is usually thought of as divided into three categories:

- skilled
- semi-skilled
- unskilled.

TOP TIP

Blue-collar and white-collar work once had some connection to what people wore. Men in offices usually wore white shirts and those in manual work did not because the nature of their work meant their clothes could get dirty. Nowadays people in many jobs wear a wider variety of clothing and the differences between blue- and white-collar work are in any case not so clear.

Working-class people are sometimes referred to as blue-collar or manual workers (unlike white-collar workers, who are in non-manual work). Blue-collar work includes manufacturing, construction, mining, mechanical work and other types of physical work, often needing physical strength. Educational qualifications are not usually needed for this kind of work, though training is needed for skilled work.

Mechanisation and automation have reduced the number of manual jobs. Tasks that once required people can now be done largely by machines. For example, manufacturing cars in factories requires fewer workers because some of the tasks involved have been mechanised and automated. The working class in most modern industrial countries has therefore declined as a proportion of the population, with fewer unskilled jobs and also a fall in employment in manufacturing, which has often moved to developing countries. There has been a shift towards a service and white-collar economy. The living standards of all classes have risen but income differences between classes remain. Growing affluence, including the ownership of housing and consumer goods, has changed working-class culture and ways of life but this is not the same as a change in its class situation.

The embourgeoisement debate

Living standards in Europe rose dramatically in the 1950s and 1960s as the continent recovered from World War Two. In the UK the Conservative Party won three general elections in a row, which it could not have done without substantial working-class support. Some have argued that greater affluence was breaking down the old class divisions, making the working class indistinguishable from the middle class, and that the working class (or at least the most affluent part of it) was going through a process of **embourgeoisement**. This is an anti-Marxist view. If it is true that class divisions are disappearing, there will be no class conflict or revolution.

KEY TERM

Embourgeoisement: the theory that the higher levels of the working class are becoming middle class.

The underclass

The underclass is a disadvantaged and marginalised group at the bottom of society. The term is a relatively new one but the idea is not. In the 19th century Marx said that there were other groups besides the working class at the lower end of society. These included older workers who had lost their jobs, farm workers trying to move into industrial work, those in casual and irregular employment, those who could not work (such as the disabled) and also the lumpenproletariat of criminals, prostitutes and vagrants.

The term underclass began to be used in the 1980s but there is no agreement as to exactly who belongs to the underclass. In the USA the underclass is associated with ethnic minorities but in Britain the term is used to refer to several groups. The idea of an underclass is not just that it is below the working class but also that it is in some way cut off from it. The underclass miss out on some of the things that everyone else takes for granted. Among groups that have been said to be in the underclass are:

- long-term unemployed people
- people dependent on state pensions
- people dependent on benefits
- disaffected teenagers without qualifications or prospects.

The underclass is a controversial term. Marxists prefer not to use it at all. They say that the underclass is a part of the working class which has suffered most during an economic downturn and been pushed out of work. The use of the term has been criticised because:

- it is vague – there are too many different definitions
- in some uses, it implies that members of the underclass are to blame for their situation; this goes back to an old distinction between the deserving and undeserving poor and to the idea of a culture of poverty – that people believe that they cannot change their situation and become fatalistic
- it lumps together different phenomena (pensioners and disaffected teenagers have little in common, for example)
- it draws attention away from the disadvantages experienced by the working class by excluding those who are most disadvantaged from it
- it implies that the underclass is stable – in fact, people move in and out of the underclass very quickly; therefore perhaps 'class' is the wrong word for a temporary experience.

The American Charles Murray, from a New Right perspective, offers a cultural view of the underclass by defining them by their behaviour. For Murray the signs of an emerging underclass are:

- a growth in illegitimacy (births to unmarried mothers)
- a rising crime rate, increasing anti-social behaviour and increasing use of illegal drugs
- the unwillingness to take jobs (related, he says, to the availability of state benefits).

This kind of approach seems to blame members of the underclass for the position they are in, and also to blame governments for providing benefits that encourage people to be irresponsible. Many sociologists are far more sympathetic to the underclass. They blame society for creating the underclass and would like to see measures that improve members' situation.

KEY TERMS

Social mobility: the movement of individuals or groups from one class to another.

Intergenerational social mobility: movement between classes in society from one generation to the next, so that when a child grows up she is in a different class from her parents.

Intragenerational social mobility: movement between classes within one generation, so that an individual is born into one class and moves into another.

Open society: a society in which it is possible to move easily from one class to another.

Social mobility between classes

Social mobility is movement between classes. The types of social mobility are:

- upward social mobility, which involves moving up the class ladder, for example from the working class to the middle class
- downward mobility, which involves moving down the class ladder, for example from the middle class to the working class
- block mobility, which is the movement of a whole class or occupational group; if proletarianisation occurs, the lower middle class is downwardly mobile; if embourgeoisement occurs, the skilled working class is upwardly mobile
- individual mobility is the movement of an individual or family from one class to another
- **intergenerational mobility** takes place between generations; for example the child of working-class parents who is successful in education and enters a middle-class profession is mobile in this way
- **intragenerational mobility** takes place within one generation; for example, a man may start his working life in a working-class job but move up to become a manager.

If there is a lot of social mobility we say that the class system is **open**; if there is not, then it is relatively closed. In a meritocracy, where people are able to achieve the position in society that their talent and effort deserve, we expect to find a lot of mobility, both upward and downward.

Education can improve your chance of being upwardly mobile

Factors that lead to social mobility include:

- getting education and qualifications to improve your chances of being upwardly mobile
- getting promotion and career advancement
- marrying someone of a different class
- changes in wealth, for example becoming wealthy through inheritance or winning a lottery.

Upward social mobility for a lucky few

Marxists see social mobility as a sort of safety valve. If people could not move between classes there would be greater anger and more chance of class conflict. However, the fact that there is some mobility persuades some people that the system is open and fair and reduces the chances of class conflict.

Upward mobility has been more common than downward mobility. This is because of changes in the numbers and proportions of different kinds of jobs. There are fewer unskilled manual jobs and more middle-class jobs in contemporary society. Because of this change and greater educational opportunities people have been able to move up. Most mobility is short range, not from the top to the bottom or vice versa but rather, for example, from the top of the working class to the bottom of the middle class. It could be argued that this is not really mobility at all since it involves little change in life style, life chances or class identity.

From the right-wing perspective it is natural that most middle-class positions will be taken by those from the middle-class origins because they tend to be more talented, as a result of the earlier upward mobility, based on ability and talent, of their parents or grandparents. This assumes that intelligence is to a large extent inherited, which is a controversial idea. Those who believe that ability and intelligence are spread equally throughout the classes argue that the present system prevents a lot of talent from being realised leading to a waste of human resources.

The Oxford Mobility Study

The most important survey of social mobility in the UK was the Oxford Mobility Study led by John Goldthorpe and based on interviews with more than 10,000 men. Goldthorpe found high rates of mobility. In no social class did more than 50 per cent of his sample originate from that class. Although there was a lot of movement there were big differences in the relative chances of different classes. It was much more likely that a working-class boy would be upwardly mobile than that an upper middle-class boy would be downwardly mobile. Goldthorpe concluded that Britain had not become more open despite high social mobility, because most of the mobility could be attributed to the changes in the number of jobs available.

Critics of Goldthorpe have noted that:

- he does not acknowledge the existence of the upper class – this seems to recruit largely from within its own ranks, confirming the impression of little mobility
- he tends to assume that class can be based on the occupation of a male breadwinner; there is less research on female social mobility – upward social mobility has been harder for women because of the glass ceiling effect, but has always been possible by marrying a man of a higher class.

TASK

1. What was the main reason for upward social mobility?
2. In what ways does this research now seem dated?

It has become harder to move up the career ladder after starting work. For example, it used to be possible to start work as a clerk in a legal office and end up as a solicitor. Now you need a degree in law at the start of your career. More qualifications are needed in contemporary society and this makes promotion more difficult for those who started in a low position. The implication of this is that upward mobility happens early in people's careers or not at all, making success at school and college all-important. There are few second chances.

ACTIVITY: *data interpretation*

The Great Gatsby curve: inequality from generation to generation: the United States in comparison, by Miles Corak, 2013

Note: The vertical (up and down) axis shows the likelihood of a child having the same income as their parents. The higher a country is, the less intergenerational social mobility there is. The horizontal axis shows how equal or unequal the country is, with least inequality to the left.

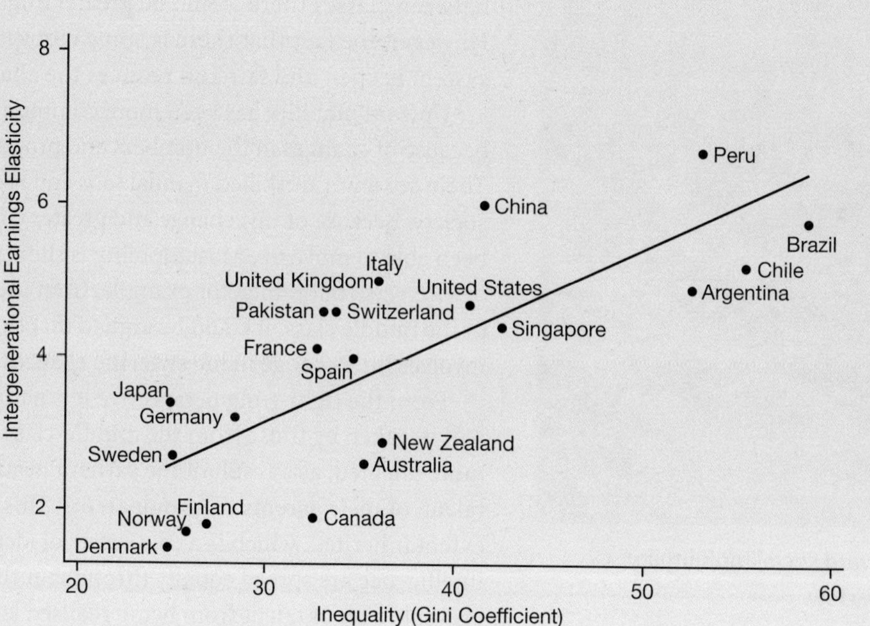

1 Which country has (a) the most intergenerational social mobility and (b) the least?

2 The graph shows that there is a correlation between inequality and social mobility. Describe the correlation shown by this graph.

TEST YOURSELF

1 What are the main similarities and differences between Marxist and Weberian accounts of class?

2 Why has upward social mobility been more common than downward social mobility?

3 Proletarianisation is usually thought of as a Marxist theory. Why is this?

4 Class inequalities seem to attract less attention than gender inequalities. Why do you think this is?

Is class still important?

The media tend to give the impression that social class is less important and even a matter of personal choice. In sociology, the continued importance of class has been questioned by the following ideas:

- The idea that we are all middle class now. This assumes that because older working-class occupations are less common and because many people's living standards have risen the working class has largely disappeared.
- A closely related idea is that consumption (what we buy and consume) has become more important than production (what we produce in our work) in shaping our identities. However, what people can consume is decided by their wealth and income, which depends on their class.
- The meritocracy – the idea that everyone reaches the level that their ability or effort deserve. In a meritocracy, although people are at different levels in society they do not pass this on to their children and so class membership does not continue over time. In the UK there is strong evidence that important advantages for the already privileged are continuing suggesting that class is still important.
- The idea that class has been overtaken by other inequalities, such as those based on gender, ethnicity, age, employment sector and region. Of these the most significant is gender. The growing influence of feminism in sociology has meant that it is no longer taken for granted that class is more important than gender.

Most prominent sociologists working on stratification believe that research has proved the continuing importance of class. Evidence of the distribution of income and wealth support this, although sociologists do not always agree where the boundaries between the classes are.

Revision checklist

Make sure that you know all the key terms listed in this unit and that you understand the following:

- The main forms of social stratification are class, age ethnicity and gender.
- Status can be ascribed or achieved.
- Individuals have life chances that are related to their position in stratified groups.
- Wealth and income are unequally distributed in different societies.
- Governments have created welfare states and have used other measures, such as equal opportunities legislation, to try to reduce inequality between classes.
- Wealth and poverty can be defined in different ways, such as absolute and relative poverty and social exclusion.
- Poverty has a number of causes and effects and can be difficult to escape.
- Globally, there are both rich and poor people with very different life chances.
- Ethnic groups can face prejudice and discrimination, for example in education, employment and housing.
- Racism can lead to ethnic groups being blamed for social problems (scapegoating).
- The life chances of both males and females is affected by their gender.
- This is particularly significant for women in employment.
- The role of women in modern industrial societies has changed.
- Gender discrimination can be explained in different ways.
- There are different ways of defining and measuring social class.
- The different classes and class cultures are changing.
- Modern societies have some social mobility, which can be analysed in terms of its nature, extent and significance.

Exam practice questions

In traditional societies there is often very little social mobility. Today, high levels of social mobility mean that a society is making use of the talents of its members; no one is unable to achieve the position they deserve because of discrimination or poverty. However, research tends to show that individuals are more likely to stay in the same class as their parents than to have moved to another class.

a What is meant by the term 'discrimination'? [2]

b Describe two ways in which individuals can achieve upward social mobility. [4]

c Explain how governments can try to reduce social inequality. [6]

d Explain why sociologists find it difficult to define and measure social mobility. [8]

e To what extent is class still the main form of stratification in modern industrial societies? [15]

Total marks available 35

Unit 4: The Family

Objectives

At the end of this unit you should be able to:

- describe the main types of family
- discuss the influence of social stratification and ethnicity on family diversity
- describe the functions of the family and understand the 'loss of functions' debate
- describe alternatives to the family
- describe cross-cultural differences in marriage and alternatives to marriage
- explain roles and relationships within families, how these have changed and how they vary, reflecting social stratification and ethnicity
- discuss negative aspects of family life
- explain how industrialisation and urbanisation affect families
- outline demographic trends and how they affect families, including the consequences of an ageing population.

Introduction

Sociology is about how people interact with others in social groups. Those social groups come in many forms and sizes: nations, organisations of different kinds, communities, schools and so on. But perhaps the most important social group in our lives is our family. This unit explores the sociology of the family, looking at different kinds of families, family structures and patterns and at how roles and relationships in families are changing.

Because people live in families we might assume that we know a lot about them. But the sociology of the family shows that there are several types of family. Over a lifetime, each person will probably live in several different types of family as the family is changed by births, marriages, deaths, divorces and separations, remarriages, adoptions and changes of residence. In modern industrial societies such as the UK, over the last 50 years or so there has been an increase in the number and proportion of different types of family and a decline in nuclear families.

What are the different types of family?

The nuclear and extended family

This section describes the nuclear and extended family. Different family types include the reconstituted or stepfamily, the single-parent family and same sex family. Not everyone lives in a family; for example, sometimes groups of friends live together. A group of people living in the same home are called a **household unit**, whether or not they are related.

KEY TERMS

Household unit: the group of people living together in the same residence and sharing living space.

Nuclear family: made up of an adult man and an adult woman who are married, or in a relationship, and living together with dependent children.

Extended family: a nuclear family living with other relatives such as grandparents or great-grandparents or aunts, uncles and cousins.

The nuclear family

A lot of sociological writing about the family in the 20th century took it for granted that there was one normal kind of family; the **nuclear family**. This was seen as the normal kind of family in the USA, the UK and other modern industrial societies at the time. It was thought to be both the most common kind of family and also the best. But from the 1970s onwards, other types of family became more noticeable.

The functionalist George Murdock argued that the nuclear family of a mother, father and dependent children was the basic family unit worldwide. He based this claim on research carried out around the world on many different cultures and societies. Types of family that seemed to be different, he argued, had a nuclear family at their heart. For example, family units of mother, father and children exist within **extended families**.

Extended families

It is usually thought that extended families were more common in the past and are now in decline because they seem less suited to life in modern industrial societies. Extended families include more relatives than the mother, father and children unit of the nuclear family. If there are more than two generations this is called a vertically extended family. If there are aunts, uncles and cousins (that is, people of the same generation as the parents and children) this is a horizontally extended family. Sometimes the term extended family is used for all the relatives sharing a household, that is, living together under one roof. Sometimes, however, we call several nuclear families living close to each other in the same street or area extended families. These are both classic extended families and seem to have been common in working-class British communities in the past. In modern industrial

TOP TIP

The way that people in different societies think about their families and kinship varies enormously. In this book, the terms used are those from the Eskimo system of kinship classification, which is used in Europe, North America and elsewhere. Although this system has become the most common, it is only one among six systems described by the anthropologist Lewis Henry Morgan. For example, in the kinship system of Hawaii before explorers arrived the brothers and sisters of your parents, who would be your aunts and uncles under the Eskimo system, were called their mother and father (so individuals had several mothers and fathers) and the children of these aunts and uncles (or rather, mothers and fathers) were your sisters and brothers (rather than cousins). The Eskimo system emphasises the nuclear family bond rather than extended kinship ties.

KEY TERMS

Kinship: when the ties between people are related by descent (having a common ancestor) by marriage and by adoption.

One-parent or single-parent family: one parent and their dependent children living together.

Divorce: the formal, legal ending of a marriage.

Reconstituted family: after the death of a partner or a divorce, a new family that is created by someone remarrying.

Step-parent: after remarriage a step-parent shares with their new partner parental responsibility for children from previous marriages.

Step-child: a child who lives with one biological parent and one step-parent.

societies, with better communication and transport, relatives who live far apart are better able to stay in contact, and where there is regular contact (for example, by phone or e-mail) and mutual support between them we describe this as a modified extended family.

Marriage creates new **kinship** ties

Single-parent family

There have always been **single-parent** or **one-parent** families. In the past these were usually the result of the death of one of the parents, leaving the other parent to raise the children on their own. This was often a temporary situation, while the surviving parent looked for a new partner. However, there has been a marked increase in the number of single-parent families in modern industrial societies since the mid-20th century. Some still result from death but many now result from separation or **divorce**.

Here are some reasons why there are more single-parent families these days than in the past:

- Divorce has become common and it leaves one parent looking after the children.
- Women have greater financial independence. They are more likely to have qualifications that allow them to work to support their family and they may be able to receive welfare benefits, so they do not need a man as a breadwinner.
- Some women now choose to raise children on their own, without the father around.

Reconstituted or stepfamily

If a person marries for a second time after the death or divorce of their first partner, a new family is formed that is called a **reconstituted** or stepfamily. There are many possible variations of this kind of family: for example, one or both partners may have been married before, one or both partners may have children, and these children may live in the new family or with the previous partner. New relationships are created by remarriage: such as **step-parents, step-children**, step-siblings

TOP TIP

Although these types of families have become more common, there is little agreement about the language we should use to talk about them. They are referred to as blended families as well as reconstituted or stepfamilies.

and step-grandparents. This situation is relatively new and so the norms and values are often not clear and may need to be negotiated. For example, a stepmother may not be sure to what extent she should correct bad behaviour in the children of her husband and his former wife. Equally, the children may be unsure what authority this new person in their lives should have.

New relationships, such as step-grandparents, are created by remarriage

Same sex family

Same sex families are when the two adults are of the same sex; that is, a male or female gay couple, usually raising their own or adopted children. In the past arrangements like this were often not accepted but increasingly modern industrial societies allow same sex couples to adopt children and give same sex couples the same or similar rights and responsibilities that opposite sex couples have, for example property rights and rights to welfare benefits. In the UK unions of two people of the same sex are formally recognised by a ceremony that creates a **civil partnership**. In other countries that do not recognise such relationships, same sex couples may still cohabit but do not have the same rights.

KEY TERM

Civil partnership: a relationship between two people usually of the same sex that has been formally registered giving them similar rights to married couples.

Women who have left their husband to live with a lesbian partner are finding it easier than in the past to gain custody of their children. This is because research in the UK and in the USA has found that children raised by gay parents are no more likely than others to grow up gay or to suffer bullying at school. Parents' sexual orientation is increasingly seen as less important in deciding who should bring up a child than factors such as the strength of the mother–child bond. Research also suggests that children brought up in same sex families are no different from children from opposite sex families in their intelligence, their gender roles and identities and their attitude to life.

Same sex couples with children remain a contentious issue, with many people still firmly believing that this situation can only damage the children. Lesbian couples are more likely to be accepted as parents than male homosexuals because of the perceived importance of the mother to her children. However, even with male couples there is a growing opinion that at least in some cases this may be the best available option for the children.

TOP TIP

The law has changed recently in some countries and in some states of the USA. There may well have been further changes by the time you read this book. As with all information in textbooks, it is worth finding out what has happened since the book was published.

ACTIVITY: *data interpretation*

Statistical table

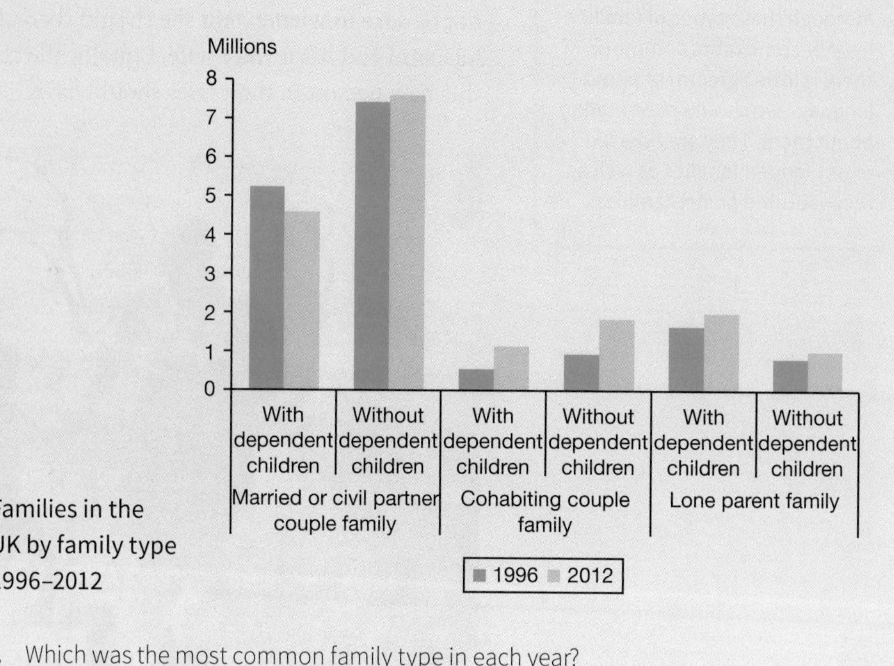

Families in the UK by family type 1996–2012

1. Which was the most common family type in each year?
2. Which type of family declined in numbers between 1996 and 2012?

TEST YOURSELF

1. What different types of extended families are there?
2. Give three reasons for the increase in single-parent families.

The influence of social stratification and ethnicity on family diversity

KEY TERM

Family diversity: the increase in the number of different types of families.

The changes in the number and types of different families, or **family diversity**, are related to both social class and ethnicity.

Stratification and family diversity

The extended family in the UK was strongly associated with the working class. Areas with old industries such as coal, steel and shipbuilding had strong working-class communities in which it was normal for young men and women to marry and stay in the area, close to their parents. With secure jobs there was no reason for them to move away. These industries declined in the late 20th century. When men lost their jobs as factories were closed, women often became the main breadwinners and some men took on domestic roles they were not prepared for. The strong communities declined as people moved away in search of work and surviving extended family ties were weakened.

Ethnicity and family diversity

In some societies some ethnic groups are associated with particular types of families. In the UK the two main minority ethnic groups are African-Caribbean and South Asian (with family origins in India, Pakistan and Bangladesh).

KEY TERMS

Matrifocal family: one in which the mother heads the family and the father has a less important role in the family and in bringing up children.

Matriarchy: when the mother is the head of the household, with authority over the men and children in the household.

African-Caribbean

In the African-Caribbean minority in the UK there is a higher-than-average number of **matrifocal** families where the father, if present at all, plays a reduced role in the family and in bringing up children. The word matrifocal is used for this situation rather than **matriarchal**. In a matriarchy, women would have power and a central role in both the family and wider society. In matrifocal families, mothers are the breadwinners and are often strongly supported by their own mothers and female relatives. It has been suggested that this pattern of family life may have begun with slavery, when the male ancestors of today's African-Caribbean population were, as slaves, unable to provide for and protect their families. Later, poverty and unemployment, partly because of racism, may have meant that the men still could not take on fully the instrumental role. This led to high rates of single-parent families and absent fathers.

South Asian minorities in the UK

South Asian minority ethnic groups in the UK are associated with the following:

- Strong extended families and extended family ties. This may be linked to migration from the South Asian subcontinent, when one family member would come to the UK first and then family members would join him when he was established.
- Large families. The average number of children that women have in the countries of origin is higher than that in the UK and, although this is falling, women from South Asian minorities still have more children than the UK average.
- Traditional gender roles. With women less likely to go out to work, paid work is often done at home. This is often for cultural reasons but may also be a defence against racism.
- **Arranged marriages**. Parents or other family members decide who their children will marry or provide them with a limited choice. The bride and groom have usually agreed to their parents doing this, often with the help of a matchmaker. Arranged marriages should not be confused with forced marriages, in which one or other partner has not given their consent. Forced marriage is viewed by the United Nations as an abuse of human rights.

KEY TERM

Arranged marriage: marriage partners are chosen by older family members rather than people choosing their own marriage partner.

European ethnic groups

Migrants, including immigrants to the UK from Eastern European countries such as Poland, are often young adults. Because of their age, and sometimes because of cultural and religious differences, the birth rate of these groups tends to be higher than that of native British people.

The functions of the family and the 'loss of functions' debate

Functions of the family

Functionalists argue that in order for societies to survive and work, certain essential tasks or functions must be performed. They argue that it is the family that carries out several vital functions and is therefore the bedrock of every society. Different writers give different labels to these functions, but the following functions of the family are agreed upon by most functionalists:

- Reproduction. Societies must produce new generations of children in order to survive; and marriage and the family are closely associated with having children. Reproduction is encouraged. Not having children may be regarded as a misfortune.

- Socialisation. Children need to learn the norms and values of their society, and this happens through **primary socialisation** in their families. Families transmit the culture of the society to the next generation; they are the vital link between individuals and the wider society.
- Social control. Closely related to socialisation, this refers to how the behaviour of children is controlled so that they conform to norms. For example, they may be punished for being 'naughty' or rewarded for behaviour their parents define as 'good'.
- Care of children. Children need to be fed, clothed, sheltered and nurtured intellectually and emotionally. In the family people are given responsibility to ensure that this happens.
- Status. Families provide status for children; they involve children in a web of interpersonal and group relationships.
- Regulation of sexual behaviour. All societies seem to set rules about what kind of sexual behaviour is accepted, with whom and in what circumstances. Although sex outside marriage is often tolerated, most societies insist that children are born to people in a socially approved sexual relationship.

KEY TERM

Primary socialisation: the process by which infants and young children absorb the basic norms and values of their culture (see Unit 2).

Functionalists argue that all these functions are performed best in the nuclear family. In such families the main responsibility for emotional and home-based needs is given to the mother, and the economic and material well-being needs of the family are given to the father. This gender division, say functionalists, suits the natures of men and women, and so nuclear families are the most common family arrangement because they are the best. Against this, however, it can be argued that these functions can be met by other types of family, and perhaps by arrangements that are not families at all. For example, in modern industrial societies part of the socialisation and childcare functions are undertaken by schools and other institutions.

Functionalists have also studied how institutions and other parts of society can have negative consequences or dysfunctions. Sometimes, even as they fulfil wider functions, they may be dysfunctional for some people. The anthropologist Edmund Leach suggested that the nuclear family in modern industrial societies was, in fact, dysfunctional. The image of a happily married couple with healthy children was found everywhere in advertising and the media; it set up an ideal that many families could not reach. Leach called this the '**cereal packet** image of the family'.

KEY TERM

Cereal packet family: the stereotypical nuclear family of mother, father and children with traditional gender roles that is often shown in advertisements.

> In the past kinsfolk and neighbours gave the individual continuous moral support throughout his life. Today the domestic household is isolated. The family looks inward upon itself; there is an intensification of emotional stress between husband and wife, and parents and children. The strain is greater than most of us can bear.
>
> (Reith Lectures 1967, 'A runaway world')

Leach means that the demands made on the nuclear family are too great, and this leads to conflict within the family. The conflict is often expressed in feelings of suspicion and fear of the world outside the family. So for Leach, the modern nuclear family is less functional than an extended family that is closely embedded in a community.

Other evidence that nuclear families can be dysfunctional comes from looking at the extent of abuse and violence within families. This is discussed in the section on the dark side of family life on page 146.

The Marxist view of family functions

KEY TERM

Family functions: the functions the family has, that is, what roles it plays and for whom, according to functionalist theory.

Marxists agree with functionalists that families are important because they carry out **functions** that are vital for individuals and society. However, they disagree with functionalists on what these functions are. For Marxists, the family is functional for capitalist society; that is, as an institution the family contributes to the continuation of an economic system. Engels, who lived at the same time as Marx and collaborated with him, showed that the family could only be understood by considering how it fitted into the economic system of a society.

Functions of the family, according to Marxists:

- The family is where each generation is socialised into accepting capitalism and its values so that, for example, many working-class people believe that the system is fair and that their failure to succeed is their own fault.
- The family brings up children to be the next generation of workers, producing profits for capitalists.
- Having families makes it difficult for workers to go on strike because then they would not be able to support their families.
- Men who are oppressed and alienated at work can compensate for this in the family, where they are in control. They take out the anger and frustration from work on their wives and children.
- The family is the main unit of consumption; that is, families buy and consume and in doing so support the system.
- Part of women's role is to look after sick and old people, so they help keep the workforce healthy and capitalists avoid responsibility for health care.

KEY TERMS

Feminism: a theoretical perspective that is mainly interested in issues of gender inequality and on the position of women in the family and in society.

Patriarchy: a term used by feminists to describe societies and organisations (including the family) in which men are dominant and women are subordinate.

The main focus of Marxists has always been on the economy and the world of work, and for many Marxists the family is a relatively insignificant side issue. Marxists tend to take a rather narrow view of the family, concentrating on its economic significance. It was Marxist feminists who saw this as inadequate and brought together the insights of both Marxism and feminism.

The feminist view of family functions

Feminists take the view that the nuclear family is functional for **patriarchal** society. The institution of the family gives men a powerful and privileged role, so it is a patriarchal institution.

Feminists see the family as having several functions. Traditional gender roles make men the breadwinner and head of the household. Men benefit from the family because they have a wife whose expected role is to look after their needs: to cook, clean, support their husbands emotionally and to put her interests behind those of her husband's. Families socialise both boys and girls into gender roles. A son or male heir traditionally inherits the family's wealth, so that wealth and power stay with males. Patriarchy in the family, according to feminists, is the basis of patriarchy in the wider society. The overall function of the family is to maintain the patriarchy so families are functional for men.

There are three main strands in feminist thinking: liberal, Marxist and radical feminism. Liberal feminists believe that equality can be achieved without fundamental changes to the nature of society. Progress can be made by, for example, persuading men to do more housework, bringing up children in non-sexist ways and by encouraging women to have careers. To both Marxist and radical feminists, such changes would be unlikely to achieve much, because society would still be patriarchal. For radical feminists, society needs to change completely. If the relationships between men and women are based on male superiority, then women need to stay out of such exploitative relationships and live separately from men. For them the exploitation of women within families is part of a wider exploitative system.

CASE STUDY

A Marxist feminist view of the nuclear family: *The Anti-Social Family* (1982) by Barrett and McIntosh

The authors imply in the title of this book that the nuclear family is antisocial. It is antisocial, they argue, because it is so widely seen and argued to be (by functionalists, for example) the only good kind of family. The media promote the idea that we should all aim for a nuclear family and state that the alternatives do not work. Barrett and McIntosh say that in reality, however, it is the nuclear family that does not work for many people. Their relationships fail because families are unequal and create stress, but people – especially women – are made to feel that they are to blame. Women are even paid less than men because of the family. This is because in the past men argued for pay increases on the grounds that they had to support their families so that even today women's paid work tends to be seen as an extra for her family (pin money) and be underpaid and undervalued.

TASK

1 What do Barrett and McIntosh mean by describing nuclear families as antisocial?
2 What is it about Barrett and McIntosh's views that make this a Marxist feminist work?

Part of the traditional female role in many cultures

What has happened to the family's functions?
The 'New Right' and family functions

The functionalist view of the family was strongest in the middle of the 20th century, when the nuclear family with its traditional gender roles seemed normal. Since then the family has undergone many changes. The New Right theory of the family argues that we need to return to the nuclear family because the new diverse types of family are unable to fulfil the functions needed in contemporary society. In particular, they argue, children need to be raised in nuclear families. Among the changes that, according to the New Right, have undermined the family's functions are:

- the growth of one-parent families
- the easy availability of divorce
- cohabitation (seen as a sign of instability and impermanence)
- the rise of feminism (seen as responsible for making women unhappy with their role)
- legal abortion (the New Right strongly supports the idea that foetuses have a right to life)
- women going out to work (seen as having negative effects on children and depriving women of their 'natural' role of housewife/mother)
- homosexuality (seen as deviant and a sign of moral decadence).

The New Right believes these changes are related to or responsible for children failing in school, rising rates of crime and delinquency and a dependency culture (in which people rely on welfare benefits and are not interested in working for a living). The welfare state, together with the other changes, disturbs the 'natural' order of family life, interfering both with relationships between men and women and with the raising of children. New Right politicians advocate cutting welfare benefits, encouraging women not to work and strengthening the nuclear family and the idea of a male breadwinner. New Right thinking and policies have been advocated mainly by journalists and politicians, by right-wing think tanks and by pressure groups such as Families Need Fathers, which oppose divorce.

The New Right approach has been strongly attacked by, among others, Pamela Abbott, Claire Wallace and Melissa Tyler, who take a feminist approach. They favour tolerance and diversity in the way people live together, and argue in favour of the rights of people to choose to live alone, in a homosexual couple, in single-parent families or with a female breadwinner supporting a househusband who cares for the children.

TEST YOURSELF

1. Name three functions that the family has, according to functionalists.
2. Why does the New Right argue that we need to return to traditional families?

Alternatives to the family

This section describes alternatives to the family, including other types of households and communes.

Not everyone lives in a family. Some people live alone or with friends who are not their family. Sociologists are interested in the different living arrangements people have. When a family lives together there is a family household but there are other types of household and ways of living that are in some ways strikingly different from families, such as **communes**.

KEY TERMS

Commune: a group of people who choose to live together and share at least some of their property.

One-person household: when only one person lives in a residence.

One-person households and singlehood

In the UK and some other modern industrial societies, there is a growing number of **one-person households**. Three main types of people live alone:

- About half of these are older people who are widowed and whose children have moved away.
- People who choose to live alone are often middle-class women who have chosen to focus on a career rather than a family. Some of these women marry later in life, but the age at which people settle down has been rising, so that at any time more people are living alone than with other people.
- Men who are separated and divorced. The wife often stays in the family home with the children, becoming a lone parent family, while the man moves out.

The number of one-person households has increased as a result of greater opportunities for women and the increase in the number of divorces.

Divorce

Communes

Communes are groups of individuals who choose to live together, sharing their living space and meals and also usually some property. They often begin in an idealistic attempt to find a better way of living, based on religious or political beliefs. In some communes all the adult members of the commune act as the parents of all the children in it. In the 1960s and 1970s groups of hippies trying to find an alternative to the mainstream lifestyle they rejected set up communes and some of these still survive.

CASE STUDY

Case study of the Oneida community

An example of a commune was the Oneida community in the USA in the 19th century. The community was led by John Humphrey Noyes and based on his religious beliefs. Noyes attracted a group of followers who believed, with him, that they could practise a lifestyle that was perfect and free of sin. They lived communally, sharing possessions. All community members worked according to their abilities and routine unskilled work was rotated so that everyone took a turn. The community practised free love; that is, any adult could have a sexual relationship with any other adult who consented. Noyes discouraged close couple relationships. Children stayed with their mother until they were weaned but from then on they lived in the children's wing and were not allowed to develop close bonds with their parents. The commune lasted for more than 30 years. It ended when Noyes tried to pass on the leadership to his son and community members began challenging some of the practices, including free love. At its height there were three hundred members and several branches of the Oneida community.

TASK

1 What characteristics of communes did the Oneida community have?
2 Why do you think the Oneida community did not last longer than it did?
3 What challenges do you think face communes today?

Friends as family and shared households

Some sociologists have argued that family life is more uncertain than it used to be. People have much greater freedom of choice about their family lives. For example, the norm of marriage for life has changed to a choice among alternative arrangements such as periods of cohabitation, serial monogamy and choosing to remain unmarried. Some believe that family ties are less permanent than they were in the past, and it has been suggested that people may rely more on their friends than on their family. For example:

- Friends have become very important for young people establishing their independence from their parents.
- Friends may play a greater part in emotional, practical and social support.
- Friendships with other unattached people become important for divorced and separated people.

(Allen, 2009, 'Family and friends in today's world', Sociology Review)

Young people in particular tend to rely on friends of their own age group. Groups of young people sharing a house have become more common. Shared households often exist for economic reasons; taking out a joint mortgage with a group of friends or renting with them may be the only way they can afford housing. But the change also reflects the importance of friends in young people's lives.

Friendships are different from family ties in several ways. Families are very unequal, while friendships are often based strongly on equality and reciprocity. However, the family is still important in many ways, with commitments in which friends would rarely be involved; for example, care of older people and the inheritance of property.

KEY TERM

Traditional societies: non-modern societies, contrasted with modern industrial societies.

Other alternatives

Anthropological studies of **traditional societies** show a range of living arrangements that are unlike the family in some ways. One well-known example is the Nayar people of southern India. Traditionally large numbers of women and children descended from a female ancestor, lived under a single roof, with an older man or *karnavan* as the head of the group or *tharavad*. Women were allowed to take several *sambandham* husbands who visited the *tharavad* at night but did not live there. The paternity of the children would not be known and the *karnavan*, the woman's brother, was responsible for bringing up her children, with the 'husbands' playing no part. This system seems to have developed as a response to the lifestyle of the Nayar, as most of the men were away a lot of the time fighting as mercenary soldiers.

Cross-cultural comparisons and variations in marriage

This section discusses different types of marriage across cultures, including monogamy, serial monogamy, polygamy and polyandry.

Monogamy

Monogamy is a marriage between only one man and one woman. In many countries it is the only legal type of marriage. The increase in divorce in the UK and other modern industrial societies has led to **serial monogamy** becoming more common; that is, a person has several marriage partners over their lifetime, but only one at a time.

KEY TERMS

Monogamy: being married to one person at a time.

Serial monogamy: when someone has more than one marriage partner during their life, but only one at any given time.

Polygamy: being married to more than one person at the same time; for example, a man with several wives or a woman with several husbands.

Polygyny: when a man has more than one wife at the same time.

Polyandry: when a woman has more than one husband at the same time.

Polygamy and polyandry

Polygamy is a marriage that involves at least three people. It can take two forms: **polygyny**, when a man has several wives, and **polyandry**, when a woman has several husbands. These can be rational adaptations to unusual circumstances if, for example, there is an imbalance between the numbers of men and women. After a war has reduced the numbers of men of fighting and marrying age, a group can regain its former numbers more quickly if the surviving men are allowed to marry and have children by several women.

Polyandry seems always to have been rare. Examples that are known usually involve a woman marrying two or more brothers. This is known as fraternal polyandry. It has been practised in Tibet, where it helps to prevent the division of scarce farming land into areas too small to support a family. The Nayar family and marriage system described above is polyandrous, although the husbands did not live with their wives.

Polygyny is far more widespread, and is allowed by law in most of Africa and the Middle East and in parts of southern Asia. Islam allows a man to have up to four wives. However, even in these countries most marriages are monogamous because it is expensive for a man to support several wives and their children. It is usually the wealthy men who take more than one wife, and the number of wives can be an indicator of status and wealth. The first wife is usually regarded as senior to other wives and has a higher status. Each wife may have separate living quarters within a larger compound.

TOP TIP

Monogamy, and related terms like polygamy, have in the past always referred to marriage. Today they can be applied more generally to long-term relationships involving cohabitation (see page 134).

Group marriages are a fourth way, after monogamy, polygyny and polyandry, in which relationships between husband and wife may be structured. In a group marriage there are two or more husbands and two or more wives. Although unusual, this may be a recognised form of marriage, and being unfaithful with someone outside the marriage would be treated as just as wrong as infidelity would be in another form of marriage.

Jacob Zuma, the President of South Africa since 2009, is one of the world's best known polygamists. In April 2012 he married for the sixth time, with his other three current wives (one having died and the other divorced) present. Polygamy is allowed in South Africa by the Customary Marriages Act.

President Zuma on official business, accompanied by his fourth wife

Serial monogamy

In most modern industrial societies only monogamy is allowed. However, over the course of their lives many people are married more than once because they remarry after the death of a partner or after divorce. Serial monogamy is when someone has more than one marriage partner over their lifetime, but only one at a time. It became more common with the rise in the **divorce rate** in the late 20th century. A number of well-known celebrities and others in the public eye have been serial monogamists. In history, the English King Henry VIII is known for having married six wives in succession in the hope of having a son to succeed him.

> **KEY TERMS**
>
> **Divorce rate:** the number of divorces per year per 1,000 people.
>
> **Cohabitation:** two people who are not married to each other living together in an intimate relationship.

Alternatives to marriage

This section looks at alternatives to marriage, such as **cohabitation** and civil partnerships.

Cohabitation

Cohabitation is when two people live together in a sexual relationship but are not married to each other. In the UK until about the 1970s this was unusual and was strongly disapproved of, being referred to as 'living in sin'. However, values changed and cohabitation became widely accepted and is now considered normal.

There are three different types of cohabitation:

- permanent or long-term relationships differing from marriage only in that a formal ceremony has not taken place
- short-term relationships without commitment
- trial marriages: living together before marriage.

(Fulcher and Scott, 1999, *Sociology*)

While the first type is prevalent in Scandinavia, it is the third type that seems particularly significant in the UK. More than half of all couples in the UK now cohabit before marriage. This does not suggest a rejection of marriage but a change in marriage practice. Marriages are delayed, perhaps for economic reasons; more people are in higher education in their twenties and for years they may not feel they are financially independent enough for marriage. There is, however, continued social disapproval of extramarital sex and social pressures make many couples marry eventually.

Civil partnerships

Same sex families were explained in the opening section of this unit on different types of family. In a small number of countries and areas same sex couples are allowed to marry. This is the case in, for example, Spain, Portugal, Denmark, Norway and Sweden. Other countries recognise a formal union of same sex partners, which is the equivalent of marriage, giving the same rights to same sex couples as heterosexual married couples have with regard to tax, pensions and inheritance. These are called civil partnerships in the UK and elsewhere. In other countries there is no legal recognition of same sex partnerships or relationships and these may be socially disapproved of or even illegal.

Trends in marriage and divorce

Marriage trends

A significant development has been a fall in the number of **marriages**. For example, in the UK the number of first marriages in a year (that is, between people getting married for the first time) fell by 50 per cent between 1970 and 2000. Over the same period the number of second and subsequent marriages rose but overall the total number of marriages fell considerably.

These figures on the decline of marriage reflect several trends. Compared with the period before 1975 more people have been getting married later in life, never marrying at all or ending a marriage by divorcing and not remarrying. Feminists might argue that this shows that women are realising the disadvantages of marriage but against this is the fact that most people do marry and many remarry after their first marriage ends.

KEY TERM

Marriage: the formal joining of a man and a woman in a relationship with rights and responsibilities; some countries now allow same sex marriage, that is, of two men or two women.

ACTIVITY: *data interpretation*

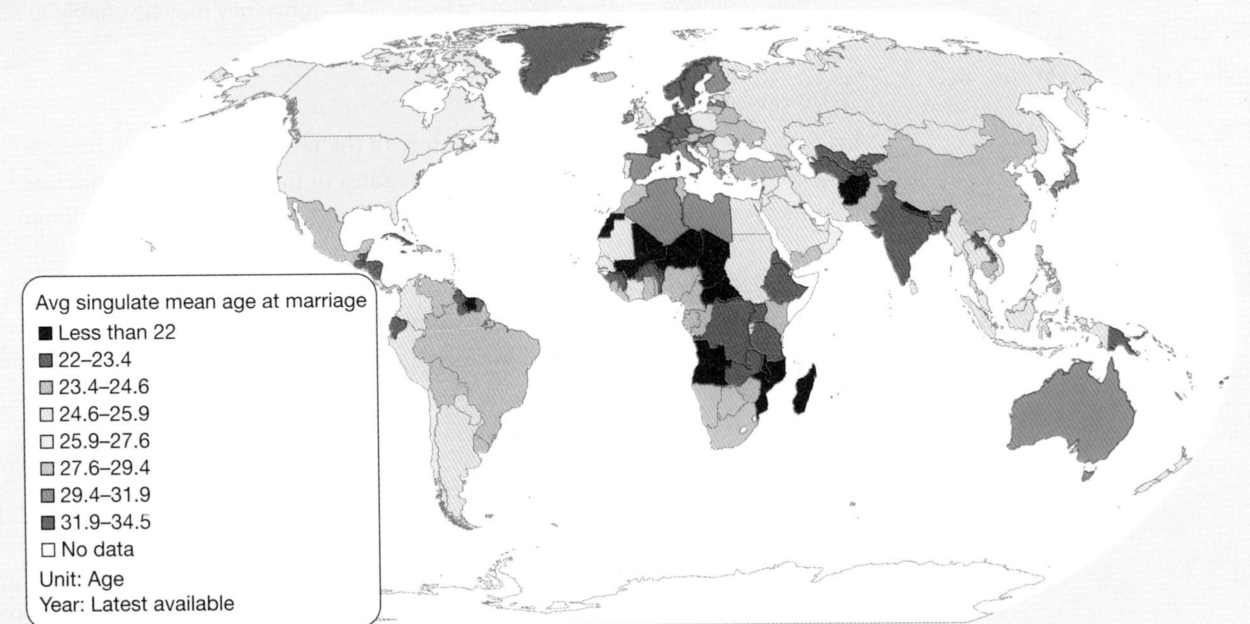

1. In which countries or parts of the world do people tend to marry at the age of 25 or below?
2. In which countries or parts of the world do people tend marry at the age of over 30?
3. Choose one developed society and one developing society and study the following date: (a) currently married (b) ever married (c) marriage rate. In groups offer a hypothesis to explain the correlation, if there is one.

Follow the links from the following web page to find the data: http://chartsbin.com/view/3232

Remarriage

A growing proportion of all marriages in modern industrial societies are now remarriages; that is, one or both partners have already been married at least once. Because of the death of a spouse this has always happened to some extent but many people now remarry after a previous divorce. Remarriages create new reconstituted families, also called stepfamilies, with individuals acquiring new relatives and new roles and relationships.

Marital breakdown

There has been a big increase in the divorce rate in many modern industrial countries. The main reason for this is often that the law has been changed so that divorce becomes easier and more affordable. This suggests that until the law changes there will be many couples who would divorce if the law of their country allowed them to or made it easier. Because divorce involves a formal ending of the marriage, usually by a judge, the number of divorces can be accurately recorded. Does the rise in divorce rates mean that there are more **breakdowns** of marriages? There are alternatives to divorce that make it difficult to know how many marriages break down:

> **KEY TERMS**
>
> **Marital breakdown:** when a marriage has broken down so that the couple are no longer living as husband and wife; some breakdowns lead to divorce.
>
> **Empty shell marriage:** a married couple continue to live together but without love or affection.

- Separation: the partners stop living together. This can often lead to divorce but it does not have to. Because separations are not recorded it is difficult to know how many couples separate.
- Desertion: a type of separation in which one partner leaves the family. Again, there are no reliable figures for desertions.
- **Empty shell marriage**: the couple continue to live together and continue to appear to the outside world to be a married couple, even though there is now no substance to their relationship. This may be for financial reasons; they may be unable to afford to live apart.

Divorce trends

There are now three times as many divorces in the UK each year as there were in 1969. The UK has one of the highest divorce rates in Europe but it also has one of the highest marriage rates. In 2010 there were about 120,000 divorces although this figure has fallen in recent years.

In the UK today it is usually women who decide to divorce their husbands rather than the other way around. About two and a half times as many divorces are granted to women as to men. Women are also less likely to get remarried after divorce than men.

Other features of divorce today are:

- those who marry young are more likely to divorce
- middle-class people are less likely to divorce than working-class people (this is a reversal of the situation in the past when only the well-off could afford divorce)
- those with strong religious beliefs are less likely to divorce; Catholicism still forbids divorce and a divorced person cannot remarry in a Catholic church.

Reasons for the rise in divorce rates

Changes in the law have made divorce possible, or easier, in many countries. In the UK the biggest change in the law was the 1971 Divorce Reform Act. Until then, in order to get divorced, the partner initiating the divorce had to prove matrimonial offence as the grounds for divorce. These included desertion, adultery (by a woman, not a man), cruelty and sodomy. After this Act couples only had to prove that there had been an irretrievable breakdown of their marriage. We still need to know why so many people are willing to take advantage of the Divorce Reform Act. Some of the factors that have been suggested that lead more people to divorce each other are:

- Changes in moral attitudes. Some people see the rise in divorce as part of a more general decline in moral standards, with individuals putting themselves first and no longer feeling tied by the marriage vows.
- The decline of religion, referred to as **secularisation**. The religious vows in marriage are no longer taken as seriously, at least by some, and more weddings are now civil, not religious, ceremonies.
- The decline of communities. In the past, when there was less geographical mobility, communities had informal controls to prevent people breaking social rules and conventions. Divorce no longer brings a couple shame and disapproval.

KEY TERM

Secularisation: the process by which religion has become less important in the daily lives of many people in modern industrial societies.

The points above all come from the New Right view of the family. Two other kinds of explanations see divorce positively as a method of giving people greater freedom:

- Feminists would say that women are now less willing to stay in a marriage that does not meet their hopes and expectations. Women no longer have to accept the expressive role or the housework and chores that are part of the traditional role of women. Women are more likely to be able to support themselves after divorce than used to be the case.
- Changes to the law on divorce have made it possible for working-class people to divorce. Previously only wealthy people could afford to divorce.
- Because people live longer they are married for longer and also for longer periods after their children have left home. Some couples may divorce after many years of marriage.

Lone-parent families

Divorce and separation have led to an increase in the number of lone-parent families. Some children have two living parents and may have regular contact with the parent they do not live with and some can be said to have two homes. The amount of contact children have with a parent they do not live with can vary enormously, from every day to never. The amount of support, financial or otherwise, that an absent parent gives can also vary enormously. This makes it difficult to generalise about lone-parent families. In the UK today, a large minority of lone parents, about 40 per cent, have never been married.

Most lone parents are women. High proportions of lone parents marry or remarry and form two-parent families. Being a lone parent is therefore often a temporary, if common, stage in life.

Because, for functionalists, a family needs two adults, one taking the breadwinner role and the other the caring and nurturing role, they saw the lone-parent family as a broken family, damaged by the absence of one parent and therefore dysfunctional, sure to create problems for both the children and society.

Among the problems that have been alleged to be associated with lone parents are underachievement at school by children from such families and a higher than average risk of problems later in life, such as criminal behaviour and the inability to sustain a relationship. The views of the New Right sociologist Charles Murray on lone parents are part of a wider account of the development of an underclass, a group at the very bottom of the social scale, which Murray characterises by crime, unemployment and antisocial behaviour.

One important aspect of the underclass, according to Murray, is the large number of single mothers, especially teenage girls. These girls, he says, do not see pregnancy and raising a child as problems; they know that they will get welfare benefits from the government to support them. For Murray it is a greater problem if a boy, rather than a girl, is being brought up by a lone mother. Society needs men who will be breadwinners, able to support a family and show loyalty and commitment to their wife and children. Boys who do not grow up seeing men behave as they should will be unable to be good husbands and fathers themselves. Like their fathers, they will get a girl pregnant and then abandon her, frightened of the commitment and unable, because they are unemployed and even unemployable, to contribute financially to raising their child. This damaging pattern of behaviour is passed on from one generation to the next, creating a cycle that is difficult to break. Murray sees this underclass of antisocial young men as a serious threat to social stability.

Both functionalist and right-wing theorists argue that lone-parent families have negative effects on both the children and on society in general. Other writers challenge these views:

- Is it essential to have two parents? A lone parent may be supported by family members, neighbours and friends, and be able both to support the children economically and to provide a loving, nurturing family environment. This may even be better for the children than remaining with two parents in an empty shell marriage characterised by arguments and bad feelings.
- Many children of lone parents experience no problems, while some children raised by two parents do experience them. The main factor involved is not the type of family but poverty. A whole range of social problems is associated with poverty and lone parents in the UK are more likely to be in poverty than two-parent families.

Feminists therefore reject the idea that a lone-parent family must be dysfunctional by its nature. They see the rise in the number of lone-parent families as being partly a result of more women recognising the oppressive nature of patriarchal families and deciding to raise children without a man.

TEST YOURSELF

1. Show the different types of family and marriage arrangements in a visual or diagrammatic form. Include for each type a definition or explanation and examples.
2. Give three reasons why more people now live alone than used to be the case.
3. 'There is more family diversity than in the past'. What does this mean? Use examples in your answer.

ACTIVITY: *evaluation*

Make a table showing the theories of the family. For each one, list their strengths and limitations. The limitations can include criticisms that would be made of them by the other theories.

ACTIVITY: *discussion*

Is it important for children to be brought up by two parents, one of each sex?

ACTIVITY: *discussion*

Is the nuclear family dying out?

How are family roles changing?

Roles in the family

This section considers **family roles**. They include **conjugal roles**, maternal and paternal roles and the roles of children and members of the extended family, including grandparents.

KEY TERMS

Family roles: the parts played by different members of the family.

Conjugal roles: the roles taken by the husband and wife within the family resulting from the domestic division of labour.

Joint conjugal roles: the husband and wife carry out many tasks and activities together, so that there is no clear separation of roles; the opposite of segregated roles.

Traditional conjugal roles: the segregated roles assumed to be normal in the traditional nuclear family.

Symmetrical family: a family in which the conjugal roles have become more equal.

Dual worker families: families in which both the man and woman do paid work.

Conjugal roles

The functionalist view of gender roles within the family is that the arrangement that works best is to have two clearly separate roles. The natural role of the man is said to be instrumental and the natural role of the woman is expressive. This division of labour is seen as natural. It follows that it is the man coming home from work who is most in need of comfort and security. His wife's role is to provide a warm, loving environment where he can relax and forget the cares of the world outside. This has been called the warm bath theory. Feminists argue that this situation benefits men and shows that the family is patriarchal.

Roles in a marriage can be classified as either segregated or **joint conjugal roles**. The segregated or separated roles are those associated with the **traditional** nuclear family, with clearly different roles for the man and woman. Joint or integrated conjugal roles mean that the man and woman share instrumental and expressive roles, so their roles are not separate. A family in which the roles have become more equal in this way is called a **symmetrical family**. Many families today are **dual worker families**, in which both the man and the woman have paid work.

The female role limits what women can achieve at work. Their responsibility for children means that women need to limit the amount of paid work they do so, for example, they work part time so they can collect their children from school. By taking time out of paid work to have children women can miss out on opportunities for training and promotion. The perceived greater importance of the male role means that a family is more likely to move to a different town or even country for the man's work, such as a promotion, than for a woman's promotion.

These features of the female domestic rolc make it different from paid work:

- It is unpaid.
- There are no starting and finishing times.
- There are no benefits such as a contract, holidays and pensions.
- It is not seen as real work so it has low status.
- It is solitary and gives little sense of achievement because there is always more to do.

Maternal roles

In many modern industrial societies there are clear expectations of what mothers' roles should be like. Mothers are expected to devote themselves to their children (while also taking care of their child's father). It is assumed that women have a mothering instinct so that they will always want and be able to raise their children. In fact, the role of mothers varies between cultures. In some societies it is not always taken for granted that the biological mother will raise the children. For example, grandparents or other close kin may adopt the children of a young, unmarried mother. In modern industrial societies many children from a few months old spend some of their time at a nursery or similar institution while the mother works.

There are three variations from the stereotypical mother in the traditional nuclear family:

- Working mothers. Many mothers in modern industrial societies do paid work even before their children are old enough to start school. Children whose mothers work may be cared for by a relative such as a grandparent, a childminder or nanny or they may go to a nursery. The UK has less childcare provision than most other European countries. For example, very few companies and organisations have workplace nurseries in the UK. Some studies have found evidence that children whose mothers work full time may not do as well at school as those with mothers who do not, but other scholars have found no evidence of this. Moreover, being with a group of children at a nursery or similar institution helps children learn to get on with others and is a good preparation for school.
- Teenage mothers. In the UK and some other countries there is concern about the number of unmarried teenage girls who become mothers. In traditional societies girls would often marry and become mothers as teenagers, but in modern industrial societies this is seen as a problem. It is thought that the teenage mothers are too young to cope with raising children, that they will not be able to continue their education and that they are less likely to provide stable family lives for their children.
- Lone mothers: this is discussed in the section on page 137.

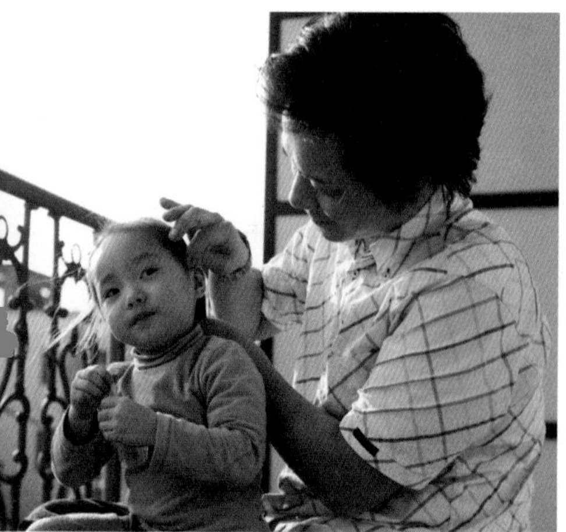
Fathers are now expected to be more involved in bringing up their children

KEY TERM

Gender equality: when men and women have equal roles, status and rights.

Paternal roles

The instrumental role of the man as head of the family and as breadwinner meant that as a father he was often away from the home and did not spend much time with his children. Tasks such as feeding a baby or pushing a pram were not seen as appropriate for men in the past and fathers were also expected to impose discipline on the children. This made it difficult to achieve a close emotional relationship between fathers and their children.

Fathers are now expected to be involved with children more often and in more ways than before. At the same time they are still expected to be the main provider, so some men, like women, have a dual role. Ideas about **gender equality** have become more widespread and more fathers are playing an active part in the emotional (expressive) side of child-rearing and spending more time with their children, though often this is when the mother is present as well. On the other hand, the need to earn money to support the family often leads to men working long hours and this limits the time that can be spent with children.

Roles of children

To understand the roles of children today we need to compare different societies today and in the past and to appreciate that the terms children and childhood mean different things at different times.

What is meant by childhood?

In the UK today children are defined as people under the age of 16. Their lives are regulated by laws that organise their lives in ways that are very different from adult lives. For example, they must go to school from the ages of 5 to 16 and they cannot work until they are 13 (and then they may work only for limited periods and only at certain times). Adult rights and responsibilities are gradually acquired throughout childhood. Some rights are not given until after childhood (driving at 17, voting at 18, serving on a jury at 21). Ages at which rights and responsibilities are gained vary between societies.

Traditional societies mark the change from childhood to adulthood by a ceremony, a rite of passage. Adolescent boys were removed from their family homes for a period during which they underwent a series of rites; a ritual of initiation into adult life. Before the ceremony, the individual is a child, after it he is a man, a full adult member of the community regardless of his age. For girls, the first menstruation is often taken as the sign of achieving womanhood. Among the Yanomami people of the Amazon rain forest, girls are treated as adult women and marry at their first menstruation. In Shona society in central southern Africa women are traditionally not treated as adults until they have a child: if they die before they have a child they are given the ceremony appropriate to the burial of a child.

Childhood was also very different in the past. According to the historian Philippe Ariès, in the European Middle Ages children worked alongside adults, dressed like adults, took part in the same games and festivals as adults and were even punished for crimes in the same way as adults. There was no idea that they should be protected from the facts of death and sex. Many people did not know their exact ages and so status did not depend on age. The small size of children was seen as making them suited for particular types of work rather than making them fundamentally different from adults. Because what is meant by childhood varies between cultures it is not just a matter of biological immaturity and we can say that childhood is socially constructed.

Children's rights and responsibilities

Children are subject to the authority of adults such as parents and teachers and are expected to be respectful and obedient. They are expected to accept that adults have greater knowledge and that this will be used to their benefit. In modern industrial societies children's time is closely controlled by their parents (for example, the time they spend on activities such as schoolwork, watching television and times for bed and meals) and there are places where they can and cannot go.

This amounts to a high degree of control over children, reinforcing the extent to which childhood is different from adulthood. This difference is social, not natural. Much of this control is of recent origin and is a response to the increased dangers to children that parents and other adults perceive. For example, the freedom children have to move around their home area in cities has been restricted because of fears about traffic and stranger danger. Whether the control is for the child's protection or not, the outcome is the shaping by society of a particular form of childhood.

On the other hand, new laws and regulations give some power to children and children are able to find ways to win greater freedom – to get their own way. Corporal punishment is no longer allowed in schools in most countries, and even physical reprimands by parents – 'smacking' – are often no longer acceptable and may be seen by the authorities as abuse. Most countries have signed the United Nations Convention on the Rights of the Child, which says that children must have

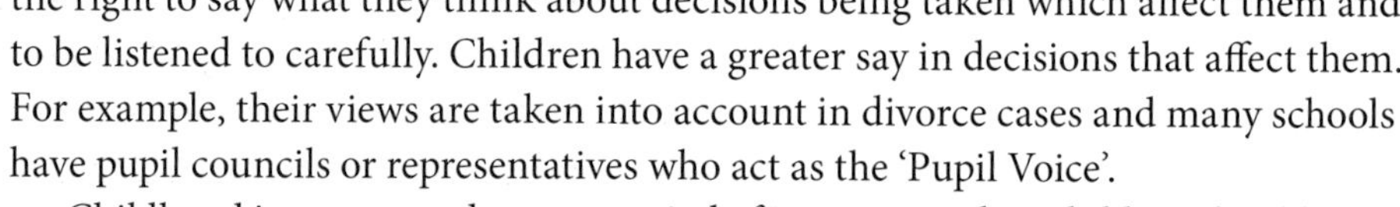

the right to say what they think about decisions being taken which affect them and to be listened to carefully. Children have a greater say in decisions that affect them. For example, their views are taken into account in divorce cases and many schools have pupil councils or representatives who act as the 'Pupil Voice'.

Childhood is seen nowadays as a period of innocence when children should not have to work or experience other aspects of the adult world. There are new industries that reinforce children's special status by producing specialised goods for them such as clothes, toys and games, television programmes and later, whole channels aimed at children and even snack foods. Far from being producers as they were in the medieval period, children have become important consumers. Modern industrial societies are now **child-centred** societies where children have a much more central place in society and in the lives of many adults than they did in the past and in traditional societies.

> **KEY TERM**
>
> **Child-centredness:** when the child's needs and wishes are the most important considerations.

Adult children

Parent–child relationships continue after the child is 18. In modern industrial societies adult children usually leave the family home, living independently and eventually marrying and starting a new home. This led to what has been called **empty-nest families**; that is, the parents living at home together after their adult children have moved out.

Recently, it has become more common for adult children to remain with their parents. Those who do leave home, for example to go to university, but who then return are sometimes described as boomerang kids, and the family as a **boomerang family**. In Italy well over half the 18 to 34-year olds live with their parents. Families in this situation have a 'full-nest syndrome' rather than 'empty-nest syndrome'. This is sometimes because the young people cannot find employment and cannot afford to move out or to marry. One result of this is that parents may continue to be financially responsible for their children for more years than used to be the case. In some societies this practice is disapproved of. In China graduate children are expected to make a substantial contribution to their parents' living expenses: it is thought to be a disgrace if when you are an adult and your parents are retired you are still being financed by them.

> **KEY TERMS**
>
> **Empty-nest families:** parents living at home together after their adult children have moved out.
>
> **Boomerang family:** a family in which the adult children have left home but then return.

Roles of grandparents and extended family members

The role of the grandparents

The survival of more people into old age means that more people today know their grandparents than was the case in the recent past. Grandparents used to be a rarity because fewer people lived long enough to become grandparents. Today, though, in modern industrial societies most children know their grandparents and grandparents often live long enough to see their grandchildren become adults. It is no longer very unusual to have four generations of the same family alive at the same time.

There is a very wide variation in the ages at which people become grandparents, from the late thirties to advanced old age. The role of the grandparent – especially the active, healthy grandparent – is a new and newly important one. The full range of developments in families that we have studied earlier have affected the role of grandparents:

- Many grandparents have children who divorce, become lone parents or remarry.
- Divorce and separation also affect the relationship between children and their grandparents; grandparents can 'lose' their grandchildren. Family feuds can also separate grandparents from their grandchildren.

- There are now many step-grandparents – that is, parents of those who have married someone who has dependent children.
- There are grandparents of the children in lesbian and gay families, of children who have been adopted or are in care, or who have been neglected and abused.
- Many children have grandparents from more than one ethnic group.
- Grandparents are themselves more likely to be divorced and remarried. They may start new families and new chapters in their lives at an age when in the past they would have been considered too old to do so.

While some grandparents live close to their children and their families and help out on a daily basis (for example, taking the role of an unpaid childminder while the mother works) many live too far from their children for this. Both parents and children tend to lead full lives and time with grandchildren may have to be planned and may involve specific activities.

Different generations within families support each other in many ways. The direction of support is not always from older to younger. As grandparents age they receive more help from their grown-up children but they often continue to give support as well. These are some of the main forms of support between grandparents and their children:

- economic – including giving and lending money and gifts
- accommodation – grandparents may live with their children and grandchildren
- personal care – this form of support is most likely to involve grandparents as receivers of support; children, especially daughters, are a major support for their elderly parents
- practical support – for example, grandparents may look after their grandchildren with working parents
- emotional and moral support – listening, talking and giving advice; in particular, many mothers rely on their own mothers for advice about childcare.

For some of these forms of support, it is more likely to be the grandmother giving the support than the grandfather. Because less research has been done on this topic, far less is known about the role of grandfathers. It is also probably the case in most societies that the mother's parents (maternal grandparents) play a bigger role than the father's parents (paternal grandparents).

Some parents experience a period in their lives when they are giving considerable support both to their own parents and to their own children. They are known as the pivot generation.

TEST YOURSELF

1 What kinds of evidence are there for the claim that childhood is socially constructed?

2 What roles can grandparents play in families?

Changes in family relationships and conjugal roles

This section examines the changes in family relationships, including the symmetrical family debate and issues relating to gender equality within the family.

Changing conjugal roles and the symmetrical family debate

According to the functionalist view, there should be a clear separation of gender roles. The man should go out to work and be the breadwinner; the woman should look after the home and the children. It is assumed that the growing employment of women over the 20th century has had negative consequences. For functionalists, a gendered division of labour is natural and desirable.

Some household tasks are carried out by other family members; for example, children may be given specific jobs to carry out around the home. Some families also employ others to carry out some domestic tasks; they may employ a cleaner, for example.

Men have always done some household work and tasks such as heavy gardening work, house repairs and car maintenance are clearly seen as men's work today. We do not usually count these as housework in the way we do chores such as cleaning and cooking, which have traditionally been seen as women's work. The wide range of tasks that can be carried out at home needs to be considered when we talk about work in the home. Women do paid work more than in the past, but many women have always worked. Women's paid work was, however, seen as less important than their domestic duties.

In some societies it is common for families who can afford it to employ nannies or other staff to help with childcare and housework. The division of tasks by gender can be seen here too; looking after children is seen as women's work.

The British sociologists Willmott and Young found evidence of a new and more equal division of domestic labour based on joint rather than **segregated conjugal roles**. While there was still to some extent a clear division of labour by gender, both husband and wife were contributing equally to the family – hence the term symmetrical.

KEY TERM

Segregated conjugal roles: the husband and wife have clearly different roles within the family and different interests and activities; the opposite of joint roles.

Reasons for more symmetrical families

- Nuclear families became privatised, which means that the couple organises their lives around the family home rather than work and community. This encouraged a more equal partnership.
- The decline of the extended family meant that there was less pressure from other family members to conform to their norms.
- Women have a higher status in society, so men are more likely to treat them as equals and women to insist that they do so.
- Women have greater independence arising from paid work, which leads to more equality, such as joint decision-making, within the family. Women became more able to have paid work as the number of children they had on average fell.
- It has become easier for both men and women to choose their roles and to negotiate them with each other.
- Labour-saving devices in the home have reduced the time and effort involved in some housework and made the home a more attractive place to be.

KEY TERM

Domestic division of labour: the way in which tasks in the home (such as cooking, cleaning, childcare and repairs) are divided between the man and woman.

Has the change to symmetrical families been exaggerated?

Research suggests that there has been some change towards more equal families but this has been quite slow and has not gone as far as some writers suggest. Feminists argue that as long as society remains patriarchal the **domestic division of labour** will be unequal. Some men will agree to help their wives more with housework and childcare but the main responsibility will stay with the woman.

TOP TIP

Domestic work can be done by the children and some families also employ people to do some domestic work, such as cleaning. If a middle-class woman employs a working-class woman to do some domestic work for her, then the middle-class woman will not be doing as much domestic work but it will still be done by a woman.

KEY TERM

Dual burden: women who do paid work as well as look after the home and family are said to have a dual burden – the term 'triple burden' or 'triple shift' is also sometimes used, adding to work and the home the expressive role of looking after the emotional needs of family members.

This view is supported by research showing that even when men and women work for the same number of hours, the woman still does considerably more housework.

Other writers on domestic labour have noted other ways in which Willmott and Young seem to be too optimistic about equal gender roles. Men tend to take on tasks they have selected and choose those that are less dull and repetitive, such as preparing a special meal for guests, perhaps, rather than the day-to-day necessity of getting children fed. Men still take most of the important decisions in the family, such as moving house or substantial spending; women take less important decisions such as home decoration.

Although the domestic division of labour is still unequal, both men and women are now usually expected to do paid and domestic work. For women, this can mean a **dual burden** or even a triple burden – paid work, domestic work and emotional work.

Women who are successful in their careers and manage to raise children as well are sometimes called supermums in the media. An example is Nicola Horlick, who had a high-flying career in finance, responsible for investing huge amounts of money, while raising six children. Men with successful careers who also find time to be fully involved in their family life can be superdads.

Research on the domestic division of labour has several problems. Researchers have to decide what tasks should be covered and how they should be measured. It is also important who is asked about housework; a husband and wife may give completely different accounts of who usually does what. These problems mean that different research findings can sometimes seem to contradict each other.

ACTIVITY: *research*

Who is responsible for domestic work in your family? Draw up a list of tasks, including those that are needed only occasionally rather than regularly. By observation or asking, find out who carries out these tasks.

ACTIVITY: *data interpretation*

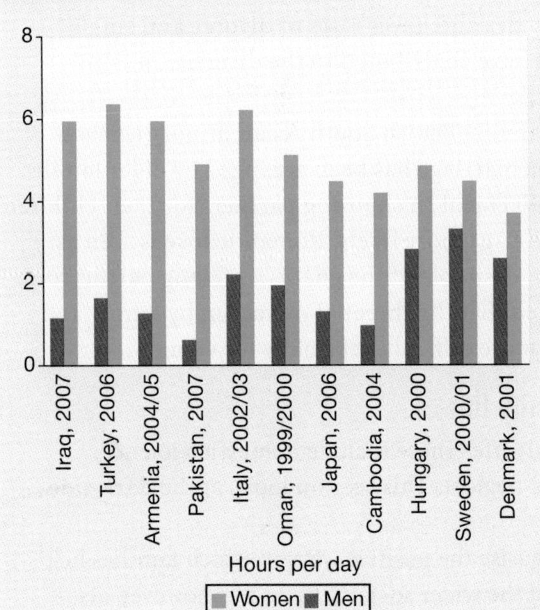

Average time used for housework, caring for family members and community/volunteer work, by sex, selected countries

In all countries women spend more time on these activities than men.

1 In which countries do men spend about or less than one hour a day on these activities?

2 In which two countries do women spend more than six hours a day on these activities?

3 In which two countries is there least difference between men and women?

TEST YOURSELF

1. Make a list of those household tasks traditionally done by women and girls, and those traditionally done by men and boys in your society. Is this situation changing?
2. Give three reasons why families are becoming more symmetrical.

Variations in family relationships

This section looks at the influence of social stratification and ethnicity on variations in family relationships.

Social stratification and family relationships

Willmott and Young found the symmetrical family was more common among working-class families than middle-class families. They suggested that this was because working-class men had less rewarding jobs so were more willing to become involved in home life. On the other hand, they found that business men such as managing directors were more work-centred than home-centred; they found their work satisfying and spent long hours on their work, earning money to support their families but being less involved with them in other ways. Willmott and Young suggested that changes in family life started among the high-status classes and then worked their way down to the working class. They called this stratified diffusion.

Willmott and Young thought that the work-centred, asymmetrical middle-class family would spread to the rest of society as more people's work became interesting and rewarding because of new technology. This does not seem to have happened. However, there is one major difference between the classes; middle-class families are able to pay for more of the housework to be done by others, employing cleaners or childminders, for example.

Ethnicity and family relationships

Ethnic minorities in the UK have adapted their family lives to British circumstances but they are still influenced by the family patterns of their countries of origin. The UK's African-Caribbean minority has high rates of single parenthood and matrifocal families. The South Asian minorities often have strong extended family ties and lower rates of divorce and single parenthood. The minority groups have contributed to the diversity of family types and relationships.

Divorce rates are much lower among British South Asian minorities than in the majority culture. Where the marriage has been arranged by older family members, their experience and judgement in choosing partners for their children is seen as making a successful marriage more likely. Romantic love is seen as unnecessary and perhaps not even desirable, if the goal is a lifelong partnership. On the other hand, it can be argued that the threat of ostracism by family and community makes divorce much more difficult, especially for women.

The negative aspects of family life

KEY TERM

Dark side of family: the negative aspects of family life such as arguments, abuse, neglect and violence.

There are negative aspects to family life. These include domestic violence, gender inequality, child abuse and neglect. This section looks at the **dark side of family** life.

Functionalist sociologists emphasise the positive ways in which families help both their individual members and the wider society. There are, however, also negative aspects to family life. The failure to fulfil their functions may be because of conflict, bad behaviour, neglect or abuse or for other reasons. Alcoholism, drug abuse and mental health problems are often involved. In the functionalist approach, **dysfunctional families** are seen as exceptions; most families function as they should but something has gone wrong to make the family dysfunctional. An alternative view is that the dysfunctional aspects of families – and specifically of the traditional nuclear family – are part of the nature of the family. For example, radical feminists see the nuclear family as patriarchal, and therefore that controlling and coercive behaviour by men is to be expected.

KEY TERMS

Dysfunctional family: a family that fails to carry out the functions expected of it; for example, where the children are neglected.

Domestic violence: violence within the family, usually but not always by males against females; refers not only to physical violence but also to patterns of controlling behaviour that may include emotional manipulation.

Domestic violence

In modern industrial societies, **domestic violence** was for a long time a subject that was not often talked about or dealt with effectively by the authorities. There was a widespread belief that what happened in the family home was private; a matter for the family and not for, for example, the police and social workers to become involved in. It was also sometimes believed that men had a right to use physical force against their wives if there was some justification. In the 1970s two sociologists, Russell and Rebecca Dobash, researched domestic violence in Scotland and showed that it was widespread, so that it could not be explained as just the behaviour of a few disturbed individuals. They found examples of women being pushed, slapped, beaten, raped and even killed by their husbands. These were often the result of what the man saw as a challenge to his authority, for example being asked by his wife why he was home late. Feminists argue that within marriage the man has power and authority and that this can make violence against wives seem acceptable. Although many men condemn violence against women, some feminists argue that all men benefit from it because it reinforces the patriarchal nature of the family and of society.

Men are offenders in most domestic violence, and the victims are usually women and sometimes children. However, men are sometimes the victims. It has been suggested that these cases of domestic violence are the least likely to be reported, because men may not want it known that they are victims and may not seek help.

Domestic violence is now recognised as a crime and the police and courts in most countries have taken a stronger stand against it. It can be difficult for them to act, however, because much domestic violence is not reported. Victims may not have friends or family to discuss the problem with, and may not have the money or independence to be able to leave the relationship.

Reasons why victims of domestic violence may not report it to the police:

- They may feel that the police will be unable or unwilling to do anything.
- They may fear that the violence will become worse.
- They may be afraid of losing contact with their children.
- They may believe that the abuse is normal or that they deserve it.
- They may believe that they will be able to change the abuser's behaviour, or that he is still really a good person.

Most victims are assaulted many times before they report the violence.

Child abuse and neglect

Not all children experience the family as a loving place of safety. For some it is dangerous and exploitative. Modern industrial societies have had an increase in known cases of child abuse and neglect, much of it by parents or step-parents, often but not always by males. Some of these cases have had a lot of news coverage and have become national scandals. It is probably the case, as with domestic abuse, that this increase is largely due to increased reporting; that is, more cases are known about rather than there simply being more cases. There is greater awareness of abuse and parents are more watchful and strive to protect their children from real and imagined dangers.

Child abuse is usually seen as having four possible forms:

- sexual abuse
- physical abuse
- emotional abuse
- neglect.

In addition, many children are in difficult and even dangerous situations, for example living with someone with mental problems or being a carer for an adult or for other children. Many children grow up in poverty and in some countries not all get the chance to go to school. In some civil wars, such as those in Sierra Leone and Uganda, children have been recruited as soldiers. They are often forced to do appalling things, even to their own families, so that they become hardened for fighting. Both boys and girls have been recruited in this way. When the war is over it is very difficult for child soldiers to return to civilian life.

ACTIVITY: *research*

How have people in your family been affected by changing roles and relationships? Interview one or more of your older relatives about changes they have seen. Present your findings to the class.

TEST YOURSELF

1. In what ways do the family structures and relationships of ethnic minority groups in your country differ from those of the majority?
2. Why is it difficult to get accurate information about the dark side of the family?

What are the changes affecting the family?

Industrialisation, urbanisation and family change

Functionalists argue that the modern nuclear family evolved from earlier types of family as society evolved. An extended family suited the needs of pre-industrial, traditional societies while the nuclear family is the most appropriate and beneficial form of family for **modern industrial societies**. The theory that the type of family fits the needs of a society is referred to as the fit thesis; while because of its emphasis on gradual evolutionary change the functionalist account of the history of the family is referred to as the march of progress.

KEY TERM

Modern industrial societies: created by industrialisation; societies that today have industrial economies and high urban populations.

The functionalist sociologist Talcott Parsons offered reasons why the nuclear family can be said to fit modern industrial societies so well. In the past people had to rely on the family to meet many needs, for example to care for them when they were sick or old, to lend or give them money when they had none and to teach them. A large family made it more likely that help would be available. Today these functions have been taken over to a large extent by other institutions. It is no longer necessary to have a type of family that can fulfil these functions. Modern economies also need workers who are willing to move to where the jobs are; nuclear families can move more easily than extended ones (see Table 4.1).

Function	Traditional societies	Modern industrial societies
	Extended families	**Nuclear families**
Care of very young	Parents supported by extended family members	Parents supported by professionals such as nurses and nursery teachers
Care of elderly	Extended family	Pensions, residential care, health and social services
Care of the sick	Extended family	Health services, doctors, nurses, hospitals
Help with work, e.g. on a farm at harvest time	Family and neighbours	No longer usually required
Education	Family, community	Schools and media
Financial support in time of crisis	Extended family	Welfare state, savings, borrowing from banks and other institutions

Table 4.1: Functions of the family

The change from reliance on the extended family to delegating its functions to a range of other institutions is called structural differentiation. According to Parsons the family in modern industrial societies now has just two main functions:

- the primary socialisation of children
- the stabilisation of adult personalities; the family provides comfort and security to its members in a world of impersonal, bureaucratic institutions.

KEY TERMS

Industrialisation: the process in history in which societies changed from being mainly rural and based on agriculture to being urban and with more people working in industries.

Urbanisation: the growth of cities, so that a higher proportion of the population live in cities.

At the same time as **industrialisation** took place, so did **urbanisation**. This means that a growing proportion of the population lived in cities, with cities growing rapidly in size and extent. For example, in the UK, in 1800 four-fifths of the population lived in small villages but by 1830 half the population lived in towns. Farming became more difficult and manufacturing and trade became more important, so that people moved from villages to the new cities to earn a living. Urbanisation and industrialisation brought huge changes to the way people lived – including their family life.

The historian Peter Laslett found that in the UK the average size of households did not change very much until the period of industrialisation. Laslett worked out what family structures were like over the period 1564 to 1821, using evidence such as parish registers of births, marriages and death and census data. He found that the average size of households had changed little and extended families were not common. People married late and started a family late, waiting until they had the means to set up house together. High mortality rates and low life expectancy meant that three-generation households were unlikely. Moreover, the English inheritance system of primogeniture (in which the eldest son inherits property and title) did not encourage siblings to stay together in horizontally extended families as probably happened in countries where inheritance was shared. There were some important differences between these and modern families, however. The households of the nobility were larger than those of poorer people because they contained servants and many people did live in large households. People probably also lived closer to more of their kin than is common today, with brothers and sisters and their families living close by.

When considering Laslett's findings we need to bear in mind the limitations of his evidence. The official records do not always tell us how many people are living in one household at the same time. Some records have not survived; others that have may not be accurate or complete. Where households were small we do not know how much they depended day to day on kin outside the household. Laslett's work is also about only England. In other countries where there were different rules about inheritance, such as elsewhere in Europe, the situation may have been different.

With industrialisation came urbanisation, which led to a much greater proportion of the population moving to newly developing cities to work in factories. Perhaps the availability of people – younger sons who would not inherit – to move to where the work was helped the UK to industrialise. In this case, the existence of nuclear families before industrialisation may have encouraged industrialisation rather than being a result of it.

According to the evolutionary view, extended families would have begun to disappear at the time of industrialisation. In fact, Anderson, studying the 1851 census for the industrial town of Preston, found that extended families actually became more common than they had been before, at least in towns and cities. Laslett found that about 10 per cent of households contained kin other than the nuclear family (co-residence) while Anderson found 23 per cent of families were co-residing. Extended family relationships would have been useful to people newly arriving in the city. They might provide someone to stay with until they found their feet, help in finding a job and help in sickness or poverty that the rural community they had left could provide but the more impersonal city could not. Extended families have played this kind of role in contemporary immigrant communities.

Anderson was not claiming that the extended family was widespread; only that in this particular situation this form of family suited the circumstances. Anderson's approach suggests a need to be alert to what may be local circumstances. There need not be any single overall national trend at a point in time. It does seem, though, that there was far more continuity between historical periods than the functionalists suggested. Nuclear families have always been common and extended families less common (at least in England) and extended families were at least as useful in the new cities as in the countryside.

The sociologists Willmott and Young found that a hundred years later in the mid-1950s there were still strong extended families in working-class areas of London. There were strong relationships, particularly between mothers and their married daughters, who would live on the same street or very close by. This was possible because the men in these families worked in the same place, such as the docks. But then these old working-class areas were redeveloped and the families moved out to suburbs. The extended family bonds weakened. Women had less contact with their mothers because they lived further away and it was harder to keep in close contact than when they had lived nearby. The strong working-class communities were fragmented. On the new housing estates there were fewer places to meet and fewer chances to socialise; further weakening extended family ties. The nuclear family became the main form of family. Without the community and extended family ties, these became privatised nuclear families. The husband–wife bond became the main bond, replacing the mother–daughter one and the nuclear family had less interaction with neighbours, community and wider kin.

The changes are sketched in Table 4.2 on page 151.

Dates	Main family type	Evidence and research methods	Writers
Before the Industrial Revolution (c. 1750)	Small households – mainly nuclear families	Parish records	Laslett
1850	Extended families in cities	Census	Anderson
1950	Extended families still found in working class areas in cities but beginning to decline as these areas were redeveloped and people moved to new housing estates	Sociological surveys and interviews	Young and Willmott
1970	Privatised nuclear families	Sociological surveys and interviews	Young and Willmott

Table 4.2: Changes over time in family structure

1

Name of the Institution Buckingham Palace

NAMES of each Person who abode therein on the Night of Sunday, June 6th.	Age of Males.	Age of Females.	OCCUPATION, if any.	Where Born: Whether Born in same County.	Where Born: Whether Born in Scotland, Ireland, or Foreign Parts.
The Queen		20	✓	Y	
H.R.H. Prince Albert	20		✓	~~N~~	F
The Princess Royal		6 months	✓	Y	
Earl of Aboyne	45		Lord in Waiting	N	
George Thos Keppel	40		Groom in Waiting	Y	
Edward Praetorius	30		Secretary to H.R.H. Prince Albert		F
Thomas Batchelor	55		Page of the Backstairs	N	
Augustus Fredk Gerding	40		Page of the Backstairs		F
William Peel	30		Page of the Presence	N	
George Wakeley	50		Queen's Messenger	N	
Thomas Hill	40		Queen's Messenger	N	
Isaac Cart	30		Valet		F
Andrew Dehler	30		Valet to H.R.H. Prince Albert		F
Thomas Cooper	25		Valet	N	
Charles Woolger	30		Valet	N	
James Woods	30		Valet	N	
Joseph Martin	35		Cabinet Maker	N	
Charles Benda	20		Jaeger to H.R.H. Prince Albert		F

Census form for the British royal family, 1841

ACTIVITY: *evaluation*

What does studying industrialisation, urbanisation and family change tell us about the difficulties of research on the history of the family? Are there any potential problems about the historical data that are used?

TEST YOURSELF

1. In what ways were extended families suited to life in pre-modern societies, according to Talcott Parsons?
2. How can we explain why extended families became more common during industrialisation and then less common again?
3. What changes are occurring to family structures and relationships in the country you live in?

KEY TERMS

Demographic trends: patterns in the changes of demographic measures such as the birth rate and death rate.

Birth rate: the number of live births per 1,000 people in the population in one year.

Fertility rate: the number of live births per 1,000 women of child-bearing age in the population.

Demographic trends

The family is affected by **demographic trends**. Here we discuss family size and birth rates, mortality rates and life expectancy.

Family size and birth rates

Historians have argued that in the past children were seen as an economic benefit to the family. From an early age they contributed to the work the family did and would look after their parents in sickness and old age. There was then only a short period – up until the age of 6 or 7 – when parents had to support children; thereafter children were expected to work. This argument has also been applied to less developed countries today.

In modern industrial societies the **birth rate** has fallen dramatically and, with mothers having fewer children (that is, a falling **fertility rate**), so has family size. Here are some reasons for this:

- Children have become an economic cost rather than a benefit. It is very expensive to raise children. They can no longer do paid work and instead depend on their parents over a long period of education.
- Fewer children die, so that parents can have fewer children and be fairly sure they will survive.
- It is no longer essential to have children to look after you when you are old; pensions and investments mean that older people can support themselves and health and social services can provide care.
- Contraception techniques are widely available, especially the contraceptive pill for women, which has allowed them to control the number of children they had. Contraception was also more widely used because of secularisation so that the advice from religions not to use contraception has had less effect.
- Having a smaller family makes it easier to move geographically, for example for a new job opportunity.
- The greater opportunities for women in paid work are restricted if they have many children.

Having a smaller number of children in a family means that children have fewer siblings, if any, and then for the next generation there are few, if any,

KEY TERM

Beanpole family: a family with only one child or very few children; combined with rising life expectancy this leads to family trees that look very tall and thin with few people in each generation, rather than bushy, with lots of siblings, aunts, uncles and cousins.

aunts and uncles. This new kind of family, with several generations but only a small number in each generation, is called a **beanpole family** and is a new development.

Some married couples choose not to have children. They may adopt a lifestyle focused on success in careers and shared leisure activities that leave little time for children. There may be less pressure than in the past from other family members to have children. Couples who both work and who do not have children are referred to as DINK families – 'double income, no kids'.

Recently the birth rate has gone up, though it is still low by historical standards and there has been talk of a new baby boom. This is thought to be due to the numbers of recently arrived immigrants, mainly from Eastern Europe, who are often young adults and so more likely to have children. There are also women who, having had children and divorced, are having children with a new partner, perhaps when they are close to middle age.

CASE STUDY

DINKs in China

A survey in China's main cities in 2003 found a significant increase in DINK families, with an estimated 10 000 such families in Beijing alone. Only 37 per cent of families in Chinese cities are now nuclear families.

> Childbearing was in ancient China a family's top priority, but now it is regarded as a personal choice by many young couples. Zheng Jian, a 38-year-old businessman, and his wife Xiao Yan, a graphic designer, think their two-person family is one of the happiest in the world. They have been married for more than 10 years and have no children. We always have so many plans to do things together,' Zheng said. 'It seems like we are two kids who like playing together.' They insist: 'We are satisfied with our present lives, so why bother with children?'

(Source: http://english.peopledaily.com.cn/200307/16/eng20030716_120372.shtml)

TASK

1 In what ways does this trend in China suggest that traditional values may be changing?

2 What are some of the likely consequences if more couples decide not to have children?

Births outside marriage

Just as living together was known as living in sin, in the past a social stigma was attached to 'illegitimate' children and their mothers. Social disapproval was so great that in the last century there were cases in which young girls who became pregnant were committed to asylums. In recent years, however, there has been a big increase in the number of children born outside marriage so that they now account for nearly half of all births in the UK. Many babies are born to cohabiting parents who may well marry in the future. This kind of family is arguably not very different from the nuclear family as the only thing that is missing is the legal bond of marriage. This is not, however, the whole story. About four in ten births outside marriage are to parents who do not live together. While this can be partly attributed to relationships breaking down during the pregnancy, it is also the case that more women are deciding to raise children on their own.

KEY TERM

Death rate: the number of deaths per 1000 people in the population in one year; also called the mortality rate.

Mortality rates and life expectancy

As the birth rate has fallen, so has the **death rate**. In particular, the infant mortality rate (deaths of infants less than 1 year old) and the child mortality rate (deaths of children aged 1 to 5) have fallen dramatically over the last century. Some reasons for the fall in the death rate are:

- improved running water, sewage disposal and sanitation
- advances in preventing and treating diseases
- higher living standards, especially better diets
- fewer deaths related to work because of safer, healthier conditions
- better education and health care.

Developing countries tend to have higher death, birth and fertility rates than developed ones. These usually fall during industrialisation. The death rate falls first, so that there is a growth in population, and then the birth rate falls later. High birth rates are due to factors such as mothers' lack of education and access to contraception and high infant and child mortality rates, so that parents cannot be sure their children will survive to adulthood.

The consequences for the family of an ageing population

TOP TIP

Just as childhood is socially constructed, so is age and ageing. These categories are decided by social customs more than biology. In modern industrial societies people are living longer and are healthy for longer, so it is no longer the case that people are thought of as old when they reach the traditional retirement age of 65.

In 1901 under 5 per cent (1.7 million) of the British population were aged 65 and over. By 2010 this was one in six people, about 10 million. Over the last 150 years life expectancy has almost doubled. The UK, like many other modern industrial countries, has an ageing population; that is, the average age is rising and there are more old people as a proportion of the total.

Old age is associated with retirement. In the UK the official age for retirement for many years was 65 for men and 60 for women, but this age has been raised because people are living longer and are healthier for longer. Men and women will retire at the same age in the future. Status depends to a considerable extent on occupation, so retiring brings a loss of status. This affects men more than women, for even women who were working full time before retirement are likely to have had periods in their adult lives when they were not working (for example, when they had young children) and because their status may be less dependent on their occupation.

Despite pensions, many older people rely on their children and, in particular, their daughters. One of the strongest reasons in the past for having children, that there will be someone to care for you in old age, remains important today. Many people – often those who have young children too, in the pivot generation – spend a lot of time and resources caring for ageing parents.

The consequences for families of population ageing are likely to be:

- more older people living alone (single-person households) after the death of the partner
- a greater role for grandparents in supporting their children and grandchildren
- a greater burden for adult children looking after their ageing parents, perhaps even after they have reached retirement age themselves
- greater isolation and loneliness among older people
- a return in some families to the extended family with three generations sharing the household.

Several generations of one family together

ACTIVITY: *data interpretation*

Statistical table

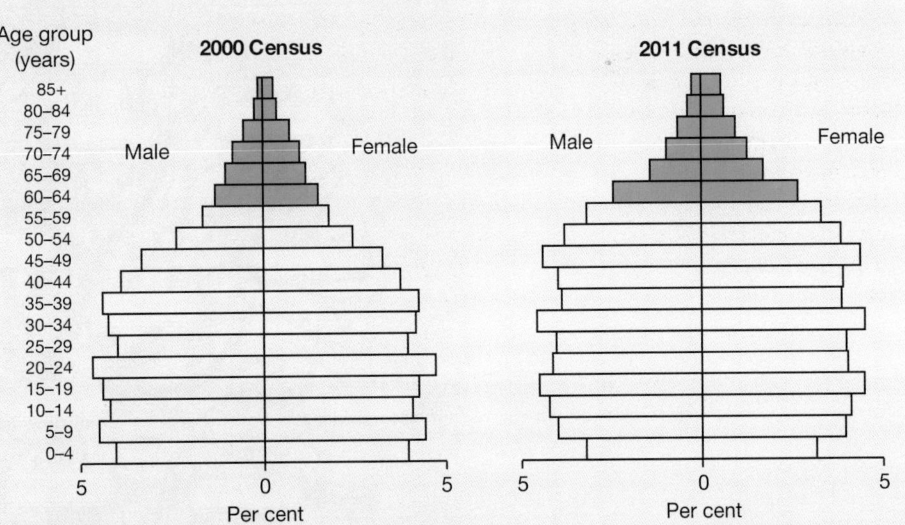

Population pyramids for the Republic of Mauritius, 2000 and 2011. The darker areas for ages 60 plus show how the proportion of people in this age group is increasing. Ageing population is now an issue affecting many countries

Note: Child population goes down while elderly population increases dramatically. The population is also ageing as a result of a decreasing number of births and longer life expectancy. Consequently, the proportion of:

- the child population aged under 15 years went down from 25 to 20 per cent and
- the elderly population aged 60 years and above increased from 9 to 13 per cent.

Use what you have learnt above to make a hypothesis about the reasons why these population changes occurred in Mauritius.

ACTIVITY: *evaluation*

What changes have there been to birth, death and fertility rates, family size and life expectancy in your country? Research this using the internet or other resources. If you do not live in the UK compare your findings with those for the UK. Suggest and evaluate reasons for the changes.

ACTIVITY: *research*

Has anyone drawn up a family tree for your family? If so, study it and see how long people lived, at what age they got married, how many children they had and so on. Then decide to what extent what has happened in your family fits the trends outlined in this unit.

TEST YOURSELF

1. What were the factors that led to changes in (a) the birth rate and (b) the mortality rate?
2. What are some of the likely consequences of an ageing population?

A family tree can be represented in many formats

Revision checklist

Make sure that you know all the key terms listed in this unit and that you understand the following:

- The main types of family are nuclear, extended, reconstituted, single parent and same sex families.
- Social stratification and ethnicity are associated with different types of families.
- Functionalists see nuclear families as having important functions, especially primary socialisation.
- Marxists see nuclear families as important for the continuation of capitalist society.
- Feminists see nuclear families as important for patriarchy.
- New Right writers argue that families today no longer carry out their functions and we need to return to the traditional nuclear family.
- Alternatives to the family include households, singlehood and communes.
- There are cross-cultural variations in marriage including monogamy, serial monogamy, polygamy (which can be either polygyny or polyandry) and group marriage.
- Alternatives to marriage include cohabitation and civil partnerships.
- Trends in marriage include fewer people marrying, marrying later, and more divorce and remarriage.
- Roles in families include conjugal roles, which can be joint or segregated, maternal and paternal roles and the roles of children and grandparents.
- Childhood is socially constructed.
- The domestic division of labour is changing, with a move towards more symmetrical families, but women still do most housework.
- Social stratification and ethnicity are associated with different roles and relationships within families.
- Nuclear families have negative aspects including gender inequality, domestic violence and child abuse and neglect.
- Families changed during industrialisation and urbanisation.
- Birth rates and death rates have fallen, families are smaller and life expectancy has increased.
- Populations are ageing, with important consequences for society.

Exam practice questions

More women in modern industrial countries now work outside the home. This has led to changes in the domestic division of labour, as women are now likely to have a dual burden. It has also probably led to changes in marriage patterns, as women marry later and have fewer children on average.

a What is meant by the term 'dual burden'? [2]

b Describe the difference between segregated and joint conjugal roles. [4]

c Explain how the fall in the fertility rate is affecting families. [6]

d Explain why birth and death rates fall during industrialisation. [8]

e To what extent have families become more equal between men and women? [15]

Total marks available 35

Unit 5: Education

Objectives

At the end of this unit you should be able to:

- understand the difference between formal and informal education
- describe how education can be an agent of socialisation and of social control
- describe the relationship between education and social mobility
- describe different types of schools
- assess explanations for different levels of achievement by gender, social class and ethnicity, including cultural, material and linguistic factors
- assess the influence of schools, teachers and peer groups on achievement
- understand issues about the measurement of intelligence and the relationship between intelligence and achievement
- describe the official curriculum, the hidden curriculum and vocationalism.

Introduction

At home and in their families children learn through socialisation the skills, knowledge and values they need to live in their society. This carries on throughout life; we all continue to learn every day. But in modern industrial societies much learning happens in schools and in other institutions such as colleges. In not much more than a hundred years we have moved from a situation where few children went to school to one where nearly all children do. The sociology of education is concerned mainly with schools. The problems it addresses are what education is for, what happens in schools and why some groups seem to do much better than others in the education system. In a world where education is seen as all-important and the key to a successful life questions like these have become very important.

KEY TERMS

Formal education: takes place in classrooms, where there is a syllabus and set content to be taught and learnt.

Informal education: takes place outside classrooms at home or work or through daily interactions.

What is the function of education?

Informal and formal education

For most of history, in traditional societies children learnt what they needed to know from their parents, families and communities, watching, listening and being shown what to do. There were usually no schools. With schools and colleges came a new style of education with courses, teachers and content that had to be taught and learnt: **formal education** had arrived.

The passage below is taken from a reply in 1744 by leaders of Native Americans to a suggestion by White European settlers in what is now the USA that they should send some of their boys to be taught at a college. It shows that the two cultures saw education very differently. For the Native Americans, it seemed that in colleges their boys learnt nothing of use. Note that the passage makes no reference to the education of girls. In both cultures at that time girls would learn what they needed to know as women from their mothers and other older women:

> But you, who are wise, must know that different Nations have different Conceptions of things and you will therefore not take it amiss, if our Ideas of this kind of Education happen not to be the same as yours. We have had some Experience of it. Several of our young people were formerly brought up at the colleges of the Northern Provinces: they were instructed in all your Sciences; but, when they came back to us, they were bad Runners, ignorant of every means of living in the woods . . . neither fit for Hunters, Warriors nor Counsellors, they were totally good for nothing. We are, however, not the less oblig'd by your kind Offer, tho' we decline accepting it; and, to show our grateful Sense of it, if the Gentlemen of Virginia will send us a Dozen of their sons, we will take Care of their Education, instruct them in all we know, and make Men of them.
>
> (Canassatego, 1744, 'Response of the Indians of the Six Nations to a suggestion that they send boys to an American college', from *Treaty of Lancaster*)

Although most children now go to school, **informal education** continues. We use the term informal education today to refer to education outside the classroom, for example after school activities, but also for what children learn in lessons that is not part of the formal content of the lesson. For example, children may learn that

KEY TERM

Hidden curriculum: attitudes and behaviour that are taught through the way the school is run and how teachers act, rather than through the taught content of a lesson.

they need to be on time or to follow instructions given by those in authority. This informal learning during lessons is called the **hidden curriculum** and is discussed later in this unit.

Education is still not provided throughout the world for all children. In many countries not all children go to school or complete their education. The United Nations has set primary education for all children as a goal to be achieved by 2015 but not all countries will succeed in reaching this and universal secondary education is a long way off.

ACTIVITY: *data interpretation*

Mali 2001: School attendance by location

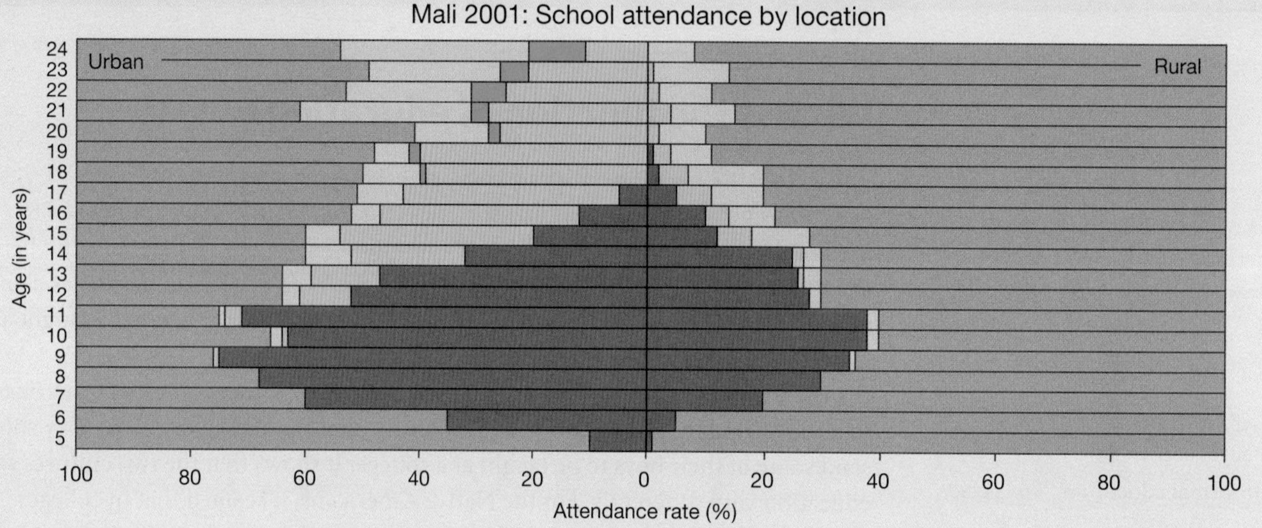

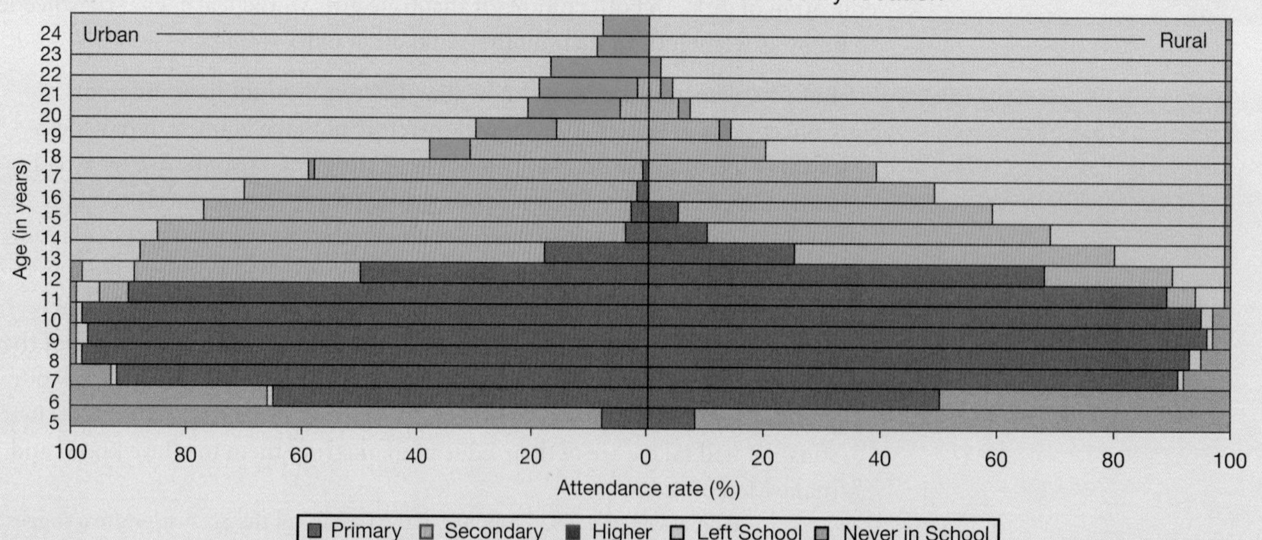

Primary · Secondary · Higher · Left School · Never in School

School attendance by age and residence, Mali and Indonesia

These graphs compare the numbers of children and young people of different ages in education in Mali, one of the poorest countries in the world, and Indonesia, an emerging economy.

Summarise the main differences between the two countries' statistics and the main differences between the figures for urban and rural areas.

TEST YOURSELF

Make a chart showing the arguments in favour of and against home schooling.

TOP TIP

Even where there is an education system open to all, not all children go to school. In the UK some parents decide to have their children educated at home by private tutors or by the parents themselves.

KEY TERMS

Socialisation: the process of learning culture.

Secondary socialisation: socialisation after the period of primary socialisation, that is, after the basic norms and values have been learnt.

Social expectations: the ways in which people are expected to behave in a particular social situation.

Social control: any way in which people are persuaded or forced to behave in particular ways.

Sanctions: any way in which children are reprimanded or receive something negative for something they have done.

Rewards: any way in which children are praised or receive something positive for something they have done.

Functions of education: the ways in which education contributes to society.

Education as an agency of socialisation and social control

Education is an agency of **secondary socialisation**. Primary socialisation happens within the family; agencies of secondary socialisation include the media and peer groups as well as schools. In schools, children learn not only what is taught in lessons, but also **social expectations** and, for example, how to get on with other children who often have different backgrounds and abilities.

The agencies of socialisation (such as the family, school and the media) can also be seen as agents of **social control**. At the same time as education allows people to become more knowledgeable and to develop skills, it is also a way in which the thoughts and behaviour of children can be influenced or even controlled. Children may be punished when they break rules or displease teachers or others in authority and **sanctions** such as detentions, loss of privileges and even physical punishment may be imposed. Behaviour that is approved of may lead to **rewards**, such as praise, badges or stickers and certificates.

Those who have power in a society may control the rest of the population through schools, the media, religious institutions and so on. Children may be taught that a particular view of the world (perhaps that their country is the best or their leaders the wisest) is correct. Marxist sociologists are interested in how the ruling class maintains its power by persuading the working class to accept ideas and values that are against their interests. Feminists argue that education can lead both boys and girls to have stereotypical and mistaken views of what the two sexes are like and can achieve. The ideas and values taught through the agencies of social control are part of an ideology. Marxists believe that education conveys the capitalist ideology and feminists believe that it conveys a patriarchal ideology.

The functions of education: the functionalist view

Functionalist sociologists focus on the ways in which education contributes to the continued well-being of society and they believe that education has several **functions**. Firstly, schools pass on the norms and values of a society from one generation to the next. They continue the process of socialisation that begins in the family and they therefore act as agencies of socialisation. Because children are socialised into a shared set of values, education can help them feel they belong to a particular society and that they have shared interests with other members of that society. The shared values may be based on a religion, but do not have to be. This can be particularly important in societies that are ethnically diverse. Here are some examples of ways in which individuals may learn in school to identify with their society:

- Being in the school with many other children, sharing the same experiences and learning and all being together in assemblies.
- Singing the national anthem.
- Seeing the national flag or other national symbols, such as the President, in classrooms and around the school.
- Learning patriotic slogans.
- Being taught in lessons about their society, its history and culture.

In most modern industrial societies one of the main values that children learn, according to functionalists, is the importance of individual achievement. At home each child has an ascribed status (where their role is set, for example by their gender or their place in the order of the children in the family) but at school they are judged mainly by what they achieve, measured by universal standards such as exams. For functionalists, schools perform an important function in enabling children to be judged by and accept universal standards, as these are essential for a modern industrial economy.

A second function of the education system is to produce people with the skills and abilities needed for the economy of that society. This is called sifting and sorting or the allocation of roles for future life after school. By assessing the children's abilities and how they do in tests and exams the school allows them to follow different paths. An intelligent child who passes exams may go on to study at university and then get a well-paid career as a result of their qualifications. Other children with different abilities may train for more practical work, learning a trade such as electrical work, or they may go into office work and administration. Those who achieve little in school may leave with few if any qualifications and may have to accept low-paid jobs that have little status or may be unable to find work at all. If the system works well it will produce the right numbers of people for the number of jobs available – a certain number of doctors, engineers, teachers and so on, but also craftspeople and manual workers. The system is seen to be fair as everyone seems to have an equal opportunity of succeeding.

Criticisms of the functionalist view come from different sources, including from Marxist and feminist perspectives. Among them are the following:

- There is no set of shared values to be passed on. For Marxists the values passed on are those of the dominant ideology, for feminists they are patriarchal values.
- There is no strong connection between schools and work. Pupils will not need most of what they learn in school when they are working as adults. Some companies even complain that the literacy and numeracy skills of school leavers are not good enough.
- People are selected for jobs not by their ability but more by their social class, ethnicity and gender.

The functions of education: the marxist view

Marxist sociologists see the functions described above in a very different light. Firstly, they agree that the education system instils a common value system but they see this common value system as the ideology of the ruling class. For Marxists, working-class people are not educated so much as indoctrinated. Working-class children are taught a set of values that will make them good workers for the capitalist system, where they are good only from the capitalists' point of view. This means they are willing to accept inadequate wages and not to question orders from a superior. Working class people suffer from false consciousness and are unaware of how they are being used. The sense of sharing a culture with others in the same country seems, from a Marxist perspective, to be no more than persuading people to work hard, and perhaps even to fight in wars and give their lives for a country (in reality, for its ruling class) when they really have more in common with working-class people in other countries. Much of this indoctrination is done through the hidden curriculum. For example, children learn in schools to be punctual and to do as they are told by those in authority (teachers). This is preparation for the world of work.

Socialisation into a common value system through schooling works differently for the middle and upper classes. The children of the bourgeoisie attend different types of schools from working-class children and are taught a different set of values. For example, they learn that they are superior to other classes and that they deserve privilege and respect. In the UK, there are public schools (fee-paying independent schools) for those wealthy enough to pay, which make it easier for them to gain access to places at top universities and to well-paid positions. In this way, according to Marxists, the ruling class is able to ensure that its sons and daughters inherit its power and wealth and that the class system survives over time. Public schools now often take children from less privileged backgrounds on scholarships but Marxists say that they do this to recruit the brightest working class children to the ruling class.

The functions of education: the feminist view

Where Marxists see a division between classes, feminists see a division between the two sexes. Education and schooling have always been affected by gender. In the past, and even today in some countries, education is thought to be more important for boys than for girls and the content of education has often been different for boys and girls. Feminists argue that schools, like other secondary agencies of socialisation, send the message to both boys and girls that boys are superior, and girls may learn to lower their expectations and be more likely to accept the traditional gender roles. This may happen for the following reasons:

- Girls are taught different knowledge; for example, subjects seen as more appropriate for the traditional female role such as sewing and needlework, cookery and childcare. Girls may even be discouraged from taking 'harder' subjects such as the sciences.
- Teachers have higher expectations of boys and encourage them to aim for a career, while assuming that the future for most girls is marriage and motherhood.
- Gender role models in schools where the head teachers and senior staff are often male, although there are many female teachers in most countries, give the impression that men are better suited for leadership roles.

KEY TERM

Social mobility: the movement of individuals or groups up or down the social hierarchy.

TEST YOURSELF

1 What differences are there between functionalist and Marxist views on the functions of education?

2 Give two ways in which girls may be treated differently from boys in schools.

The relationship between education and social mobility

KEY TERMS

Equality of opportunity: when everyone has the same chance of succeeding.

Meritocracy: a system in which individuals reach the social positions they deserve, based on their educational achievement, talent and skills.

Functionalists believe the education system permits **social mobility**. If there is **equality of opportunity** people are able to reach the level they deserve based on their natural ability and the effort they make to succeed. This is called a **meritocracy**. In a meritocracy social background should be irrelevant; a bright child from a working-class background who works hard should be able to do as well as one from a privileged background. Because a shared value system is taught in schools, most people accept the education system as a fair one. Those who are successful are said to deserve their success and those who are not blame themselves (for example, for not working hard enough) rather than the system. In a meritocracy there is social mobility. People from working-class and underprivileged groups like those with ethnic minority backgrounds can be upwardly mobile if they merit this, while those from privileged backgrounds will become downwardly mobile if they do not merit success.

Sociologists using other perspectives, however, challenge the idea that a meritocracy exists and the possibility of social mobility, pointing to evidence that sex, class and ethnicity play a bigger part than ability in children's achievements, and that therefore schools reproduce ascribed inequalities. If children are competing with each other in a race to obtain prized occupations after school, those from working-class backgrounds, in particular, start with a handicap. Upward mobility is possible when there are new positions in the professions to be filled. Then some working-class people will be able to move up. This was the case in Britain in the 1950s and 1960s. There was a big increase in the number of professional jobs as this sector of the economy grew, and able pupils from the working class, winning places in academically oriented grammar schools, were able to gain qualifications and enter these professions. But there is little downward mobility so that when these new opportunities dried up it became harder for others from the working class to join them. Marxists believe that the capitalist system recruited the most able of the working class and this made the system stronger. Most working-class children were still, however, unable to escape their situation.

Marxists therefore reject the idea that the education system is meritocratic; success depends less on talent and effort than on class background. Middle- and upper-class parents can provide advantages for their children like independent schooling, private tutors, access to books and other resources. Any mobility that is allowed is a safety valve, taking away from the working class its potential leaders.

TEST YOURSELF

1 What is meant by a meritocracy?
2 Why do Marxists not think that the UK is a meritocracy?

Different types of schools

In modern societies there are different kinds of schools. This section discusses state, private, single-sex and faith schools.

Muslim children in class at a primary school in Indonesia

The Green School in Bali, Indonesia, which is known for promoting eco-friendly concepts to its students

There are many different types of schools and school systems vary between countries. Types of schools are also often known by different names. It is possible that not all the types of schools described here exist in your country.

One way of categorising schools is by the age of the pupils they take. Primary schools (called elementary schools in the USA and some other countries) are where children receive their first years of academic education. In the UK children usually start their primary education at the age of 5 and move on to another school at the age of 11. The starting age is higher in some countries; for example it is 6 years in China and Australia. Primary education usually involves an emphasis on reading, writing and mathematics and an introduction to some other subjects. All the subjects may be taught by one class teacher.

Many children will already have had some education in a school-like setting before they start primary school. This is known as pre-school, pre-primary education and is designed to help very young children get used to learning in a school-type environment. Such learning usually focuses on the children developing cognitive, physical, social and emotional skills. The schools are usually known as kindergartens or nursery schools.

Secondary schools involve the second period of education and are usually for children aged 11 to 16 years or more. The term high school is used in some countries, though because education systems vary so much the term does not mean exactly the same as secondary school. In this stage pupils study a range of different subjects, with a different teacher for each. Secondary education often ends with a series of examinations that determine whether the pupil can move on to the next stage of education. In modern industrial countries, secondary education is compulsory. Pupils cannot leave to go to work until they have reached the school-leaving age. In the UK at the age of 16 pupils may either stay in their school to enter the sixth form or they may go to a sixth form college. Examinations at 18 years of age decide whether the pupil can continue further.

Tertiary education, the third period of education, is not compulsory and involves going to a university or college. It is also referred to as **post-compulsory education** or higher education. It is typically for people aged 18 years and over and it also may attract students who are much older and are returning to education (mature students). Universities offer both first or undergraduate degrees and higher or postgraduate degrees, including doctorates. University staff members carry out research as well as teaching students. The proportions of people in different countries who study at this level vary.

KEY TERMS

Post-compulsory education: education after the school-leaving age, where individuals choose to stay in education when they could have left.

State schools: schools that are run, directly or indirectly, by the government.

Private school: a school that is not run or controlled by the government.

Another way of categorising schools is by who runs and is responsible for them. The two basic types are **state schools,** which are run directly or indirectly by national or local government, and **private schools,** which are not. In many countries these two types of school exist alongside each other. State schools are funded from taxation; private schools are funded mainly by the tuition fees paid by the students. Private schools are usually free from restrictions placed on state schools, such as having to teach certain subjects or having to have qualified teachers. Private schools are mainly for children whose parents can afford to pay for their children's education but there may also be scholarships or schemes so that some other children can get places without having to pay. In many countries there are also some schools that are partly state and partly private.

In the UK about 7 per cent of children go to fee-paying private schools. There is a wide variety of private schools, some of which are very small and some are religious in character, including schools for religious groups that are small in the

UK, such as Buddhists and Seventh Day Adventists. The small group of the most expensive and prestigious private schools are often called public schools, although they are not public at all. These are usually long-established and have traditionally taught the children (usually boys) of the wealthiest families. The two most famous are probably Eton and Harrow. Children educated at these schools are virtually guaranteed access to highly paid careers that attract power and status.

For private schools
■ They have smaller class sizes and better resources and facilities than state schools.
■ Parents have the right to spend their money as they wish and so should be able to spend it on a better education than others can get. Parents will still contribute to state education through taxes, so they are paying for something they then opt out of.
■ Private schools can make some places available without fees to children from less wealthy backgrounds.
■ For parents, the biggest advantage is that attending a private school is beneficial however well the child does in exams. Someone who has been to a private school stands a better chance of a good job than someone who has the same exam results but who went to a state school.
Against private schools
■ Most parents cannot afford these schools. It is wrong that the wealthy can buy a better education.
■ Private schools are charities, so attract subsidies and benefits although they educate only a wealthy minority.
■ Teaching is often no better than in state schools. Exam results are often better but this is probably due to the smaller classes and more individual attention than in state schools.
■ Top private schools spend about four times as much a year on each student as state schools do. This money could be better spent on improving education for all.
■ Private schools play an important role in ensuring that higher classes can pass on their privileges to their children.

Table 5.1: Arguments for and against private schools in the UK

CASE STUDY

Study these facts

- Eton is a British public school
- Independent boys boarding school, founded in 1440
- One of the 100 largest charities in the UK
- Educated nine British prime ministers, including David Cameron (Prime Minister from 2010)
- Close links to the British royal family; educated Princes William and Harry
- Fees £29,862 per year (2010–2011), which is more than the average person's earnings in one year
- Many pupils are from outside Britain, including at times members of African and Asian royal families

Eton College, Windsor, United Kingdom

TASK

What advantages does an education at Eton give a pupil?

ACTIVITY: *evaluation*

What arguments can be made for abolishing schools like Eton?

The Krishna Avanti School, a London-based faith school

Some private schools, as noted above, are religious, but so are state schools in many countries. In the UK the main churches have always run many primary schools and some secondary schools. These schools are mainly part of the state system. There is also a growing number of schools run by smaller religious groups and organisations in the UK. Religious schools are referred to as **faith schools** or sometimes as parochial schools. Faith schools are usually at least partly selective in that they are able to give priority to children who are members of the school's faith, and faith schools often have a distinctive ethos based on their faith. For example, the ethos of the Krishna Avanti School in London involves a lacto-vegetarian diet, based on compassion for animals and an awareness of the ecological consequences of our diet.

In many countries primary schools usually take most of the children in a local area. At secondary level there is a much wider range of types of schools. One of the main distinctions between types of schools is whether they select their pupils or accept all who apply. **Selective education** means a system in which schools select their pupils, usually by ability. The following section discusses the main types of secondary school in England and Wales.

KEY TERMS

Faith schools: schools controlled by a religious organisation.

Selective education: pupils are selected (and others excluded), usually on the basis of their academic ability.

Comprehensive system: non-selective secondary schools accepting all the children of that age in an area.

Comprehensive schools are those that cater for all the children in a local area. In England and Wales comprehensive schools were introduced from the 1960s onwards. They replaced an earlier system of three types of secondary schools:

- Grammar schools: for 'academic' children, selected by a test at the age of 11 years or afterwards. Grammar schools taught the classics (Latin and Greek), maths, science and other demanding subjects for the GCE O (ordinary) level examinations.
- Technical schools: specialised in technical education, helping pupils prepare for manual occupations.
- Secondary modern schools: for most children, offering a basic education with often few opportunities to take exams.

These three types of schools existed alongside independent schools. This system was known as the tripartite system. It was based on the assumption that children could be classified into different types with different abilities and that they needed different types of education, which was best provided in different schools. Grammar schools often enrolled mainly middle-class pupils, while working-class children went to the other types of schools. Grammar schools were also often able to attract the best teachers. Pupils in secondary modern schools had little chance of success and knew that they had in effect been labelled as failures at the age of 11. This reduced their motivation to work well and to behave. In this way their **life chances** were already limited at this age.

KEY TERM

Life chances: the opportunities that individuals have to improve their lives.

Comprehensive schools were introduced because of a big change in thinking about schools. Comprehensive schools are based on the idea that all children should be given the chance to succeed.

There has been a move away from comprehensive schools and there are now other types of schools in England and Wales today including:

- Specialist schools – secondary schools that specialise in one or more subjects such as sports, arts, business and enterprise, engineering, maths and computing, music, humanities, science, technology and languages.

- Academies – these were first introduced by the Labour government in 2000 and allowed businesses and other sponsors to start schools, usually to replace schools with very low GCSE results. The sponsors decide how the school is run. In 2010 the government began to encourage all schools to become academies, allowing outstanding schools to do this very quickly. Academies are not under the control of the local authority as they are funded directly by government and can set their own curriculum, salary levels and ethos.
- Free schools. The current government also allows parents, teachers, charities and other groups to set up schools and be directly funded by the government.

In favour of comprehensives	Against comprehensives
They allow equal opportunity – all pupils study the same subjects and have an equal chance of succeeding.	They bring down standards because the brighter students have to work at the same speed as the less able.
They have a strong community spirit, bringing together all the children in an area regardless of class, ethnic group or ability.	In practice, comprehensives were often not very diverse; for example, if the school had a mainly working-class catchment area most of the pupils would be working class.
Children are no longer labelled as failures at the age of 11 and those who develop as learners after this young age have a chance to succeed.	Comprehensives tend to be large and impersonal and may have discipline problems.
Fewer pupils leave without any qualifications.	Some comprehensives have not been true comprehensives because they have used streaming and setting, providing a different education for pupils with different abilities and in effect selecting.
The comprehensive system benefits working-class pupils as they are the least likely to be able to get into grammar schools.	Some comprehensives have not been able to take all the children in an area, because some have been creamed off by private and grammar schools nearby. This was possible because governments failed to abolish private schools and allowed the tripartite system to continue in some areas.

Table 5.2: Arguments for and against comprehensive schools in England and Wales

The range of different schools now existing means that schools are increasingly competing against each other for pupils and resources. Previously, apart from the privileged minority who went to fee-paying schools, most children went to the state school nearest their home. Each school had a catchment area. These still exist but parents can now choose to apply to other schools. Nowadays parents can access more information about schools to help them choose. Schools have websites, prospectuses and open days to try to persuade parents to send their children to the school in question and league tables of exam results and school inspection reports are published so that parents can compare schools.

Schools are under pressure to get good results, as measured by national tests and exams. To achieve this, they try to select the most able pupils because they will do well, and to exclude those with learning difficulties as they need expensive extra resources and may not do well at school.

Supporters of competition between schools argue that it forces schools to improve and so raises results, and that it gives parents choice. Opponents point out that not all parents have an equal ability to choose. Those with economic and **cultural capital** can get their children into the right school; for example, they can afford transport to send them to a better school or can move into the catchment area. Working-class parents are much less able to take advantage of the choice. Also, while some schools become successful, others who cannot attract 'good' pupils fall into a downward spiral of fewer pupils, fewer resources and worse results.

KEY TERM

Cultural capital: the knowledge, language, attitudes and values that give those who have them an advantage in the educational system.

CASE STUDY

Summerhill School

This school in Britain was started by A.S. Neill, who believed that normal schools failed to turn out people who were free and happy, and tried to make Summerhill a school that was different and would achieve this. It is run democratically and each member of staff and each pupil has one vote in school meetings. Pupils attend the subjects and lessons they want to, at the level they want to study at. It is a boarding and day school offering both primary and secondary education. Summerhill has been very controversial and in 2000 it had to go to court to fight criticisms made by inspectors from OFSTED. Visit this web site for more information: www.summerhillschool.co.uk.

TASK

1 In what way is Summerhill different from normal schools?
2 Why is Summerhill controversial?

ACTIVITY: *evaluation*

Make a table to compare and contrast the functionalist, Marxist and feminist views of the functions of education.

TEST YOURSELF

1 What kinds of schools exist in your country? Which of the kinds of schools discussed above are not found in your country?
2 Outline two arguments in favour of, and two arguments against, the comprehensive school system.

ACTIVITY: *discussion*

'Pupils of different abilities and backgrounds should attend different types of schools.' Do you agree?

ACTIVITY: *research*

Interview an older member of your family about their education. Find out how schools and education have changed, ask what subjects were taught, what lessons were like, what resources were used, how teachers interacted with pupils and whether boys and girls were treated the same. Report back to your class comparing your own experience and your family member's.

KEY TERM

Educational inequality (based on class, gender and ethnicity): when different groups are treated differently or have different levels of educational achievement.

What factors help to explain differences in educational achievement?

Patterns in educational achievement and experience

This section discusses the patterns of educational achievement in relation to gender, ethnicity and social class. These are patterns of **educational inequality**. Different groups are treated differently and have different levels of educational achievement.

Gender

In the past most schooling was reserved for boys and most girls received very little education. It is still true in some developing countries that boys are more likely to go to school than girls. This is often because parents think the education of their sons is more important. The future of a boy is seen in terms of a successful career and perhaps being able to support his ageing parents. A girl, however, may be expected to marry, and on marriage she will join her husband's family, perhaps taking their family name, and her main responsibility is to them. For a family with limited income, paying for a daughter's education may seem an unnecessary expense.

The United Nations and its member governments are strongly committed to education for girls. It is seen both as a human right and as essential to a country's development. To achieve the second Millennium Development Goal of universal primary education, more girls need to be educated in schools. For example, 57 per cent of the children who do not go to primary school are girls. It has been shown that educating girls has positive outcomes in improving the living standards, health and nutrition of families. Girls who have been to school will have fewer children.

In schools in most modern industrial countries, boys and girls now follow the same curriculum. In the past, however, some subjects were set aside for girls, such as domestic science and textiles, while others, such as woodwork and metalwork, were thought to be for boys only. Girls also tended to stop studying science before boys did. When children have choices about what to study, girls do still make different choices from boys in many countries and schools, and are more likely to choose arts subjects than technology, for example. These differences come from earlier socialisation into gender roles, where, for example, girls and boys play with different toys at home and are encouraged to have the interests seen as appropriate for their sex.

Girls taking part in a science experiment

Girls may find that some classrooms, such as science laboratories, are dominated by boys. Textbooks in subjects like science and technology may show boys rather than girls in the illustrations and the lessons may be taught by a man. All these factors can give girls the message that the subject is not for them. Equally, boys may be put off subjects such as dance and domestic science and also, perhaps, sociology. In England and Wales about two-thirds of pupils taking sociology at school are girls.

In the UK the main concern about gender and education until about 1990 was that girls were underachieving. Girls did better than boys in the early years of education but then tended to fall behind and were less likely to get the exam grades they needed for entry to university or to high-paid careers. However, by the 1990s girls started to do better than boys at every level of education. For example, girls do better than boys on average in almost every subject at GCSE level and more girls go on to university. In 2012, 64 per cent of girls taking GCSEs got five passes at grade C or above, including English and mathematics, compared with 54 per cent of boys. Both boys and girls are doing better than in the past, but there is still a gap.

ACTIVITY: *data interpretation*

Percentage of students gaining 5+

Boys Girls

Percentage of school leavers achieving 5+ A–C (or pass) O-level or A*–C GCSE by gender (1962–2006)

1. In what year did girls begin to achieve higher grades than boys?
2. Has the gap between boys and girls narrowed, widened or stayed the same since 1993?

Why do girls now do better than boys at GCSE level?

1. The attitude and motivation of girls has increased because there are more opportunities for girls and more successful women who act as role models. Girls know that they do not have to become housewives and mothers.
2. Schools make an effort to ensure that girls get the same opportunities as boys to study and succeed, and advice from teachers and others is now more likely to encourage them to aim to have careers.
3. Some schools used schemes to encourage girls to aim higher, especially in science and technology. They used **positive discrimination**, for example ensuring that girls had priority over boys in accessing laboratory equipment.
4. Girls seem to be better motivated and to work more consistently over long periods. For example, they spend more time than boys doing homework, they concentrate better in class and are better organised. Girls seem to benefit more than boys from coursework and continuous assessment, which have become more common in many countries.
5. It has been argued that girls mature earlier than boys, so that by the age of 16, when schoolchildren in many countries take exams, they are more likely to recognise the importance of studying hard.

KEY TERM

Positive discrimination: giving disadvantaged groups better treatment than others in an attempt to make up for their disadvantage.

Why do boys underachieve compared to girls?

1. Boys may be treated differently in schools; teachers may believe that poor study habits and behaviour is normal for boys when similar behaviour would not be tolerated from girls. Boys probably also behave worse overall; they tend to be sent out of the classroom and punished more than girls are.
2. Boys tend to be too confident. They overestimate their ability and believe they can do well without working hard. Girls are more likely to underestimate their ability and believe that they have to work hard to have any chance of success.

3 Laddish behaviour. Boys may belong to or be affected by an anti-learning subculture. They may think they will lose status in the eyes of their peers if they work hard or do well. Instead, they may attempt to gain status through exuberant and boisterous behaviour that may get them into trouble at school and will stop them making progress.
4 In many modern industrial countries there are fewer traditional male jobs, such as those in engineering and mining. Boys may feel that there is little point in working hard to pass exams when there are few job opportunities for them. They may also have unrealistic ambitions that do not require success at school, such as being a star footballer.
5 Boys and girls spend their leisure time differently. Girls are more likely to talk, which helps develop language and reasoning skills, whereas boys are more likely to play sports or games. While these activities develop skills they are less helpful for academic success.
6 Most school work is based on reading and writing. Boys tend to have different skills and interests. They would do better if more school work was active and practical. Reading can also be something that boys believe is more appropriate for girls than for themselves. It has been suggested, for example, that mothers are more likely to read to their young children than fathers and that because of this both boys and girls come to see reading as a female activity.

Ethnicity

Many individual pupils from all ethnic backgrounds do well but in many countries there is concern about how some minority ethnic groups do in the school system. Pupils from these groups tend to do less well than the average for that country. For example, in the USA there has been concern about African-American pupils, whereas in the UK children from Pakistani and Bangladeshi backgrounds and African-Caribbean pupils achieve less on average. This section concentrates on the achievement of minority ethnic groups in the UK but the factors suggested as explanations may apply in other countries and to other ethnic groups.

In 2012, 59 per cent of pupils taking GCSEs in England and Wales got five passes, including English and mathematics, at grade C or above. For White British pupils the figures were very close to the national figure, as would be expected, since White British pupils make up about two-thirds of the total. The two minority ethnic groups that performed well above the national figure were Chinese pupils at 76 per cent and Indian pupils at 74 per cent. The lowest achieving groups were Gypsy (Roma) at 9 per cent and Travellers of Irish Heritage at 16 per cent, then African-Caribbean children at 50 per cent. After concerns in the past about the achievement of Pakistani and Bangladeshi pupils, they are now close to the national figure at 54 per cent and 62 per cent, respectively.

Why do some ethnic groups do less well than others?

1 Ethnicity cannot be separated from class and gender. African-Caribbean pupils in British schools are often from working-class backgrounds. This is because when their families arrived as immigrants it was mainly for employment in working-class occupations such as working on trains and buses. This would help to explain the relatively low achievement of African-Caribbean pupils. Immigrants from Pakistan and Bangladesh were often from rural and poor backgrounds. On the

other hand, those with Indian and East African Asian backgrounds included a high proportion of professionals and business people. With regard to gender, it has been suggested that girls from some Asian backgrounds are socialised into stronger traditional female roles and that this may limit their aspirations, so that they do not have the incentive to work hard to achieve qualifications.

KEY TERMS

Social factors: things that affect lifestyle and life chances, such as wealth, religion and occupation.

Discrimination: when one group is treated unfairly.

Ethnocentrism: seeing other cultures from the point of view of your own, so that the other culture is devalued.

Intelligence: how clever someone is; a very difficult idea to measure.

2 Wider **social factors**. If there is prejudice and **discrimination** against a minority group in the wider society, for example in access to jobs and housing, then they would be expected to achieve less than average in schools. The society may have failed to eliminate racism. For example, pupils from an ethnic minority may be aware that they and their families face discrimination and may react against this by rebelling against the school, which represents the authority of the racist society in their daily lives.

3 Factors within school. Schools need to ensure that all pupils have equal opportunities to succeed. This may require tackling racism in the school. Schools may themselves be racist:

- There may be discrimination by the school, for example in allocating pupils to streams and sets. Pupils from minority ethnic groups may be put in lower streams or sets because of assumptions that are made based on their ethnicity rather than their individual ability.
- Teachers may assume that pupils from the minority ethnic group are unable to do well or label them 'troublemakers'.
- What is taught in lessons may be **ethnocentric**; that is, treating the culture of the majority as more important and implicitly telling pupils from the minority groups that their own culture is of less value. This can show, for example, in the teaching of history, where pupils from ethnic minority groups may learn nothing about their own people's experiences. This may lead such pupils to believe that the lessons are not relevant to them and they may do less well than those from ethnic majority groups because they lose interest.
- The authorities may not deal with racism by other pupils against the minority, perhaps by treating it as unimportant despite the damage it may do.

4 Cultural differences. If the values at home clash with those of the school this may hold up pupils' progress. For example, the dress, appearance or way of speaking of a pupil may reinforce a stereotype held by teachers. Cultural factors are considered in more detail in the next section.

5 Genetic difference. Another possible explanation is that different ethnic groups have different levels of ability. This view has been discredited. It is explained in the section on measuring **intelligence**.

Social class

KEY TERM

Social stratification: the different levels into which societies are divided, such as upper class, middle class and working class, based on differences in wealth, power and status.

Social stratification by class is a major influence on educational achievement. Schools in the past were largely for the rich and powerful. Until the 20th century, even in modern industrial societies, only a minority of lower-class children received an education, and what they did get would be short and basic. There was essentially a two-tier system, with basic schooling for most children and a privileged education for the few.

The development of schools in the UK was very much based on social class. There were private schools for the wealthy, grammar schools for the middle class and secondary moderns and technical schools for the working class. Comprehensive schools attempted to remove this class divide but the continued existence of private schools and also of grammar schools in some areas made this difficult.

Of the 44 per cent of pupils eligible for free school meals 36 per cent got five grade Cs or above, including English and mathematics, in their GCSEs in 2012, compared to 63 per cent of other pupils. Eligibility for free school meals is only one possible way of measuring social class, but these figures suggest that class is a bigger factor in influencing **educational achievement** than gender or ethnicity.

The relative lack of achievement by working-class pupils is usually seen as a problem by governments, who want to have well-educated workforces who will attract companies to invest. There have been many different attempts to raise the school-leaving achievements of working-class pupils. These are referred to as compensatory education (compensating for perceived shortcomings in the child's background). It includes any extra support given to those from disadvantaged backgrounds to help them overcome the disadvantages they face in education. An example in the UK is the Education Action Zones (later renamed Excellence in Cities Action Zones). These were schools in working-class areas in inner cities that were given extra funding and resources.

Working-class pupils may underachieve for the following reasons:

- Factors within schools, such as **labelling**, setting and **streaming**, lead to their underachievement. These are examined on page 181, where the influence of schools and teachers on educational achievement is discussed.
- Inherited intelligence. It has been suggested that middle-class children do better in schools because they have inherited intelligence from their parents, who by definition have been successful. This is examined in the section on measuring intelligence.
- Home background. It has been suggested that working-class children are hampered by cultural or **material deprivation** or both. This is examined in the section on material influences.
- Low self-esteem and low expectations of themselves, which may be reinforced by teachers. Working-class pupils may be aware from an early age that they need to limit their hopes and aspirations and so they may be more willing to accept jobs that require few qualifications.
- Language differences (see linguistic influences in the next section).
- Cultural capital (see cultural influences in the next section).
- Class position. The French sociologist Raymond Boudon pointed to the importance of considering the class position of pupils when assessing the costs and benefits of choices about education. For example, a boy from a middle-class background may see himself as a failure if he does not go to university, as his parents may well have assumed all his life that he would enter a profession such as medicine. On the other hand, a student from a working-class background might well be the first person from their family to go into higher education and might have to loosen ties with their community and move away socially from friends who do not go on to higher education. People from a working-class background who go into clerical work may well have moved further up the occupational ladder than their parents, and so could be seen as more successful than someone from a middle-class background who becomes a doctor or lawyer. This suggests we need to consider class position when deciding how well people have done in the education system.

KEY TERMS

Educational achievement: how well individuals do in the school system, usually measured by exam results.

Labelling: defining a person or group in a particular way so that certain behaviour is expected from them.

Streaming: when children are taught in classes of similar ability for all subjects.

Material deprivation: problems in the standard of living in the home background of some children that prevent them from achieving in education.

TOP TIP

Gender, ethnicity and social class are discussed in separate sections here, but in practice all three are aspects of each individual's identity, so as factors they overlap and are not easy to separate. For example, people in the UK generalise by saying that girls do better than boys, but middle-class girls do much better than working-class girls.

- Working-class pupils in general underachieve in comparison to middle- and upper-class pupils, so another set of factors relates to the advantages higher class pupils have. These include access to better schools, resources at home to support education and the cultural capital of their families.

TEST YOURSELF

1. Suggest two reasons why girls overtook boys in educational achievement in the UK in the 1990s.
2. How could governments and schools help working-class pupils to achieve better results?

Material, cultural and linguistic influences on educational achievement

This section discusses the influence of material, cultural and linguistic factors on family background and educational achievement.

Material influences

Social class

Material deprivation refers to factors in the standard of living of children, especially those from working-class backgrounds, that may lead to them underachieving in school. Children living in or on the margins of poverty are likely to be educationally disadvantaged in several ways, even when education is free. These disadvantages include:

- not having a quiet place to work because the home is small or crowded
- getting an inadequate diet so they have problems in concentration and tiredness
- being unable to afford extras – although education is free, parents are expected to provide school uniforms, sports kit, writing and other equipment and to contribute to the costs of trips
- not having gone to preschool education, as the family does not have the money to pay for this – they may then start primary school behind other children
- having few resources at home like educational books or materials in the home, and no access to a computer
- having part-time jobs when they are old enough and trying to combine earning a wage with studies – this is likely to affect how well they do in school
- attending a disadvantaged school in a poor area that cannot offer as good an education as those in more prosperous areas, where parents may raise extra money for the school
- coming from a family that is not financially able to support a son or daughter through university or other higher education – students may be aware of this from an early age and limit their ambitions accordingly.

KEY TERM

Home factors: factors in the home background of children that affect how they do in school.

These **home factors** tend to reinforce each other, making the problems wor children of middle-class parents are less likely to suffer from these disad Middle-class parents are more likely to be able and willing to afford e help their children do well, buying books or even arranging a tuto outside lessons.

Ethnicity

Some minority ethnic groups have a high proportion of their members in the working class, so they suffer from material disadvantages more than the majority ethnic group. This has often been the case for groups of immigrants who take low positions in their new home country, establishing themselves and then moving up the social ladder in the second or later generations. Some immigrant groups are from relatively poor backgrounds and this disadvantage can continue in the education system of their new country. This was the case for people from Bangladesh moving to the UK in the 1960s and 1970s.

Gender

Material deprivation is related more to class and ethnicity than to gender. However, where a family has limited resources to spend on education, girls' education may be seen as less important than that of boys and the resources that are available are used to educate sons rather daughters.

Cultural influences

Social class

Some researchers have claimed that the working class has a culture or subculture that is different from the rest of society. The cultural background of working-class pupils may then help to explain their underachievement in school. This is referred to as cultural, rather than material, deprivation. **Cultural deprivation** comes from values and attitudes rather than a lack of money and resources. Aspects of culture that have been alleged to be part of working-class culture and that stand in the way of success in education include:

KEY TERMS

Cultural deprivation: aspects of the values and attitudes from the home and family background of some children that prevent them from achieving in education.

Immediate gratification: having short-term aims and wanting rewards straight away.

Deferred gratification: having long-term aims and being willing to postpone rewards.

- a fatalistic attitude; that is, not believing that you are in control of your own destiny and can change your prospects
- the need for **immediate** rather than **deferred gratification**; this means being unable to see the benefits of putting off rewards – for example, staying in education when you could work for a wage involves a belief that further education will improve your situation in years to come, but not yet
- for boys, a liking for thrills and excitement, which may get them into trouble
- having parents who do not value education, perhaps as a result of having had negative experiences at school themselves
- loyalty to the group – it may be seen as wrong to want to move away from your origins by moving up the class ladder
- an absence of successful role models in the family who benefited from education and community; this may contribute to seeing education as unimportant or irrelevant or simply not for 'people like us'.

However, the evidence that there is a different working-class culture can be questioned. Working-class parents do see the benefits of education and may be ambitious for their children to succeed. However, they may lack the knowledge and confidence that middle-class parents may have, for example, to push for extra support for their child. Some working-class parents are reluctant to have contact with schools because of their own experience at school and so, for example, may not attend parental consultations. Their children may wrongly interpret this as a lack of interest in their education.

Working-class parents may also lack the cultural capital that middle- and upper-class parents have. The concept of cultural capital was developed by the French sociologist Pierre Bourdieu. In this theory the advantages middle-class and upper-class pupils have derived not only from being better off financially, because their parents can buy them a good education (financial capital), but also because they have cultural capital, which includes such things as tastes, values and behaviour. The advantages parents can give to their children in terms of cultural capital include familiarity with books and reading, visits to museums and art galleries and a sense of the importance of education. These parents will also know how the education system works and how to use it to help their children. Working-class children will have less cultural capital. Pupils with high cultural capital will be judged favourably by teachers and are likely to be among the most able students.

Pierre Bourdieu

Ethnicity

The ethnic background of pupils can influence their achievement. For example, this background may or may not place a high value on learning and academic success. The British sociologist Louise Archer researched why children with Chinese backgrounds were so successful in schools compared to those from other ethnic groups. She found that working hard at school was an essential part of the Chinese ethnic identity. Parents valued education highly and invested time and money in their children's education, regardless of how well off they were. Children were socialised into seeing educational success as very important. Their parents talked with them frequently about their school work and about planning their career so that they had clear goals. One of the Chinese pupils Archer interviewed summed this up by saying that while White British children were told to do their best, Chinese children were told to be the best. This strong motivation from Chinese pupils' cultural background was a strong reason for their high achievement.

Gender

Boys and girls are socialised into gender roles, starting in the period of primary socialisation. By the time they start school both sexes have clear ideas about the behaviour and attitudes appropriate to both sexes, learnt from the culture they are growing up in. Girls may be influenced to see their future in terms of marriage and motherhood rather than a profession and career. Most boys will marry and become fathers but see their future in terms of work. Girls may feel that qualifications are unnecessary for them and not work hard. On the other hand, a good education can sometimes help the girl find a high-status husband.

In modern industrial societies there has been a shift away from the traditional gender roles and girls are now much more likely to have career aims and to be motivated to work hard in school to reach them.

KEY TERMS

Restricted code: a form of language used with close friends and families, where there are shared meanings; compared to the elaborated code it is informal.

Elaborated code: a form of language used in careful explanation and detail, and in formal contexts such as in examinations.

Linguistic influences

Social class

In 1971 Basil Bernstein argued in *Class, Codes and Control* that languages had two codes. The **restricted code** is used for informal everyday spoken communication with family and friends. Its vocabulary is limited and meanings are not always made explicit because the two parties share knowledge and assumptions. The **elaborated code**, on the other hand, makes meanings explicit and can be used to express complex and abstract ideas. It is the code used for formal occasions in schools by teachers and in textbooks, and it is what pupils get marks for using in written work. Bernstein suggested that, because of their different exposure to types

Basil Bernstein

of language, middle-class children were more likely to be proficient in using the elaborated code than working-class children. This allowed middle-class children to do better in schools, as well as making them seem to be more able to their teachers. It is important to note, however, that the restricted code has its own strengths and uses, and that everybody uses it (including middle-class people): it is not simply working-class speech. The advantage middle-class children have is being able to switch between the two codes easily.

Ethnicity

Minority ethnic groups may be taught in a language that is not their home language. This is the case for many children in developing countries, where schools use the official language, which is usually the language of the former colonial rulers, such as English or French. The pupils will, however, speak different languages at home and with their peers, so in school they face problems of understanding, for example subjects that are explained in a different language. It also sometimes happens that their own language is devalued and seen as inappropriate for school. In the UK there are many schools with pupils who speak languages other than English at home. This may cause some disadvantage to recently arrived immigrants with little English but this is usually temporary. Being able to use more than one language (being bilingual) may give them an advantage in developing the ability to learn.

The kind of language spoken by some minority ethnic groups may be thought by teachers to be ungrammatical and even wrong, indicating a lack of education or backwardness – 'broken English'. This might apply, for example, to patois or creole languages. For example, the American linguist William Labov showed that the language used by African-Americans – African-American vernacular English (AAVE) – had a grammatical structure and could be used to express complex and abstract ideas. Until Labov's work was published it had been widely assumed that AAVE was a substandard form of English and teachers discouraged or even punished children for using it. African-American pupils expressing their thoughts in AAVE might have the same level of understanding as pupils using standard English but this would not be recognised by teachers. Their language, therefore, held them back from achieving.

TEST YOURSELF

1. What is meant by cultural capital and why is it important in education?
2. Outline two ways in which the language children speak may affect how well they do in school.

The influence of school, teachers and the peer group on educational achievement

Social class

The explanations of working-class underachievement discussed so far have centred largely on the structural material and cultural factors outside the school that shape children before and during schooling. It is almost as if those from upper- and middle-class backgrounds are born to succeed in education, while those from the most disadvantaged, poor backgrounds are born to fail. However, many would argue that **school factors** are important. Schools can make a difference to the life chances of students whatever their background as, for example, Rutter's work has suggested.

KEY TERM

School factors: factors at school that affect children's educational achievement.

Michael Rutter and his colleagues in *Fifteen Thousand Hours: Secondary Schools and their Effects on Children* (1979) reported research that showed, in the face of much previous research suggesting the opposite, that good schools can make a difference to the life chances of all pupils. Rutter suggested that it is the features of the school's organisation which make this difference. The positive features are as follows:

- Teachers are well prepared for lessons.
- Teachers have high expectations of pupils' academic performance and set and mark classwork and homework regularly.
- Teachers set examples of behaviour; for example, they are on time and they use only officially approved forms of discipline.
- Teachers place more emphasis on praise and reward than on blame and punishment.
- Teachers treat pupils as responsible people, for example by giving them positions of responsibility in looking after school books and property.
- Teachers show an interest in the pupils and encourage them to do well.
- There is an atmosphere or ethos in the school which reflects the above points, with all teachers sharing a commitment to the aims and values of the school.
- There is a mixture of abilities in the school, as the presence of high-ability pupils benefits the academic performance and behaviour of pupils of all abilities.

Research has suggested that social patterns of underachievement in education are affected by what goes on in school classrooms and the way in which meanings are constructed in the classroom (how teachers and students come to see each other) affects student progress. For example, it is possible that sociological evidence demonstrating a link between working-class origin and underachievement may have led teachers to expect working-class pupils to perform poorly and these low expectations may be an important factor contributing to their failure.

Much of the research in this area is based on the interpretivist perspective. From this perspective, pupils are not seen simply as passive victims of structural, material or cultural forces outside the school that cause them to underachieve. The emphasis is on how, through interaction with others, teachers or pupils come to interpret and define situations and develop meanings that influence the way they behave.

Teachers are constantly involved in judging and classifying pupils in various ways, such as bright or slow, as troublemakers or ideal pupils or as hardworking or lazy. This process of classification or labelling by teachers has been shown to affect the performance of students. The stereotype held by the teacher (good/bad or not bright/bright student and so on) can produce a halo effect, in which pupils become stereotyped on the basis of earlier impressions and these impressions influence future teacher–student relations.

According to Howard Becker, teachers judge pupils on non-academic factors such as speech, dress, personality (how cooperative and polite they are), their enthusiasm for work, conduct and appearance. Together these make up a stereotype of the ideal pupil and influence the teachers' assessments of a student's ability. The social class of the student has an important influence on this evaluation. Students from working-class homes are often seen as being poorly motivated and lacking support from the home, and as engaging in disruptive behaviour in the classroom. This may mean they are perceived by teachers as lacking in ability, even if they are very able. By contrast, those from middle-class backgrounds most closely fit the teacher's stereotype of the ideal pupil and teachers may assume that children who enter school already confident, fluent and familiar with learning, who are more likely to be from middle-class homes, have greater potential and will push them to achieve accordingly.

The way teachers assess and evaluate students affects their achievement levels, as pupils may gradually bring their own self-image into line with the one the teacher holds of them ('what's the point in trying – the teacher thinks I can't do it'). Those labelled as bright and likely to be successful in education are more likely to perform in line with the teachers' expectations and predictions, while those labelled as slow, difficult or of low ability and unlikely to succeed are persuaded not to bother. In both cases the teachers' predictions may come true. This suggests the difference between bright and slow or good and bad students, and the progress they make in school, are created by the processes of typing and labelling. This is the **self-fulfilling prophecy**.

KEY TERM

Self-fulfilling prophecy: when people act in the way they have been expected to, making the expectation come true.

The self-fulfilling prophecy and the self-negating prophecy

Research by Rosenthal and Jacobson (1968) in California provided useful evidence of the self-fulfilling prophecy. They found that a randomly chosen group of students whom teachers were told were bright and could be expected to make good progress, even though they were no different from other students in terms of ability, did in fact make greater progress than students who were not so labelled. If teachers are more likely to negatively label working-class pupils and have low expectations of them, this suggests that a self-fulfilling prophecy will lead to low achievement by those pupils.

It is also possible to have a self-negating prophecy. This is when a pupil is labelled as unable to do well, but reacts against the label by setting out to prove that it is wrong, and succeeds.

Another way that pupils are labelled is by being put into streams or sets according to their predicted ability. Streaming is when pupils are in one class for all lessons with others of similar ability so there is a top stream for those seen as high achievers and a bottom stream for those seen as low achievers, with a hierarchy of other grades in between. Critics say that streaming involves prejudging success and failure. Those who are put in the top streams will become confident, high achievers; those in low streams will see themselves as failures and may be found among disruptive pupils and will struggle to do well even if they work hard. Being placed in a low stream or set may undermine pupils' confidence and discourage them from trying, and teachers may be less ambitious and offer less information to lower-stream children than they would to others. Since streaming is often linked to social class – the higher a pupil's social class, the greater their chance of being allocated to a top stream – it contributes to the underachievement of working-class pupils. On the other hand, those placed in top streams are being rewarded by the school so are more likely to conform to the school's values.

KEY TERM

Setting: when children are taught in classes of similar ability for a particular subject.

The opposite of streaming is mixed ability classes where there is no selection. Many schools also have banding or **setting**, which fall in between streaming and mixed ability. In banding pupils are placed in wide ability groups that are then randomly divided into teaching groups. In setting pupils are placed in a class based on their ability in one subject only. So a pupil might be in a top set for maths but a bottom set for English.

Ethnicity

Teachers may make assumptions about pupils from different groups by labelling them and possibly by creating self-fulfilling prophecies. Pupils from minority ethnic groups may be more likely to be put in low streams and sets, perhaps because of language differences or teacher stereotypes rather than their actual ability. Some interpretivist studies in schools have found evidence of teacher racism.

In the UK African-Caribbean pupils have been subjected to the processes of labelling and stereotyping by the school. Much higher proportions of African-Caribbean boys than other ethnic groups are excluded from schools. While there may initially have been bad behaviour in some boys in this group, this can create an expectation in teachers of poor behaviour from all such boys and lead to a self-fulfilling prophecy. The boys, often from working-class backgrounds, may not be doing well in school, and their extrovert behaviour, which might be accepted in other contexts, leads to their being labelled troublemakers. It can be very difficult to reject labels such as these as they can become what interpretivists call a master status. This means they pinpoint the single most important thing about the person in the eyes of others, which is then internalised by the person so labelled (who comes to believe that the label describes them correctly). Once labelled a troublemaker, a boy may be under suspicion when something goes wrong at school even if he is completely innocent.

The Chinese pupils studied by Archer found that teachers had high expectations of them. This was not necessarily good, because it meant that they received little praise or effort for doing well (because their success was only to be expected) and also when they did have difficulties teachers gave them little help because they assumed the Chinese pupils could help themselves.

KEY TERM

Single-sex schools: schools that take either only boys or only girls.

Gender

Schools often treat boys and girls differently and some schools are **single sex**. The organisation of schools can reinforce the importance and significance of gender roles. For example, registers may be separated into boys and girls, seating plans may be based on gender. Girls may take different subjects or play different sports from boys. Teachers have assumptions about the two sexes and may give boys and girls different kinds of attention. Girls are praised for their appearance, good behaviour and neatness of work but these features are valued less highly than what is seen as individuality or creativity in boys.

Boys are more likely to be seen by schools as problems. Less than one in five of the pupils excluded from British schools each year are girls. Almost all concerns and policies to deal with excluded pupils focus on boys. This does not mean, of course, that girls do not have problems, but rather that girls are less likely to act out their problems in a way that demands attention.

Teaching is a female-dominated profession in many countries. The senior levels in teaching and in education are, however, still male dominated. Although most secondary school teachers in the UK are women, most secondary school head teachers are men. Even in primary schools, which tend to have even higher proportions of female teachers, half the head teachers are male and women who are head teachers are more likely than men to be in infant schools or smaller schools. The result is that boys have few role models among teachers, but those that they do have are likely to be senior staff.

While girls have more role models, in many schools women teachers are noticeably missing from some subject areas, especially science and technology. One outcome of this may be that girls do not believe that science and technology are subjects for them and choose other subjects when they are able to. This can be reinforced by textbooks and other resources that were published some time ago, which may not show girls and women, although newer books will avoid such sexism. The use of resources such as science equipment can also be dominated by boys. Teachers do not always challenge the physical domination of spaces by assertive boys.

Growing awareness of the ways in which racism and sexism can be present in schools has led many schools to adopt new policies, to train staff to be aware of these issues and to take positive action to ensure equal opportunities. Schools that do this, however, face the problem that these attitudes may still be present in the wider society.

ACTIVITY: *research*

If your school is co-educational, find out whether boys get into trouble more than girls, and whether the things the two sexes get punished for tend to be different. Choose your own method for this, using ideas from Unit 1. Then write a brief report outlining your main findings.

Influence of peer group and pupil sub-cultures on educational achievement

Social class

Most schools generally place a high value on things such as hard work, good behaviour and exam success. One of the effects of streaming and labelling is to divide students into those who achieve highly and who more or less conform to these aims and therefore achieve high status in the eyes of the school, and those who are labelled as failures by the school and are therefore deprived of status. In response to this, some pupils rebel against the school and develop an alternative set of values, attitudes and behaviour in opposition to the academic aims of the school. This is the **anti-school** or **counter-school sub-culture**. Anti-school sub-cultures provide a means for pupils to improve their own self-esteem by giving them status in the eyes of their peer group that has been denied them by the school. These sub-cultures often, but not always, involve boys rather than girls. They involve a **culture of masculinity**, in which the accepted ways of behaving for males, taken too far, lead to their being labelled. These sub-cultures are usually:

KEY TERMS

Anti-school sub-culture: the norms and values of a group of pupils that reject the school's values.

Culture of masculinity: norms and values that involve supposedly masculine characteristics, for example preferring sports to reading.

- hating school
- truanting
- avoiding work
- cheating when they have to do some work
- being insolent and aggressive towards teachers
- despising pupils who work hard at school
- often being openly racist and sexist
- being involved in delinquency and sometimes serious crime outside school.

TOP TIP

Some research on anti-school sub-cultures has been criticised for making the pupils come across as heroes rebelling against authority but it is clear from the books of Willis and others that they were not pleasant characters.

Members of the sub-culture generally disrupt the smooth running of the school as a way of getting back at the system and resisting a schooling that has labelled them as failures and denied them status. These are responses to the labels that have been placed on pupils by the school, and because it is working-class pupils who are labelled as failures it is working-class pupils who are more likely to belong to anti-school sub-cultures.

CASE STUDY

One of the classic studies of an anti-school sub-culture was by Paul Willis, who followed a group of working-class boys in a secondary school in England. The lads, as they were known, came to school not to learn but only to 'have a laugh', enjoying breaking the school rules and messing about in and out of lessons to annoy teachers. They knew that qualifications were not needed for the work they would do in local factories so they saw no point in learning at school. They could be violent and racist. The lads looked down on other pupils who did not rebel against the school, including a group of boys they called 'ear 'oles' (because they always listened to the teacher).

TASK

1. What are likely to be the common features of anti-school sub-cultures?
2. Why is this kind of sub-culture more common among boys than girls?

Anti-school sub-cultures and peer groups are less likely to exist among middle-class pupils or in schools with large numbers of middle-class pupils. The peer groups here may be supportive of learning and lead to **conformity** with the school's values.

KEY TERM

Social conformity: fitting in with social expectations for behaviour.

Ethnicity

Sometimes it is pupils from minority ethnic group who are labelled as failures and allocated to low streams. The same processes as for working-class pupils can also apply to minority ethnic groups, such as failing to meet the ideal pupil stereotype, being labelled and conforming to a self-fulfilling prophecy of failure.

The Chinese pupils studied by Archer were often too few in number to form a peer group in any one school. The other pupils tended to have high expectations of the Chinese pupils and saw them as geeks. This shows that labelling can be done by peers as well as teachers. A label like 'geek' suggests academic ability but the attitude behind it tends to devalue that ability, so it is a label that some pupils would try to reject – and that could be done by not working as hard and risking failure.

Tony Sewell in a book titled *Black Masculinities and Schooling* (1997) studied African-Caribbean boys in a British secondary school who were an anti-school sub-culture. He referred to them as rebels. They were so opposed to the school's rules that they smoked cannabis on school premises and were sometimes violent towards other pupils and staff. They were very aggressively masculine. Sewell saw their behaviour as partly a response to racist teachers and racism in schools. He found other African-Caribbean students responded to the school in other ways, so the rebels should not be taken to be normal or typical of African-Caribbean boys.

TOP TIP

A lot of research looks at unusual sub-cultures that attract attention through their behaviour but it can be just as interesting and rewarding to try to research normal behaviour.

Anti-school sub-cultures can be more complicated than involving a simple rejection of the school and its authority. Martin Mac an Ghaill described a group of young women from minority ethnic groups who succeeded in their education despite being strongly critical of it. The 'Black sisters' were from African-Caribbean and Asian backgrounds and were in an inner-city sixth-form college. They did not like the college or the schools they had been to before; they were critical of the way in which streaming had discriminated against them and of the teachers' failure to recognise their ability and the ethnocentric curriculum they had had to learn. However, they decided that succeeding in education was important to them and they did well, working hard at the same time as rejecting the college's authority.

TOP TIP

In popular culture boys who were hard working at school were often negatively stereotyped as geeks or nerds. For boys there is often a culture of masculinity that emphasises the importance of sports and physical activity and a laid back attitude to school work. This has begun to change and the geek stereotype has become a positive one, perhaps because pupils are now more aware that working hard can have positive outcomes.

Gender

Both studies by Sewell and Mac an Ghaill outlined above are about gender as well as ethnic differences. Girls' peer groups are more likely than those of boys to be in tune with the school and with learning, and girls often support each other in their studies. It is also thought that the time that girls spend socialising and talking with their friends may be more helpful to their studies than the way boys spend their time playing sports or computer games, because girls develop their language skills more in their activities.

One study of girls' peer groups in British schools was done by Valerie Hey. She found that cliques (tight, closed friendship groups) tended to form among girls from the same class background, based on a core of best friends, with other girls moving in and out of favour. Working-class girls used their attractiveness to manipulate boys and male teachers, by wearing make-up (even against school rules) and acting in very feminine ways. They resisted school by various methods, including truanting. In some ways these girls misbehaved as much as boys but the ways in which they did this were less visible and less confrontational than those adopted by the boys.

Valerie Hey

A recent development in the UK, according to research by Carolyn Jackson, is that more girls in British secondary schools are behaving in ways previously associated with boys, such as fighting, swearing and being aggressive. This involves only a minority of girls but it seems that working hard has become seen by some girls as uncool, as it has often been for boys. Jackson suggested that being seen not to work was a way of protecting from the effects of failure. If pupils did not do well, they could always claim that they could have done well had they tried, so it was better not to try. This might be the result of greater pressure on both boys and girls to do well.

TEST YOURSELF

1 How do peer groups affect educational achievement?
2 What are the arguments for and against streaming and setting in schools?

Measuring intelligence

This section discusses the impact of measuring intelligence and selection on educational achievement.

It can be argued that some people are simply more intelligent than others and that this explains how well people do in school. This would have to mean that middle-class children were more intelligent than working-class children, since their school achievements are higher. If this were true schools would not make much difference. This view is not accepted by sociologists, who say that the patterns of underachievement by social class, ethnicity and gender must be due to a large extent to material and cultural factors both in and out of school.

It is likely that intelligence is partly inborn (innate) but that how it develops depends on the child's environment. For a young child this would involve stimuli such as toys to play with, interaction with parents and other adults, their diet, the family home and so on. Intelligence develops rather than being fixed. In practice, it is impossible to separate the innate from the environmental influences. There are also probably different kinds of intelligence. We know that someone who is good at mathematics, for example, is not necessarily as good at learning languages. Gardner has suggested that there are multiple intelligences. What we usually call intelligence, which involves mainly verbal and logical reasoning, is just one form of intelligence, though it is the form that is most valued and tested in the education system. There is also, for example, emotional intelligence, involving the ability to empathise with others and to work cooperatively.

KEY TERM

IQ tests: intelligence quotient tests involve answering questions that are then used to work out a score which supposedly indicates how intelligent the person is.

Intelligence is measured by intelligence quotient (**IQ**) **tests**. These have been used by schools as a way of selecting pupils. Pupils who get high scores are deemed to be intelligent. IQ tests have shown there is a pattern of results between different groups; for example, middle-class people tend to score higher than working-class people. Most controversially, IQ has sometimes been linked to racial and ethnic differences, with some researchers claiming that there is a link between IQ and ethnicity so that, for example, African-Americans have lower scores than White Americans. There are, however, problems with IQ tests that mean these claims should be questioned:

- If intelligence depends partly on environment, then higher scores may indicate a very positive environment in early childhood rather than innate ability, while lower scores may suggest a less stimulating environment.
- IQ tests are based on a fairly narrow range of reasoning skills and exclude other types of intelligence.
- IQ tests are written by people who inevitably build into the tests their own assumptions drawn from their culture; those from other cultures will find the test more difficult.
- IQ scores are taken at one moment in time but intelligence develops so the scores should not be taken as predicting future achievement (this would rule out their use in selection for schools).
- Performance in IQ tests can be affected by factors such as feeling nervous or ill.

Intelligence tests

- Performance in IQ tests improves with practice. Parents whose children are going to take tests for school selection will want them to practise so as to improve. This raises the question of whether IQ tests actually measure intelligence or just the skill of doing well in tests like this.
- Some people with low scores go on to do well in their education and career, while those with high scores do not always succeed in later life.

The roles of the official curriculum and the hidden curriculum

Official curriculum

KEY TERM

Official curriculum: the subjects and lessons and their content.

The **official curriculum** consists of the subjects taught and their content. In most countries the first years of primary education concentrate on reading, writing and mathematics, with an introduction to some other subjects. At secondary level pupils study a wider range of subjects, often taught by a teacher specialising in that subject and then, if they continue to post-compulsory education, they study only a few subjects, often choosing between arts and science subjects. At university level it is normal to study only one, or possibly two, subjects.

Many countries have a national curriculum in which the subjects to be taught and their content are decided by the government. This means that all the pupils of a certain age are taught the same things in different schools. There can then be national tests taken by all pupils of that age, and the results can be used to see how well schools are doing. This has been important in countries such as the UK, where the government has tried to make it possible for parents to choose between schools. Test differences between schools are important information that parents would like to have when choosing a school.

England, Wales and Northern Ireland have had a national curriculum since 1988. It sets out not only the subjects to be taught and their content but also the standards pupils are expected to achieve. English, mathematics and science are the three core subjects and there are other subjects that all pupils are expected to study. Academies and private schools do not have to keep to the national curriculum, so as more schools become academies the national curriculum will be compulsory for fewer pupils.

Having a national curriculum allows a government to decide what subjects and skills it wants for its future citizens and to assess how both pupils and schools are doing using a national testing system. The way that lessons are taught in schools assumes that knowledge can be taught in chunks labelled history, science and so on. These divisions are social constructions; that is, they are not natural but are the result of decisions made by people about how to divide up knowledge. This way of organising education may prevent pupils from understanding the many ways in which different areas of knowledge are connected and overlap. Interesting and important areas of knowledge fall into the gaps between subjects and are neglected in schools.

Hidden curriculum

All pupils know the official curriculum; it is the timetable of the lessons that they follow. But the experience of going to school is also a form of education; pupils learn norms, values, beliefs and attitudes through their school experiences. This is the hidden curriculum.

Part of the hidden curriculum is the physical structure and organisation of the school. Schools are physically separate from the home and from places of work.

Classrooms are usually set out so that the teacher is at the front, with all the pupils seated, often in rows, so they can see the teacher and the teacher in turn can see them all. This reinforces the message that the teacher is in control and the centre of attention. The ways that teachers interact with pupils and the assumptions they make about them are also part of the hidden curriculum. Schools are also hierarchies and pupils learn their place in this hierarchy and the norms that go with the pupil role.

Other features of the hidden curriculum include:

- competitive sports and testing individuals, giving the message that doing better than others is more important than cooperating with them
- the importance of punctuality by being on time for lessons, meaning that your time is not your own
- school rules and having to concentrate on school work, teaching that you have to do what you are told by those in authority, even if you do not agree.

Is the importance of doing better than others part of the hidden curriculum?

Functionalist, Marxist and feminist sociologists all use the idea of the hidden curriculum, but they have different ideas about the main values and attitudes that are conveyed and how these should be interpreted. For functionalists the hidden curriculum gives skills and attitudes essential both for the smooth running of society and for the individual's future; it helps education fulfil its functions.

For Marxists the hidden curriculum is about social control – how the working class is controlled by the ruling class through ideology. Through the hidden curriculum, working-class children learn not to have high expectations of work or of life and learn to expect to be told what to do, to have their opinions ignored and to be bored a lot of the time. They become passive and conformist. They are likely to accept the message that they have failed in school through their own fault, when in fact the system has been designed to ensure that they – or at least most of them – fail. Schools do give them access to knowledge, but the division of the curriculum into subjects makes it harder for pupils to gain understanding, especially of the way capitalist societies work. The most important knowledge is made available only to those who stay in education after the age of 16 (and who are likely to be middle class and so to have a stake in the system). The hidden curriculum in a top public school is very different. Here higher-class children learn to expect to have a high-status occupation in which they will tell others what to do.

Feminists see the hidden curriculum as conveying messages about gender and gender roles. For example, boys and girls may have different uniforms, take different subjects and be treated differently by teachers. This encourages both boys and girls to conform to the traditional gender stereotypes.

TOP TIP

The basic skills taught in the official curriculum (reading, writing and arithmetic) are sometimes called the three Rs. Jackson suggested there are three Rs in the hidden curriculum too – rules, routines and regulations.

KEY TERM

Vocationalism: vocational education prepares people for work or trains them for particular jobs or careers.

Vocationalism

Vocationalism or vocational education is education in which you are prepared for a particular trade, craft or profession. Most schooling is general academic schooling, and most of the students who succeed at school go on to higher education and higher qualifications such as degrees, and afterwards look for work. Vocational education gives people another route into work. In secondary education and above, courses may be available that lead to careers in, for example, car vehicle maintenance or in health care.

In the UK vocational education has always had a lower status than academic education. It is seen as better to take A levels and go to university than to take vocational training, and those who do vocational training are sometimes seen as having failed to do any better. Many of those who do vocational courses are from working-class backgrounds, which reinforces the divisions between the classes. Governments have tried in many ways to improve the status of vocational education by introducing new qualifications and methods of assessment. They have done this because of the needs of the economy, in an attempt to match more young people to the jobs available and to overcome the criticism from some companies and businesses that school-leavers do not have the level of skills needed for work. All secondary school pupils have some preparation for working life, including work experience.

Critics of the new vocational courses and training have argued that:

- they are ways of keeping young people who are not suitable for academic courses occupied and of avoiding counting them as being unemployed
- they have been used by some employers as a source of free or cheap labour, with young people working for little or no pay and no real job at the end
- the purpose of education should not just be to produce workers but to increase the potential of individuals to lead fulfilling and constructive lives, and for that a more rounded and wider education is needed.

ACTIVITY: *evaluation*

In what ways do social class, ethnicity and gender interact as influences on educational achievement?

TEST YOURSELF

1 What are the differences between what functionalists and feminists think are the most important aspects of the hidden curriculum?
2 How can the lower status of vocationalism be explained, and what can be done to improve its status?

Revision checklist

Make sure that you know all the key terms listed in this unit and that you understand the following:

- Education can be either formal or informal.
- Education is both an agency of socialisation and of social control.
- Functionalist views of education focus on the role of education in socialisation and in allocating roles as well as providing opportunities for social mobility.
- Marxist views of education focus on the role of education in social control and in maintaining class privilege. Marxists believe education allows only very limited social mobility.
- There are many different types of schools, including state/public and independent/private, selective and non-selective, single-sex and mixed and faith schools.
- There are differences in educational achievement between boys and girls, between different ethnic groups and between different social classes.
- These differences can be attributed to differences outside school, in cultural, material and linguistic influences from family life.
- They can also be attributed to the influence of schools, teachers and peer groups.
- Attempts to measure intelligence via IQ tests can affect achievement through labelling and allocating pupils to different schools or streams.
- There is a hidden curriculum as well as the official curriculum; most secondary schools now also have some vocational education.

Exam practice questions

How pupils do in school is influenced by both home factors, such as cultural background, and school factors. Processes in schools, such as the hidden curriculum, labelling and the presence of sub-cultures among pupils, can lead to some groups underachieving.

a What is meant by the term hidden curriculum? [2]

b Describe two ways in which the cultural background of pupils may affect their achievement in schools. [4]

c Explain how labelling by teachers may influence educational achievement. [6]

d Explain why some boys may belong to anti-school sub-cultures in schools. [8]

e To what extent do schools reproduce social inequalities? [15]

Total marks available 35

Unit 6: Crime, Deviance and Social Control

Objectives

At the end of this unit you should be able to:

- understand the difference between crime and deviance and how definitions of these vary between societies and across time
- explain the difference between informal and formal social control and the role of agencies of social control such as the media, religion, the police, courts and the penal system
- understand and describe the strengths and limitations of the ways in which crime can be measured
- explain patterns of crime by age, class, gender and ethnicity and assess explanations of these patterns
- describe policing, law enforcement and policing strategies such as targeting, surveillance and crime prevention
- describe crimes related to new technologies such as the internet
- explain ways in which crime is dealt with, including community sentencing, punishment, prison, rehabilitation and deterrents
- assess sociological explanations of deviant and criminal behaviour
- explain the role of law enforcement agencies and the media in defining crime and deviance
- explain the development of sub-cultures and how these link to crime and deviance, with particular reference to youth.

Introduction

All societies and cultures set expectations and rules for the behaviour of their members. Behaviour has to be controlled as part of living with people; we cannot just do whatever we like. But there are many occasions and situations when these expectations and rules are broken and the social group may then punish the rule breakers. Sociologists of crime and deviance are interested in how rules and laws are made and how they are kept or broken; in who makes the laws, who breaks them and who decides what happens as a result.

Modern industrial societies have many laws. They have police forces and a legal system of courts and judges, and a series of punishments, including prison, awaits lawbreakers. Governments and the media express concern about rising crime rates. For sociologists, it is interesting that most people break laws at some time yet most are not labelled criminal. There are also very clear patterns as to which types of people are most likely to be labelled criminal and also which are most likely to be victims of crime. This section explores some of the research and discussion about crime, deviance and social control.

What are crime, deviance and social control?

The difference between crime and deviance

Deviance refers to any act that does not follow the norms and expectations of the social group. **Crime** involves acts that break a law set by the government or rulers. **Deviance** is a wider category of behaviour than crime because it includes acts that do not involve breaking a law.

Deviance includes acts that are positive and may be **rewarded** (positively sanctioned). For example, an act of heroism may be rewarded with a medal. Some deviance is not sanctioned; for example, eccentric behaviour may be tolerated. Most sociologists use the term deviance for behaviour that is negatively sanctioned. Marshall Clinard said deviance should be used to refer to 'those situations in which behavior is in a disapproved direction and of a sufficient degree to exceed the tolerance of the community'. The most obvious form of deviance is therefore crime. However, sociologists of deviance have often studied deviance that is not necessarily criminal, such as suicide and mental illness.

Deviance and crime are relative, that is, what is considered to be deviant or criminal varies from time to time and place to place. They go against the **dominant values** of the society. Actions can be deviant only in terms of the standards of a particular society or in a particular time in its history. No acts are deviant by their nature. Even killing someone is not always considered a crime, for example it is not a crime for soldiers to kill enemy soldiers in wartime. There have been arguments as to whether incest and cannibalism are always deviant, so that all societies have punished them. However, there seem to have been a small number of occasions when in particular societies even these have been allowed or expected.

In sociology, most early research and theory was about crime but from the 1960s onwards there was a greater interest in deviance, especially in some deviant sub-cultures. Sociologists were often sympathetic to the deviant sub-cultures they studied and showed how this behaviour was labelled deviant rather than assuming that it actually was either deviant or wrong.

KEY TERMS

Crime: acts that break formal written laws.

Deviance: behaviour that breaks (or violates) the norms or values of a group.

Rewards: positive benefits received for an act (also called positive sanctions).

Dominant values: beliefs that form a basis for action and are held by most people or by those with the power to force their values on others.

TOP TIP

The words deviance and deviancy are used interchangeably. There is no difference in their meaning. Be sure, however, not to confuse crime, deviance and delinquency.

Formal and informal social control

This section discusses formal and informal social control including agencies of social control such as the media, religion, the police, the courts and the penal system.

Social control can be informal, through using various techniques of persuasion by family, friends and colleagues, or it can be imposed more formally by a wide range of institutions such as social work departments, medical authorities and the police. Some groups feel the force of social control more than others, especially young people.

Informal social control includes comments, ridicule, sarcasm and disapproving looks as **sanctions** and words of praise as rewards. It also includes the internalisation by people of norms, so that people control their own behaviour and conform even when they are alone. **Formal social control** is enforced by government or its agencies, such as the police and courts, or by people in positions of authority, such as teachers in enforcing school rules. These agencies can impose punishments. They can often use both formal and informal methods of controlling behaviour; for example, schools control the behaviour of pupils formally through rules with punishments such as detentions for breaking them but also through informal social control.

The agencies of socialisation (see Unit 2) also act as **agencies of social control**. These include:

- The media: reporting criminal behaviour and court cases in the newspapers or on television informs people about behaviour that will be punished and often reinforces shared social feelings about what is right and wrong behaviour. Much of the content of the media is about crime and deviance. The role of the media is explored later in this unit.
- Religion: religions have rules about behaviour for their followers. For example, in Christianity the Ten Commandments forbid certain actions. Some of these may become part of the law in countries where Christianity is dominant and in other countries help to shape a general set of values on which laws are based.

KEY TERMS

Informal social control: ways in which people get others to conform to norms, for example by ridiculing them or with looks of disapproval.

Sanctions: penalties imposed for not conforming to norms and values.

Formal social control: ways in which a government or its agencies, such as the police and the law courts, get people to conform to laws.

Agencies of social control: organisations, institutions and groups that guide or coerce people into conforming to norms.

Police in riot gear

KEY TERM

Policing: the ways in which the police carry out their work such as investigating crimes and arresting offenders.

There are also agencies of social control that deal with criminal acts. These include:

- the **police**, who are responsible for investigating criminal acts and catching offenders

- the law courts that hear charges brought against people, decide on their guilt or innocence and impose punishments
- the **penal system**, including **prisons** and other institutions, that are responsible for overseeing the punishment that has been imposed by the law courts.

KEY TERMS

Penal system: the formal organisation of punishments for crime in a society.

Prison: a place for physically confining offenders, depriving them of their freedom.

A prison cell – part of the penal system

KEY TERM

Conformity: matching attitudes and behaviour to those of the group.

Today, informal and formal social control together ensure that most people conform to social expectations most of the time. The extent of **conformity** today would shock someone from a few hundred years ago. In *Visions of Social Control* (1985) Stanley Cohen identifies several ways in which the nature of social control has changed over the last 200 years:

- The state is increasingly involved in social control. We now have institutions and systems such as police forces to deal with criminals and other deviants. Recently the state has begun to hand over control to private organisations and this has led to private prisons and companies with their own security guards rather than relying on the police.
- We have developed detailed classification systems for criminals and deviants with explanations of their behaviour, and we use these to decide what to do with them.
- Deviants are increasingly segregated. Deviants have been taken out of the community and put in institutions such as prisons. In earlier times deviants were often punished physically and then allowed to return to the community.
- There has been a shift in the type of punishment deviants are given, moving away from inflicting pain on them in public towards greater control of their mind to try to prevent people reoffending.

KEY TERM

Surveillance: monitoring individuals and groups by governments or others, collecting information with the intention of preventing crime.

- Families, schools and local communities are increasingly being expected to help enforce conformity.

Cohen points to the growth of video **surveillance** and discussed how public spaces have been replaced by private ones (high streets by arcades and malls, parks by theme parks) where people are often watched over more than they would have been in the past. This can be presented as being for public safety and in the interests of people but it also has the effect of closely monitoring behaviour.

TEST YOURSELF

1. Identify how social control is imposed, both formally and informally, in your school or college.
2. In what ways can religions act as agents of social control?

ACTIVITY: *research*

Find out how attitudes towards one or more of the following are different in different societies. Are they considered deviant or criminal, or neither and what sanctions, if any, are imposed:

- the use of cannabis (marijuana)
- drinking alcohol
- attempting to commit suicide.

What are the patterns of crime?

This section deals with the ways of measuring crime and their strengths and limitations. They include official statistics, self-report studies and victim surveys.

Official statistics

KEY TERM

Official crime statistics: official figures of the number of crimes and offenders.

One of the main sources of information about crime is **official statistics**. These are often taken at face value and assumptions are made from them about the extent of crime and the characteristics of offenders. The statistics are, however, socially constructed and need to be treated with caution. Interpretivists argue that they tell us more about the decisions made by those who compile them than about the actual extent of criminal activity.

The main sets of official statistics on crime are usually:

- police counts of the total numbers of different types of offences
- court records of the total numbers of convictions for different offences and records of the characteristics of offenders such as their age, gender and ethnic group, and also their other convictions, if any
- the Home Office statistics in the UK, published each year, compiled from figures submitted by all police forces.

KEY TERM

Dark figure: the unknown number of crimes not included in official statistics.

Many crimes do not appear in these figures. The police statistics are the tip of the iceberg. Unreported and unrecorded crimes are known as the **dark figure** of crime. However, the official statistics are often seen as reflecting reality and influence governments, the police and others in deciding how to deal with crime.

Sociologists see the police statistics as a social construct and have used two techniques to try to get the full picture:

KEY TERM

Self-report studies: research that asks people what crimes or deviant acts they have committed.

1 **Self-report studies**. These are confidential questionnaires or interviews asking respondents whether they have committed listed criminal acts. People may, in research that is anonymous and confidential, reveal crimes that are unknown to the police. While official statistics show that most crime is committed by men and by working-class people, self-report studies reveal that significant numbers of crimes are committed by women and by middle-class people. This calls into question the implication that theories based on the official statistics (for example, those assuming that most crime is committed by working-class people) are true.

However, the data in self-report studies can also be questioned:

- Validity: how accurate are the responses? Respondents may exaggerate to impress their peers or the researcher or there may be reasons why different types of people admit or do not admit to crimes. Researchers cannot be sure how many and which responses are valid.
- Relevance: some self-report studies have asked about relatively trivial offences, such as travelling on public transport without paying, and can be seen as a test of honesty rather than criminality. If, for example, women are admitting mainly to these lesser offences, the view from police statistics that most serious crime is committed by men may still be true. Questions on trivial offences are included because without them there would be very few useful answers from most respondents.
- Representativeness: many self-report studies have been of adolescents in school, so whole categories of crime such as **white-collar crime** are ignored.

TOP TIP

Validity and representativeness are key concepts in evaluating research methods. Look again at the explanations of these terms in Unit 1.

2 Victimisation studies. These ask a sample of people what crimes they have been victims of, usually over the previous year. Respondents are likely to be more willing to report crimes they have been victims of than those they have committed themselves, as in self-report studies. **Victim surveys** uncover unreported crimes and can show new patterns. A good example of this is the British Crime Survey, which has found there is massive underreporting of many crimes and revealed, for example, that the group thought to be the main offenders – young working-class men in inner cities – are also the most likely to be the victims of crime. Victim surveys have these problems:

KEY TERMS

White-collar crime: non-violent crime committed by middle-class people for financial gain, such as fraud, embezzlement, bribery and identity theft.

Victim surveys: research that asks people what crimes they have been victims of.

- They cannot cover all types of crime. For example, they do not cover victimless crimes, such as drug use or crimes against organisations or businesses. They also do not usually cover crimes against children, as children are not often respondents in these surveys, although it is thought that children are at high risk of being victims of some types of offences.
- It is thought that some types of crimes, such as sexual offences, are still underreported.
- Victim surveys rely on the memories of respondents, which may be faulty; for example, they may have forgotten whether an offence occurred in the past year.

ACTIVITY: *data interpretation*

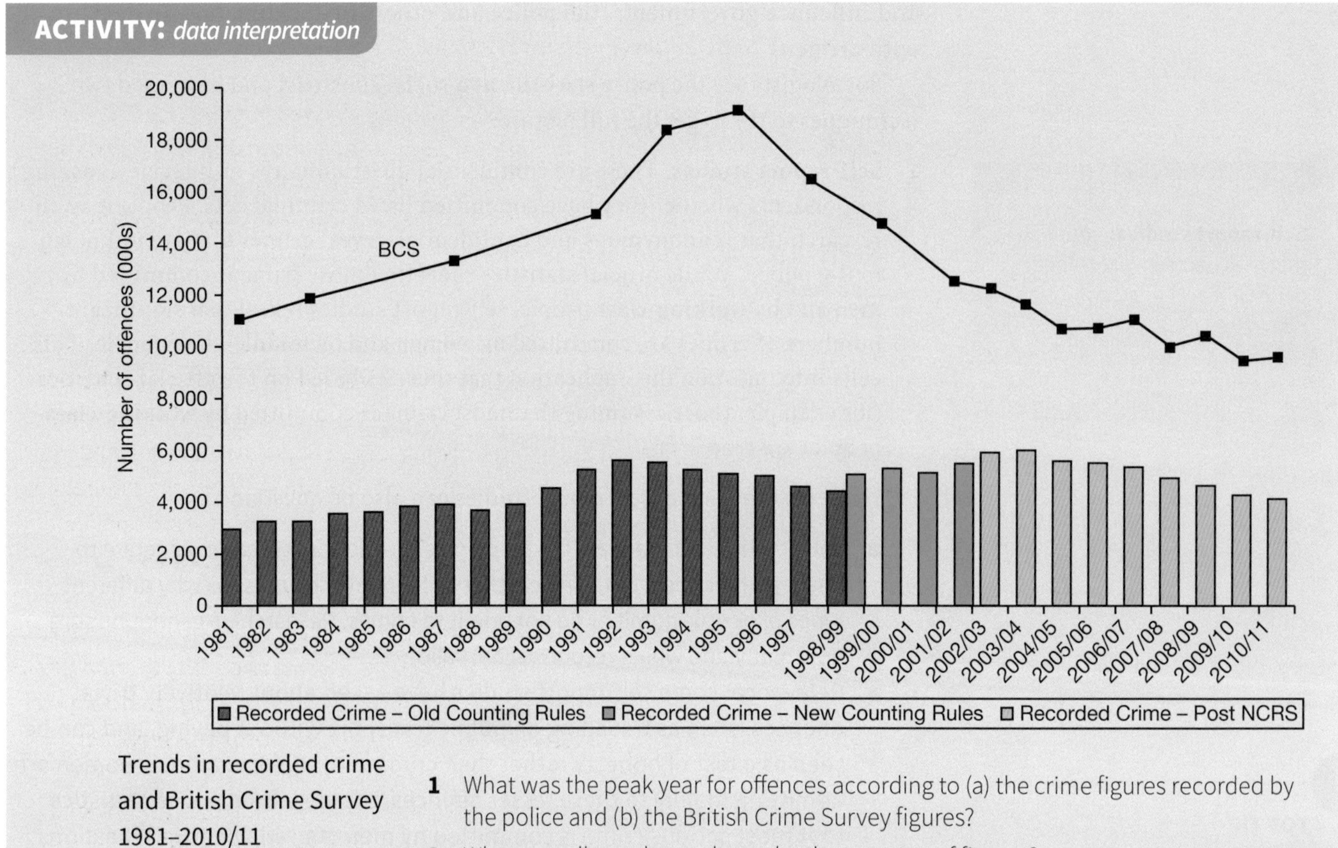

Trends in recorded crime and British Crime Survey 1981–2010/11

1. What was the peak year for offences according to (a) the crime figures recorded by the police and (b) the British Crime Survey figures?
2. What overall trends are shown by the two sets of figures?

The official police statistics have been shown to under record crime but to different extents for different crimes and types of offenders. There are several reasons for this:

1. Most crimes that reach the statistics are reported to the police either by the victim or by a witness. Few crimes are uncovered by the police. These are some of the factors that influence whether or not victims and witnesses report crimes to the police:

   - People do not report crimes they regard as trivial or when they do not believe the police can do anything to help.
   - Victims may report crimes if it will benefit them. For example, the theft of an insured item may be reported to the police as the insurance company may require this but if there is no realistic chance of the stolen goods being recovered the victim may decide there is no point reporting the theft.
   - Some crimes are seen as private matters between individuals in which the police should not be involved.
   - Victims may not want to report a crime because they may not want the offender to be punished or they may be too embarrassed to report it.
   - Witnesses may not report a crime as they may not want to get involved in, for example, giving a statement to the police or appearing in court.
   - Victims and witnesses may be threatened with reprisal by the criminal if they report the offence to the police.
   - Some communities distrust the police and may be reluctant to have any contact with them.

KEY TERM

Corporate crime: crime committed by corporations or organisations, usually in pursuit of profit for the corporation rather than the benefit of individuals.

2 Invisible crime. Some white-collar crimes (crimes related to work) and **corporate crimes** are unlikely to come to the attention of the police. For example, there are some areas of work where fraud and theft are normal. These are often 'fiddles' of which the victims may be unaware, such as being charged for a service that has not been provided. Credit card frauds, even those involving large sums of money, are usually dealt with by the credit card company rather than the police. A lot of shoplifting is not detected and even when it is the shop or store may not involve the police. The companies that own the shops will have planned for a certain amount of loss of stock or wastage.

The police play a crucial role in deciding which acts are defined as illegal and which complaints should be recorded as a crime. The police have discretion on whether to arrest someone and what to charge an offender with. They have ideas of where trouble is likely to occur and deploy their resources in these places accordingly, so they are more likely to be aware of offences in these areas. There are differences between the different police forces depending on the priorities of senior police officers. For example, some are stricter on drugs and prostitution and when they 'crack down' on these they may uncover offences that would otherwise be unrecorded. Police forces are often under pressure to achieve targets and to clear up a high proportion of crimes. Some use practices known as cuffing to manipulate the statistics to create a good impression. In cuffing crimes are made to disappear, as if up the police officer's sleeve, by either recording them as a false report or by downgrading their seriousness.

KEY TERM

Moral panic: exaggerated social reaction to deviance, creating a demand for action against it.

The recording of crime is also shaped by wider media and political pressures. For example, police forces may be under pressure to clear up particular crimes or to act on something about which there is a **moral panic**.

ACTIVITY: *data interpretation*

Comparing police and victim survey statistics

In the year ending September 2012, the police in England and Wales recorded 3.8 million crimes, a fall of 7% from the previous year. The Crime Survey for England and Wales, based on a sample of the population, estimated that there were 8.9 million offences. A survey of businesses as victims of crime produced an estimate of 9.2 million crimes, and it was also estimated that there were 0.8 million crimes against children, who were not included in the main victim survey. See: http://www.ons.gov.uk/ons/rel/crime-stats/crime-statistics/period-ending-sept-2012/index.html.

1 What do these figures suggest about the extent of the dark figure of crime?
2 Calculate the total number of crimes suggested by these figures and the percentage of these that were recorded.
3 What other crimes or types of crimes are likely to still be missing from these figures?

TEST YOURSELF

1 Court records show that most convicted offenders are young working-class men. Using information about police statistics, self-report studies and victim surveys, assess the extent to which this is likely to be an accurate reflection of offending.
2 What steps could researchers using a victim survey take to try to increase the validity of responses?

Patterns and explanations of crime by age, class, gender and ethnicity

Age

Most crimes are committed by young people. The age group most likely to commit a crime is 15 to 25 years of age. Crimes by young people attract a lot of media attention and pressure put on governments to prevent crimes by young people is increasing.

KEY TERM

Juvenile delinquency: deviant acts by young people that would be treated as crimes if they were older.

Juvenile delinquency refers to people under the age of majority (18 years old in the UK) who commit offences that would have led to criminal charges in an adult court if they were older. Most countries have separate systems, such as juvenile courts and juvenile detention centres to deal with juvenile delinquents. This is to try to prevent juveniles from coming into contact with and being influenced by older offenders, and to try to ensure that young people do not damage their futures by having criminal records. In most countries, more serious offences by juveniles are dealt with in adult courts.

Some offences by young people are status offences; that is, they are offences only because of the age of the person committing them. Examples might be smoking or drinking alcohol under age. Most offences by juveniles, though, would also be offences if they were committed by adults, such as theft and damage to property.

High proportions of young people commit offences, but despite media concern these are almost always non-violent and are not repeated. It can be argued that such limited, small-scale offending is a normal part of growing up. In modern industrial societies young people have an extended period of adolescence when they feel they are neither children nor adults. This is in contrast to traditional societies where a rite of passage is usually performed, after which the individual is accepted as an adult member of the community. There is now a drawn-out period of transition in which young people need to find their emerging adult identity and to test the freedoms they are acquiring. Anti-social and delinquent acts can be seen as a way of testing the boundaries of their new status. However, some juvenile offenders are persistent offenders and commit multiple offences. These young people are at high risk of becoming adult offenders.

Many explanations for offending by young people have been suggested. Many of the theoretical explanations discussed in the next section, such as labelling theory and strain theory, can be applied to young people. Some of the factors associated with higher rates of offending among young people are listed below:

- Boys are more likely to offend than girls. This has been explained by the greater likelihood in most cultures for males to behave in ways that demonstrate their masculinity by being aggressive and competitive. However, rates of offending by young women are increasing. The peak age for delinquency is also slightly lower in girls than in boys.
- Boys from minority ethnic groups are more likely to offend than boys from majority ethnicities. This is likely to be related to the greater chance that they live in poverty, their fewer qualifications and the lower likelihood of their being employed compared to the majority ethnic group.
- Parenting styles that are very lenient or very strict seem more likely to lead to delinquent children.
- Criminal parents or older siblings influence delinquency. Young people in single-parent families are more likely to offend. This factor is linked to the greater risk of poverty and unemployment.

CASE STUDY

Juvenile delinquency

The American sociologist William Chambliss studied two delinquent gangs in an American city. Chambliss called the working-class gang the 'roughnecks'. They were involved in fights, stole petrol from cars, shoplifted and had all been arrested at least once. The other gang were middle class. They were also involved in serious delinquency such as truancy, drinking, wild driving, petty theft and vandalism but none of them was ever arrested in the two years of Chambliss's research. Their acts were seen as harmless pranks and if the police took notice of them the 'saints' had the support of influential parents. Chambliss said that the police did not take middle-class delinquency seriously because the middle-class youths did not conform to their image of typical delinquents.

TASK

1 What differences would official statistics have shown on delinquency between working-class and middle-class youths?

2 What is the importance of police stereotyping of offenders?

ACTIVITY: *discussion*

Is a certain amount of deviance a natural part of growing up? What should society do about teenage deviance if it is a temporary phase?

Older people

Very little crime is committed by older people. High-profile cases are occasionally reported in the media but these are exceptional. Sometimes the reports are about crimes committed when the person was younger. Examples of this include people charged with war crimes at international criminal courts, who are often brought to trial many years after the events.

As modern industrial societies experience ageing populations (see Unit 4) crimes by older people may make up a growing proportion of all crimes. Japan is already experiencing more crime committed by older people. In 2007 one in seven of all crimes, including 150 murders, were committed by people aged over 65. The Japanese government has begun building special prison accommodation for elderly people. The rise in crime by older people in Japan may be linked to growing economic problems and to older people feeling less connected to their families and communities. See: http://www.telegraph.co.uk/news/worldnews/asia/japan/3213349/Japan-struggles-with-elderly-crime-wave.html 'Japan struggles with elderly crime wave'.

Social class

Working-class crime Official statistics suggest that most crimes are committed by members of the working class. This has led to research into why there should be higher rates of criminality in this social group. Working-class crime is also referred to as blue-collar crime. Some explanations for blue-collar crime are listed below:

KEY TERM

Socialisation: the process by which individuals learn the norms and values of a social group.

- They have been **socialised** into a different set of values from the middle class. It has been suggested that working-class people have a separate culture with different values that are more likely to lead its members into crime. Such values include a focus on short-term and immediate goals rather than deferred gratification.

KEY TERM

Relative deprivation: the feeling of having less than others with whom a comparison can legitimately be made.

- **Relative deprivation**: for example, members of the working class may be more likely to steal consumer goods that they see the middle class enjoying but that they cannot obtain legitimately.

Marxists argue that the official statistics are misleading because they only show what has been defined as a crime. The ruling class decides the laws and who should be punished for what crimes. Some actions of the working class are criminalised and the law is also selectively enforced so that the powerful are less likely to have their actions defined as criminal. This is in the interests of the ruling class and supports the capitalist system for these reasons:

- By punishing and blaming individuals from the subject class it deflects attention from those who are really to blame for social problems and reinforces the belief that individuals, not institutions, are responsible for social problems.
- It neutralises potential opposition. Working-class leaders who might challenge the system can be charged with offences and imprisoned.

For Marxists, the true criminals are those who benefit from a system based on exploitation. It is only to be expected that the working class will be overrepresented among criminals.

Middle-class crime Statistics show that less crime is committed by the middle class than by other classes. However, this may be because crimes committed by the middle class are less likely to be recorded. White-collar crimes are those that middle-class people are able to commit because of their occupation. The middle classes usually have more opportunities for occupational crime because their jobs may give them access to money, resources and information. For example, a person working in a finance department may have opportunities to defraud the company and to conceal the evidence of doing so. White-collar crimes are non-violent and the motive is usually financial gain.

White-collar crimes have always been less likely to be defined as crimes and to be treated differently. White-collar criminals do not fit the stereotypes of offenders. Their crimes are dealt with differently. For example, tax evasion is dealt with by Her Majesty's Revenue and Customs (HMRC) rather than the police. When HMRC decided in 2011 to crack down on tax evasion with the aim of recovering £15 billion in lost revenue, this was done not by arresting and charging people but by offering an amnesty to middle-class professionals who agreed to pay up. Working-class people who falsely claim benefits are much more likely to be tried in a court, although the amount of money involved is much smaller than in middle-class tax evasion.

White-collar crimes may not be recorded in official statistics because companies prefer to avoid the publicity of a criminal case. An employee caught stealing from the company, for example, may be dismissed without involving the police. Middle-class people may be more skilled at negotiating the criminal justice system. They understand their rights and will be well represented. If found guilty, they may be given a community sentence or treated leniently because they do not fit the stereotype of a typical offender.

Ruling-class crime Crime is defined by the ruling class. Many actions of the ruling class are therefore not defined as crimes. As with white-collar crime, those that are treated as crimes are usually treated less severely. Crimes

Former President Charles Taylor of Liberia, found guilty of war crimes and crimes against humanity

committed by those in power and authority include state crime and corporate crime.

State crimes are crimes committed by the state or its representatives. In such crimes the laws of the country are ignored or broken, or international laws or treaties are broken, such as the treaty on human rights to which the country has agreed. Some definitions also include acts by states that have not accepted these international agreements but to which all states might be expected to conform: that is, they violate widely accepted international norms. International crimes committed by states include:

- terrorism
- war crimes
- torture
- genocide.

Corporate crime is law breaking by companies and businesses. It overlaps with white-collar crime but corporate crime is usually in the interests of the company as a whole, rather than individual employees. Corporate crime includes:

- bribery and corruption
- breaking health and safety and environmental protection laws such as those controlling pollution
- false and deceptive advertising
- false accounting, such as concealing profits to avoid tax.

CASE STUDY

Breaking laws on safety at work

An analysis by sociologists Steve Tombs and David Whyte of the 2008 Health and Safety Executive figures showed that in the UK every year there are 30 000 major accidents in the workplace including deaths, amputations, blindings or maimings yet only 5 per cent of them are investigated by the police. This compares with an investigation rate of over 90 per cent for serious injuries suffered outside the workplace. Some of these cases involve negligence and some involve the deliberate flouting of health and safety laws in pursuit of profit. Moreover, the laws are not very stringent. Corporations have been able to influence the law-making process in their own interests.

TASK

1. Why are deaths and injuries in the workplace not usually counted as crimes?
2. In what ways are corporate crimes dealt with differently from blue-collar crimes?

TOP TIP

State crime is a relatively new area of study for sociologists of crime and it raises questions about definitions of crime. State crimes are often claimed to be justified and there is unlikely to be a court hearing that can decide on this.

Corporations often do not have to break the law to achieve their interests because they can get the law made to suit their interests. Groups of companies working together can make it difficult for governments to act against them. For example, tobacco companies have been able to hold up moves to control and reduce smoking.

Large multinationals can use their size to evade the law, for example by transferring money within their companies and departments to avoid taxes.

Prosecutions of corporate crimes are unusual. In cases that attract attention, one employee often takes the blame while the company is not charged. For example, a manager may be blamed for not following health and safety regulations even when these regulations have been ignored throughout the company. In the last resort companies will pay fines as a sort of tax but they can insure against this and the fines can count as a tax-deductible expense or can be passed on to customers.

Gender

Official statistics show that males are responsible for several times as many crimes as females and that there are far more male than female criminals. There are differences between the types of offences men and women commit, though these vary between societies. One crime for which numbers of offences by men and women are similar is shoplifting. It has been suggested that women engage in shoplifting because of the traditional female role of providing for the family.

Female crime Some writers have noted that the statistics do not reflect the true rate of female crime. Pollak in 1961 suggested that crimes by women such as prostitution and shoplifting were often not reported to the police and that women were very skilled at evading detection for other offences. Self-report studies show that the number of female offences is underestimated in official statistics but for serious offences the statistics are fairly accurate.

Another possibility is that women are less likely to be convicted of crimes because they receive different treatment from the police and courts. This is called the 'chivalry factor'. It is said to make juries and judges more lenient towards women by taking into consideration their responsibility for running a home or a pregnancy. However an alternative view suggests that courts are in fact harder on women because they are seen as committing offences that are against their true nature (as wives and mothers). Similar behaviour by males may be seen as wrong but not unnatural. There has been a similar debate over police attitudes, suggesting that the police may have stereotypical ideas about girls being led astray by male companions and may be more likely to caution them than bring charges against them.

Early explanations of female crime tried to explain why those few women who did commit crimes did so and why they were different from most other women. Some of these early explanations were based on biology or on dubious assumptions about differences between men and women. Talcott Parsons suggested that the answer might lie in the different patterns of socialisation between girls and boys. Both young boys and girls have a home-centred life until adolescence, but boys move towards a job-centred role outside the home while girls as adults continue a home-centred life. Delinquent girls may perhaps be reacting against their role because they lack a role model. Explanations like this tried to show why some women acted in a supposedly masculine way by commiting crimes. Later sociologists, including feminists, did not accept that the low rate of female criminality needed no explanation.

To explain the low rates of female crime, they suggested factors including those listed below.

- Girls and boys are socialised differently. Girls are not socialised into the values generally associated with delinquency such as aggressiveness.
- Females have fewer opportunities to commit crime. In many cultures they spend a lot of their time at home. Even when they are at work they are less likely than men to be in a situation to commit a serious white-collar crime.

- Females experience greater social control in public than males: public life is dominated by men who generally have greater freedom; for example, they are more often out alone at night.

The result of these factors is that women have less desire and less opportunity to engage in deviancy or crime. In the last few decades the number and proportion of crimes committed by females has been increasing. Suggested reasons for this include the following:

- The changing position of women in society. More women spend more time outside the home, for example. Work provides opportunities for occupational crime.
- Changes in gender roles and attitudes. It has become more acceptable in some modern industrial societies for females to behave in ways previously associated with males, such as drinking alcohol to excess and engaging in rowdy public behaviour.
- A link to a widespread questioning of patriarchal society. Some feminists suggest that women are rejecting male domination in work, politics and so on. They may also reject the rules that a male-dominated society imposes on them.

ACTIVITY: *discussion*

Why are girls less deviant and why do girls commit less crime than boys? Or do they commit the same amount of crime but they are better than boys at concealing their wrongdoing?

Male crime Why is it that males commit more crime than females? One argument put forward is that criminal behaviour is a way of achieving or asserting masculinity. Men show that they are men in different ways, such as working hard and supporting a family. But some may turn to crime and deviance to achieve this or to compensate for their inability to support a family. Examples of this may include:

- Adventurous, risk-taking behaviour to display masculinity may involve criminality (for example, stealing, football hooliganism).
- Asserting masculinity by showing aggression towards other men or towards women (for example, domestic violence by a man to his female partner).

Using the concept of masculinity to explain crime is discussed later in this unit.

Ethnicity

Official statistics for the UK show that some minority ethnic groups commit more crimes than would be expected, given their numbers in the population. However, as you have learnt, police statistics and self-report studies need to be handled very cautiously. Victim surveys, otherwise a useful additional source of information, are of limited value: the information is gathered from victims who often do not know the offender. The central research problem for sociologists is whether the different rates of arrest and imprisonment for ethnic groups reflect different levels of crime or the practices of the crime control agencies (such as the police, the courts and the media).

The police, especially in London, have claimed that rates of certain street crimes are much higher for young African-Caribbean people, especially males, than for the population in general. The police are aware that their arrest rate is not an objective measure and could reflect their own racism; however, the identification of victims by assailants bears out their claim. There are, however, some problems with assuming that the statistics show their greater criminality:

- Most crime is committed by young people. Ethnic minorities have a higher proportion of young people than the majority group, so more crime would be expected of them.
- The victims may be biased. They may be more likely to report crimes committed by Black people because of racial prejudice. Against this is the fact that most crime is committed within an ethnic group.
- Policing patterns affect crime statistics. If the police put resources into certain areas or target certain offences and, for example, stop and search people from some ethnic groups more often than others, then it is to be expected that more crime in these ethnic groups would be uncovered.
- Police racism can explain those offences uncovered by police rather than reported to them.

CASE STUDY

Policing the Crisis by Stuart Hall *et al.*

This research shows how moral panic over mugging led to aggressive stop and search methods by police unfamiliar with the area they were policing. As a result of their prejudiced stereotypes the police arrested large numbers of Black youths. 'Mugging' is a term the media use for street robberies with the threat or use of violence: it is not a legal term. The media used this term to associate it with young African-Caribbean men and news reports led to a demand by the public for the police and government to crack down hard on this supposedly new crime. In fact, there was no increase in this type of offence. The police, many of whom had been brought in to areas such as Brixton, where people of ethnic minorities lived, where they did not know or understand the community, saw all African-Caribbean people as possible offenders and the African-Caribbean residents saw the police as victimising them, motivated by racism. This research adopts a Marxist perspective and explains these events as a deliberate attempt by the state to distract people from deeper problems by focusing on a relatively minor problem that it could claim to be dealing with.

TASK

1. Explain how this research shows how a minority ethnic group can be labelled as criminal or deviant.
2. To what extent do police statistics on crime reflect the assumptions of the police about crime and who commits a crime?

ACTIVITY: *research*

Find out about the murder in 1993 of Stephen Lawrence, an A-level student in London, and the way the police responded to this murder. The government's inquiry into this murder looked at the actions of the Metropolitan Police and described it as 'institutionally racist'.

Stephen Lawrence

KEY TERM

Crime rates: statistical measures of crime.

Explanations for higher **crime rates** for minority ethnic groups:

- Marginalisation and relative deprivation. Where minority groups share the same values and aspirations as the rest of society but the normal routes to achieving these goals are blocked, such as success in education, they may turn to crime in response.
- Racism and racial discrimination. Crime may also be a response to experiencing racism, prejudice and discrimination. These may lead to disillusionment and rejection of society and its values.
- The historical context. Many minorities in modern industrial societies emigrated from countries that were once colonies of these societies. Resentment and resistance to colonial authority where the indigenous people were excluded from power and from participation in politics may continue in the original colonising country.

There is a range of possible responses to the situations in which minority ethnic groups find themselves, most of which do not involve crime. For example, an alternative reaction to experiencing racism and discrimination may be religious, by participating in an evangelical Christian church or one with roots to the person's country of origin.

Much of the research in the UK and USA has been on African-Caribbean and African-American minorities. Some other minority groups attract less attention because they are, or appear to be, more law abiding. Some communities are relatively closed and deal with their problems, including criminal behaviour in the group, internally rather than involving the police and courts. Other minorities may have low crime rates because of their greater economic success, their stronger family and community ties or distinct cultures, sometimes based on religion, which offer alternatives to mainstream culture so that their members are less likely to feel marginalised or deprived.

Victims of crime by age, class, gender and ethnicity

The groups that are shown by official statistics to be most likely to be offenders are often also those most likely to be the victims of crimes. This applies to young people, working-class people, females and some minorities. The victim and offender often share the same group membership; for example, young working-class men are often victims of crime by other young working-class men.

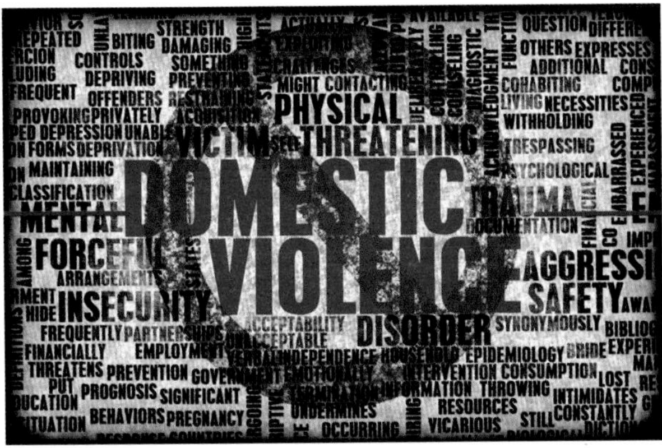

Anti domestic violence poster

Women as victims

Victim surveys show that many women are afraid of crime, especially when they are out at night, but also that their chances of being attacked are actually very slight. So some sociologists argue that women's fears of being attacked are exaggerated and arise from the media's interest in coverage of crime. However, this can lead to a self-fulfilling prophecy. If fewer women go out at night, those who do are more vulnerable because there is less chance of the attack being seen by other members of the public, and so the risk of attack increases and the media image becomes the reality. Women are more likely to be victims of the most underreported of crimes, such as sexual assault, including rape, and domestic violence.

- Rape. A common view of rape is that it happens at night in a dark alley and is committed by a stranger. In fact most rapes are committed by someone who is known to the victim and often takes place in her own home. The traditional explanation is that some men are unable to control their sexual desire and are encouraged by a woman's manners or style of dress to commit this crime. These assumptions may be made by the police and law courts dealing with rape cases. This attitude may discourage rape victims from reporting offences, feeling that they will not be treated well. Women may feel partly to blame and unsure whether the act, by a 'normal' man who is known to them, really was rape. Most men see rapists as significantly different from other men. This stereotype is contradicted when a man accused of rape seems normal and is known to the victim. This tends to make men distrust the accusation. Feminist approaches challenge the traditional view, pointing out that in a patriarchal society rape is a way in which men demonstrate power over women, reinforcing gender power differences in ways that benefit all men, even those who condemn rape.

- Domestic violence. This is underreported because victims may be afraid of further violence or they may see it as a personal matter. Alternatively, they may feel they are themselves to blame and may believe the police will not be able to help. Victims may not want to get the offender arrested (they may have loved him and his support may be needed for their children) and they may have no other means of support. Police attitudes in the past were that the family home was private and that this affected their right to intervene. Older explanations of domestic violence looked for faults in personality or sub-cultural values. More recent approaches, like those for rape, tend to focus on the power relationships in the context of a patriarchal society.

TEST YOURSELF

1. Why are young men more likely to be offenders than other groups of people?
2. Assess the reasons for the recent increases in crimes committed by females.
3. Why are some minority ethnic groups more likely than others to have high rates of criminality?

Policing and law enforcement

Police forces are organisations formed by states to enforce the law and to impose social control. They protect private property. The police are allowed to use force in some situations and they may carry weapons such as firearms. Police forces vary considerably between societies in their size and functions.

For Marxists, police forces are part of the repressive state apparatus; that is, they are used by the ruling capitalist class to protect itself against the working class. The police are often used to control protests and demonstrations and so they have an openly political role. According to Marxists, the police are the first line of defence when ideology fails to keep the working class under control. In situations where the police are unable to cope with demonstrations the army may be called in. For riot control, the police may use weapons such as batons, rubber bullets and electroshock weapons. Because more crime now transcends national borders there has been an increase in cooperation between police forces in different countries, especially in sharing information.

Because of the nature of policing, it is inevitable that the police will tend to focus on some types of crimes and offenders rather than others. Police **targeting** is when the police focus on a particular group of people, believing them to be more likely to be involved in criminal behaviour than other groups. Examples of groups that are often targeted in this way include young males, the working class and members of some minority ethnic groups. In particular, in the United Kingdom, young Afro-Caribbean men are more likely to be stopped and searched. Targeting of young Muslim men has probably also increased because of fears of terrorism by radicalised young men.

KEY TERM

Targeting: when the police focus on a particular group of people, believing them to be more likely to be involved in criminal behaviour than others.

One way in which the police can target particular groups and places is through surveillance. New technologies have led to surveillance being widespread. Sometimes surveillance is of individuals or groups who are suspect, but it can also be far more general; in modern industrial societies, everyone is under surveillance in some way.

Types of surveillance include:

- computer surveillance: by monitoring websites visited, e-mails and instant messaging
- telephone surveillance: by monitoring telephone calls (often called phone tapping)
- surveillance cameras
- aerial surveillance: for example, by helicopters, satellites or unmanned aerial devices (drones)
- identity card systems
- tracking use of credit cards or other sources of information about people
- biometric surveillance: monitoring people for behaviour or traits that may indicate their emotional state or likely behaviour
- use of social networking behaviour (Twitter, Facebook and phone calls) to track contacts, interests and connections between individuals and groups
- electronic tagging of people, animals or goods
- in the UK, police surveillance of protest groups has included police officers joining groups under false identities and becaming deeply involved in the groups' activities.

There has been a growth in interest in ways of designing out crime. This is based on the right-wing realist view that there are always some bad people in a society so it is impossible to eliminate crime. But individuals can try to greatly reduce the chance that they will be victims, and the environment can be designed so as to deter potential criminals by making it more likely that they will be caught. There has been a big growth in **crime prevention** goods available for consumers to buy so they can protect themselves, their property and their homes from crime, such as alarms and security locks for windows and doors.

KEY TERM

Crime prevention: attempts by governments to reduce crime, enforce laws and maintain criminal justice.

The design of the environment can also reduce the likelihood of crime. Designers and architects can try to minimise crime by designing buildings to ensure that entrance doors are visible, well lit and can be monitored, or planting thorny bushes outside ground-level windows. Measures to protect property and people in this way are called target hardening.

Situational crime prevention involves changing the calculation that a potential criminal makes in deciding whether or not to commit a crime. Examples include:

- Closed circuit television cameras. These may provide evidence that will help to catch offenders and, perhaps more importantly, they may also prevent an offence being committed in the first place.
- Cameras used for traffic control. Drivers are less likely to break the speed limit or drive through red traffic lights if they know that they will be identified by camera evidence.
- Control of credit card fraud through a series of calculations and checks for irregular use and other patterns. This does not prevent all fraud but it makes it hard for the thief to profit much before the fraud is detected and the card cancelled, so the effort involved in stealing the card details becomes less worthwhile.

In some cities well-off people now protect their luxury lifestyles by segregating themselves from the urban poor. They pay for private protection using security guards and others rather than relying on the police force. Those who can afford it live in gated communities with a strictly controlled access that keeps out those who do not belong. Such privileged people may rarely come into contact with people from other classes.

A sociological theory that led directly to changes in policing and policy was the broken windows theory. This was based on the observation that if there were signs in an area that no one cared, such as a broken window being left unrepaired, there would soon be other problems such as litter, graffiti and vandalism. A small incident could result in growing deviance. This led to the zero tolerance policy, in New York and elsewhere, in which the police and authorities acted against minor deviance such as begging, dropping litter and selling goods on the street without a licence. The idea was that this would give a message to criminals that more serious deviance would not be tolerated either. The policy was hailed as successful because the crime rate, including the rate for the most serious crimes, fell in the cities where zero tolerance was tried. However, the approach has been controversial:

- Homeless people were removed from the centre of New York but the underlying problem remained: these people were still homeless.
- Crime rates fell in other cities where zero tolerance policies were not brought in. The reason was probably a reduction, in New York and elsewhere, in the proportion of young men in the population.

KEY TERMS

Cybercrime: crime involving use of new technologies such as computers.

Internet crime: crime involving use of the internet.

Crime related to new technologies such as the internet

New technologies have led to new types of crime, usually referred to as computer crime or **cybercrime**. These are often the computer equivalents of crimes that existed before the new technologies; for example, new forms of fraud, scams and harassment. Some are more specific to new technologies; for example, sending spam (unsolicited bulk e-mails) is illegal in some countries. As with other crime, computer crimes can be committed by individuals, groups or organisations or by the state. Some cybercrimes involve targeting victims through their computer, such as infecting their PC with a virus. Others involve use of computers as a means of carrying out the crime. Crimes that use the internet are often referred to as **internet crime** or netcrime. Cybercrime is a wider term that covers all new forms of technology that might involve, for example, e-mails, forums, chat rooms and notice boards as well as websites and also mobile phones and other portable devices.

There are many types of cybercrime. They include:

- Spreading computer viruses and malware.
- Fraud and identity theft.
- Internet scams targeting individual users.
- Websites with obscene or offensive content, and the spread of obscene or offensive content by e-mail and mobile phone.
- Harassment by cyberstalking or cyberbullying.
- Trade in illegal drugs and other illegal goods (the internet makes it easier for buyers and sellers to contact each other).
- Cyberterrorism; in cyberterrorism the internet is used for deliberate, widespread attacks on computers or computer networks. For example, an activist group may try to hack into and disable the website of a government or a corporation. Some attacks of this kind are thought to have been carried out by governments of other countries. One possible example of this was in 2007 when a coordinated attack on Estonian government and banking websites forced them offline. This was widely thought to have been a response by the Russian government to the

Internet crime

dismantling of a Russian war memorial in the Estonian capital Tallinn, but this was never proved.

Policing cybercrime is difficult because cyberspace exists outside national boundaries. The victims of hacking or other cybercrimes may live in another country from the offender. Cybercrime is global and aspects of it require a global response. But countries do not all have the same laws and they may not agree, for example on what is offensive or obscene, and may not cooperate in developing regulations and policing cybercrime. Some countries try to control the expression of political opinions on the internet; other countries might see this as preventing free speech. The internet developed without any central coordination or control and remains today to a large extent beyond the control of governments.

An example of this is Anonymous. Anonymous is the collective name of a loose and decentralised group of hacktivists with constantly changing membership and without leaders. They see themselves as defenders of internet freedom, opposing surveillance and censorship of the internet. They have hacked government, financial and security organisation websites, for example to retaliate against attempts to crack down on sharing films and music online. File-sharing websites such as the Pirate Bay and Megaupload have been labelled pirates and condemned for infringing copyright. Anonymous breaks laws in its retaliatory attacks in defence of these 'pirates' but has also acted as an online vigilante group, tracking down, for example, child pornography on the internet. Some see Anonymous as a form of cyberterrorism, whose sometimes apparently positive actions against netcrime should be discouraged because they are taking on the role of governments. Others see them as social and political activists using their expertise for the public good.

KEY TERM

Community sentencing: punishments that involve non-custodial sentences, such as carrying out work for the community.

TEST YOURSELF

1 In what ways has the development of new technologies changed the nature of crime and deviance?

2 In what ways has surveillance increased as a result of new technologies?

Dealing with crime

This section explains how societies deal with crime through punishment, prison, **community sentencing**, rehabilitation and other **deterrents**.

In the past people who committed a crime were punished physically, often in public. Other punishments included **exile**, when the offender had to leave their home and community, and **ostracism**, when the offender was shunned by the community. Today, **judicial systems** – the system of courts, trials and judges that deal with crimes – use a wide range of punishments. Reasons for punishment include:

- Incapacitation: to prevent the offender from committing more crimes, for example by imprisoning them or banning them from an area or activity. The death penalty is the extreme form of this.
- Deterrence: to deter the offender or others from committing the offence again but making them aware of the consequences. Punishing one person can be a deterrent to others.
- **Rehabilitation**: to prevent the offenders from committing further crimes by changing their attitudes and behaviour or by giving them opportunities for education and training so that they have other ways of making a living than by crime. This is different from deterrence as it is based on changing offenders, not just stopping them from committing a crime. Recent developments in

KEY TERMS

Deterrent: when a punishment is intended to stop the offender or others from committing the offence so as to avoid the punishment.

Exile: punsihment involving the offender having to leave their home and community.

Ostracism: punishment involving being excluded from the community.

Judicial system: the system of courts that apply and interpret laws.

Rehabilitation: when the punishment involves work or education to help offenders realise they were wrong to commit the crime and to help them resume a law-abiding life.

rehabilitation include restorative justice, which involves the offender and their victim meeting and the offender paying the victim back and apologising. This has been used, for example, to show thieves the effects of their actions on families in the hope that they will feel remorse. It also allows victims to be involved in the process of dealing with the offence.

Common punishments today for crimes include:

- Imprisonment: offenders are confined to a prison and deprived of some of the freedoms that those outside prison enjoy. Prisons in modern industrial societies usually try to rehabilitate offenders; for example, offenders may have the chance to study and gain qualifications that may make it easier for them to find work and less likely to return to crime. However, many offenders who go to prison commit offences again after being released.
- Conditional sentences: the offender is not sent to prison and is allowed to live in the community but with restrictions on what they can do, where and when. For example, the offender may have to be at home between certain times each day. Electronic monitoring, in which the offender wears a 'tag', is often used to enforce this.
- Fines: for less serious offences, offenders may pay a sum of money to the court as punishment.
- Community sentences: the offender is made to do unpaid compulsory work for a set period. Often the punishment is related to the offence; for example, someone convicted of vandalism may be made to repair property.

What are the explanations of crime?

Sociological explanations

This section discusses the different **sociological explanations** of deviant and criminal behaviour. They include labelling theory, Marxist theory, socialisation (by the family and **peer groups**), lack of opportunity, relative deprivation, masculinity and **status frustration**.

> **KEY TERMS**
>
> **Sociological explanation:** attempts to account for phenomena such as crime that rely on sociological (as opposed to, for example, psychological or biological) insights.
>
> **Peer group:** a group that individuals identify with because they share characteristics such as age or status.
>
> **Status frustration:** when people are unable to achieve the socially approved goals because of their position in society.

Functionalism

Functionalists always look for functions and they see crime as having a function. A limited amount of crime is seen as socially necessary, inevitable and beneficial. There cannot be societies without crime. Durkheim imagined a society of saints in which, he said, very minor lapses in behaviour would be punished. Too much crime, however, is dysfunctional and can bring about social collapse.

For functionalists, society is based on shared values and beliefs; there is agreement about what is right and wrong and people act accordingly. Laws make clear to everyone where the boundaries of behaviour lie and the punishment of crimes reinforces this. People can also express their opinions about a crime to further reinforce these boundaries (for example, through condemnation in the media and in conversations). Sometimes values change and this shows that a change in the law is needed. Criminals therefore perform a useful function in helping the law reflect the shared values of society, reinforcing the boundaries of behaviour and allowing for changes in the law to prevent a dysfunctional mismatch between values and laws.

People follow their own interests when they can but they are prevented by the law and, even stronger, by the collective conscience, the set of shared norms and values. The collective conscience can be weakened in periods of change and stress so that people no longer feel integrated into society. Durkheim was concerned about the effects of industrialisation and urbanisation and whether the collective

KEY TERM

Anomie: when the social bonds and shared value system between a society and individuals are broken, so people do not respect these social values and feel they are outside society.

conscience might be weakened through this, leading to disorder. Durkheim called situations in which the collective conscience no longer held **anomie**.

Merton's theory of deviant behaviour

The ideas of Durkheim and early functionalists were developed further by the American sociologist Robert K. Merton. He also uses the concept of anomie but uses it to refer particularly to a disjunction between goals and means, between what societies encourage people to want and how far they allow them to achieve this. In the 1930s in the USA there was a great emphasis on the American Dream, which mainly meant achieving material success and becoming prosperous through hard work and study, which, it was believed, would also bring happiness. All Americans accepted this as a goal but not all were equally able to achieve it. Those from wealthier backgrounds were more likely to be able to achieve it, while for most Americans the goal was unattainable however hard they studied and worked. Some turned to socially unacceptable ways of getting money. The goals thus actually promoted deviant behaviour. Merton suggested there was a range of possible responses to anomie. Conformists continued to work hard and believed (wrongly) that they could achieve the goals. Innovators found new ways, most of them considered to be deviant, to achieve the goals. Ritualists carried on working hard but knew they could not achieve them. Retreatists rejected both the goals and the means, and were resigned to failure. Rebels adopted both new goals and new ways to achieve them.

Robert K. Merton

Attitude to goals	Attitude to means		
	Accept	Reject	Accept/reject
Accept	Conformity	Innovation	–
Reject	Ritualism	Retreatism	–
Accept/reject	–	–	Rebellion

Table 6.1: Merton's theory of deviant behaviour: modes of adaptation

Merton therefore introduced the idea that people choose different patterns of deviant behaviour. Much working-class crime could be explained by the difficulty this group experienced in achieving the goal of success through legitimate means. This approach is often known as strain theory because it sees crime as the outcome of strain between what people wish to achieve and what is possible.

This theory has been criticised for assuming that everyone in a society shares the same values. It is useful for explaining crimes for material gain like theft and fraud but it cannot explain other types of offence that are not motivated by gaining wealth and property nor can it explain crimes committed by those who have achieved the goals.

Albert Cohen used the idea of status frustration to explain why some people turned to crime and delinquency. Young working-class males, in particular, feel frustrated that they face disadvantages and inequalities and they may react by becoming criminal or delinquent. Cohen saw this as a collective response by a group, unlike Merton, who focused on individuals.

ACTIVITY: *evaluation*

How useful is Merton's theory in explaining crime and deviance today? Think about the economic situation today and people's chances of achieving goals and what goals society seems to set us.

Socialisation: families and crime

Early longitudinal research suggested there was a link between poor parenting and offending. Offenders were more likely to come from poor families and single-parent families. New Right sociologists extended this thesis to argue that changes to the structure of families have contributed to a rise in crime. They contrast the family of the 1950s and before with modern families. The older type of family, they say, provided stability and moral values. Families no longer do this as well as they once did. Several changes indicate the moral fabric of society is weakening:

- Increases in cohabitation (living together without being married) have undermined the idea of marriage.
- Increases in divorce have undermined the idea of marriage as a partnership for life and created instability and uncertainty in families.
- Greater independence of women so they are no longer devoting themselves to the home and family and so the socialisation of children is less effective.
- More families without fathers so that more boys grow up without appropriate role models and may struggle to live as men are meant to, according to this view, as breadwinners.

Together these developments are claimed to have weakened the bonds that prevent people, especially young men, from offending. Alternative interpretations of the same findings see the root of the problem not as families but as poverty.

Charles Murray, an American New Right sociologist, sees the failings of modern families in the context of failing communities. In some inner city areas communities have been replaced by what he calls the underclass. The underclass, whom he calls the new rabble, are unemployed and do not want to work, preferring to live on welfare benefits or the proceeds of crime. Young people have short-term relationships so that children are routinely born outside serious relationships. Fathers do not stay with mothers to look after their children because they do not see it as their responsibility. Children grow up without sharing the wider values of society. In areas where the underclass becomes a strong presence, law-abiding working-class people are driven out so that local communities are destroyed. The result is rapidly increasing crime rates in these areas.

Murray first developed his ideas referring to Black inner city areas in the USA: the underclass is African-American. When he visited Britain in the early 1990s Murray claimed he could see an underclass emerging here, too. The New Right accounts of both families and communities involve an assumption that there was a golden age and that things are now worse. However, the golden age family was patriarchal and not at all golden for women, who were obliged to sacrifice a chance of higher education and challenging work to devote themselves to their family.

Marxist theories of crime

The Marxist view is that laws are made by the state and reflect ruling-class interests (because the ruling class controls the state and uses it to protect its interests). Laws criminalise the actions of the working class; in particular, they protect private property, which is essential to capitalism. Marxists point out that some crimes involving property are punished more severely than crimes involving violence or even death. Where functionalists see a shared set of values, Marxists see an ideology that the working class is effectively tricked into accepting, so that it is in a state of false consciousness. Marxists also argue that at least as significant as the laws passed are those that do not exist, such as laws that might limit inequalities or prevent corporations from exploiting workers and consumers. Law creation is as important as law enforcement.

TOP TIP

Marxists argue that some actions that ought to be illegal are not, such as some activities of capitalists and companies. Marxism therefore raises important questions about how we define crime.

One objection that can be made about the Marxist view that laws are made to serve the interests of the ruling class is that some laws are clearly in everyone's interests. There are even laws that give the state powers to control industry and commerce, when Marxists would expect capitalist enterprises to be allowed to make profits without being controlled. Marxists would reply that even laws that appear to be against ruling-class interests in fact favour them. The capitalist system needs a healthy, safe population of workers and consumers who are loyal to their workplace. This explains, for example, laws about health and safety at work. There may also be some concessions to radical causes as a way of preventing even greater dissent that may threaten the survival of the system. An example of this would be the concessions made by the US government to the civil rights movement in the 1960s.

More recent Marxist approaches combine the structural perspective of traditional Marxism with many of the insights of labelling theory, especially the importance of individuals' perceptions and societal reactions to perceived deviants.

KEY TERM

Urban crime: crime in cities or associated with the lifestyle people have in cities.

CASE STUDY

Urban crime – 2011 England riots

In August 2011 there were serious riots in London and in several other British cities. The crimes committed included arson, looting and destruction of homes and property. The police were deployed on a large scale to try to control the disorder. Those involved seemed to be mainly young people from all ethnic groups, broadly reflecting the make-up of inner city populations. The media and politicians tended to condemn the riots as simple criminality while others linked the riots to poverty and social exclusion, government spending cuts and corruption at the top of society that showed up in the scandal of the expenses of members of parliament and bankers' bonuses. There were also claims that media reporting encouraged more riots through copycat acts. Analysts who were more sympathetic to those involved described the events not as riots but as protests or insurrections. More than 3,000 people were arrested and many were given sentences that were thought to be harsh.

TASK

1 How might a functionalist interpret the riots?
2 How might a Marxist interpret the riots?
3 How similar were these riots to events in the Arab Spring of 2011?

KEY TERM

Material deprivation: being short of the material goods needed in a society.

Relative deprivation

Material deprivation, that is lacking resources and money, does not directly lead to someone turning to crime. Some sociologists use the idea of relative deprivation particularly for explaining crime in cities and among groups suffering disadvantages, such as members of minority ethnic groups. Relative deprivation theory claims that it is not the fact of being deprived that leads to crime. It is when individuals or groups see themselves as deprived in relation to others that they choose to compare themselves with that crime is fostered. Where others seem to be doing well there will be more resentment and more possibility of crime in the group that sees itself as deprived. This is similar to Merton's theory. A related idea is marginalisation, which is when a group does not have organisations or representatives to protect their interests, so they have no outlet for their feelings of anger other than violence and rioting. This is in contrast to, for example, workers organised in trade unions with the aim of achieving higher wages and improved conditions.

Lea and Young argued that some people turned to crime because they were marginalised and relatively deprived. They were often young men from minority groups in inner cities. The victims of their crimes were usually from the same area

Howard Becker

and community. They argued that the Marxist view of crime did not recognise that most victims of crime, as well as most offenders, were working class. Crime was a very real problem for its victims, they said, and could not be explained away as something invented by the ruling class to distract attention from other issues. They criticised earlier Marxist approaches for not recognising the reality of crime for most people and for concentrating on white-collar and corporate crime. These are harmful, they said, but the kind of crime that concerns working-class people most is more directly harmful.

Interactionist explanations: labelling theory

These explanations start with a very different assumption: that everyone at some time does things that could result in their being labelled as criminal or deviant but in fact only some people are so labelled. Interactionists do not try to explain the initial act but the responses to it that may result in a label being applied. Their concern is with how individuals become labelled as deviant and the consequences of this for the person labelled, and how certain acts come to be defined as deviant. Howard Becker argued that a deviant is a person who has been labelled deviant, and deviant behaviour is behaviour that people label as deviant. A good illustration of this is how in Cicourel's research working-class youths were more likely to be labelled than middle-class youths although the acts they committed were similar.

KEY TERMS

Labelling: the way in which acts and people are defined as deviant by the social reaction to their behaviour.

Master status: a status that overrides all others and becomes the way that individuals see themselves and are seen by others.

Deviant career: in labelling theory this term described the choices that individuals make which lead them to behave in ways labelled as deviant and they go on to follow a deviant path or career.

Deviancy amplification: when responses to deviance create further deviance.

Labelling can give someone a **master status** that overrides all others and can even lead to the reassessment of that person's life in terms of the label. An individual's self-concept is largely derived from the views others have of them so they tend to see themselves in terms of the label. This can produce a self-fulfilling prophecy. Public labelling leads to rejection, the loss of family and friends and encourages further deviance. Having been denied the ordinary means of carrying on everyday life, the labelled person's self-concept may change. They may eventually fully adopt a **deviant career** and identity and join an organised deviant group with values and beliefs that justify the group's identity and activities. This can lead to an increase in the amount of deviance; which is known as **deviancy amplification**. It is also possible for the labelled individual to try to reject the label and not see themselves in terms of the label.

Some labelling theorists make a distinction between primary and secondary deviance. Primary deviance refers to acts before they are publicly labelled that have little effect on self-concept and status. Secondary deviance develops in response to society's reaction and begins the process that can lead to deviancy amplification, a change in self-concept and a new master status.

Howard Becker also applied labelling theory to the process of rule creation. He studied the laws about marijuana use in the USA. It was legal until 1937, although opiates and alcohol had been made illegal. He said that there were three important American values that led to the disapproval of marijuana use:

- The ideal of self-control and taking responsibility for your own actions. Under the influence of drugs people are not responsible for their actions.
- The disapproval of states of ecstasy.
- The value of humanitarianism. Drugs that are addictive deprive people of free choice.

In order for these values to lead to the banning of marijuana a moral crusade has to be waged against them by moral entrepreneurs. In this case the entrepreneurs were the US Treasury's Bureau of Narcotics, who identified an area of wrongdoing and felt it should be under their jurisdiction. They lobbied for and won support from other government departments and from the public by releasing to the press stories about the supposed effects of marijuana use. There was opposition to making it illegal from seed oil manufacturers, who were eventually allowed to continue to use marijuana seed provided it was sterilised. There was no organisation of marijuana users to campaign against the law, and so marijuana use became defined as criminal in a law that was passed against it.

Labelling is most likely to have an effect when those who make the label have power over the labelled person. Judges, teachers and parents are in positions of power and as a result the labels they use can stick. Labels are also more effective when the labelled individuals do not have other sources of information about themselves so that no one can tell them that the label does not apply to them.

Labelling theory was very popular in the 1960s and remains very influential, but a number of limitations in it have been identified:

- The definition of deviance ignores the meaning that the act has for the person committing it. Some acts, such as murder, are always deviant whether or not there is a social reaction against it.
- Although Lemert says primary deviance is so common it does not need to be explained, the acts committed vary and people also know they are breaking norms and laws even if their actions are not detected.
- Labelling theory tends to imply that deviants are the victims of the labels that are applied to them but individuals can choose to be deviant regardless of whether they have been labelled or not.
- Labelling does not explain why some people are labelled and others are not, and why some activities are against the law and others are not.
- Labelling theorists have been criticised for taking the side of the labelled, and in doing so ignoring the deviance that led to the label.

Masculinity

KEY TERM

Masculinity: the attitudes and behaviour associated with being a man in a particular culture.

Feminist sociologists have drawn attention to the importance of gender differences in crime and deviance. Official statistics and other sources all suggest that males commit more crime and more serious crime than females. The idea of masculinity has been used to explain this. **Masculinity** refers to the attitudes and behaviour associated with being considered a man in a particular culture. It has been argued that the dominant form of masculinity in modern industrial societies is hegemonic masculinity. This ideal form involves, for example:

- controlling emotions (except anger); for example not crying in public
- being physically strong
- being willing to use violence to resolve problems
- being competitive.

As boys grow up they become aware through socialisation of what is expected of men in their society and they try make others see them as masculine, for example through success at sport or by showing dominance over others by bullying. Hegemonic masculinity is not possible for many or even most boys. There are alternative forms of masculinity but these have a lower status because they involve being less 'male'. Some boys may be labelled effeminate if they cannot show at least some aspects of hegemonic masculinity. The idea of hegemonic masculinity can be applied to crime and deviance because some ways of expressing it can be violent or involve breaking rules. The kind of behaviour that is expected of men can result in crime. Society seems to encourage some behaviour that it then condemns. This seems to apply particularly to teenage boys, who are trying to negotiate and create their own identities.

Girls are under equivalent pressures to acquire a feminine identity but the expected behaviour – care over appearance such as use of make-up and so on – is less likely to lead to deviance. Explanations of crime based on masculinity can be criticised for:

- assuming that all men are socialised into the same set of values that stresses hegemonic masculinity
- not recognising that some aspects of masculinity and the masculine role, such as acting with restraint and protecting the weak, are positive and do not lead to crime
- not recognising that males have choices in how they express their masculinity; for example, some will reject hegemonic masculinity.

KEY TERM

Inadequate socialisation: socialisation that fails to fully instill social norms and values and so makes individuals more likely to become deviant.

TEST YOURSELF

1 How might **inadequate socialisation** lead to crime and deviance?
2 How does Lea and Young's approach differ from Marxist theories of crime?

ACTIVITY: *evaluation*

Consider each of the explanations of crime above and assess which types of crime each is best at explaining and why you think this.

Defining crime and deviance

This section explains the role played by **law enforcement agencies** and the media in defining crime and deviance. It discusses **stereotyping**, labelling and deviancy amplification.

KEY TERMS

Law enforcement agencies: government agencies with powers to make people conform to the law in their area, such as police forces or, in the USA, the Federal Bureau of Investigation.

Stereotyping: representations of groups in popular culture or views held by individuals that assume that all members of a group have the same characteristics.

The media and law enforcement agencies

The media play an important part in shaping what we know about crime and deviance. Most people have little direct contact with crime and so they rely on the media for their knowledge. Crime in the UK, as recorded by the police and by the British Crime Survey, has been falling steadily for more than 20 years. It has continued to fall during the economic problems since 2008, although this was unexpected as crime rose in previous recessions. In spite of this fall in crime, many people think crime is rising and is a serious problem. As a result, governments do not claim credit for reducing crime and feel they cannot cut spending on the police and criminal justice system. The belief in rising crime probably comes from media reporting. Many headline news stories are about crimes. Many of those that attract the most attention in the news are unusual but the news coverage can persuade people that they are more common than they are.

Some results of this belief in rising crime include:

- putting pressure on the government to act strongly against particular types of crime, regardless of whether the benefits would justify the cost
- people changing their behaviour through fear of crime; for example, they may avoid places that are perceived as dangerous or stop going out at night
- a growing market for goods that offer protection from crimes.

One sociological explanation of the role of law enforcement agencies and the media in defining deviance is the concept of moral panic. The way that the media report some crime and deviance can result in attaching labels to a group, who then function as folk devils. A stereotype is created so that all the members of the group are assumed to have the same characteristics. The media define the group as a threat to social values and overreact, as the initial deviant behaviour is fairly minor. Media reporting in moral panics involves the following:

- Exaggeration. The behaviour of the group is reported as worse than it is, using exaggerated language; for example, a small fight is reported as if it were a pitched battle.
- Prediction. The media claim that the deviance will happen again and will be worse unless strong action is taken.
- Symbolisation. The media show how folk devils can be recognised, for example by their appearance or clothing.

KEY TERM

Stigma: a label that changes the labelled person's positive self-image into a negative one.

Folk devils are represented by the media as being totally different from 'us', the supposed majority to which readers or viewers are made to think they belong. They are **stigmatised**; that is, regarded by others as different in a negative way. Media reporting in moral panics encourages a strong response by the police and courts. This has the effect of changing the group's perception of themselves so that they increasingly act in the way they have been defined, thus actually increasing the amount of deviance. A deviancy amplification spiral can develop in which the media response leads to more deviance, which leads to a stronger media response and even greater deviance, and so on. However, after a while the media interest ceases and the moral panic ends.

Media reporting is an important aspect of moral panic but the role of the police and courts is also important. In Jock Young's study *The Drugtakers* the media started by establishing a stereotype of hippy drug takers but it was primarily the police reaction that led to greater deviance. Young found that at first using marijuana was a relatively unimportant part of the hippy **sub-culture**. The police disapproved of hippies, who had a very different lifestyle from the mainstream, but found that drug taking was the activity they could arrest hippies for. The police reaction led to the hippy group reassessing itself, creating a new self-concept by wearing their hair long and dressing in distinctive ways that made them appear even more different from mainstream society. Using marijuana became the central concern of the group and a test

KEY TERM

Sub-culture: a group of people in a culture who have sufficiently different norms and values to be seen as a separate group.

of whether people really belonged to it. The group then became small and closed, excluding outsiders (for security). Previously people had joined and left the group easily but over time doing so became more difficult. The police arrested more people for drug use and when the media reported the arrests this suggested that drug use was increasing, prompting even stronger police action and more arrests.

The term moral panic was first used by Stanley Cohen to describe the media reaction to two teenage sub-cultures in the 1960s, the mods and the rockers. Minor vandalism and fighting were reported with sensationalised headlines, as if they were threats to society. The teenagers came from similar backgrounds and had different styles of dress and taste in music but the media reported the sub-cultures as rival gangs and this became a self-fulfilling prophecy. Moral panic has since become a widely used term in both sociology and the media. In some cases when it is used, not all the elements of a moral panic described by Cohen are present.

The links between sub-cultures and crime and deviance

This section describes the development of sub-cultures and their links to deviance, with particular reference to **youth culture** and **youth sub-cultures**.

KEY TERMS

Youth culture: the ways of life of young people between childhood and adulthood.

Youth sub-culture: a distinct group within the general youth culture, such as Goths.

The idea of sub-cultures to explain some kinds of deviance can be seen first in Merton's theory, where one possible reaction to status frustration is the development of new goals. When a group shares such feelings, a new sub-culture may emerge that has values that are different from those of wider society. This idea was later applied to teenage boys in schools in which those in lower streams were looked down on and seen as failures. They would sometimes deliberately reverse the school's value system, acting in whatever ways the school disapproved of. This was useful to them in two ways:

- It created an alternative set of values through which they could gain status and respect from their peers.
- It gave them a way of hitting back at society.

The introduction of the idea of sub-cultures filled in two gaps in Merton's theory: it offered an explanation for collective deviance and it explained why much deviance was not done for economic gain.

Cloward and Ohlin suggested there was an illegitimate opportunity structure in society. This had three aspects:

- A criminal sub-culture. In some working-class communities there were successful role models for criminals and a career structure for aspiring criminals (for example, in areas where the mafia was strong), so some young men chose crime as a career.
- A conflict sub-culture. Where there was no sub-culture with role models and opportunities to be a successful criminal, so that both legal and criminal ways of achieving goals were blocked, young men might turn to violence and gang warfare among each other.
- A retreatist sub-culture. One response to double failure (failure to achieve success either legally or by crime) was to turn to drugs as an escape.

These early sub-cultural theories assumed that everyone in society shared the same goals of financial success. The next step in the development of sub-cultural explanations of crime and deviance, by Walter Miller, saw the working class as having a distinct sub-culture, the values of which could lead people into deviance. Deviance was the outcome of the normal values of the sub-culture. The values that encouraged deviance in teenage gangs were:

- accepting fate: feeling that you have little control over your life, so you need to make the most of any chances
- seeking autonomy: trying to control your own life and so resisting authority
- views on trouble: confrontations with authority and with others are normal and unavoidable
- attractions of excitement: looking for fun and enjoyment
- virtues of smartness: looking good, making a public display
- virtues of toughness: being masculine by being aggressive.

However, some research suggests that delinquents have the same values as everyone else. They disapprove of crime in general and when they are caught will justify their actions and show remorse. David Matza suggested that everyone has two sets of values: as well as the values that dominate our everyday lives, we also have hidden, subterranean values that we only indulge on certain occasions, such as at a party. There are some situations where these subterranean values of sexuality, greed and aggression are tolerated but Matza suggested that delinquents behave according to subterranean values in the wrong situations. Youth is a difficult period in which young people feel they have no control over their destiny. This weakens the bonds between them and society and can lead to delinquent acts that are attempts by individuals to exercise control over their life. Youths drift in and out of delinquency. They use techniques of neutralisation, which show that they acknowledge that what they did was wrong but that there are reasons why they should not be condemned for their actions. These include:

- denying responsibility by saying that they were not responsible because they were drunk
- denying there was a victim by claiming that this victim deserved it even if the act was wrong
- denying harm was done, for example saying the victim could easily afford to replace something that was stolen
- condemning the condemners by claiming that everyone does it, even the authority figure accusing the offender
- appealing to higher loyalties by saying that the wrongness of the act was outweighed by other factors such as the need to protect their friends.

The term sub-cultures is also applied to groups of young people with distinctive styles, for example in dress and music. Some of these have been Teddy Boys in the 1950s, mods and rockers in the 1960s and punks and skinheads in the 1970s. Youth sub-cultures are discussed on page 55, with a case study of the skinhead youth sub-culture on page 57. Since then sub-cultures have become less clearly defined and many now recreate or borrow from earlier sub-cultures. Some writers interpreted the original sub-cultures as expressions of the anger of young working-class people at a society that seemed to offer them little. Anti-social behaviour, resisting authority and delinquency were often part of these sub-cultures. Today it is harder to identify sub-cultures and there is not always a clear connection between them and deviance.

Sub-cultures

One recent sub-culture that has caused much public concern is juvenile gangs, associated with knife crime in London and other UK cities. Marginalised young people join gangs for a sense of purpose and identity. The gangs wear 'hoodies' to conceal their faces and sometimes carry knives and even guns. These may be intended for self-defence (often against members of other gangs), but having a knife is an offence. Gang members are seen as deviant and commit offences that can lead to getting a criminal record.

TEST YOURSELF

1. Explain how the police reaction to deviance can lead to even greater deviance.
2. In what ways can belonging to a sub-culture encourage deviant behaviour?

Revision checklist

Make sure that you know all the key terms listed in this unit and that you understand the following:

- Crime, deviance and delinquency are related but different concepts.
- Definitions of crime and deviance vary between societies and across time.
- Social control can be formal and informal and there are agencies of social control including the police, the courts and the penal system.
- Measurements of crime include official statistics, self-report studies and victim surveys; each of which has strengths and limitations.
- There is no accurate count of the number of crimes because statistics are socially constructed and there is always an unknown dark figure of crime.
- Official statistics suggest most crime is committed by young working-class men but some sociologists suggest crime and deviance occur in all social groups.
- White-collar, corporate and state crimes often do not appear in statistics and are dealt with differently.
- The internet and other new technologies have led to new crimes, new ways of committing crimes and problems in policing crimes.
- The main explanations of crime are functionalism, Marxism, labelling theory, inadequate socialisation, lack of opportunity, relative deprivation, masculinity and status frustration.
- Law enforcement agencies and the media define crime and deviance through stereotyping, labelling and deviancy amplification.
- Some crime and deviance is linked to sub-cultures and especially youth sub-cultures.

Exam practice questions

Official statistics do not record all the crimes that are committed, only those recorded by the police. The extent of the dark figure of crime is unknown. Sociologists have tried to estimate it using methods such as self-report studies and victim surveys. The statistics tell us not only the number of crimes but also who commits them. The typical offender, according to official statistics, is a young working-class man.

a What is meant by the term 'dark figure of crime'? [2]

b Describe two ways in which self-report studies may not give the true extent of crime. [4]

c Explain how decisions taken by the police may influence the official statistics on crime. [6]

d Explain why official statistics show that most crime is committed by young working-class men. [8]

e To what extent can criminal behaviour be explained by Marxist theories of crime? [15]

Total marks available 35

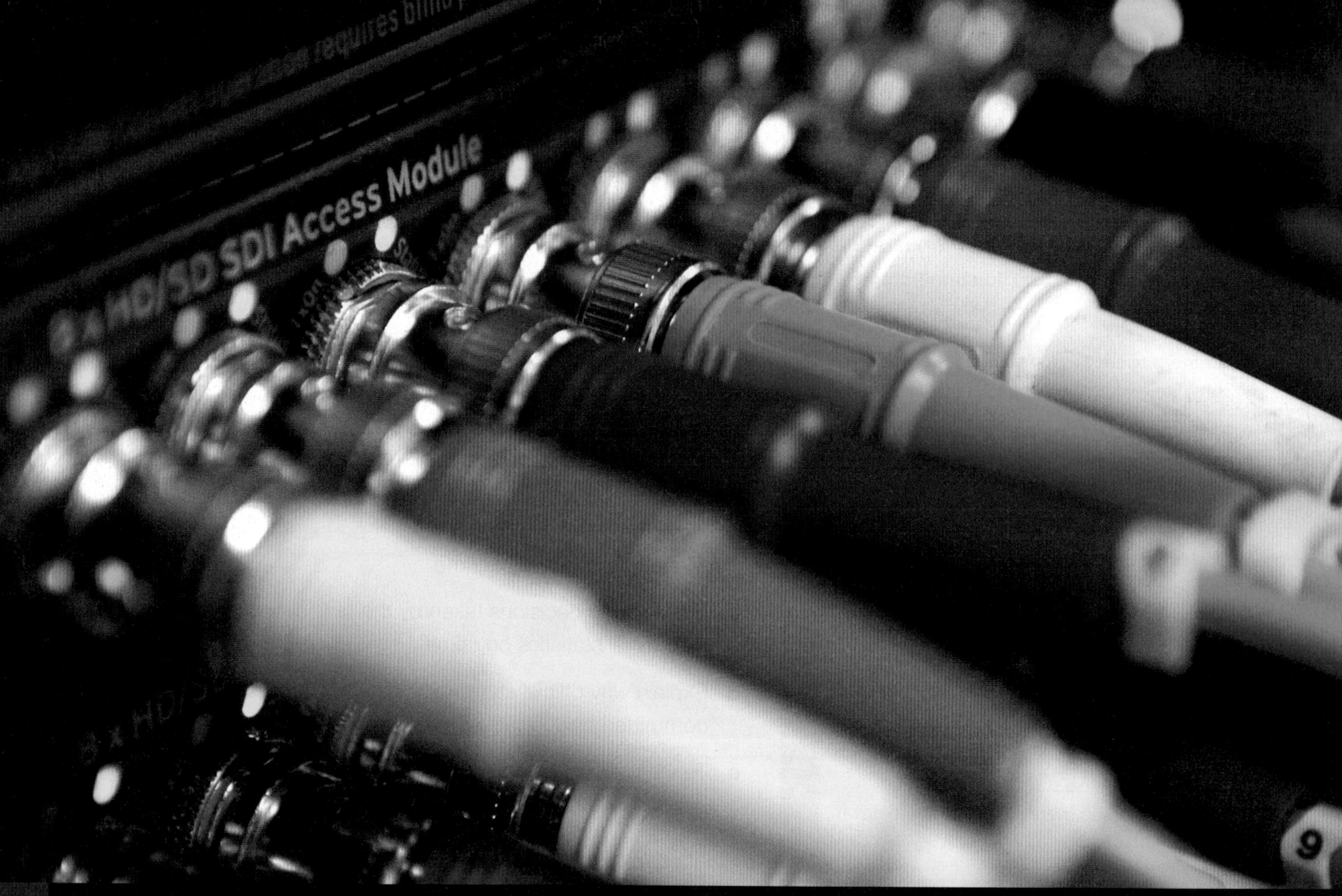

222

Unit 7: The Media

Objectives

At the end of this unit you should be able to:

- understand the various forms the media take, including differences between old and new media
- explain the role of advertising in the media
- understand the debates about ownership and control and freedom and censorship in the media
- understand Pluralist, Marxist and postmodernist perspectives on the nature and role of the media
- explain patterns of media use by gender, age, social class and ethnicity
- explain media representations of social groups and their influence on audiences
- assess the role of the traditional and new media in shaping values, attitudes and behaviour
- explain the selection and presentation of news, including agenda setting, gate-keeping and stereotyping
- assess different explanations of the influence of the media
- explain bias and distortion in the media
- explain developments in the media
- discuss the influence of media representations on the audience.

Introduction

The media are the ways in which people communicate with each other, and so they are essential to societies and cultures. As societies have become more complex, so have the media. Once children only heard stories from adults they knew personally, perhaps told round campfires by hunter gatherers in pre-industrial times. Later came books, newspapers and comics, then sound recordings and then television and film. Now, a huge range of media content is available from many different technologies. The internet may have begun a revolution in communication, as it seems to be breaking down some of the old certainties about the media. New media are more interactive, more flexible and more global. This unit considers both the older, now traditional media of newspapers, the radio and television, and also the ways in which new media are transforming both the media and the world.

KEY TERM

Media content: the content of one of the media, such as a television programme.

Who controls the media?

The forms of the media and media content

This section describes the different forms of the media and **media content**. Media content refers to the content of one of the media, for example a television programme rather than the television set or other device on which it is watched.

The media are channels of communication; the ways in which people send and receive information. Face-to-face communication using language and gestures is the most basic medium but as societies developed so people used a wider range of media. The media today include:

- newspapers
- magazines
- television
- radio
- films
- books
- advertising, such as billboards and posters
- the internet
- telephones
- social media
- recorded music.

TOP TIP

The word media is the plural of medium. So television is one medium, television and radio are media.

A newspaper is printed and distributed so it may be read by millions of people and a television station broadcasts to a wide area. **Mass communication** can be distinguished from interpersonal communication, which is one-to-one rather than one-to-many. It was once easy to be clear about what the mass media were but the distinction between mass communication and interpersonal communication is no longer straightforward. This is because some new forms of media have the potential to be both. These changes have also created the possibility of many-to-many communication, for example in chat rooms and forums on the internet, where the people who produce the content also consume it.

KEY TERM

Mass communication: communication from a single central point to a widely distributed mass audience.

The term old media is now used to describe the mass media that are a one-way channel of communication between the producer and a mass audience, such as

KEY TERMS

New media: new media technologies, usually digital, and involving greater interactivity and on-demand access.

books, newspaper, magazines and television. **New media** means the media where there is two-way (or more) communication, in which the distinction between producers and consumers is no longer clear. New media include:

- websites
- forums, chat rooms and message boards on websites
- social networking sites such as Facebook and Myspace
- instant messaging and e-mail
- Twitter
- video-sharing websites such as YouTube
- blogging.

When new forms of media have developed in the past, there have often been predictions that older media will die out. For example, it was thought that the arrival of television in most people's homes in the USA in the mid-20th century would mean the end of the film industry, as people would no longer go to the cinema. In fact, people continued to go to the cinema and films found new markets and audiences as films could be shown on television, video and DVD, and later on the internet. So it seems that old media often survive by adapting to new technologies.

Old media or **traditional media** include:

KEY TERMS

Traditional media: print and other older media such as radio and film with little, if any, interactivity.

Advertising: use of the media to persuade the audience to buy or to do something.

- Newspapers. Newspapers publish news of current events including politics, entertainment and sport, opinion, general articles of interest, editorials expressing the newspaper's opinion and diversions such as word games and **advertising**. Many newspapers are published daily but some are published at other intervals, such as weekly. They may be national, regional or local. Until recently all newspapers were printed on paper and distributed physically to readers. All newspapers now have websites. The arrival of the internet and new media has been a huge challenge for newspapers because people have become used to getting news without paying for it. Some newspaper websites now have paywalls so that only those who pay for it can access the content, but while news is available free on other websites readers will be reluctant to pay. Newspaper websites carry advertisements, just as their paper versions do but the income to the newspaper company from this may not cover costs. In the UK the number of newspapers has stayed roughly the same for many years although sales and readership have been falling. In the UK, newspapers are conventionally classified as either broadsheet or tabloid. This originally referred to the size of paper used but became associated with the content as well. Tabloid newspapers such as *The Sun* are associated with over reporting celebrity gossip, scandal and sports. Broadsheets are concerned more with serious news and analysis.
- Television. Older television channels broadcast a wide range of programmes usually intended for a national audience, including news, current affairs, entertainment and sports. Changes in technology then led to a huge increase in the number of channels broadcast by satellite or delivered to homes by cable. Where new channels have a small, specialised audience, such as fans of a particular sport, this is called **narrowcasting**. The increase in channels has meant a fall in audiences for the old main channels and also that there is no national audience, in the sense that it is now unlikely that most of

KEY TERM

Narrowcasting: transmitting radio or television to a narrow or niche audience.

KEY TERM

Broadcasting: transmitting radio or television signals to large audiences.

TOP TIP

With some media you need to consider whether the technology or the content is being discussed. For example, television can mean either the physical television set (the original way of watching television) or the content, the television programme, which can be watched on DVD or streamed or downloaded on a computer as well as on a television. Recorded music is a type of content that can be consumed through many different media.

the population in a country has watched the same programme. Television programmes could be watched once only, as they were broadcast, but later it was possible to record them on video to watch and now they can be streamed or downloaded from websites. In the UK the BBC was the first television channel and before satellite television there were only four channels. Today, most households in the UK have access, through digital **broadcasting,** to more than a hundred channels, and many pay subscriptions for extra channels.

- Books. Books are probably the oldest form of mass media, but they also face challenges in the age of new media. Books can now be read on computers and e-book readers. This has led some people to wonder if books as physical objects will survive. Even if they do not, books will continue to be written and read.

Role of advertising

Advertising is usually the main source of income for the privately owned media and it has therefore been essential to the development of the media. Advertisers try to stimulate demand for their products. The importance of advertising income has encouraged media industries to concentrate on attracting audiences with spending power. This means either trying to reach a mass audience, so that viewing or reading figures will justify the high prices charged for advertising, or a smaller audience with spending power. The needs of audiences with little spending power are likely to be ignored by the media. Advertisers have a choice as to where to place adverts, so the media need to be careful to avoid controversial content that advertisers may not want to be associated with.

Advertising can be seen as a kind of propaganda. It is powerful and it is all around us and almost impossible to avoid. As well as traditional advertisements such as billboard posters and 30-second commercials on television, it includes sponsorship. For example, in any media coverage of sporting events the names of the sponsors will almost certainly feature. Advertisements have always used many tricks to appeal to audiences, such as using humour and appeals to pity and other emotions. They associate their products with things to which we attach positive values; for example, a car advertisement may show a car in an unspoilt natural landscape (which the car will pollute and help to destroy and which is totally unlike the urban streets where the car will inevitably be driven most often). Increasingly, advertisements make use of the audience's awareness of advertising tricks and play endless reflexive games with them.

The boundary between advertising and content is becoming less clear. For example, many television programmes and films contain product placement, where a company has paid for its product to be featured (for example, a character is shown drinking a brand of soft drink). There is also an overlap in employees. Many media workers such as film directors spend part of their career in advertising.

Advertising also appears on websites and other new media. For example, most websites have banner advertisements and pop-ups. Websites also track what internet users do online through cookies, and are able to make the advertising appropriate to the user.

Advertising informs audiences about things they might want to buy and tells them about new products. Audiences are free to interpret advertisements and to choose to ignore them but advertising has also been much criticised for these reasons:

- Advertising encourages people to always be dissatisfied and to want more than they have. It encourages materialism, consumerism and a wasteful **lifestyle**.
- Advertising often portrays a successful Western lifestyle and culture. Accepting this is good poses a threat to traditional cultures and is also socially and environmentally damaging.
- Many heavily advertised goods are overpriced, unnecessary and have planned obsolescence (that is, they will not last).
- All companies feel the need to advertise because their rivals do but this adds to costs and pushes up the prices that consumers have to pay for goods.
- Advertising often uses images of women, and sometimes men, that put pressure on people to trying to achieve a look that is impossible and undesirable. It can encourage dissatisfaction with one's self-image and may lead to anorexia and other eating disorders.
- Advertisers have sometimes aimed their advertisements at children, who then put pressure on their parents to buy things for them.

KEY TERM

Lifestyle: the typical way of life of an individual, group or society.

TEST YOURSELF

1. Old media are often referred to as mass media but new media are not. Why is this?
2. Why is advertising important to media industries and how does it affect the content of the media?

ACTIVITY: *evaluation*

Draw a table to show the main similarities and differences between old and new media.

Ownership and control of the media

The world's media are increasingly dominated by a small number of giant conglomerates. These are constantly changing and becoming fewer through mergers and acquisitions. Although the media now operate globally, the USA is still the centre of the media companies, and most conglomerates are American originally even if now they operate all around the world. They are transnational corporations. The biggest six media conglomerates in the world are:

- AOL Time Warner
- Disney
- Bertelsmann
- Viacom
- News Corporation
- Vivendi Universal.

Many well-known brands are owned by these corporations, although the public are not always aware of this. Some conglomerates have interests outside the media – for example, Vivendi owns many water companies. The conglomerates cooperate at times, sell brands to each other and reconfigure themselves as circumstances change. They constantly shift alliances and jockey for advantage over rivals.

As an example, Disney is the largest media conglomerate in the world in terms of revenue. It was founded in 1923 when it started making short cartoon films but has grown and diversified enormously. Its interests include:

- films including Pixar Animation Studios
- network television and cable channels including ABC, ESPN (sports) and the Disney Channel
- toys, clothing and other merchandise, with Disney stores
- theme parks and resorts
- Hyperion books
- sports teams.

The trend towards the restriction of ownership of the media to a small number of companies is called the concentration of media ownership.

The BBC

KEY TERMS

Private funding: the costs of the media are covered by private individuals or companies.

Public funding: the costs of the media are covered by payments from the government or other public body.

Public service broadcasting: radio and television funded by the public.

State ownership of media

In some countries the state owns some of the media, such as newspapers. In some countries these are monopolies; in others they compete with media that are **privately funded** and owned. Countries with mainly state-owned media tend to be less economically developed and are less likely to have democratic political systems. There are different degrees to which the state uses its ownership to influence people's views, depending on the extent to which the state controls content or whether editors or producers have some independence.

Most media today are privately owned, but in many countries the broadcasting media were first set up as state-owned monopolies (that is, they are **publicly funded**). This meant that all television and radio stations were state owned and they had no competition from other companies but were run as a public service. They were funded by general taxation, licence fees or by other means. The initial reasons for establishing **public service broadcasting** were the cost of the technology and the limitations of the media.

Public service broadcasting has been implemented in different ways in different countries. In the British model the British Broadcasting Corporation (BBC) and Channel 4 were the first publicly owned media. The BBC was set up by an Act of Parliament and has to adhere to its charter. Its income is largely decided by the licence fee, the level of which is set by the government. Beyond this, however, the BBC is largely independent of government. The BBC's public service mission is to inform, educate and entertain. In the past the BBC saw entertainment as taking third place. The first director-general of the BBC, Lord Reith, said that to the extent that the BBC was intended to entertain, it was also intended to educate listeners and viewers in matters of taste as regards entertainment. So BBC entertainment was meant to improve people, too. As a result the BBC broadcast classical music and Shakespeare's plays. The BBC has always been independent of the government of the day and has a reputation for impartiality that has made the BBC respected throughout the world. However, there is always a danger that an organisation funded by the government is likely to favour the government line. That is just what happened in the 1926 General Strike when Reith argued that the BBC was the people's service and the government was the people's choice, so it followed that the BBC supported the government against the strikers.

KEY TERM

Bias: being one-sided in the selection of which events and stories are reported and how.

Here are some advantages of public service broadcasting:

- They are free from commercial interests and the **bias** these may lead to.
- They can play a role in creating a sense of national unity.
- They can address minority groups who may lack the spending power to attract media aimed at them.
- They can focus on the quality of programming rather than the need to make a profit.

Private ownership

Many media businesses are owned by individuals, families or shareholders. They exist to make a profit rather than to provide a service, as public service broadcasters do. Perhaps the best known example of an individual controlling a large conglomerate is Rupert Murdoch's News Corporation. In the UK newspaper ownership is entirely private and is heavily concentrated. Of all national daily newspapers sold 96 per cent are produced by just five companies.

Ownership versus control

The media can be either state-owned or privately owned. Ownership is not, however, the same as control. Controllers are those who make day-to-day decisions on behalf of the company, such as editors of newspapers, heads of film studios and television producers. Controllers are sometimes also owners in that senior managers may have shares in the company. The distinction between ownership and control is important because it raises questions about who decides the content of the media.

The importance of owners varies:

- Owners may sometimes directly control the content by giving orders to their staff.
- Owners may appoint as editors and senior staff only people who agree with their point of view and can be relied on to do the editor's bidding.

The importance of controllers:

- Controllers have to take the main day-to-day decisions because in large corporations the owners have too many media so have to delegate decision-making.
- Controllers may be allowed by owners to take decisions themselves as long as the profitability of the company is not damaged.

The different theoretical approaches to the ownership and control of the media are discussed on page 226.

TEST YOURSELF

1 Why is the distinction between owners and controllers important?
2 What is meant by public service broadcasting and how is it different from privately owned media?

KEY TERM

Social control: the ways in which society regulates individual and group behaviour.

Freedom and censorship in the media

The media can be used for **social control**, that is, to influence the ways that people behave. In countries where there is state control of most media with few, if any, privately owned media, there is a concern that the media can be used for

KEY TERM

Propaganda: use of the media to influence people to accept a particular point of view.

Walt Disney – Disney's film studio made propaganda films for the Allied war effort in World War Two

KEY TERM

Censorship: control or suppression of what is published in the media.

TOP TIP

Sometimes self-censorship is important. Makers of a media text often think ahead to what a censor might object to and leave that out. For example, film directors who want their film to be seen by young people may delete scenes of sex or violence from the script or screenplay rather than wait for a censor to decide those scenes cannot be shown.

KEY TERMS

Pluralist perspective: approach to the media that emphasises choice and competition.

Socialisation: the process of learning the norms and values of a culture.

Norm-setting: the process by which norms are established.

propaganda. Propaganda involves giving a one-sided, even untrue version of events, without allowing people access to alternative views, so that they will accept the view being presented.

State-controlled media may:

- present the government and its polices favourably
- present opposition parties and policies unfavourably
- not report issues or events which would show the government unfavourably.

In the past, examples of use of the media for propaganda include:

- Nazi Germany. Hitler used the media of the time – newspapers, magazines, posters and radio – for propaganda to demonise Jews, communists and others.
- The Soviet Union. Under Stalin, propaganda for the communist government included a propaganda train with a cinema that visited remote areas.
- The USA during World War Two. Walt Disney made propaganda films for the American war effort against Nazi Germany, including some featuring characters such as Donald Duck.

Public service broadcasters such as the BBC have considerable freedom over what to report and how. They are usually required, however, to report with due impartiality, which means in an appropriately balanced and fair way. This does not mean giving equal time and prominence to every opinion but it does involve a duty to report fairly different points of view.

Censorship of the media in modern industrial societies can take many forms, including:

- laws protecting the state, such as the UK's Official Secrets Act, which prevents the reporting of state secrets
- laws on obscenity
- libel and slander laws, which prevent the media from making unfounded allegations against individuals
- laws preventing the unfair treatment of ethnic and other minorities
- the certification system for films and computer games
- the watershed for television which prevents some sex, violence, swearing and drug use being shown before 9 pm, so that children should not be watching.

Pluralist, Marxist and postmodernist perspectives

This section describes pluralist and Marxist perspectives on the nature and role of the media.

Pluralism

There are two contrasting approaches to the media, pluralism and Marxism. There are also two rather different approaches within Marxism. Pluralism is also called the liberal or market view and takes a very positive view of the role of the media. **Pluralists** believe the media plays an important role in society. The media are one of the agencies of secondary **socialisation** and as such help to establish the **norms** of the society. The main argument put forward by pluralists is that the media can only reflect and respond to their audiences: the audiences shape the media, rather

TOP TIP

The main theoretical perspectives in the sociology of the mass media are slightly different from those in other areas of sociology, but you can think of pluralism as being closely related to functionalism

than the other way round. Pluralists therefore reject the view that the media can strongly influence their audiences. It is the audience who have the power, through choice and competition. This is made possible by the diversity of media. A very wide choice of media is available and is growing all the time as new technologies provide new ways to access information and entertainment. Although ownership is concentrated in large companies like Murdoch's News Corporation, pluralists point out that there are also many small independent companies. Even the large media conglomerates like that of Murdoch have to produce what people want because that is what will bring them profit.

Two key ideas used by pluralists are competition and choice. Competition refers to the fact that media corporations are constantly trying to outdo each other and to produce what people want. For example, each Hollywood film studio is trying to produce the next successful blockbuster film, newspapers compete for readers and television channels for viewers. A company that fails to produce what audiences want will not make profits and may be driven out of business. Pluralists argue that this means that standards are always rising and that the media cannot afford to produce poor-quality content. Competition also means that the prices to audiences are kept low.

The development of new and social media supports the pluralist approach. They have increased the choices available to audiences. The distinction between audiences and producers also becomes less clear as users can create content, by having websites, writing blogs and uploading videos to YouTube and so on.

Opponents of the pluralist view point out that each company's aim is to drive competitors out of business. If they are successful there will then be reduced competition and the surviving companies will not need to care about what audiences want. Opponents also point out that there is bias in the media; for example, few newspapers support left-of-centre political views. Pluralists accept that the media are biased but argue that this does not matter because it is what the public wants, and the range of media output is so wide that different types of bias are available. This reflects what modern industrial societies are like – there are groups with different political beliefs, different religions and different values. If one point of view or ideology seems to be **dominant**, that is simply because it is the one that most people hold. If much of the content of the media seems to be dumbed down, with little serious reporting of politics and economics, this simply reflects what people want.

KEY TERM

Dominant values: the main beliefs in a society, held by most people and/or spread by the media.

Reasons why media corporations are not all-powerful:

- Media companies have to ensure that what they make is wanted by audiences. If it is not they will go out of business.
- Most media companies are owned by shareholders, who through pension funds and other investments can represent many people. It is shareholders who have the ultimate power, not individual owners like Murdoch.
- Governments have rules preventing monopolies and cross-media ownership.
- There are also rules in some countries on the quality of programming, for example requiring a certain amount of news reporting.
- There are laws such as the libel laws that prevent the media from telling lies about people and organisations.

Pluralists think it is good to have a range of media from which audiences can choose. They favour private ownership and do not believe this leads to a restriction on points of view expressed in the media.

Marxism

KEY TERMS

Marxist: an approach to the media that emphasises how the media help the ruling class to retain their position and control over society.

Indoctrination: giving information or ideas to people in ways that they accept uncritically.

From the traditional **Marxist** perspective the media convey the dominant ideology and so keep the population ignorant and in a state of false consciousness. The media do this because they are owned and controlled by the capitalist class who deliberately use them to keep power and prevent social change. For example, Ralph Miliband in *The State and Capitalist Society* described the media as an agency of conservative **indoctrination**.

Marxists argue that people can be manipulated by the media. For example, people in the UK were manipulated into supporting the invasion of Iraq in 2003 because the media repeatedly told them that Iraq could launch an attack within 45 minutes. It was difficult for people to evaluate this claim or to find alternative views. The media also help capitalism by creating false needs. They make people passive consumers who are willing to work hard to buy things they have been persuaded that they need. This leads to constant demand for new products and to profits for businesses.

The media divert attention from really important issues, feed the audience with trivia and gossip and ignore or ridicule radical ideas. The media do not offer reports and programmes that help us to understand the world better. Increasingly, all we are offered is entertainment (like reality television, celebrity gossip and sports) that distracts us from real issues. When important issues are reported, it is in ways that make it seem that nothing can be done anyway.

KEY TERMS

Labelling: applying a term and an associated set of assumptions to an individual or group.

Distortion: the changing of accurate reporting into a biased or inaccurate report.

Democracy: a political system in which all eligible citizens have a say in the decisions affecting them.

Alternative views will sometimes be allowed because this makes it possible for capitalists to claim that the media are free and impartial. But these alternative views are restricted to small media outlets or presented in a way that marginalises and ridicules them, and makes it clear to the audience that they should ignore them (for example, they will be **labelled** extremist).

This Marxist view of the media has been criticised for making it seem that there is a conspiracy by a small group of rulers to control everyone else. Another variation on Marxism seems to be more aware of the complex ways in which the media and audiences interact. From the neo-Marxist or hegemonic perspective, the media convey the dominant ideology not through conscious intent but by the way in which the media industries are organised and media controllers are socialised. The dominant ideology is a set of beliefs involving a **distortion** of the truth, which serves the interests of the ruling class. Attitudes in the media that reflect the dominant ideology include the approval of business, inequality of wealth, parliamentary **democracy** and the monarchy, as well as disapproval of trade unions, feminism and protesters and a suspicion of ethnic minorities, young people and radicals. From their own experiences and other sources of knowledge, people are able to see that some of this is untrue. The media are, however, most people's main source of information so they tend to accept the ideological messages the media convey.

Rather than a conspiracy by the owners of the media to deceive people, the hegemonic Marxist view is that it is editors, producers and journalists who have attitudes that lead them to report only the dominant world view or ideology. The media carry the dominant ideology not because they are conspiring to deceive the public (which is how the traditional Marxists make it seem) but because decision-makers in the media (the editors and producers) actually have a world view that supports the ideology. This is because they tend to be:

- White
- male

- middle class
- middle aged.

As a result, the media give us a consistent view of the world, an ideology. There is room for disagreement within this; for example support for different political parties. But hegemonic Marxists see how much is common in the media, rather than differences that they believe are fairly minor.

The ruling class can protect its power by force. It can use the repressive state apparatus (such as the police, army and criminal courts) to silence those who oppose it. It is far more effective, however, to control people's thoughts and beliefs. This is done by the ideological state apparatus. The media convey an ideology, a world view, that justifies the way things are and persuades people that alternatives are not possible.

Where the working class accepts this ideology, even though it is fundamentally against its interest, a situation of hegemonic control exists. This means that the ideology that is transmitted seems to be simple common sense – normal and natural. The ideology then achieves hegemony, a situation in which people are content to accept things as they are. They know it does not have to be that way but the alternatives are made to seem too threatening or difficult. Gramsci argued that hegemony is never complete and that there is always the possibility of the dominant ideology being rejected, so this is not the state of false consciousness that the traditional Marxists describe.

For Marxists, the ruling class use the media at two levels to maintain their power:

- concealing the truth from the working class and spreading misinformation
- distracting the working class from important issues by cultivating an obsession with trivia and celebrities.

The hegemonic Marxist view can be found in the writings of the Glasgow Media Group, which are considered on page 253.

KEY TERMS

Postmodern: changes in the media and society have produced a new type of culture and society that we call postmodern.

Postmodernist: someone who accepts the postmodern view of the media and society.

Postmodernism

Postmodernism is a relatively new perspective on the media. This is partly because, far more than pluralism and Marxism, it focuses on the ways that the media have become more interactive, with users producing content. **Postmodernists** say that information now moves between points in a network rather than top down, as was the case with traditional media. This means that the media cannot be controlled, or used for propaganda, or convey a dominant ideology. This means that the world today has moved beyond being modern – it is postmodern.

TEST YOURSELF

1 Explain some of the forms that media censorship can take.
2 What different explanations would pluralists and Marxists have of the dumbing down of the media?

ACTIVITY: *evaluation*

Draw a table to show the main similarities and differences between pluralist and Marxist views of the media.

CASE STUDY

A radical view of the media: *Manufacturing Consent: The Political Economy of the Mass Media*

This is the title of a book by the American writer Noam Chomsky. Chomsky argues that in a democracy the rulers cannot do what they want to without the people's consent. So that consent has to be manufactured and this is done using the mass media. It is only because the mass media are so effective at doing this that we are allowed to have a democracy. The media ensure that we will not vote for radical changes. They tell lies so that we do not have the information to understand what is really going on.

Chomsky says the most important media are the quality broadsheets, the **agenda setting** media, because these are read by the people who shape policies. Here there is an illusion of differences of opinion and debate but these are always within the range of opinions that is considered acceptable. Chomsky's own books are published only by small publishers and he rarely appears on the mainstream media. He has been said to be the most important thinker alive yet his ideas are not widely known.

Noam Chomsky

TASK

1 According to Chomsky, how do the media effectively spread propaganda in a democracy like the USA?

2 Chomsky's books are published by small publishers and he rarely appears on the mainstream media. Is this because the system suppresses his views – or because few people think his views are worth reading?

KEY TERM

Agenda setting: the ability of the media to make some topics important.

Patterns of media use

This section describes media use according to gender, age, social class and ethnicity.

Gender

Gender issues affect the use of media technologies. The clearest example of this is that males use computers and video games much more than females. This goes back to the early days of these technologies. Many early games focused on fighting and violence and involved identifying with male characters. This has begun to change with the development of games that appeal to females.

There are clear gender differences in, for example, use of television. Men tend to prefer documentaries, sport and action adventure; women prefer soap operas and costume drama. For example, David Morley's UK-based research published in *Family Television* found other differences:

- In the family men almost always have control over programme choice.
- Men prefer to view attentively, in silence, uninterrupted; women see viewing as a social activity, combined with conversation and household tasks.
- Men carefully plan their viewing; women tend not to.
- Most women left video recording to their husbands or children.

Age

The amount of television people watch goes up when they are over the age of 50. For people with visual or hearing difficulties television is better than newspapers because it has both visual and verbal information. Some writers have suggested that watching more television is a way of compensating for being less engaged in society (for example, not going to work any more) while others see it as a way of keeping in contact with society.

People tend to be most confident and comfortable with media technologies that they have become used to when they were young. The arrival of the internet in all its forms has been accepted by many older people but some have found it difficult to get used to the new technologies. Older people are less likely to use the internet and older women less likely than older men to do so. According to research in 2012, only 30 per cent of people in the UK aged 75 or over had used the internet (http://web.orange.co.uk/article/news/most_elderly_never_use_internet).

Teenagers and young people tend to visit the cinema more than other age groups. This is because the cinema involves going out and is an opportunity for socialising. The importance of these age groups to the film industry can be seen in the types of films made by the main studios, which are designed to appeal to these age groups and to have characters they can identify with. Young people watch television less than older people but increasingly the moving images they watch are short videos, for example on YouTube, rather than traditional films and television programmes.

Social class

More than other media, newspapers are associated with particular social classes. For example, in the UK the tabloids such as *The Sun* and the *Daily Mirror* are seen as working-class newspapers while the quality, ex-broadsheet newspapers such as *The Times* are read by middle-class people and above. This also applies to television; the mainstream television channels, with a lot of soap operas, reality programmes, game shows and other popular entertainment, are aimed at mass audiences that are primarily working class. Many working-class families pay for satellite and cable channels which provide football and other sports traditionally seen as working-class diversions. Marxists would see in this the media's function of distracting the working class from the important political and economic issues by providing entertainment. In the use of the internet, there is still a digital divide between classes in some countries because of cost.

Ethnicity

Immigrant communities in modern industrial countries have greater opportunities than in the past to access the media from their country of origin or in their native language. For example, television channels from their home country may be available by satellite and they can visit websites of newspapers when the physical newspaper may not be available. This means there are greater chances to preserve their culture and may mean that such communities are less likely to be assimilated into the host culture. For example, Bollywood films are watched all around the world by families of Indian origin.

As minority groups become established in new home countries, they are likely to be able to produce their own media. These may well be successful, especially if representations of the group in the mainstream media are stereotypical or absent, but the group may not provide a large enough audience for this. In the UK, The Voice is a newspaper for the African-Caribbean community which has been published weekly since 1982.

Minority groups will also of course use mainstream media, but they may sometimes read content in a different way to majority groups. For example, Marie Gillespie, who carried out participant observation research with Punjabi families in London, found that teenagers enjoyed watching both Punjabi programmes and mainstream programmes such as the Australian soap opera *Neighbours*. They took ideas from these programmes and through sharing ideas made sense of their own lives as part of two cultures.

Media representations

This section describes how the media represent ethnicity, gender, age, class and disability.

KEY TERM

Media representation: the ways in which ethnic/gender/age/class/disability groups are portrayed in the media.

This section deals with what you should know about **media representations** of ethnicity, gender, age, class and people with a disability. A representation in sociology refers to the way in which we imagine or picture things. The concept can be applied to people as well as other things: for example, it can be applied to places. A city can be pictured as dangerous and full of crime and poverty or as a place of opportunity where you can make your dreams come true. The media represents reality rather than reflecting it by giving us images (whether paintings, photographs or a film still) or pieces of text about something. This representation has been constructed and put together by someone. All media texts are constructed by people with a specific purpose and a specific audience in mind. They are never simple reflections of reality even though they are often presented as if they were.

Representation is an important concept in theories about the media. It is used when we try to understand what media texts mean and how the meanings they offer us are constructed. We need to ask about what we see and read in the media: who constructed it, where and when, for what purpose and for what audience?

Key concepts in discussing representation

In discussing the different areas of representation – ethnicity, gender, age, class and people with a disability – a number of concepts must be used:

KEY TERMS

Invisibility: when a group is not present in the media.

Stereotyping: representing people and groups in a simplified and misleading way.

Traditional stereotyping: well-established and enduring stereotypes, now existing alongside more recent representations.

TOP TIP

Many of the examples of underrepresentation and stereotyping in textbooks are now quite old. Representations change and you may feel that the examples are out of date. But you always need to ask how much has really changed. Remember that with television and films, old images and stereotypes are continuously recycled through repeat showings (which is happening more than ever before because of the proliferation of new channels).

- **Invisibility**. Some groups are absent from areas of the media and are said to have been made invisible.
- Underrepresentation. Some groups appear less than you might expect, given their numbers in the population. For example, people with disabilities do not often appear in the media other than in texts specifically for or about disabled people although one in five people in the UK has a disability of some kind (http://www.papworth.org.uk/downloads/disabilityintheunitedkingdom2012_120910112857.pdf).
- Tokenism. When a member of an underrepresented group appears in the media, this can sometimes be criticised for being tokenism, meaning that it has been done to create an illusion of being fair without making any genuine attempt to achieve an even balance.
- **Stereotyping**. The media often use these one-sided, exaggerated images because they are a widely understood shorthand way of conveying ideas. Stereotypes often have some basis in truth and can be positive as well as negative. Often one person is shown in a way that suggests that their characteristics also apply to other members of the group (such as all disabled people or all people from a particular country). They are often, but not only, applied to minority groups. They can be repeated so often that they come to seem natural and can be hard to break away from. They involve judgements – the characteristics that the group are assumed to have are seen as clearly good or bad. Some stereotypes are **traditional**, such as the male provider and female housewife; others are more recent, such as the career woman.
- The gaze. This idea was first developed by Laura Mulvey, a feminist writer on films. She wrote about the male gaze, by which she meant the ways in which films are made from a male perspective – by men, for an audience assumed to be male and making the audience take the position of male characters.

The concept has since been applied more widely. For example, it has been argued there is a White gaze. Most films are made by White directors so what we get in those films is a White person's ideas of what people from other ethnic groups are like.

- Binary oppositions. These were first noted by the anthropologist Claude Levi-Strauss in myths and in literature. Stories are built around opposed forces (good versus evil, day versus night, civilised versus barbarian and so on). In the study of representations this idea has been used to show how a group may be defined as the opposite of another. For example, men and women are often represented as opposites when in fact the two genders have much in common.

TOP TIP

When writing about representations you can use examples from any media texts (including films, television programmes and magazines) that you are familiar with. It is better to do this than to use the examples given in textbooks that you do not otherwise know. The following sections make extensive use of *The Simpsons* television programme and the *Harry Potter* films, as these are widely known.

Representations of ethnicity

Ethnic groups are represented in different ways in the media. In the media from Europe and the USA, where the majority is White, minority ethnic groups have often been represented in stereotyped ways. In the USA the main focus has been on African-American people and in the UK the focus is on the African-Caribbean population and Asian people (with family origins in India, Pakistan, Bangladesh and Sri Lanka). These have in the past been underrepresented. Other representations that are relevant include those of people in developing countries in the media of the developed world and representations of indigenous peoples such as Native Americans and Aborigines in Australia. Taking all these together, we can say that there is often a binary opposition between White and non-White. The representations of non-White people have often been offensive and are examples of the White gaze.

Some stereotypes of non-White people that have been noted include:

- The dangerous savage. This is a stereotype of uncivilised people who want to attack and harm White people, especially women and children. Attacks are shown as the result of a savage nature (rather than the last resort of those whose lands are being stolen and lifestyle destroyed, which was often the case in the real events on which the representations are based). An example is the genre of old Western films (cowboys and Indians) that portrayed Indians in this way. It is often found in films where the White hero or explorer, such as Indiana Jones, deals with natives.
- The noble savage. This is a positive stereotype that is the contrary of the dangerous savage. The noble savage is shown as living a simple life in harmony with nature but unchanging and without a history. This is an idealised and romanticised view of other cultures, based on projecting Western ideas and values onto them. It is present in some Western films sympathetic to Native Americans, such as *Dances with Wolves*.
- The childlike primitive. This is closely connected to the noble savage stereotype. Non-Whites are seen as amusing but stupid and unsophisticated and so need to be looked after by White people. This stereotype is present in much reporting of wars and famines, especially in Africa, that uses images of starving, defenceless and helpless children.
- The entertainer. One of the main ways in which Black people have been able to win cultural acceptance from White society is through music and dance, based on a stereotype of having natural rhythm. This has made Black people more acceptable if they are funny or sing and dance.
- The sexually exotic and alluring woman. Non-White women are often shown as more daring and more dangerous than White women. White men have to tame or avoid

such women. This stereotype can be seen in media texts that rework historical or mythological figures such as Cleopatra, Salome, Delilah and Kali.

- The rich, evil tyrant. Non-White leaders are often shown as corrupt and despotic, oppressing their people. This stereotype suggests that non-White people are incapable of being good rulers (in the past, this helped justify colonialism). This can be present in news reporting and in films.
- The clever, devious trickster. These villains are often shown as having acquired Western education or culture but are using this for their own evil purposes. Some older Hollywood films had Chinese villains who were clever but evil.

Overall, these stereotypes are negative and even those that are sympathetic suggest inferiority in some way. The binary oppositions involve categories in which non-White is defined as opposite to White:

Non-White	White
primitive	civilised
savage	sophisticated
body	mind
irrational	rational
natural	cultural
ancient	modern
magical	scientific
heathen	Christian
evil	good
exotic	ordinary
erotic	repressed

Table 7.1: Binary oppositions defining stereotypes of non-white culture (adapted from O'Shaughnessy 1999)

The UK has minority ethnic group populations that together make up about 10 per cent of the population. This proportion grew in the mid-20th century through immigration. News media during the main period of immigration treated immigrants as trouble. Prejudice among White people was treated as funny (for example in the television sitcoms *Till Death Us Do Part* and *Love Thy Neighbour*) and understandable, not as a serious problem. People from minority groups were seen in the media but often in minor or stereotypical roles, rarely as main characters, and they were made fun of. Examples include the television sitcom *Mind Your Language*. Representations have improved in music, entertainment, sports and comedy but there is still underrepresentation in some areas.

Some of the main stereotypes present in the late 20th century about minority groups are listed below:

- African-Caribbean people are shown as potentially thieves and criminals, with young men ready to use violence and drugs and become involved in gangs. Stuart Hall and his colleagues showed how news media labelled young Black men as muggers and created a new stereotype.

- Asian people are shown stereotypically as having unusual accents, large extended families and appear in a limited range of roles, such as owning small shops. In *The Simpsons* the character Apu brings together several aspects of this stereotype: he is a semi-legal immigrant, speaks in a stilted way, has a long unpronounceable surname (Nahasapeemapetilon), an arranged marriage and many children, and works long hours in his store.

In the Hollywood film industry African-American actors were for many years restricted to minor and stereotypical roles. Even successful actors such as Will Smith felt that they were given stereotypical roles. In a police film featuring a White policeman and a Black policeman as buddies, it would always be the Black cop who was killed early on so that the White hero could seek revenge. This has now changed as some top African-American actors play leading roles where their ethnicity is irrelevant. However, there are still few successful African-American directors. The Hollywood film industry is now rivalled globally by Bollywood (based in Mumbai in India) and Nollywood (Nigeria) where ethnic groups that would be treated as minorities in American and European films are the majority.

Representations of people in developing countries

Developing countries are underreported in American and European media and when they are reported it is often in negative ways. It has been suggested that there is a coup-war-famine syndrome, meaning that the only news that can be reported from developing countries has something to do with death, disease and disaster. The media's coverage of aid and disaster relief also contributes to a stereotype of victims living off charity from the West and needing to be saved by heroic White doctors and others. Africa often features in Hollywood films as a setting for war and adventure stories with White main characters.

Representations of gender

Men and women are often represented through binary opposition as being totally different from each other.

Male: tough, hard, sweaty, sports loving, strong, physical
Female: soft, warm fragrant, weak, emotional

However, in recent years there has begun to be a wider range of representations of both genders. This is related to changes in wider society, where the roles and expectations associated with gender have changed.

Representations of females

In the media females tend to be:

- underrepresented in most areas; for example, few action-drama shows and films have women as the main characters
- shown in a very narrow range of roles; they tend to be shown in the home rather than at work and the roles of wife, mother and girlfriend (that is, their relationship to the men in their lives) are shown as the most important aspects of who they are
- shown in ways that emphasise their physical appearance
- shown in ways that most women cannot attain; the media are full of images, often digitally altered, of women that leave women feeling inadequate because they cannot achieve the same level of physical beauty – this has raised concerns,

for example, that images of very thin models may encourage eating disorders such as anorexia
- shown as passive, weak and helpless; for example, waiting to be rescued by the hero – this often involves the woman being shown as a victim.

The interest in representations of women grew with the impact of feminist ideas in the 1970s and 1980s. One content analysis study during this period was Diane Meehan's *Ladies of the Evening: Women Characters of Prime Time TV* (1983). She analysed the content of American drama serials of the time. She found that:

- essentially only 10 female character types were used: the imp, the good wife, the harpy, the bitch, the victim, the decoy, the siren, the courtesan, the witch and the matriarch
- women are portrayed as either good or evil, never with more complex personalities
- good women are submissive and domesticated (so, for example, they like cleaning)
- bad women are shown as being rebellious and independent
- evil male characters are always counterbalanced by good ones but this does not happen for women
- women are shown in a very limited number of occupations (secretary, receptionist, primary school teacher and prostitute); men are also shown in a limited number of occupations compared to reality but these tended to be more exciting.

These stereotypes are based on late 1970s television and it is hoped that representations are now more balanced, positive and realistic (though it is worth noting that many of the old series are still being repeated so the stereotypes in them get extended lives). Marge Simpson in *The Simpsons* is more intelligent than her husband but she is represented in quite a traditional way in that her life is totally focused on her home and family.

ACTIVITY: *research*

Areas of the media in which women have been said to be underrepresented include cartoons, news and current affairs and some comedies. Media texts with more representations of women (though they are still not equal to men) include soap operas, talk shows and quiz shows. Carry out content analysis to check whether this is the case in the media you have access to in your country.

Feminists argue that sexist representations are still common in the media. These occur in different ways in media aimed both at men and at women. In media aimed at men, including some newspapers, there are sexual images of women that draw attention to their bodies in ways that are not usually used for men. This is the male gaze.

There are now many examples in the media of representations that break away from the older stereotypes of females. For example, there are films and television dramas that feature females in traditionally male roles as detectives and police officers, spies and business executives. These representations establish new **role models** for girls today that were rarely available for previous generations.

KEY TERM

Role models: individuals who act as examples to others who try to follow their attitudes and behaviour.

Representations of males

Representations of men tend to concentrate on:

- strength and power
- sexual attractiveness based on strength
- independence.

Together these give an idea of what has been called hegemonic masculinity, discussed in Unit 6. This is an extreme form of what men are supposed to be like in modern industrial societies. A hegemonic male character in an action movie, for example, is strong, athletic and a man of action; willing to use violence, not saying much and not showing emotions. Film characters such as *Rambo* and Bruce Willis's character John McClane in the *Die Hard* films are hegemonically male. These characteristics are meant to be admired for their masculine qualities. It has been suggested that these representations, like those of beautiful women, encourage audiences to have unrealistic expectations. Just as most women cannot have the body shape of famous models, so most men cannot achieve the levels of strength, fitness and emotional control that media representations seem to suggest they should have.

Men are also often shown in the traditional gender role of head of the family and breadwinner, supporting the others. A male hero will protect the weak and the innocent.

Increasingly, there are other male characters whose representation challenges the dominant assumptions about masculinity. The footballer David Beckham has been represented as a real man in terms of male good looks, football skills and competitive spirit, but these have been balanced by images that move away from this. For example, he has been shown as a model father, devoted to his children. Representations that suggest men should be more emotional and more concerned with relationships and so on are linked to the idea of the new man. A related new type of representation of men and masculinity is the metrosexual, a heterosexual man living in a modern city who is concerned with his appearance and with fashion, shopping and lifestyle. This character type brings into representations of heterosexual men some of the traits usually associated with gay men. In the media, as well as new character types in films and on television, this has meant that new magazines have been published aimed at men and focusing on appearance and fashions.

Representations of age groups

Age groups tend to be represented in these ways:

- children as innocent and vulnerable
- teenagers as rebellious and irresponsible
- middle-aged people as responsible and law-abiding figures of authority
- older people as vulnerable and a burden to society.

These representations reflect the roles of these age groups in modern industrial societies where most media are produced. In some cultures, these age groups are constructed in very different ways.

There can be differences between the ways males and females are represented within these age groups; for example, teenage girls may be shown as less rebellious than boys or rebelling in different ways from teenage boys.

Early advertising using representations of children

KEY TERMS

Moral panic: exaggerated social reaction to deviance, creating a demand for action against it.

Folk devils: a group who act as scapegoats in a moral panic.

Despite the negative representations of some young people, especially teenagers, overall the media are strongly biased in favour of the young. Magazines and advertising give the message that signs of growing old are bad and a range of cosmetics and treatments is available to try to disguise signs of ageing. This happens although ageing is inevitable and we do not expect people to try to hide their gender or their ethnic identity.

Representations of children

Modern societies usually see childhood as a period of innocence and helplessness in which children must be protected by responsible adults. The media can be seen both as reflecting this image and helping to create it. For example, in the early part of the 20th century, advertisements such as those for Pears Soap used images of children as helpless and vulnerable with large round eyes and chubby cheeks (they were also usually blonde, blue-eyed and White).

However, sometimes children are shown as having greater wisdom and sense than adults and their parents (especially fathers) are seen as useless and stupid. In some Hollywood films and other media, children understand more than adults (perhaps about some kinds of danger) and have to solve the problem themselves because the adults are unable or unwilling to act. Children are shown as able to deal with complex issues. Sometimes children are represented as bad or even evil. This forms a binary opposition with the more common representation of innocence.

Representations of teenagers

Teenagers and youths are often represented in stereotypical and negative ways. They are represented as rebellious juvenile delinquents who may be involved in petty crime, and become gang members. Groups of teenagers over the years, known as youth sub-cultures, have been reported in news media in **moral panics** as **folk devils**, acting as symbols for the changes in society that older people find worrying. This has contributed to the generation gap in which young and older people feel they have little in common and do not understand each other.

However, teenagers are sometimes represented more positively, especially in film and television dramas for young people where there is a need for characters that the audience can identify with. A good example of this is the Harry Potter series of films. In these films Harry and his friends Ron and Hermione are teenagers, shown growing up over the series and facing some of the problems of adolescence that all young people face, but using their qualities and magical powers to get the better of the older villains. In appearance Harry himself fits the geek stereotype.

Representations of older people

Older people tend to be underrepresented in the media. Many of their representations involve negative stereotypes of their being physically weak, needing help and being forgetful and confused. Grampa Simpson in *The Simpsons* tells long, rambling stories about his life that make little sense and are probably untrue but his family humour him. He lives in a nursing home with other older people who are doddering and even senile.

More recently there have been more positive representations of older people. This partly reflects the need for the media to reach an older audience. Older people are a fairly new and large market because of the growth in:

- the numbers of older people both absolutely and as a proportion of the population, because the baby boom generations are ageing

- the spending power of older people; many older people in modern industrial societies have disposable income from savings, pensions and investments so are a significant market for media industries – this is a change from the middle of the 20th century when, with higher proportions of young people, there was a cult of youth and older people tended to be ignored or shown negatively.

JK Rowling's Harry Potter stories have been very successful all around the world

These trends are likely to continue and more media will be aimed at older audiences. The negative representations of old people may become less common as the media will want to avoid insulting and alienating an important part of the audience.

One representation of old age that is partly positive is the rebellious older character in a struggle for freedom against bureaucracy and social expectations. There is a similarity between these characters and rebellious teenagers in films and television programmes from the 1950s to 1970s. A strongly positive representation of older people is the wise old person. In the Harry Potter books and films, Dumbledore is the wise old wizard and the headmaster of Hogwarts who protects everyone. Dumbledore fits a physical stereotype, with a long flowing beard but he is intelligent, compassionate and wise. The villain, Voldemort, is also old but devotes his energy and power to trying to stay young: this is portrayed as being unnatural and wrong. There are similar wise old wizard figures in other media, such as Gandalf in *The Lord of the Rings*.

There are also lifestyle magazines aimed at older people advertising the range of interests and activities that people can still have after retirement. Some recent positive representations of older people in Hollywood films include:

- The 2009 cartoon film *Up*, in which the main character is a 78-year-old widower, Carl Fredricksen, who flies by balloon to South America and has adventures there. He is shown as grumpy and difficult but he has a heart of gold, and flashbacks to his courtship of his wife Ellie, their life together and her death, help the audience to empathise with him. He also becomes friends with a young boy, showing that the generation gap can be bridged.
- The 2008 film *Gran Torino* was released when its director and star, Clint Eastwood, was 78. Eastwood's character is a widower whose grown-up children want to put him in a nursing home. He resists this and then overcomes his prejudice to help his immigrant neighbours deal with a violent gang.

Several writers have argued that older men are more likely to be portrayed positively than older women. Women in all age groups are assessed using the criteria of beauty and sex appeal, so older stars are admired for their ability to retain their good looks. Many older female actors, however, complain of the lack of leading roles for them in comparison with those for older men. In his sixties Harrison Ford can still star in films, even as an action hero, but female stars tend to fade from the industry before they reach that age. Older men are found as newscasters, as presenters and sports commentators on television and radio. The numbers of older women shown in these roles is far smaller.

Representations of social class

The way that social class is represented in the media can show the ideas that the makers of the media have about class and about how wealth and power are distributed.

Media representations do either of the following two things:

- Suggest that we live in an open, meritocratic society (where it is possible for anyone to reach the top by hard work and talent). Those who are poor or who fail do so because of lack of effort or talent: it is their own fault. This representation would be present in any drama or documentary that had a rags to riches storyline.
- Suggest that we live in a closed society, where the class holding power and wealth ensures that this is passed on to the next generation from the same class. Those who are poor or who fail do so because the odds were heavily stacked against them from the start.

It is the former representation that is by far the more common. However, most of the sociological evidence leads us to strongly question how open or meritocratic modern industrial societies are. This suggests that some of the main assumptions built into a lot of programming and reporting are misleading and are based on ignoring the strength of class power.

The USA likes to imagine itself as an open society where, for example, anyone can become the president. American film and television rarely raise issues of class and when they do they tend to suggest that the poor or underprivileged (who appear perhaps as trailer trash) deserve to be where they are. In Britain and the USA the middle class tends to be represented as normal. Representations of middle-class life are clear in a variety of situation comedies and dramas. For example, most of the period costume dramas such as *Pride and Prejudice* and *Downton Abbey* are about middle-class or upper-class characters; working people appear only incidentally, as servants or farm labourers, because they are not seen as significant enough to be main characters.

The working class is underrepresented in the media. However, the main British television soap operas, which are among the most long-running and popular programmes, are based on working-class communities:

- *Coronation Street,* which started in 1960, shows a working-class community in Manchester with storylines that tend to emphasise the strength of local loyalties and a strong community. Until recently there were few characters from minority ethnic groups or other outsiders in this series.
- *EastEnders,* which started in 1986, shows a working-class community in east London. Unlike *Coronation Street* it has always had an emphasis on the forces and issues that threaten the community rather than on what holds it together. *EastEnders* has a commitment to represent Walford as multicultural; however ethnic minority characters tend not to last as long as the main White characters.

American soap operas are different because they tend to focus on middle-class people, with the assumption that everyone is middle class. Sometimes there is a fascination with and admiration of money and power (as in *Dallas* and *Dynasty*) which do not involve questioning the ways in which the rich got rich.

Situation comedies on television often show working-class men in a very negative light, as being irresponsible and lacking in common sense. Homer Simpson in *The Simpsons* is a version of this character type. We appreciate his good intentions and he may even be likeable but he is certainly not a role model for anyone to admire.

CASE STUDY

Titanic: social class in a Hollywood film

The 1997 film *Titanic* was screened as a very popular blend of love story and disaster movie. As well as showing the huge ship sinking, using special effects, it showed social class differences in 1912, the year in which the film is set. This was a society very sharply divided by class. There were rich people living in luxury on the upper decks while down below in the steerage compartments were the poor. As the film makes clear, most of the survivors came from among the upper-class passengers while the lower classes often did not even get the chance to make it to the lifeboats.

Audiences could easily identify the rich characters by their luxury lifestyle on the ship and by their clothing, accents and topics of conversations. The film also shows how the newly rich were not fully accepted by those from families with inherited wealth. The poorer passengers' decks were overcrowded and untidy but they are shown entertaining themselves with boisterous music and dance.

TASK

1 Explain how the concept of binary oppositions can be applied to the representations in this film.

2 Identify other films that show two or more social classes and analyse the representations in them.

Representations of class are also present in the news media. Working-class people who claim benefits are often represented negatively as scroungers, with the implication that they do not deserve help. Working-class people who strike to protect their working conditions or pay are described as greedy. Often in complete contrast are representations of bankers and financiers who behave irresponsibly and whose actions can result in people losing their incomes, as well as of middle-class and upper-class people and companies who avoid paying tax. These are not shown in as negative a way. Finding a way to avoid tax may even be shown as clever and acceptable; finding a new way to claim more benefits would be condemned.

Representations of people with a disability

Media representations of people with a disability are often stereotypical. They are based on able-bodied people's attitudes towards those with disabilities and so they say more about those attitudes than about the people who are being represented. They often project fears and other negative attitudes onto disabled people. Disabled people are underrepresented in all media and often not present at all.

Some common representations of disabled people are:

- the monstrous freak or villain, common in older Hollywood films and even James Bond villains
- the object of pity – this associates disability with illness and suffering, for example children in hospitals or nursing homes
- the object of violence
- the super-cripple – this is a stereotype of a disabled person with superhuman qualities, battling against the odds; it is not a simple negative representation but can imply that disabled people need super qualities to earn respect
- the object of ridicule – in this stereotype, for example, the audience is invited to laugh at a visually impaired person who bumps into things
- a burden on society and others
- incapable of fully participating in community life.

Organisations of people with a disability and who are concerned with disabilities have strongly criticised the distortions and omissions they have found. As a result there have been improvements:

- The organisations supporting people with a disability have attacked the type of advertising by charities that feature a disabled person as an object of pity, someone to feel sorry for. As a result there have been new advertisements showing people with a disability in a positive light.
- Terms like spastic, handicapped, cripple and retard that are associated with negative attitudes towards disabled people are no longer used in the media or by most people.
- Many media organisations now have codes of practice or guidelines for their staff to work to.
- A small number of people with a disability have achieved success in the media. For example, Stephen Hawking, the leading scientist who has motor neurone disease, has presented television series based on his best-selling books. You can read his account of how his disability has affected his studies and career on his website http://www.hawking.org.uk/.
- The creation of new media texts. For example, the BBC TV series *Beyond Boundaries* followed a team of disabled people trekking across the wilderness. This was positive in showing what disabled people can achieve but was also criticised for pushing the super-cripple stereotype.

A recent development that seems to have led to more positive representations was the televising of the 2012 Paralympic Games in which athletes with a disability competed against each other. The coverage was greater than for previous Paralympics and audiences were shown how much can be achieved by such athletes.

Reasons for changes in representations

In most of the areas of representation that you have now studied, there have been changes over the last 20 or 30 years. Below are listed some of the reasons for these changes. You will need to work out for yourself which reasons apply to which changes:

- Campaigns to change representations have been launched by organisations of members of the group or pressure groups acting on their behalf.
- Social positions have changed so that women are no longer just housewives and mothers, but also workers and decision-makers, and media representations reflect this.
- More employment is available in the media so that, for example, more women and members of ethnic minorities are employed in the media and their presence may change the attitudes of editors, producers and others towards these groups. They may also be in a position to decide media content.
- Demographic changes have taken place. For example, the 1960s saw a big increase in media aimed at young people (especially music) because the baby boom meant that there were more teenagers. As that generation ages and with rising life expectancy and a fall in births, they continue to be an important target audience.
- The purchasing power of social groups has been recognised. For example, older people and minority ethnic groups are now seen as significant markets for the media and for advertisers using the media to promote products.

- The media have become increasingly diverse. The growth in the media (internet, multi-channel television and so on) has provided opportunities for a wider range of representations and for groups to produce their own media if they are dissatisfied with mainstream media.
- Changes to the law or government policy have taken place. For example, laws against discrimination in employment can increase the numbers of members of ethnic minorities working in the media.

It follows from this that groups that achieve greater status and purchasing power can effectively challenge negative representations. This has happened with women and with some ethnic minorities and, some way behind, with people with a disability. Groups that have lower status and less power continue to be represented negatively. In the UK today, such groups include Travellers, Gypsies and asylum seekers and refugees.

TEST YOURSELF

1 In what ways are teenagers represented in the media?
2 Why have representations of older people become more positive?

What is the influence of the media?

The role of the media

In this section we discuss the role of the traditional and new media in shaping values, attitudes and behaviour, with particular reference to television and violence; political beliefs and voting; patterns of consumption; traditional and gender stereotyping; and the influence of the internet in areas such as social networking.

Violence and the media

Politicians and others have expressed concern that violence in the media may lead to more violence in society. This might happen through the following means:

Imitation: observing and copying someone else's behaviour.

Hypodermic syringe model: this explanation focuses on the strong, immediate effects of the media on behaviour.

- **Imitation**. Children learn from copying others, so they may copy violence they see in the media. This concern is linked to the **hypodermic syringe** explanation of media effects.
- Desensitisation. This involves becoming so used to images of violence that people are no longer shocked. This concern is linked to the cultural effects explanation of media effects and the idea of slow drip effects.

On the other hand, it can be claimed that violence in the media may have positive effects, such as:

- catharsis – the release of strong emotions by channelling them safely, such as by releasing aggressive impulses through playing a violent computer game, which does not involved real violence or anyone getting hurt
- sensitisation – the shock effect of seeing violence in the media causes someone to take action against real-life violence; for example, the media coverage of the Dunblane shootings in the UK in 1996 led to a huge public campaign against guns and a change in the law, and which may have led to a reduction in violence involving guns.

In considering violence in the media we need to ask these questions:

- How realistic is the violence? Real images on the news and in documentaries are very different from fictional ones. Fictional violence can be realistic, as in some crime dramas, and can be made more realistic by new media effects such as computer generated images. On the other hand, violence by cartoon animals such as Tom and Jerry (satirised in Itchy and Scratchy in *The Simpsons*) is totally unrealistic and is not likely to have any influence on people.
- How is the violence represented? For example, does the character with whom the reader is meant to identify use violence and is this shown as good or necessary, or does a character get punished for being violent?
- Who is watching? Access to violent images is restricted for children and young people by the times at which programmes are shown on television and the ratings classification system for films and computer games.
- How can the effects of violent media be separated from all the other possible influences, such as the family, school and peers? Any study of violent offenders is likely to find they have seen violent media, because most people have. This does not prove the media caused the individual to be violent.

Some research has claimed to find a relationship between watching violence and aggressive behaviour. An example is the research by Bandura and his colleagues described in the section on experiments in Unit 1 in this book. However, this involved an artificial situation and if violence does affect people it is more likely that the effects accumulate over a long period. If individuals do copy an act of violence they have seen, it has been suggested that they were likely to be violent anyway but the media violence showed them a specific way of doing it. It is more likely that a society can become more violent through people becoming accustomed to violence than that individuals immediately copy something violent they have seen.

Any violence in the media will be seen by countless people yet only a tiny number, if any, then commit offences or claim to have been influenced by the media. It seems that nearly everyone can watch violence without being influenced to copy what they see. Another strong argument against media violence having effects is that appalling acts of violence have been committed throughout history, long before the mass media were invented. As a species, we seem to be capable of extreme violence against each other and any part the media play in this is minor.

Political beliefs and voting

Privately owned media often take strong political positions. The political position of newspapers can be seen in their choice of stories, the language that is used and the opinions that are expressed in editorials. Newspapers in the UK are strongly conservative. The public service broadcasting tradition and regulation of the television industry mean that television and radio are more neutral, though they are sometimes accused of bias. In the USA broadcasting is organised differently and the television channel Fox News, owned by News Corporation, is openly and strongly right wing.

In election campaigns, parties make extensive use of the media to get their messages across to voters. They use billboards and posters and make election broadcasts, as well as publishing manifestos and leaflets and ensuring they get news coverage through making policy statements and arranging press conferences. Election campaigns in the UK and USA are focused on the images and personalities of party leaders and less attention is given to the parties' policies.

The Sun newspaper in the UK, also owned by News Corporation, has the highest readership of all British newspapers and has claimed that it can influence how people vote and therefore the result of general elections. This was particularly the case in 1992 when the Labour Party was expected to win but *The Sun* backed the Conservatives, who won. Politicians seem to believe The *Sun* is influential, as leaders of both main parties have thought it more important to get positive coverage in *The Sun* than in other newspapers. It is, however, difficult to separate all the factors that influence how people vote.

KEY TERM

Opinion polls: results of survey research showing the opinions of the population.

Another way in which the media can influence politics is through their reporting of **opinion polls**. Opinion polls before general elections are based on small samples but are often interpreted as showing what the result is likely to be. For example, individuals may decide not to vote for their chosen candidate if the opinion polls show that that candidate is unlikely to win. In some countries opinion polls cannot be published in the final days before an election in case they influence the outcome.

Patterns of consumption

Through advertising and general content the media encourage a materialist, consumerist set of values. The spread of the media around the world involves the globalisation of Western values and an associated lifestyle. Advertising also establishes branding of goods and leads to a desire to own particular brands, not for their intrinsic value but for the social status that is attached to, for example, driving a particular make of car or having a particular brand of watch. Advertising carries images of what is taken to be the good life and so it encourages people to aspire to improve their lives so that they can earn the money to achieve this. However, it can be argued that this is an impossible goal for most people and is likely to make people dissatisfied and unhappy. It may even encourage crime as people turn to theft if they cannot afford to buy what they want. Marxists say the things that people learn from the media that they are supposed to want but that they do not need are false needs.

Gender and traditional stereotyping

Feminists and others are concerned by the gender stereotyping in the media and the effects this may have through the slow drip effect in shaping perceptions. For example, the gender stereotyping that young children encounter may encourage them to believe that:

- boys are able to do more than girls, for example they are more adventurous
- girls should be interested in toys and activities associated with the home and a future role as housewives and mothers
- boys are superior
- girls should spend a lot of time making themselves look attractive.

Feminists have advocated different gender representations in the media, for example, girls as main characters having the kinds of adventures that boys have always had, and showing girls in roles and occupations traditionally associated with males.

KEY TERMS

Social media: mobile and web-based media that allow people to interact more.

Digital divide: inequalities between groups in their access to media and information technology.

The influence of the internet on areas such as social networking

While traditional media involved one-way communication from the centre to the mass audience, the internet has changed the way in which people interact with each other. It is fairly cheap and easy to build a website and even easier to contribute to websites or online communities by blogging and uploading messages. New media that allow people to interact more are called **social media**. These are some of the ways in which the internet is now being used:

- social networking sites such as Facebook and Myspace
- video-sharing sites such as YouTube
- instant messaging, texting and Twitter messages
- e-mail.

Traditional media – broadcasting tower

These allow people to communicate, anonymously if they wish, with people all around the world whom they may never meet. Some groups, especially some older people and those excluded by the **digital divide**, do not use the internet. Even those who do still use traditional media as well at times communicate with others in older ways, such as by landline telephones and letters.

The internet is more difficult for governments to control and censor than traditional media. Some governments, such as in China and North Korea, manage to exercise control of the internet to the extent that it could be described as censorship. Even modern industrial societies try to police the internet by removing images such as child pornography and closing down illegal file-sharing sites but this is difficult because the internet is global and servers may be in any part of the world. Internet service providers claim they have no responsibility for the content of sites they allow their customers to visit, but governments sometimes prevent their citizens from accessing sites of which they disapprove.

TEST YOURSELF

1. Assess the view that the level of violence in a society is affected by the level of violence in its media.
2. In what ways is the internet changing how people communicate?

KEY TERMS

Gate-keeping: the ability of individuals to control access; for example, an editor controls what stories make the news.

News values: the ideas that people working in news industries have about what makes a good news story.

Selecting and presenting the news

This section deals with agenda setting, **gatekeeping** and stereotyping through the selection and presentation of the news.

The news is a social construction; that is, the news is the result of decisions and choices made by journalists and others: it does not reflect reality in any simple way. Sociologists show that the social construction of news has two stages, selection and presentation:

- Selection refers to how some events become news and others do not, and to how some news stories are then given greater prominence than others (for example, by becoming headline news). The key idea for explaining selection is a story's **news values**.
- Presentation refers to the decisions made about how news stories will appear to the reader or viewer; for example, what angle, spin or interpretation is put on the story. It can also involve decisions about what kind of story it is; for example, a story about a company declaring a large profit or loss might appear in the main news section or in the financial pages of a newspaper.

Gatekeepers such as news editors decide what to select and what to discard as news. The editor receives many stories and has to decide whether to include them in the media. Some will be passed and others will be spiked (rejected). By choosing some stories to make headline status and not covering others, the media practise agenda setting. Stories covered in the news media become talked about, including in other media, and statements and actions on the story are required from politicians and others. Sometimes whether a story makes the news or not may depend on what other stories there are on that day.

Both the selection and presentation of news happen under practical and cultural constraints. The practical constraints include time and space. News bulletins and newspapers normally have a set amount of space to fill: say, half an hour or 48 pages. Within this space there are normally set subdivisions. In a newspaper these are home news, foreign news, business news, sports news and so on. The space available has to be filled even if there are no strong news stories. Time constraints mean that a news bulletin has to be transmitted at a certain time, and the newspaper must be printed at a certain time. There are also legal constraints; for example, editors do not want to publish news that would lead to being taken to court for libel. Other practical constraints may include whether a reporter is on the spot when something happens and whether video footage, interviews or archive materials are available.

Rolling 24-hour news services and news sites on the internet do not face these constraints to the same extent as the old media do. New news media also increasingly use stories and photographs submitted by members of the public, who can often respond to breaking news stories more quickly than professional journalists. This has led to an increase in **citizen journalism**.

The term cultural constraints refers to how the news is shaped by news values; the ideas about what makes a story **newsworthy**. Marxists and others say that reporters share a professional ideology. Because of their similar background and their professional training they agree on what makes a good news story and on how to decide whether a story is newsworthy or not. While there are different lists of news values these are some that are widely agreed:

- frequency: the media report events that fit in with their schedules; long-term trends receive less coverage
- negativity: bad news is preferred to good news
- unexpectedness: events that are out of the ordinary
- personalisation: where there is human interest to the story, for example when someone in the story can be interviewed about their personal experience in a way that allows the audience to feel empathy for them
- reference to elite nations: news about the USA and other wealthy countries has a higher news value than equivalent stories from other countries
- reference to elite individuals: stories about royalty, leading politicians and celebrities can be news stories when they would not be if only ordinary people were involved
- conflict: stories that can be made dramatic because they involve a clash of ideas or people
- logistics: being able to get a reporter or a film crew to the place where an event has happened
- meaningfulness: when the story has more meaning to the audience because they can identify with aspects of it

KEY TERMS

Citizen journalism: ways in which the public can gather and distribute information.

Newsworthiness: the extent to which a news story conforms to news values.

- lack of ambiguity: events whose meaning is clear are more newsworthy than those where there is doubt and uncertainty
- continuity: once established, a story may run for a long time and minor new developments may be given prominence.

News media have been strongly criticised by Marxists and others for:

- selecting and presenting news stories in ways that suit powerful groups in society
- neglecting the interests and concerns of particular groups in society
- neglecting the wrongdoing of large and powerful corporations.

In some modern industrial countries there are alternative news media that give radically different interpretations of the news from the mainstream media. For example, the UK has a morning newspaper called the *Morning Star*. This was once the newspaper of the Communist Party and it still reports from a strongly left-wing point of view. However, it is not read by many people and is not often found in smaller shops. Pluralists would say that this is because people are not interested in this type of news and reporting; Marxists would say that few people know about the *Morning Star* because it is not kept in shops, and that if more people knew about it it would have a larger readership.

TEST YOURSELF

1. What is meant by saying that the media set the agenda?
2. Explain the difference between practical and cultural constraints in the selection and presentation of news.

ACTIVITY: *research*

Collect several newspapers or print pages from a news website. How many news values from the list in the section above can you identify? Are other, different, news values present?

Explanations of the influence of the media

Explanations of the influence of the media include the hypodermic syringe model, audience selection, cultural effects and the uses and gratifications model.

Hypodermic syringe model

The hypodermic syringe model argues that the media have direct and immediate effects on audiences. It assumes that the audience is passive and soaks in media messages, and also that everyone in the audience is affected in the same way. This theory was widely held in the first part of the 20th century. It was believed that the media, especially moving images, which were then new, were powerful enough to have a direct influence on people. There were two aspects to this:

- Companies often believed that advertising would be successful – all they had to do was put an advertisement in front of people (for example, on a cinema screen) and their sales would increase.
- The mass media were used directly for propaganda, for example in Nazi Germany and in the Soviet Union. In situations where people do not have access to alternative information, propaganda can be successful. It is much harder now to

use the media in this way because the range of media available means that we have access to alternative information.

A later variation on this model suggested that people discuss with others what they have seen, read or heard before deciding how to react. When they do so, the opinions of some people – opinion leaders – are more important than others. In this view the media have a strong effect but it is mediated by social interactions. This is called the two-step flow model.

KEY TERM

Audience selection: this explanation is based on the part audiences play in how they read and are affected by the media.

Audience selection

Later explanations of media influence did not assume that the whole audience would be affected in the same way or that audiences were passive consumers. They used the idea that audiences actively read media texts rather than simply consume a message. Producers of media texts encode a meaning (the way they intend the text to be read) but audiences may decode the text differently.

Members of the audience are not always giving the media their full attention. For example, a television may be switched on while individuals are doing something else in the room. But if something comes on the television that they find interesting, they begin to watch and listen attentively. This is selective attention. Later, people remember some things they have heard or read better than others, so some media messages have a stronger impact than others. This is selective retention. Together, they mean that a media message does not necessarily affect audience members.

One related explanation put forward by David Morley was based on research in which he interviewed groups of people of similar backgrounds about how they responded to a television news and current affairs programme. Morley found that different groups read the same programme in different ways:

- In a dominant (or hegemonic) reading, readers share the programme's code (its meaning, system of values, attitudes, beliefs and assumptions) and fully accept the programme's preferred reading.
- In a negotiated reading, readers partly share the programme's code and broadly accept the preferred reading but modify it in a way that reflects their position and interests. This allows some readers to distance themselves from the preferred reading.
- In an oppositional (or counter-hegemonic) reading, readers do not share the programme's code and reject the preferred reading. Instead they use an alternative frame of interpretation. Readers expressed this to Morley by saying that the programme did not show life as it really was.

Morley's research was based on grouping people by their class background and looking at how belonging to a class-based sub-culture shaped their readings of programmes. Other significant variables are likely to be age, ethnicity and gender. This approach works well with news and current affairs programmes but it is not always as clearly useful for other genres. Media texts differ in the degree to which they are clearly offering a preferred reading. Later writers described programmes and images that are clearly intended to be read in a particular way as monosemic. Those that are left open to allow different readings are described as polysemic.

The implication of all these approaches is that meanings are produced by audiences (which vary by class, age, ethnicity, gender and so on) but that audiences have to work on the text, which has been put together in particular ways by producers. A further implication is that the media do have the power and ability to influence audiences by pushing preferred readings, but this power is limited by the ability of audiences to produce alternative readings.

Cultural effects

KEY TERM

Cultural effects approach: this explanation focuses on the slow, cumulative effects of the media.

Cultural effects explanations cover a range of related theories and research. They are united by the idea that the media do have very real and very important effects but these are usually long term and cumulative and depend on contexts and circumstances. This is in contrast with the hypodermic syringe explanation, which sees the effects as immediate. For example, the cultural effects explanation suggests that if women are shown in a particular way by the media, then this representation will slowly but steadily shape how people think of women. Feminists have also been concerned about the long-term effects on both boys and girls of prolonged exposure to sexist stereotypes. There is particular concern about the importance of the media when audiences do not have access to other sources of information. For example, media representations of women may be particularly misleading to boys in a boarding school or other institution where they do not meet or talk often to real women or girls.

In the UK the Glasgow Media Group have for over 30 years produced the most substantial and challenging body of research on the British media showing that the media do have important effects in the ways suggested by the cultural effects approach. They have demonstrated the importance of the media in shaping people's attitudes and opinions when they do not have access to other sources of information. The Glasgow Media Group found that the following factors influence audiences in believing or rejecting media accounts:

- The role of direct experience. The media have more power to instruct their audiences when the audience does not have direct knowledge of the event. Audience members who had experienced mental distress (themselves, or in their family or friends) were very critical of media accounts that tend to link mental distress to violence and imply that mentally distressed people were dangerous (the 'mad axe murderer syndrome').
- The use of logic. For example, some people rejected the view that picketing in the miners' strike was as violent as the media portrayed it on the grounds that it was not possible for so many people to have been involved in fighting: the police dealt with it, not the army.
- Affiliations and sympathies. Audience responses are influenced by their political, religious and other beliefs.
- The source of information. For example, when the tabloid press in the UK reported that BSE (mad cow disease) could be passed to humans by eating beef products and this was being contradicted by the government, many people decided **the press** were being sensationalist and believed the government. The government later accepted that the disease could be passed to humans.

KEY TERM

The press: newspaper and magazine publishing industry.

The Glasgow Media Group research suggests that audiences do not simply absorb messages and they can distinguish between fact and fiction. But audiences are not

KEY TERM

Uses and gratifications model: this explanation focuses on how audiences use the media rather than how they are affected by them.

in the all-powerful position suggested by the **uses and gratifications** approach – the media do influence what we believe. Each case needs to be studied separately to determine the exact nature of the influence.

Uses and gratifications

The fourth explanation, uses and gratifications, is concerned with how audiences use the media. It believes that the audiences are in control, rather than being influenced by the media, and it is closely related to the pluralist approach. This explanation argues that people have needs and that some of these needs can be met by consuming media stories.

The implication is that we need to ask different questions about the media – no longer 'What effects do the media have?' but rather 'How do audiences use the media?' Different writers have given different suggestions as to what the main uses and gratifications are. McQuail suggested they could be grouped under four headings:

- Entertainment. Some media texts are used purely for entertainment: we relax, fill time and get enjoyment from the media.
- Personal relationships. There are two possibilities here. Firstly, the viewer may feel a sense of companionship, of not being alone, by identifying with characters. People sometimes express this as feeling that they really know a character, perhaps better than their own friends or neighbours. Secondly, the media text becomes a source of friendship by talking to others about it or it may even lead to a friendship group held together by interest in it.
- Personal identity**.** People make decisions about themselves and their lives and relationships by comparing themselves with characters and situations in the media. The media can reinforce our values or challenge them and can change our self-identities.
- Information. The media supply information, allowing us to choose to find out things beyond our immediate experience.

This approach concentrates on audiences and does not give the whole picture. There are three problems with this approach:

- It does not look at media messages, which it tends to assume are unambiguous, only at people's use of them.
- It does not consider that audiences may have been taught by the media to have the needs that the media then satisfy (learning to enjoy what is available), as would be suggested by Marxists.
- It does not look at the social context of audiences (such as different classes, ethnic groups and ages). Different sectors of the audience may have more or less agency in their ability to use the media in the way this model suggests.

New media have increased the ways in which audiences can be actively involved in the media and so the growth of new media has strengthened the uses and gratifications approach.

ACTIVITY: *discussion*

What media do you use and why? Analyse your own media use and discuss with others whether the uses and gratifications approach explains how you and your friends use the media.

TEST YOURSELF

1. According to uses and gratifications theory, what are some of the ways in which audiences use the media?
2. How do people decide to what extent they will trust a news story?

Bias and distortion

This section discusses bias and distortion in the media, including propaganda and moral panics.

Bias and distortion

According to pluralists, the media in modern industrial societies have a range of different biases. For example, newspapers support different political parties. Readers can then choose the bias they want. However, Marxists argue that the range of opinion on offer is in fact narrow and excludes views that are dismissed as extreme.

Research by the Glasgow Media Group has shown some of the ways in which the news can be reported in a biased way through their analysis of strikes by trade unionists. There were two sides in these disputes, management and unions:

- Managers were given more time than the union leaders to express their opinions in interview and were interviewed first.
- Managers were usually interviewed in calm surroundings such as their offices, while workers were interviewed on the street, on picket lines and so on, with noise and distractions.
- The actions of the strikers were reported more than their opinions.

Mods – a youth group about which there was a moral panic

The outcome was that the news reporting seemed to be unbiased by reporting both sides but the audience were being guided towards seeing the managers as reasonable and right and the strikers as unreasonable and wrong.

Moral panics

One result of bias in the media is the creation of moral panics. This is when a group or event is reported in an exaggerated and sensationalised way so that great public concern is created. This leads to a spiralling situation in which the response to the initial events actually leads to more trouble – a self-fulfilling prophecy. The phenomenon of moral panics was first described by Stanley Cohen, who showed how initial minor disturbances involving youth groups known as mods and rockers were reported in ways that made these young people into folk devils, with the public insisting that the police and courts should deal firmly with them. The expectation of trouble led to more young people getting involved and to bigger confrontations with the police. Often the young people involved are being **scapegoated**; that is, they are wrongly blamed, and the

KEY TERM

Scapegoats: those singled out for negative treatment or undeserved blame.

fear and anger that others have about the way society is changing is directed at them.

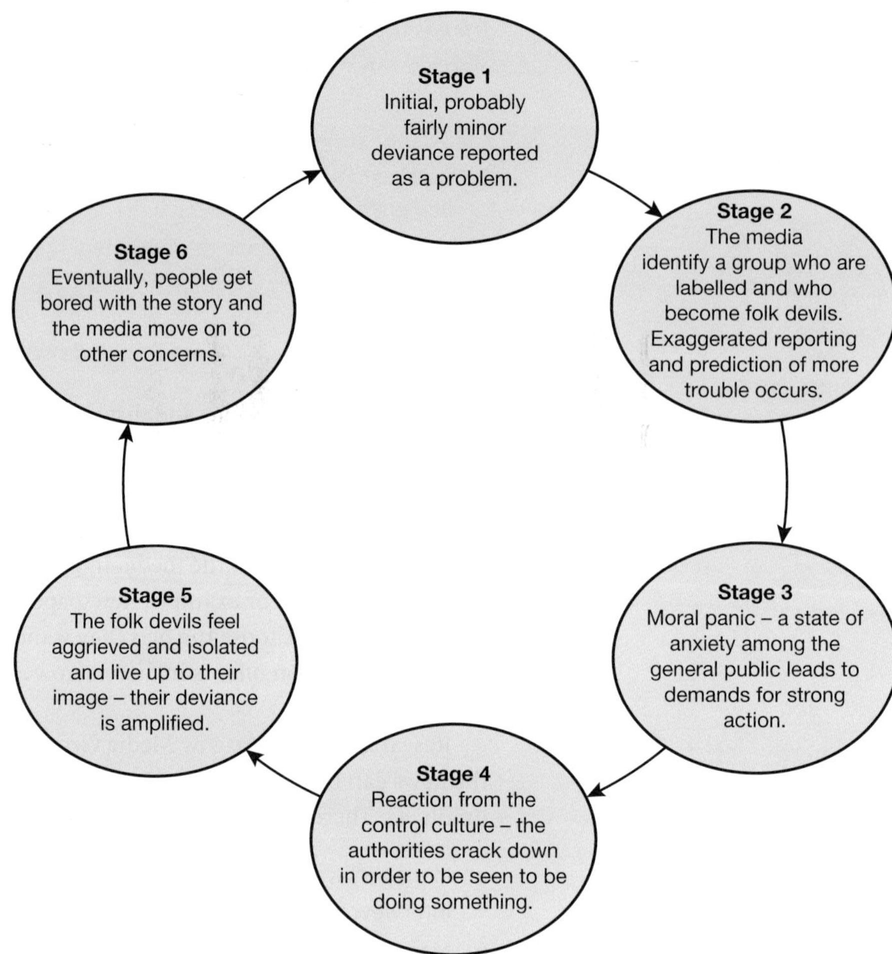

Stages in moral panics

Moral panics involve two aspects of bias in the media:

- **Exaggeration**: in the case of the mods and rockers, the numbers involved and the extent of the damage were exaggerated in news reports.
- **Sensationalism**: information and events may be deliberately misrepresented in ways designed to appeal to the audience's emotions; the media report a good story without due regard for the facts.

KEY TERMS

Exaggeration: represents things as greater than they really are.

Sensationalism: a form of bias in which stories are deliberately reported in ways designed to excite or attract viewers or readers.

Interactivity: when media respond in some way to actions of audiences and vice versa.

Developments in the media

Developments in the media include changes in ownership, globalisation, **interactivity**, the digital divide, diversification and convergence in the media.

Changes in ownership and control

Two recent trends in media ownership are horizontal and vertical integration. Media conglomerates own a range of companies in different media, and sometimes in the same media (for example, a conglomerate may own several companies producing similar content in one medium). This is called horizontal integration and offers opportunities to increase their market share and profits. For example, News Corporation can show the films it owns through Twentieth Century Fox on its Sky and Star television channels. Vertical integration is also found in the media. This is when companies under the same ownership control different stages of the production and distribution. This used to be the case in the US film industry when the main Hollywood studios also had their own cinema chains. Today some television broadcasting corporations make programmes that are broadcast on their own channels using a distribution service such as the satellite that the corporation also owns.

Synergy is the term given to the advantages of being able to move content easily between media or between different companies in the same conglomerate. For example, Hollywood film studios used to allow television companies to broadcast films only two years after their initial release and after buying the right to broadcast them. Sky wanted to show first-run films to attract new subscribers and to achieve this it bought one of the main Hollywood studios, Twentieth Century Fox. Media conglomerates are also able to subsidise loss-making parts of the business or to invest heavily in major new initiatives.

Pluralists argue that the concentration of media ownership has been exaggerated. There are many small media companies that tend to be forgotten when discussing the big ones. The biggest media corporations do not necessarily stay successful. Some of the most important companies today did not even exist a few years ago, while others have become less successful or broken up. Changes in media technologies mean that new companies (such as Google) are challenging the older ones and this competition ensures a good service to consumers. Pluralists also point out that most of the big media companies are owned by shareholders, who include, for example, pension funds investing money that belongs to millions of people. Ownership by a single person is unusual.

Marxists, on the other hand, are very concerned about the recent trends in media ownership such as concentration and vertical integration. Media ownership becomes concentrated in a few very powerful conglomerates that support capitalism and will not allow dissenting points of view. Marxists do not see choice, as pluralists do, but an illusion of choice – lots of different media products all based on the same very limited set of ideas. For example, newspapers that appear to have different political stances are in fact not very different; radical views are not discussed. The media are also seen by Marxists to be ignoring what should be important news stories, turning a blind eye to the effects of capitalism.

Globalisation

KEY TERM

Globalisation: growing integration and interdependence of countries and peoples around the world.

There are many ways in which the media are part of **globalisation**. Communication via the media is now instant around the globe. Unfolding news events can be watched as they happen, even on the other side of the world. The importance of the media, and especially the new media, may be to create a sense of sharing a common home, Spaceship Earth or a global village. Print and early broadcasting media helped people feel a sense of belonging to a nation; new media may be extending this to the global level.

Some aspects of globalisation and the media are:

- The global media are dominated by a small number of huge conglomerates.
- These are based in Western societies and spread mainly Western culture.
- Increasingly media products are made for global rather than national audiences and contain elements that may appeal globally.
- Local cultures may be swamped by Western culture spread by the media; so that, for example, people may use their own languages less often.

- Non-Western media may be able to reach new global audiences; for example, Bollywood films are watched all around the world and some non-Bollywood films, such as *Slumdog Millionaire*, adopt some of the features of Bollywood films.

Interactivity

The new media offer much greater opportunities for interactivity than the old media. For the old media, involvement was limited to such things as:

- writing letters to a newspaper
- taking part in a telephone vote on a television programme.

New media allow users to:

- personalise their media use, for example having news on particular topics e-mailed to them
- create their own media: having a website or writing a blog or uploading videos or photographs
- contribute to online discussions on forums and message boards, and reply immediately to others
- play role playing and other games with others who are physically distant and may not be known to the user.

Some of this use of the new media can be anonymous, using an assumed name and avatar. This has sometimes encouraged people to behave in ways they would probably not if their identities were known, such as trolling (making deliberately provocative comments) and flaming (being hostile and insulting on a forum).

The digital divide

A major concern associated with social class, inequalities and new media has been the idea of a digital divide. This refers to how the cost of computers and internet access makes them less affordable to the working class, so that the other classes were making much greater use of them. There is also a global digital divide, in which poor people and those in developing countries have less access to the internet and to the new media. People in modern industrial countries enjoy access to a greater range of new media and services. This gap is seen as a major problem because it tends to keep the world and individual countries unequal. Those with access to the digital media are able to improve their social capital while those without miss out on opportunities for education and acquiring knowledge to increase their chances of good employment. There are various initiatives to improve this situation, for example the One Laptop per Child project, which aims to supply children in developing countries with laptop computers, and Sugata Mitra's Hole in the Wall experiments, which showed that children in India could work out for themselves how to use computers fitted in walls in slums and rural areas and could then teach others.

In modern industrial countries, costs have fallen and new media content has become accessible in more and more affordable ways but there are still some concerns about it in modern industrial countries. For example, in the UK, although it is now common for teachers to set homework tasks requiring the use of a computer or the internet, not all pupils have computers at home and may

KEY TERM

Media culture: the idea that the development of new media means that we all increasingly live in a world dominated by the media.

need, for example, to use a public library to access one or to use school computers outside lesson time. Increasingly, people also have access to the internet and multimedia through mobile phones and other devices. There remains a digital divide between age groups, as older people are less likely to use the internet. Young people can be described as digital natives because they have grown up with digital media and find them easy to use, but some older people find it hard to get used to the new media.

Overall, these developments in the media have made the media an even more important part of most people's lives. We now live in a **media culture**.

ACTIVITY: *discussion*

How can the digital divide be reduced? Discuss the merits of different ways of getting more people on line.

ACTIVITY: *data interpretation*

World internet usage and population statistics – June 30, 2012

World regions	Population (2012 Est.)	Internet users Dec. 31, 2000	Internet users latest data	Penetration (% population)	Growth 2000–2012 (%)	Users % of table
Africa	1,073,380,925	4,514,400	167,335,676	15.6	3,606.7	7.0
Asia	3,922,066,987	114,304,000	1,076,681,059	27.5	841.9	44.8
Europe	820,918,446	105,096,093	518,512,109	63.2	393.4	21.5
Middle East	223,608,203	3,284,800	90,000,455	40.2	2,639.9	3.7
North America	348,280,154	108,096,800	273,785,413	78.6	153.3	11.4
Latin America / Caribbean	593,688,638	18,068,919	254,915,745	42.9	1,310.8	10.6
Oceania / Australia	35,903,569	7,620,480	24,287,919	67.6	218.7	1.0
World total	**7,017,846,922**	**360,985,492**	**2,405,518,376**	**34.3**	**566.4**	**100.0**

Internet users of the world: distribution by world regions, 2012

1. Which world region has the highest percentage of the population using the internet, and which the least?
2. In which region is internet use growing fastest?
3. Calculate the increase in the number of internet users globally between 2000 and the latest figures in the table.
4. What conclusions can you draw about internet usage from these statistics?

KEY TERM

Diversification: when media corporations extend their activities into different areas.

Convergence: media technologies moving towards being able to perform similar tasks.

Diversification and convergence

These two terms may sound contradictory, and this shows how complex the world of new media is becoming. **Diversification** refers to media corporations extending their interests into other areas. News Corporation began with the family of Rupert Murdoch who owned several Australian newspapers, but it has expanded and diversified and now has interests in a wide range of media. Other corporations have diversified beyond the media. Virgin is a major media

Rupert Murdoch

corporation in the UK but it also runs trains and airlines and has other non-media interests.

Convergence refers to the way that differences between media technologies are becoming unclear. With old media, the content and the technology could be treated as the same; the word 'television' stood both for the box in the corner of the living room and the programmes that could be watched on it. Today, television programmes can be watched on a television, a computer or a mobile telephone. The internet could once be accessed only from a computer; now a variety of technological equipment can be used, including televisions. The difference between computers and the latest televisions is their size and how far you sit away from them: they can be used for much the same things. Newspapers were once only physical sheets of paper; now newspaper articles are more likely to be read on websites. It is now more important than it used to be to distinguish between media content and the technology used to access it. The differences between the technologies are increasingly only about size and portability. Televisions, computers (including laptops and tablets) and mobile phones can increasingly be used to access the same media.

ACTIVITY: *data interpretation*

1 Which age group is least likely to use the internet at all?
2 For all except two types of device, it is the age group 16–24 who access the internet most. What are the exceptions, and which age groups used them most?

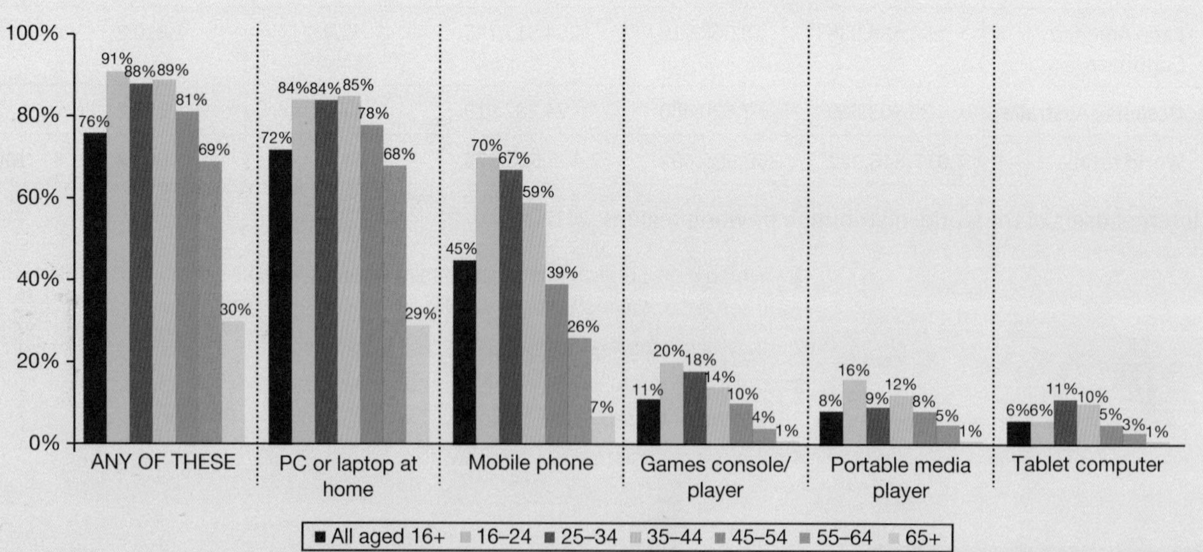

Devices used to visit internet websites in 2011 in the UK, by age

Influence of media representations on audiences

This section discusses how media representations influence the audience.

Almost all research on representations describes representations of particular groups of people or places and much of it concentrates on negative stereotypes, using content analysis. Such research on its own cannot show whether the representations have effects. Some representations may create or reinforce prejudiced beliefs about a group of people (such as that all blondes are dumb or that all mental patients are potential axe murderers). However, prejudiced beliefs do not necessarily influence behaviour. A man who believes that women are not capable of certain types of work may be able to act on this belief only if he is in a position to employ or promote people.

The media are only one source of ideas, and media representations may be contradicted by, for example, personal experience. There may be differences between the media in their ability to influence us. For example, the visual impact of television may make it more influential than radio as it may be better able to convince us that it is presenting the truth.

TEST YOURSELF

1. What is the digital divide, and what effects might it have?
2. What recent trends have there been in media industries?

Radio, a traditional form of broadcast media

Revision checklist

Make sure that you know all the key terms listed in this unit and that you understand the following:

- Traditional or old media can be distinguished from new media.
- The media are our main source of information about people and issues we do not have direct contact with.
- Advertising is important, especially as the main source of revenue for media.
- Ownership of the media is concentrated in a few large conglomerates.
- The media can be used for propaganda and can be censored so that people do not have full access to information.
- The main sociological perspectives on the media are pluralism, Marxism and postmodernism.
- Patterns of media use vary by gender, age, social class and ethnicity.
- The media represent ethnicity, gender, age, class and disability, often in negative and stereotypical ways which can influence audiences.
- Some of these stereotypical representations are changing.
- The media can shape values and attitudes in a variety of ways.
- The news is socially constructed through processes involving gatekeepers and agenda setting and selection and presentation involving practical and cultural constraints.
- Explanations of media influence include those suggesting strong effects and passive audiences (the hypodermic syringe model and cultural effects) and those that suggest weak effects and active audience (audience reception and uses and gratifications).
- Recent developments include the concentration of ownership, globalisation, greater interactivity, the digital divide, diversification and convergence.

Exam practice questions

A major area of the media studied by sociologists is representations. Representations often involve stereotypes, for example of minority ethnic groups or of age groups such as children. Representations are seen as important because the media are one of our main sources of information and because some sociologists argue that representations can have important effects, for example changing people's attitudes and behaviour.

a What is meant by the term stereotype? [2]

b Describe two examples of stereotypes of minority ethnic groups. [4]

c Explain how children are represented in the media. [6]

d Explain why representations change over time. [8]

e To what extent can representations in the media influence attitudes and behaviour? [15]

Total available marks 35

Unit 8: Examination Skills

The syllabus

You should make sure that you are familiar with the appropriate syllabus for the year you will be taking your examinations. Your teacher will be able to guide you. The syllabus will indicate the topics you will be expected to know and understand. The syllabus will also direct you to the key skills you will have covered on your course that are important to the study of sociology. These skills are in the assessment objectives (AO).

There are three assessment objectives from the Cambridge IGCSE syllabus:

AO1 Knowledge and understanding

You will show that you:

- know and understand the topics
- understand the theoretical and practical considerations influencing sociological research
- understand and use sociological terms and concepts.

AO2 Interpretation of evidence

You will show that you:

- are aware of the main methods of sociological enquiry
- can interpret and apply relevant evidence and data
- are aware of their uses and of different types and sources of evidence.

AO3 Analysis and evaluation

You will show you can:

- evaluate the strengths and limitations of particular sociological studies and methods
- recognise limitations and bias in evidence and distinguish between fact, opinion and values
- reach conclusions based on a reasoned consideration of the evidence
- organise and present evidence and arguments in a coherent and purposeful form.

Most students find the skills within AO1 the most straightforward to learn and demonstrate in examination. There is a lot to learn and understand but the other skills are more demanding. The units of this book cover all the content that is listed in the syllabus. The syllabus lists key terms in each topic area. These are given in each unit with a definition or explanation. You need to know these terms. The AO2 skills mean that you have to show that you can work out what sociological evidence and data to use in your answers, and that you understand different types and sources of evidence and data. The skills within AO3 are probably the most challenging to master. Evaluation is a difficult skill and you need to practise writing exam-style answers in which you evaluate the topic. Ask your teacher to check these practice examples.

Evaluation does not have to be all about criticisms in the negative sense. A good evaluation can also show what is useful or important about the topic. These are some ways to evaluate that you can practise and try to use:

- Point out a limitation or problem in a research study. For example, the sample may have been too small for generalisations to be made from it.

- Point out a limitation or problem in a theoretical perspective. For example, Marxists tend to focus on class divisions but there are other conflicts in societies as well.
- Point out when a sociological research study or theory does not seem to explain something well (or perhaps at all) or where there are exceptions to the findings.
- Point out the contribution that a research study has made to sociological knowledge or that a theory has made to sociological understanding.
- Point out differences between the findings of research studies or between different theoretical perspectives.

You will often be evaluating if you use words and phrases like 'however' or 'on the other hand'. These introduce different points. Your evaluation will be even stronger if you can explain why there is a difference and which point you think is stronger.

The syllabus document will also give details of how the examination is structured. The Cambridge IGCSE exam is made up of two papers. Within Paper 1, you have to answer two questions, each made up of several part questions, in two hours. You should spend the first 15 minutes of the exam reading the questions.

The first question is a data response question and is called Section A. It tests Unit 1, theory and methods and is worth 45 marks. This is the question that all students have to answer.

There will be two questions in Paper 1 – Section B on Unit 2 (culture, identity and socialisation) and Section C on Unit 3 (social inequality). You are expected to have studied both these units, because they are the basics of sociology and lay the foundations for the other topics. However, you may answer only one of the questions, so you will need to decide which one. The question that you choose to answer will be worth 35 marks, so the total mark for Paper 1 is 80.

Your second sociology exam is Paper 2. There will be four questions in this paper, one on each of:

- Section A: Family
- Section B: Education
- Section C: Crime, deviance and social control
- Section D: Media.

You have to answer two questions, each of which will be made up of questions with several parts. Each question has 35 marks available, so the total mark for the paper is 70. If you have studied more than two of these sections you will need to decide in the examination which two to answer questions on. This exam is one and three-quarter hours long. As you did in Paper 1, spend the first 15 minutes reading the questions. You will then have 45 minutes to answer each of the two questions you have chosen. Knowledge of the topics on Paper 1 may be useful in this paper.

Command words

Questions have content words and command words. Here is an example of a possible question:

Explain why positivists prefer using quantitative research methods.

In this example 'explain' is the command word and 'positivists' and 'quantitative research methods' are content words and phrases. Content words and phrases tell you what to write about; the command words tell you how you should write about them. Command words help you work out what skills you should demonstrate in your answer. This is because command words are associated with the assessment objectives.

Here are some of the command words that you may see and the assessment objectives they may be associated with:

- AO1 Knowledge and understanding: 'what is meant by', 'identify'
- AO2 Interpretation of evidence: 'describe'
- AO3 Analysis and evaluation: 'explain', 'to what extent'.

Different questions have a different number of marks for each AO. You do not have to be concerned about this because the questions will be worded so as to get you to show the skills that are required. This, however, makes it very important to do exactly what the question says.

When there is an AO3 command word, more marks will be available than for other questions and some of these marks will be for AO1. This is because you can only analyse and evaluate the sociological knowledge you are presenting. It is particularly important that you recognise when AO3 is required so that you avoid just writing everything you know about something without showing that you can analyse and evaluate.

Exam techniques

This section offers a few general points about how you should approach examination.

Timing

Make sure you know how long you have for each question paper and allocate the time accordingly. You need to allow time to read through the paper and choose questions if there are optional questions. For example, if the paper allows one hour and 45 minutes to complete two questions you may allocate 15 minutes to read and select questions and then divide the remaining time according to the number of marks allocated to each question.

Question selection

There are two possible strategies for selecting which questions to answer in examinations, on which your teachers will offer guidance. You can prepare for questions on all units and decide when you see the questions which of them you feel you can do best on. Alternatively, you might decide in advance which topic you will answer questions on and focus on that one in your revision.

Make sure that you read all parts of all questions carefully before making your selection, including any source material that is provided as part of the question. Don't be tempted to select a question just because it happens to be about a topic on which you feel confident. Look at what the question is asking you to **do**, as well as the subject matter.

Revision helps to strengthen our understanding

Revision

To do well in examination you will need to revise effectively. Throughout your study of the course, keep a file or exercise book of notes on the topics as you study them. Keep these together with any documents or other handouts your teachers give you and also the work your teachers have marked. The marks or grades your teachers have given you are less important than the comments they have made about where you have done well and where you need to improve, so take note of these.

To revise effectively as your examinations approach you need a revision plan. Your teachers may help you with this. You need to know:

- the times and dates of your sociology exams – ask your teacher if you have not yet been told
- the times and dates of any exams you have in other subjects around that time
- any other commitments you may have; for example, there may be a family occasion or other event that you are expected to go to
- times and dates when you will be in school for lessons.

On each day you also need to allow time for sleeping, eating and relaxing. Divide each day into morning, afternoon and evening, and divide each of these into two, so that you have made six time slots in the day, probably of about an hour and a half each. Block out slots where you have any commitments. Then, in each free slot, write in the name of a subject you need to revise for, giving more time to that subject as the exam approaches. You probably need about the same number of slots for each subject but you may want to vary this, for example if you are particularly worried (or confident) about a subject or if there is significantly more or less to learn for a subject.

You should now have some idea about how many time slots you have for revising sociology. If you are sitting more than one sociology exam, you may wish to divide your time slots equally between the exams.

These are the resources you will need for effective revision:

- Your teachers: they are experts in the subject and in revision and exam techniques. Ask them questions and ask for advice. You will probably find that they are pleased that you are keen to do well and will offer you full support.
- This textbook.
- Your notes from all the way through the course – in order and divided into the topic areas. Card dividers can help you organise your notes.
- Paper.
- Pens, pencils and highlighter pens.
- Past exam papers and mark schemes. Same past exam papers are available on the public website of Cambridge International Examinations, as are specimen papers, but your teachers may be able to get others.

While revising, you want to be interrupted as little as possible. Talk to your family and friends and explain when you want to be left undisturbed and why. It is good to have a space where you revise (for example, a desk or table) but it can also be good to sit somewhere else for a change.

When you are revising, it is important to do more than just reading. Most people find that if they just read notes or a textbook their mind wanders. Try rewriting the notes in a different way or summarising them.

People revise in different ways and you need to work out what works best for you. Here are some ways to revise that many people find effective:

- Do practice exams. Ask your teachers to help you find past exam papers and use the exam-style questions in this book. You can practise individual questions but you should also try a whole exam paper without breaks. This is so that you get used to how many questions you have to answer and the time that you have in which to do them. It is also important to know how much you can write in the time, and to write by hand so that your fingers are less likely to get tired when writing in the exam itself.

- Write definitions of key words or names of sociologists on cards or small pieces of paper. You will learn from writing these but you can also carry them around with you.
- Revise with a friend sometimes. Revision can be quite lonely so get together with a fellow student. Test each other with quiz-style questions about who knows the most sociology.
- Turn your linear notes into diagrams such as spider diagrams. Be inventive: use colours to make them attractive and memorable.
- You may be able to put revision notes and posters on a wall at home or perhaps on a mirror, so you constantly see and are reminded of them. This is doing for yourself what teachers do when they put posters and diagrams on classroom walls.

You will need breaks. No one can work for a very long time without a break. Set yourself targets; for example, that you will revise a topic for an hour, or write 20 definitions on cards and then reward yourself by stopping for a break or having a drink or snack. You will need self-discipline. If you think you will find self-discipline difficult, ask a family member to monitor how you are doing and tell you when you have succeeded.

Computer revision

If you have access to one, a computer can be very useful for revision. There are some good revision sources for sociology on the internet and your teachers should be able to advise you which ones to use. Some sites are less helpful and a search for something like gender will give you millions of websites, but probably not many that are relevant to IGCSE Sociology, so avoid wide searches.

Be careful about revising on a computer or laptop and think about how you use a computer. Computers can be great time wasters. Will you be constantly tempted to check e-mails or social networking sites, or to visit internet sites that are nothing to do with your revision? If so, put a strict limit on how much time you spend at your computer. You may also need to switch off your mobile phone, if you have one, while you are revising.

The exam room

Just before the examination

- Go to bed at your usual time the night before an exam or even earlier if you tend to stay up late. A good night's sleep will help you more than last minute cramming.
- Have something to eat before the exam. You will work better and you will not be distracted by your empty stomach.
- Drink plenty of water to keep hydrated. Your brain does not work at its full capacity if you are dehydrated. If you are allowed to, take a bottle of water into the exam.
- Too many fizzy drinks or chocolate and sweets can lower your concentration for a while, so avoid these.
- Try to stay calm before the exam but remember that being a bit nervous is normal and can even help you to focus.

In the exam room

Be early and be equipped. You will need to write in a black pen, and you should take a spare pen too.

There are often distractions in an exam room. People move or cough, chairs creak and there may be noises outside the room. Keep focused on the exam and try to screen out anything else. At the very start of the exam, as the papers are given out and before you can start writing, clear your mind, close your eyes and breathe deeply to prepare yourself.

Everyone goes into the exam knowing some sociology and some people know more than others but very few have managed to learn everything. Here are some of the things you can do to help yourself do the best you can with the sociological knowledge that you have:

- Use the sources: they are there to help you. Some students are so keen to get on with answering the question that they do not take time to read them carefully. The sources give you some sociological knowledge and ideas that will help you get started on some answers.
- Read the questions very carefully and try to do exactly what they tell you to do. Try to split the question up into sections, thinking about what each word and phrase means. The question will not contain unnecessary words, so each word or phrase is trying to get students to do something: work out what this is. Remember that you have to answer the question that has been set, not the question you were hoping would come up.
- Know the timings. This includes how long the exam is and how long you should spend on each question. Do not rush; work steadily. Have a watch with you as there may not be a clock in the room.
- If you feel you cannot answer a question, move on to one that you can answer and come back later to the earlier question. Your brain will continue to think about the question and you may remember something. For the same reason, it can be a good idea to read through all the sources and questions before you start writing.
- How much you write is less important than what you write.
- Try to answer every question in the sections you have to answer or choose to answer. If you write something, even if you are not sure whether it is right, there is a chance you will succeed.
- If you have to cross something out, do this with a single clear line. If you do not have enough room for your answer, use the extra pages at the back of your answer booklet and tell the examiner you have done this (for example by writing: 'continued at back of book').
- For questions that require longer answers, it is a good idea to plan. Make a list above where you will write your answer of the points you want to make, the theories, studies or sociologists you want to include and so on. Decide on the order, then start writing. Look back at your plan as you write, ticking the points you have covered. You will then be able to see how much more you have to say and you can check how much time you have left for this.
- Try to leave enough time to read quickly over your answer paper at the end. The most important thing is to make sure you have answered all the questions that you should have done. Then see if there are any good, relevant points that you could have included but did not and add them. You can also correct any spelling, grammatical or punctuation errors that you see, if you have time.

Timing is important in an exam setting

After the exam it is not usually a good idea to talk about what you wrote. Your fellow students may tell you they included something that you did not and you may begin to worry that you have not done well. But in sociology there are often different ways to answer a question and your answer may be just as good as, or better than, your friends' answers. In any case, there is nothing you can do once the exam paper is handed in. Better to start thinking about the next exam, or take a well-deserved break if you have finished your exams.

Your answers

A lot of the sociology you have learnt will have been about the UK and the USA. This is partly because a lot of sociological research has been done in these countries and they are where many important ideas in sociology were developed. Other textbooks that you may have seen, for example for GCSE Sociology, are intended for use by students in the UK or elsewhere, following syllabuses that are mainly about the UK.

It is not possible to have a different textbook for every country where students are taking IGCSE Sociology. You may have thought at times that the topic you are learning in these books seems very different from the situation in your own society. This textbook tries to be more international and global than other textbooks and we have included examples and information from a range of countries. However, you can show you have good sociological skills and understanding by taking ideas from the sociology you have learnt in the textbooks and applying them to your own society. You have to answer the question, of course, and you have to show you have sociological knowledge but do not be afraid to write about your own society.

Exam-style sample questions and answers

It is important to understand the question format of your exam before you sit it

When you see exam papers there may be topics that you have not studied. Do not try to answer the questions on these even if you think you can: keep to what you have been taught.

Examples of part questions

The first part question in a section may ask you to explain what is meant by a particular sociological concept. For example:

'What is meant by . . .'

The word or phrase that follows might be taken from the lists of key concepts in the syllabus and it might also be in the stimulus given on the exam paper.

Part question example 1

What is meant by the term 'norms'? (from Culture, Identity and Socialisation) [2]

Answer: *Norms are the rules of behaviour for specific situations in everyday life.*

Commentary on answer: [2/2] This answer shows understanding and explains what the term 'norms' means. If two marks are available and your answer shows some understanding but does **not** fully explain what the term means, it will be possible to get only one mark.

If the concept has two parts, make sure you say what is meant by both parts together.

Part question example 2

What is meant by 'minority ethnic group'? (from Social Inequality) [2]

Answer: *This is a group that is culturally or racially distinct from other groups in the same society.*

Commentary on answer: [1/2] This answer explains what 'ethnic group' means but not 'minority'. The majority group is also culturally distinct, so this is not a complete answer.

Other part questions needing only brief answers may be in this form: 'Identify two . . .' followed by a word such as groups, ways or types.

Part question example 3

Identify two ways of carrying out a social survey. (from Theory and Methods) [2]

Answer: *Face-to-face, telephone.*

Commentary on answer: [2/2] This answer makes two correct points and both would gain a mark.

Some part questions ask you to describe two things. These can be the same type of thing (such as strengths, limitations, ways, types or reasons) or different (such as one strength and one limitation).

Part question example 4

Describe two strengths of using official statistics in sociological research. (from Theory and Methods) [4]

Answer: *Official statistics are easy to access on the internet because the government makes them freely available. Because they are produced by government-funded research they are usually based on large representative samples.*

Commentary on answer: [4/4] Both points made are strengths of official statistics.

Notice that it is not necessary to explain why these are strengths because the question does not tell you to.

Part question example 5

Describe one strength and one limitation of using official statistics in sociological research. (from Theory and Methods) [4]

Answer: *They are based on research that has usually involved a large sample.*
A limitation is that they may have been manipulated for political reasons and so do not give the full picture.

Commentary on answer: [2/4] The second part of the answer is a clear limitation. The first part of the answer does not make clear if it is a strength or a weakness so does not gain a mark.

Answer: *One strength of official statistics is that they are based on research which, because it has been funded by the government, has usually involved large representative samples. A limitation is that they may have been manipulated for political reasons so do not give the full picture.*

> **Commentary on answer: [4/4]** This now gives one correct strength and one correct limitation, and makes it clear which is which.
>
> You may also be asked for more than two things.

Part question example 6

Describe two strengths and two limitations of covert participant observation in sociological research. (from Theory and Methods) [8]

Answer: *One strength of covert participant observation is that the researcher will probably not influence the behaviour of the group because they will not know they are being studied. Another strength is that the researcher will be able to get an in-depth and detailed understanding from the point of view of group members. One limitation is that the researcher will have to spend a lot of time and effort making sure that the group does not discover who he or she really is. This leads to another limitation, which is that the researcher cannot make notes without raising suspicions and so risk being uncovered.*

> **Commentary on answer: [8/8]** This answer clearly identifies two strengths and two limitations and briefly describes them. The second strength applies to all participant observation, overt as well as covert, but since it does apply to covert participant observation it would still gain a mark. The answer does not define covert participant observation but it is clear from the answer that the student knows what it means. The answer could also be set out in this way:
>
> Strength 1:
> Strength 2:
> Limitation 1:
> Limitation 2:
>
> If a part question asks you to 'explain how . . .' or 'explain why . . . ', you will need to write in sentences and make several points. You will not have the time to write a long answer but you should try to answer the question as fully as you can. The topic of the part question will have been chosen so that it is on one aspect only of the syllabus.

Part question example 7

Explain how labelling may influence educational achievement. (from Education) [6]

Answer: *Labelling is when teachers make assumptions about pupils based on their appearance, attitudes, etc. For example, a teacher may label someone as a troublemaker because they mess around in class and do not work. This may influence educational achievement if the labelled pupil internalises the message and thinks that they really are a troublemaker. This is called a self-fulfilling prophecy. The pupil will then not do well. On the other hand, if a teacher thinks someone can be good at maths and encourages and helps them, this can also be a self-fulfilling prophecy and that pupil will do better.*

Commentary on answer: [6/6] This answer shows knowledge and understanding by explaining labelling in the first sentence. It also shows understanding of the key concept, self-fulfilling prophecy. It gives two examples that show how this might work and links both directly to educational achievement (one to high achievement and one to low achievement). The answer could also have included labelling by peers as well as teachers or could discuss the self-negating prophecy, but it would still get full marks as it stands.

There may also be part questions asking you to 'Explain why . . .' Explaining 'why' requires more AO3 (analysis and evaluation) than explaining 'how' does and you should bear this in mind when planning and writing your answer.

Part question example 8

Explain why birth rates have fallen in many countries in the last 100 years. (from The Family) [8]

Answer 1: [8/8] *Traditional societies have high birth rates but they also have high mortality rates, especially infant and child mortality rates. This means that although many babies are born a high proportion of them do not survive to adulthood. This situation has changed in the last 100 years in modern industrial societies. The death rate fell because of improvements in health care, immunisations, nutrition and living standards. People no longer felt it was necessary to have lots of children because they could be sure most would survive. It also became more expensive to have children. Also, people no longer needed to have children who would look after them when they were old because pensions and welfare benefits became common. Finally, new forms of contraception such as the pill made it possible for more women to plan how many children to have.*

Commentary on answer 1: This answer covers a good range of points about why birth rates have fallen. It shows good understanding of how birth rates are related to other demographic measures such as mortality rates. The answer does not refer to any particular countries, nor does it quote any statistics, but these are not essential.

Answer 2: [4/8] *A 100 years ago the death rate and birth rate were both still high but they have both fallen since then in many countries. The death rate fell because of improvements in health care such as immunisation against diseases and also because of rising living standards generally. Because the death rate fell, families started to have fewer children. This was because before then it was always likely that a baby or child would not survive but now the death of a child is unusual so people know that all the children they have will survive, so they do not have as many.*

Commentary on answer 2: This answer covers some of the same ground as answer 1, linking the fall in the birth rate to the fall in the infant and child mortality rates (although these terms are not actually used). This is good and shows some analytical skill. However, there is really only one explanation given here for the fall in the birth rate; while answer 1 had several explanations.

Part question example 9

Explain why police statistics underestimate the true extent of crime (from Crime, Deviance and Social Control) [8]

Answer: *Police statistics do not give the true extent of crime. This is because the police do not know about all crimes. They rely on the public to report crimes to them but not all crimes are reported. For example, crimes are often reported by victims but there are victimless crimes. Sometimes people don't realise they have been a victim of crime; they may just think they have lost something that has really been stolen. Also, even when crimes are reported to the police they are not always recorded as crimes.*

Commentary on answer: [5/8] This answer makes several points, covering reporting and recording of crimes and non-reporting. The answer could be fuller and explain the points better; for example, there is no explanation of why the police do not record all reported crimes, and there are no examples of victimless crimes. These were missed opportunities.

The final part question on every section of both exam papers will have more marks available than the other part questions. The wording will be, 'to what extent . . . '. On this question you will have to show that you can evaluate. The command phrase, 'to what extent . . . ' is intended to guide you towards the AO3 skills. Note also that the question discourages you from completely agreeing and disagreeing. Whatever you are asked about there will be points to be made on either side. You need to discuss these and to try to weigh up which view is stronger than the other to show the skill of evaluation. For these part questions you should make sure you have time to write an essay-style answer in sentences and paragraphs. It is good to finish with a conclusion that sums up the main points you have made.

Part question example 10

To what extent are nuclear families declining in modern industrial societies? (from The Family) [15]

Answer 1: *In the mid-20th century functionalist sociologists assumed that in the modern world the nuclear family was the most common and the best kind of family. By a nuclear family they meant a married heterosexual couple with their own children. Today many other types of family are acceptable. For example, there are many lone parent families, same sex couples with children and cohabiting couples. There are also more people living alone so that some sociologists say we should now talk about households rather than families. As people live longer there are more generations alive at the same time, so there may be a return to extended families. If there are more types of families, then nuclear families seem to be declining. Right-wing sociologists are concerned that this may lead to social problems such as rising crime.*

However, many people still spend a large part of their lives in nuclear families. Children in lone parent families usually have two parents living together when they are born; separation or divorce comes later. Most people also want to live in nuclear families, although for more people than in the past this does not work out. It could also be argued that some families that are sometimes counted as not nuclear are in fact almost the same, such as reconstituted families where one of the parents is a step-parent, and cohabiting families where the couple is not married. These are similar to nuclear families in that there is a heterosexual couple bringing up children. If a wider definition of nuclear family is used, then the nuclear family is still very much with us.

Commentary on answer 1: [15/15] This answer has a simple but effective structure. It defines the term 'nuclear family' early on, and brings in some theory with a mention of functionalism. It then outlines some of the ways in which more diverse types of family can be found today. The penultimate sentence of the first paragraph makes it clear how this is answering the question, and there is reference to another theory, the new right. The second paragraph starts with 'however' to indicate that a different point of view is going to be explained. This second part of the answer is about the same length as the first, so the two points of view are being considered equally. Several good points are made about how the nuclear family may in fact not be declining as much as might be thought. The conclusion is that it depends what we mean by a nuclear family, implying that this may be why there is disagreement on this issue. This is a strongly evaluative end to an answer in which the skills for all three assessment objectives are clearly shown. There are no named sociologists in this answer, and no use of statistics or references to research studies. These would have further improved the answer. However, there is enough here for this answer to get full marks.

Answer 2: *Functionalists argue that the nuclear family is the most important kind of family and that it is found in all societies in some form. In traditional societies people did live in extended families but in modern industrial societies the nuclear family became the norm. This meant that the women stayed at home carrying out the expressive role, which involves looking after the house and children, while the man went to work and was the breadwinner, providing for the economic needs of the family. Today there are many other types of families and sociologists say there is greater diversity. This means, for example, that there are lone parent families, reconstituted families, cohabiting couples with children and more people living on their own. But functionalists and the right-wing sociologists would say that nuclear families are still the best way to organise our lives because they are functional for individuals and society.*

Commentary on answer 2: [5/15] This answer shows some good knowledge of sociology, for example about functionalism, roles and diversity. However, the information is not used to directly answer the question. When talking about diversity, the answer does not say what diversity means for nuclear families. It would have been good to do so and even better to have discussed whether cohabiting couples with children, for example, might be considered a type of nuclear family, raising questions about how to define the nuclear family. The answer does not focus on whether or not the nuclear family is declining, and the concluding sentence is instead about the importance of the nuclear family. This answer is considerably weaker than answer 1.

Part question example 11

To what extent can the media influence social behaviour? (from Media) [15]

Answer: *Some theories claim that the media have strong effects on behaviour. The hypodermic-syringe model suggests that the media can work like a drug, having immediate* *and dramatic effects on behaviour. For example, political propaganda may persuade people to accept an argument and vote accordingly. However, we now live in a media culture, surrounded by many different media, and they cannot all affect behaviour like this. More plausible is the cultural effects approach, which suggests that the media have long-term effects, shaping our values and general behaviour. For example, levels of violence in the media may not make individuals violent, as the hypodermic syringe model suggests, but might make us less shocked by real-life violence than we would otherwise be.*

Other approaches suggest that people use the media rather than being influenced by it. Pluralists emphasise how much choice and competition there is in the media. The uses and gratifications approach suggests that audiences use the media, for example for information and entertainment. The media then have little effect on behaviour. Audiences can decide what media to use, and not be influenced by it. However, Marxists would argue that the choices audiences make have in fact been shaped by the media. The media dominate social life to such an extent now that it seems unlikely that they do not have effects on behaviour. Even some of the norms of everyday life have been changed by mobile phones and other new media.

Commentary on answer: [12/15] This answer covers several different approaches. The brief account of each approach is followed by examples and by explicit evaluative points. The criticisms made of the different approaches are strong evaluative points. There is a contrast between the view that the media have strong effects and that they do not, but two different approaches are discussed on the 'strong effects' side, increasing the scope for evaluation. The answer ends with a well-considered point that puts the debate within the context of a media culture. There could have been more detail on the approaches, and discussion of what 'behaviour' might mean, but this answer concentrates on demonstrating the AO2 and AO3 skills necessary for a high mark for this kind of question.

Results

Results day!

After you have finished your exam it will be marked by an examiner. Examiners use a mark scheme, which tells them what marks they can give for the answers they are marking. The work examiners do is checked by senior examiners to ensure that all examiners are using the mark scheme in the same way, and awarding the same marks for the same level of work.

When your two exam papers have been marked, your grade for IGCSE Sociology is worked out. In doing this Paper 1 is worth 60 per cent and Paper 2 is worth 40 per cent. The grades, as for all IGCSEs, are A*, A, B, C, D, E, F, G and U. If you achieve a grade C or higher in IGCSE Sociology you should consider studying sociology at AS and A level. You will be well prepared for the Cambridge International AS and A level courses.

Bibliography

Unit 1

Bandura, A., Ross, D. and Ross, S. (1961), Transmission of aggression through imitation of aggressive models, Journal of Abnormal and Social Psychology, 63, 575–582; also available at: http://psychclassics.yorku.ca/Bandura/bobo.htm

Cumberbatch, G. (1994), Legislating mythology: video violence and children, Journal of Mental Health, 3, 485–494

DFID (Department for International Development) (2000), Viewing the world: a study of British television coverage of developing countries, DFID, London and Glasgow; also available at http://webarchive.nationalarchives.gov.uk/+/http:/www.dfid.gov.uk/pubs/files/viewworldfull.pdf

Durkheim, E. (1970), *Suicide: a study in Sociology*, Routledge & Kegan Paul, London

Gatrell, C. (2004), *Hard Labour*, Open University Press, Maidenhead

Goldthorpe, J.H., Lockwood, D., Bechhofer, P. and Platt, J. (1968), *The Affluent Worker: industrial attitudes and behaviour*, Cambridge University Press, Cambridge

Rosenthal, R. and Jacobson, L. (1968), *Pygmalion in the Classroom*, Holt, Rinehart & Winston, New York

Venkatesh, S. (2009), *Gang Leader for a Day: a rogue sociologist crosses the line*, Penguin, London

Webster, C., Simpson, D., Macdonald, R., Abbas, A., Cieslik, M., Shildrick, T. and Simpson, M. (2004), *Poor Transitions: how do young people from poor families make the transition to adulthood?*, Policy Press, Bristol

http://www.britsoc.co.uk/media/27107/StatementofEthicalPractice.pdf

http://www.ons.gov.uk/census/index.html

http://www.cls.ioe.ac.uk/page.aspx?&sitesectionid=724&sitesectiontitle=Welcome+to+the+1958+National+Child+Development+Study

The following are the sources for the exercises in interpreting quantitative data:

http://search.worldbank.org/data?qterm=life%20expectancy&language=EN

http://data.worldbank.org/indicator/SE.ADT.LITR.ZS

https://kings9geo.wikispaces.com/file/view/graph_megacity_development.jpg/299183052/446x296/graph_megacity_development.jpg

http://www.ufcw.ca/templates/ufcwcanada/images/directions12/september/1271/pie_chart_sept2012_en-1.jpg

Unit 2

Althusser, L. (1971), *Lenin and Philosophy and Other Essays*, New Left Books, London

Ariès, P. (1973), *Centuries of Childhood*, Penguin, Harmondsworth

Cohen, P. (1972), Subcultural conflict and working class community, Working Papers in Cultural Studies no 2, University of Birmingham, Birmingham

Durkheim, E. (1961), *The Elementary Forms of the Religious Life*, Collier Books, New York

Elias, N. (1969), *The Civilizing Process: the history of manners*, Blackwell, Oxford

Hall, S. (1996), 'Who needs identity?' (introduction), in Hall, S. and du Gay, P., *Questions of Cultural Identity*, Sage, London

McRobbie, A. (1991), *Feminism and Youth Culture: from Jackie to Just Seventeen*, Macmillan, London

Mead, M. (2002), *Sex and Temperament in Three Primitive Societies*, Harper Collins, London

Murdock, G.P. (1949), *Social Structure*, Macmillan, New York

Oakley, A. (1972), *Sex, Gender and Society*, Temple Smith, London

Postman, N. (1991), *The Disappearance of Childhood*, Vintage, New York

Said, E. (1977), *Orientalism*, Penguin, Harmondsworth

Thorne, B. (1993), *Gender Play: boys and girls in school*, Open University Press, Buckingham

The following is the source for the material used in the date interpretation exercise:

McCabe, J., Fairchild, E., Grauerholz, L., Pescosolido, B.A. and Tope, D. (2011), Gender in twentieth century books: the patterns of disparity in titles and central characters, Gender and Society, 25, 197

Unit 3

Davis, K. and Moore, W.E. (1945), Some Principles of Stratification, reproduced in Bendix, R. and Lipset, S.M. (1962) (eds), *Class, Status and Power*, Routledge and Kegan Paul, London

Ehrenreich, B. (1984), *The Hearts of Men: American dreams and the flight from commitment*, Anchor, New York

Giddens, A. and Sutton, P. (2013), *Sociology*, 7th edition, Polity, Cambridge

Goldthorpe, J. (1980), *Social Mobility and Class Structure in Modern Britain*, Clarendon Press, Oxford

Mack, J. and Lansley, S. (1985), *Poor Britain*, Allen & Unwin, London

Murray, C. (1984), *Losing Ground*, Basic Books, New York

Ryan, M.K. and Haslam, S.A. (2005), The glass cliff: evidence that women are over-represented in precarious leadership positions, British Journal of Management, 16, 81–90

Sklair, L. (1995), *Sociology of the Global System*, 2nd edition, Prentice Hall, Hemel Hempstead

Townsend, P. (1979), *Poverty in the United Kingdom*, Penguin, Harmondsworth

Walby, S. (1990), *Theorizing Patriarchy*, Wiley-Blackwell, Oxford

Weber, M. (1947), *The Theory of Economic and Social Organizations*, Free Press, New York

Westergaard, J. and Resler, H. (1976), *Class in a Capitalist Society*, Penguin, Harmodsworth

Wilkinson, R. and Pickett, K. (2010), *The Spirit Level: why equality is better for everyone*, Penguin, London

Wright, E.O. (1978), *Class, Crisis and the State*, New Left Books, London

The following are the sources for the data interpretation material:

http://www.ofmdfmni.gov.uk/gender_equality_strategy_statistics__2011_update.pdf

http://milescorak.com/2012/01/12/here-is-the-source-for-the-great-gatsby-curve-in-the-alan-krueger-speech-at-the-center-for-american-progress/

Unit 4

Abbott, P., Wallace, C. and Tyler, M. (2005), *Introduction to Sociology: a feminist approach*, 3rd edition, Routledge, London

Allen, G. (2009), Family and friends in today's world, Sociology Review, vol 19, no 1, 2–5

Anderson, M. (1971), *Family Structure in Nineteenth Century Lancashire*, Cambridge University Press, Cambridge

Barrett, M. and McIntosh, M. (1982), *The Anti-Social Family*, Verso, London

Dobash, R.E. and Dobash, R.P. (1992), *Women, Violence and Social Change*, Routledge, London

Engels, F. (1972), *The Origin of the Family, Private Property and the State*, Lawrence and Wishart, London

Fulcher, J. and Scott, J. (1999), *Sociology*, Oxford University Press, Oxford

Gough, E.K. (1959), The Nayars and the definition of marriage, Journal of the Royal Anthropological Institute of Great Britain and Northern Ireland, vol 89, no 1, 23–24

Laslett, P. (1971), *The World We Have Lost*, 2nd edition, Methuen, London

Leach, E. (1967), A runaway world, BBC Reith lectures, available at: http://downloads.bbc.co.uk/rmhttp/radio4/transcripts/1967_reith3.pdf

Morgan, L.H. (1997), *Systems of Consanguinity & Affinity of the Human Family*, University of Nebraska Press, Lincoln (first published 1871)

Murdock, G.P. (1949), *Social Structure*, Macmillan, New York

Murray, C. (1984), *Losing Ground*, Basic Books, New York

Parsons, T. (1951), *The Social System*, Free Press, New York

Young, M. and Willmott, P. (1973), *The Symmetrical Family: a study of work and leisure in the London region*, Routledge, London

Young, M.D. and Willmott, P. (1957), *Family and Kinship in East London*, Routledge, London

The following are sources for data interpretation and case studies:

http://www.ons.gov.uk/ons/dcp171778_284823.pdf

http://chartsbin.com/view/3232

http://unstats.un.org/unsd/demographic/products/Worldswomen/WW_full%20 report_color.pdf

http://english.peopledaily.com.cn/200307/16/eng20030716_120372.shtml

http://www.gov.mu/portal/goc/cso/ei977/pop2011.pdf

Unit 5

Archer, L. (2006), Why are Bitish Chinese students so successful in British schools?, Social Science Teacher, 36, 16–19

Becker, H.S. (1952), Social class variation in the Teacher-Pupil Relationship, Journal of Educational Sociology, 25, 451–465.

Bernstein, B. (1971), *Class, Codes and Control*, volume 1, Paladin, London

Boudon, R. (1974), *Education, Opportunity and Social Inequality*, John Wiley & sons New York

Department of Education and Skills (2007), Gender and education: the evidence on pupils in England, DES, London, available at https://www.education.gov.United Kingdom/publications/eOrderingDownload/00389-2007BKT-EN.pdf

Gardner, H. (1983), *Frames of Mind: the theory of multiple intelligences*, Basic Books, New York

Hey, V. (1997), *The Company She Keeps: an ethnography of girls' friendships*, Open University Press, Milton Keynes

Jackson, C. (2006), *Lads and Ladettes: gender and the fear of failure*, Maidenhead, Open University Press

Jackson, P. (1968), *Life in Classrooms*, Teachers College Press, New York

Labov, W. (1972), *Language in the Inner City: studies in Black English vernacular,* University of Pennsylvania Press, Philadelphia

Mac an Ghaill, M. (1988), *Young, Gifted and Black: student-teacher relations in the schooling of black youth*, Open University Press, Milton Keynes

Rosenthal, R. and Jacobson, L. (1968), *Pygmalion in the Classroom*, Rinehart & Winston, New York

Rutter, M., Maugham, B., Mortimore, P. and Ouston, J. (1979), *Fifteen Thousand Hours: secondary schools and their effects on children,* Harvard University Press, Cambridge

Sewell, T. (1997), *Black Masculinities and Schooling*, Trentham, Stoke on Trent

Willis, P. (1977), *Learning to Labour: how working class kids get working class jobs*, Saxon House, Farnborough

http://www.greatthoughtstreasury.com/?q=node/187187 (Canassatego, Treaty of Lancaster, 1744)

https://www.gov.uk/government/publications/gcse-and-equivalent-attainment-by-pupil-characteristics-in-england

The following are sources for data interpretation and case studies:

http://www.fao.org/mdg/goaltwo/en/ (FAO 2000)

www.summerhillschool.co.uk

Unit 6

Becker, H. (1953), Becoming a marihuana user, American Journal of Sociology, vol 59, no 3, 235–242

Becker, H. (1963), *Outsiders: studies in the sociology of deviance*, Free Press, New York

Chambliss, W. (1978), The Saints and the Roughnecks, Sociology, vol 11, 224–231

Cicourel, A. (1976), *The Social Organization of Juvenile Justice*, Heinemann, London

Clinard, M.B. (1974), *Sociology of Deviant Behaviour*, 4th edition, Holt, Rinehart & Winston, New York

Cloward, R.A. and Ohlin, L.E. (1961), *Delinquency and Opportunity*, Free Press, Glencoe

Cohen, A.K. (1955), *Delinquent Boys*, Free Press, Glencoe

Cohen, S. (1972), *Folk Devils and Moral Panics*, Paladin, London

Cohen, S. (1985), *Visions of Social Control*, Polity, Cambridge

Durkheim, E. (1982), *The Rules of Sociological Method*, Macmillan, London (first published 1895)

Hall, S., Critcher, C., Jefferson T., Clarke J.N. and Roberts, B. (1979), *Policing the Crisis*, Macmillan, London

Lea, J. and Young, J. (1984), *What Is To Be Done About Law and Order?*, Penguin, Harmondsworth

Lemert, E.M. (1972), *Human Deviance, Social Problems and Social Control*, 2nd edition, Prentice Hall, Engelwood Cliffs NJ

Matza, D. (1964), *Delinquency and Drift*, John Wiley & Sons, New York

Merton, R.K. (1968), *Social Theory and Social Structure*, Free Press, New York

Miller, W. (1962), 'Lower class culture as a generating milieu of gang delinquency', in Wolfgang, M.E., Savitz, L. and Johnston, N. (eds), *The Sociology of Crime and Deviance*, Wiley, New York

Murray, C. (1984), *Losing Ground*, Basic Books, New York

Parsons, T. (1956), '*Family structure and the socialization of the child*', in Parsons, T. and Bales, R.F. in collaboration with Olds, J., Zelditch, M. Jr. and Slater, P.E. (eds), *Family Socialization and Interaction Process*, Routledge, London

Pollak, O. (1961), *The Criminality of Women*, University of Philadelphia Press, Philadelphia

Tombs, S. and Whyte, D. (2008), *A Crisis of Enforcement: the decriminalisation of death and injury at work*, available at: http://www.crimeandjustice.org.uk/opus685/crisisenforcementweb.pdf

Young, J. (1971), *The Drugtakers: the social meaning of drug use*, Paladin, London

http://www.ons.gov.uk/ons/rel/crime-stats/crime-statistics/period-ending-march-2013/sty-crime-in-england-and-wales.html

http://www.ons.gov.uk/ons/rel/crime-stats/crime-statistics/period-ending-sept-2012/index.html http://www.telegraph.co.uk/news/worldnews/asia/japan/3213349/Japan-struggles-with-elderly-crime-wave.html

The following are sources for data interpretation and case studies:

http://ukcrimestats.com/blog/category/recorded-crime-totals/

Unit 7

Cohen, S. (1972), *Folk Devils and Moral Panics*, Paladin, London

Glasgow Media Group (1976), *Bad News*, Routledge, London

Gramsci, A. (1971), *Selections from the Prison Notebooks*, Lawrence & Wishart, London

Herman, E.S. and Chomsky, N. (2002), *Manufacturing Consent: the political economy of the mass media*, Pantheon, New York

Levi-Strauss, C. (1995), *Myth and Meaning: cracking the code of culture*, Schocken Books, New York

Meehan, D. (1983), *Ladies of the Evening: women characters of prime time TV*, Scarecrow Press, Metuchen NJ

Miliband, R. (1973), *The State and Capitalist Society*, Quartet, London

Morley, D. (2004), *The Nationwide Audience: structure and decoding*, British Film Institute, London

Morley, D. (1986), *Family Television: cultural power and domestic leisure*, Routledge, London

Mulvey, L. (1975), Visual pleasure and narrative cinema, Screen, vol 16, no 3

O'Shaugnessy, M. (1999), *Media and Society: an introduction*, Oxford University Press, Oxford

http://web.orange.co.uk/article/news/most_elderly_never_use_internet

http://www.internetworldstats.com/stats.htm

http://stakeholders.ofcom.org.uk/market-data-research/market-data/communications-market-reports/cmr12/internet-web/uk-4.22

Index

Acknowledgements

The author and publishers acknowledge the following sources of copyright material and are grateful for the permissions granted. While every effort has been made, it has not always been possible to identify the sources of all the material used, or to trace all copyright holders. If any omissions are brought to our notice, we will be happy to include the appropriate acknowledgements on reprinting.

Cover Cienpies Design/Shutterstock; p6 Oleksiy Maksymenko / Getty; p7 Pictorial Press Ltd / Alamy; p11 Georgios Kollidas / Thinkstock; p13 Cameron Whitman / Thinkstock; p13 PhotoAlto sas / Alamy; p16 © Vuk Nenezic / Thinkstock; p18 British Sociology Association; p22 Radharc Images / Alamy; p24 © Rob Marmion / Thinkstock; p26 monkeybusinessimages / Thinkstock; p33 WireImage / Getty; p42 comstock / Thinkstock; p43 Oleksiy Mark / Thinkstock; p46 Maltaguy1 / Thinkstock; p49 Getty Images / Getty; p53 Jacob Jenne / Thinkstock; p55 © Pavel Siamionau / Thinkstock; p59 michael Langley / Thinkstock; p62 moodboard / Thinkstock; p63 digital vision / Thinkstock; p73 ZUMA Press, Inc. / Alamy; p82*l* © Trevor Smith / Alamy; p82*r* © Colin Edwards / Alamy; p84 Paul Springett 05 / Alamy; p86 © CS-Stock / Alamy; p90 jeesoen / Thinkstock; p98*l* © Mark Towner / Alamy; p98*r* gary yim / Shutterstock; p100 © Africa Media Online / Alamy; p106 © ZUMA Press, Inc. / Alamy; p108*tr* Ad van Brunschot / Thinkstock; p108*l* George Doyle / Thinkstock; p108*br* Felipe Dupouy / Thinkstock; p111 © Keystone Pictures USA / Alamy; p118 Gregg Vignal / Alamy; p119 Len Green / Thinkstock; p122 Zurijeta / Thinkstock; p124 Blend Images / Thinkstock; p125 Fuse / Thinkstock; p130 Fuse / Thinkstock; p131 Jeffrey Hamilton / Thinkstock; p134 © epa european pressphoto agency b.v. / Alamy; p140 MIXA / Thinkstock; p151 © Getty Images / Thinkstock; p155 David Sacks / Thinkstock; p156 Shlapak_Liliya / Thinkstock; p158 digital vision / Thinkstock; p164 Robin Laurance / Alamy; p164 paul prescott /Shutterstock; p166 Peter Spiro / Thinkstock; p167 www.avanti.org.uk; p170 Fuse / Thinkstock; p177 Gamma-Rapho via Getty Images; p178 Francis Bernstein; p184 Valerie Hay; p185 Jirsak / Shutterstock; p187 zoonar / Thinkstock; p190 MilaBricheri / Thinkstock; p192 1000 Words / Shutterstock; p193 LOU OATES / Thinkstock; p201 epa european pressphoto agency b.v. / Alamy; p204 James Boardman Archive / Alamy; p205 kentoh / Shutterstock; p208 aetb / Thinkstock; p211 Getty Images; p214 © Sophie Bassouls / Sygma / Corbis; p220 © Gina Smith / Thinkstock; p222 Michael Austen / Alamy; p227 Justin Kase z12z / Alamy; p229 Everett Collection Historical / Alamy; p233 Bernal Revert / Alamy; p241 Hulton-Deutsch Collection/CORBIS; p242 Pictorial Press Ltd / Alamy; p249 Bhakpong / Thinkstock; p255 MalcolmFreeman.Com / Alamy; p260 david hancock / Alamy; p261 Vladimir Nenov / Thinkstock; p263 digital vision / Thinkstock; p266 Ingram Publishing / Thinkstock; p268 Fuse / Thinkstock; p269 Julio Etchart / Alamy; p270 Catherine Yeulet / Thinkstock; p276 oliveromg / Shutterstock.

The publishers would like to thank the following people who assisted in reviewing this book: Glenda Jane Clark, Ian Lantham and Om Nath Varma.